W9-DIM-209

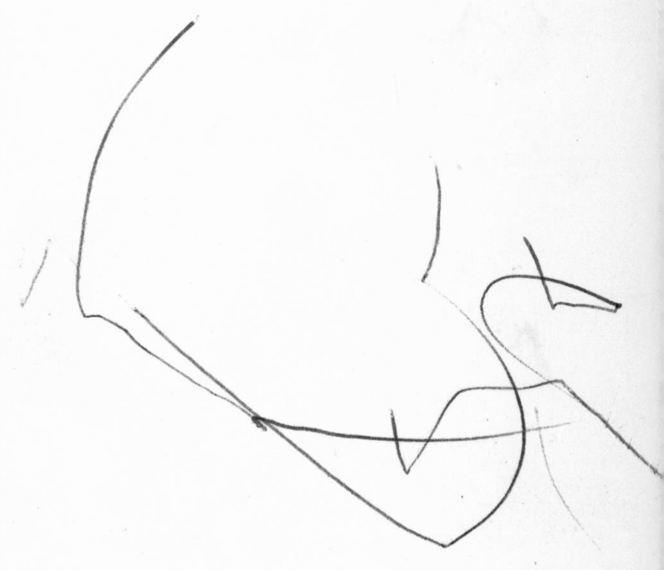

Group Dynamics

PRINCIPLES AND APPLICATIONS

Hubert Bonner

PROFESSOR OF PSYCHOLOGY
OHIO WESLEYAN UNIVERSITY

THE RONALD PRESS COMPANY • NEW YORK

Library of Congress Catalog Card Number: 59-6102

PRINTED IN THE UNITED STATES OF AMERICA

Preface

This book offers a comprehensive treatment of the dynamics of small-group behavior. It is designed as a textbook for college students and for professional reading by psychologists, social scientists, teachers, and personnel managers.

As the subtitle indicates, we are concerned with both theory and empirical example. Accordingly, we offer first a systematic presentation of those aspects of group behavior which have come to comprise the central subject matter of group dynamics; namely, group structure, group cohesiveness, intergroup tensions, group learning, group problem-solving, and group leadership. Having laid down this theoretical framework, we then trace its important emergent applications to the vital areas of industry, community relations, political behavior, group psychotherapy, and education. Although the applications of group dynamics to education have received much attention in the past decade, writers in the field of group dynamics have not made an explicit and systematic analysis of these other areas. Of particular interest here is the subject of group psychotherapy and personality dynamics—topics of especial importance to an understanding of the formation and enhancement of groups, group tensions and conflicts, mutual dependence, group change, and the ebb and flow of the interpersonal process.

The book is divided into five parts. Part I lays down the historical foundations of group dynamics, tracing the subject from its earliest discernible origins in the latter part of the nineteenth century.

Part II details the dynamic factors which underlie group behavior. It examines the psychological structure of the group, with particular reference to its individual and collective properties. It describes the cohesive and disruptive factors in group behavior, with special consideration of interpersonal and group attractiveness and the psychology of hostile relations. Group behavior is also analyzed in the light of learning theory, and the relative merits of individual and group learning are carefully investigated.

The problems of the conflict and adjustment of groups, and their theoretical and practical solutions, are sympathetically yet critically delineated in Part III. Specifically, this is achieved by devoting a separate chapter to the nature of intergroup relations, group leadership, collective problem-solving, and the application of group-dynamic principles and findings to education, industry, community relations, and political behavior.

The discussion in Part IV is concerned with the role of the person in the group, particularly the relation of individual behavior and group dynamics. A detailed treatment of role behavior is followed by an analysis of the self-enhancing and self-constricting factors in the behavior of groups. And finally, the fundamentals of group psychotherapy are set forth, illustrating the emotional intensity of the interpersonal contacts in psychotherapeutic groups.

Part V aims to bring balance and perspective to the discussion by a critical analysis of the fundamental ideas and assumptions of group dynamics. It thus affords a detailed evaluation of its basic achievements and weaknesses both as a scientific discipline and as an instrument for human betterment.

The field of group dynamics emerges from the pages of this book as a valid scientific discipline, bristling with problems but with valuable applications for the study and enhancement of human relations. Empirical research and experimental investigation make up its characteristic temper.

While it lacks theoretical rigor and rigid experimental design, it has attained the level of dependable description if not that of empirical law. If present developments are indicative of its future, group dynamics should in the next decade be able to describe group behavior by means of empirical laws in which functional relations will explain group phenomena. Today, however, experimental results permit explanations of only limited scope; hence, we are not yet able to compare the findings in metrical terms.

Like every writer on scholarly subjects, I am indebted to others, either directly through personal influence or indirectly by way of their published writings. My initial interest in group psychology was stimulated by Dr. Herbert Blumer, more than twenty years ago. The theoretical and practical researches of Kurt Lewin have been an important stimulus and have helped to crystallize my interest along systematic and empirical lines, even though I have been quite critical of many of his ideas and deplore the exaggerated claims made for his work by some of his followers. My former students in a graduate seminar in intergroup relations at Columbia University in 1953–1955 were exceedingly helpful, especially in their criticisms of fundamental concepts. Several persons read parts of the original manuscript and made helpful suggestions. Specifically, I want to thank Dr. Arthur S. Flemming, Mr. Herman M. Shipps, and Dr. Donald P. Irish. Dr. Ronald R. Greene read several chapters and made helpful suggestions for improving them. I also thank him for his generous help in the exacting task of reading proofs. I was fortunate, furthermore, in having the advice of Dr. J. McV. Hunt, general editor of the series of which this book is a part. He was quick to perceive my objectives, gave me sound advice and good suggestions for improving the original manuscript, and showed himself in every way to be an ideal editor. To my family goes the credit for infinite patience with my dereliction as a husband and father while I was absorbed in the solitary job of writing this book. I thank Mrs. Mary Alter not only for her expert typing but for her intelligent reading of the whole manuscript. Finally, I wish to thank the Administration of Ohio Wesleyan University, particularly Acting Dean George W. Burns, for much-needed financial assistance at a crucial stage in the production of this book.

Hubert Bonner

Delaware, Ohio
January, 1959

Contents

PART I
Introduction: Foundations of Group Dynamics

PART II
Group Development: Dynamic Factors in Group Behavior

PART III
Resolution of Group Tensions: Conflict and Adjustment of Groups

Part I

INTRODUCTION: FOUNDATIONS OF GROUP DYNAMICS

CHAPTER 1

Group Dynamics: Its Origins and Development

While the term "group dynamics" is new, the ideas and the knowledge which it represents are, as developments in the social sciences go, relatively old. As a matter of fact, the relevant knowledge in this area has been the concern, often explicitly, of most scholars and researchers in the domains of sociology, anthropology, and social psychology. It is difficult, if not impossible, to find sociological writings since the latter part of the nineteenth century in which the concept of social control is not a dominant one. Modern sociology, since its beginnings, has concerned itself with the processes by which individuals are compelled or induced to conform to the customs of the group. It is not an exaggeration to say that sociology is the study of the ways in which social conformity and social solidarity are achieved and maintained. So conceived, sociology has been investigating "group dynamics" almost from its beginnings.

While psychology came upon the group dynamics scene somewhat later, it has made important contributions to the subject during the past thirty years. This is particularly true of social psychology. Much of the value and importance of the psychologists' contribution to the subject lies in their experimental approach.

Probably no single individual is ever solely responsible for a new idea or discovery. Every researcher builds on the work of his predecessors. While Kurt Lewin has been the driving genius behind recent developments in group dynamics and gave it its name, there are, then, important sociological origins and parallels, as well as contributions by individuals in other disciplines, notably by psychologists and sociometrists. These developments we shall examine in the present chapter.

GROUP DYNAMICS DEFINED

Group dynamics is, quite obviously, concerned with the group. A group exists whenever two or more individuals are aware of one another, when they are in some important way interrelated. In this sense a group is not the same thing as an aggregate of individuals. The latter is a collection, a population, or a class. A group is a number of people in interaction with one another, and it is this interaction process that distinguishes the group from an aggregate.

More important, however, is the fact that the group which we study is not only interactive, it is also *dynamic*. It is a group whose members are in a continuously *changing* and *adjusting* relationship with reference to one another. The changes occur for several reasons. First, it is characteristic of interacting individuals to be in a state of tension, to be attracted or repelled by one another, to seek a resolution of the tensions, and to restore equilibrium among themselves. While the concept of homeostasis, or the return to equilibrium after any disturbance, can be and has been overstressed in modern psychology, it is useful in describing this phase of group development.

Changes occur, in the second place, when the group membership changes. The presence or absence of certain members, the introduction of new members, changes in leadership, and the like may affect the structure and the rate of change of a dynamic group. A change of membership, however, does not in itself necessarily produce changes in a group. Some groups retain their structure in the face of continuing membership changes.

The foregoing observation points to a third reason for group changes. While we do not always know why some groups change and others tend to persist, the factors of group rigidity and group flexibility are important determinants of group change. It should be apparent to the reader that a rigid, that is, unadaptable, group is more resistant to change than a more flexible and adaptable one. Ideas and influences are resisted in the interests of maintaining equilibrium. The need for stability overshadows the desire or urgency for social change. While this rigidity forestalls for a time both internal and external pressures for change, the stability is often obtained at the price of unresolved tensions.

Group changes are dependent, finally, on the degree of organization of a group. The less organized the group is, relatively speaking, the less marked are those social-psychological forces which make for a high level of motivation, for group participation and cooperation, interdependence, and a constructive morale. The leader will be far less effective in an unorganized than in an organized group. Along with these positive qualities, however, the organized group is also subject to a much greater number and degree of frustrations and aggressions.[1]

On the basis of the foregoing remarks we can now define group dynamics as that division of social psychology which investigates the formation and change in the structure and functions of the psychological grouping of people into self-directing wholes. The formation and change of the group do not take place automatically and inevitably but are a consequence of the efforts of its members to solve their problems and satisfy their needs. A dynamic group is thus in a continuous process of restructuring, adjusting, and read-

[1] Cf. J. R. P. French, Organized and unorganized groups under fear and frustration, in *Studies in topological and vector psychology* (Iowa City: University of Iowa Press, 1944).

justing members to one another for the purpose of reducing the tensions, eliminating the conflicts, and solving the problems which its members have in common.

Group dynamics is also increasingly defined in a "practical" sense. It is conceived as a technique of fostering conciliation between individuals and between groups regarding important issues and practices. Research in group dynamics aims to formulate not only the abstract principles which underlie group behavior, but to devise techniques for effecting group decisions and group actions.

EARLY DEVELOPMENT OF GROUP DYNAMICS

Scientific ideas, like most ideas, have no single origin. Practically every important formulation has its equivalent or parallel in the past. Every advance in human knowledge proceeds from a body of facts or a system of ideas already implicit in their predecessors. This is notably true of group dynamics which, regrettably, is too often treated as a subject of very recent origin.

SOCIOLOGICAL ANTECEDENTS. No attempt will be made in this section to write a comprehensive survey of sociologists' contribution to the origin and growth of group dynamics. Only enough evidence will be presented to make our assertion concerning the role of sociology more than a bald and unsupported statement.

From static to dynamic sociology. Early sociology, notably as it is represented by such famous pioneers as Auguste Comte and Herbert Spencer, was mostly philosophical, and the society which it described was largely static. Analysis, description, and classification abound in its writings. While Comte wrote vaguely about social planning, and hence by implication of social change and social control, he never followed his own suggestive lead, but bogged down on the idea of social destiny.[2] Spencer's conception was even more

[2] Auguste Comte, *Positive philosophy,* Vol. II (London: Trübner & Co., 1875–1890).

static. He believed that society evolves in accordance with fixed laws, and that any efforts to change it was not only misguided but detrimental in the long run.[3]

Later in this same period, however, Lester Ward in America was writing his *Dynamic Sociology*. His ideas marked a distinct shift away from Spencer's descriptive sociology and Comte's sentimental "prevision" to the concept of "social telesis," or the notion of society as a self-directing whole.[4]

It should be pointed out here that Ward's concept of social self-direction was posited as an explanatory principle on which to base effective social planning. It was used to explain the basis on which to direct societal forces to progressive ends. It was not conceived as a principle which would explain the behavior of small, face-to-face groups, as is done in contemporary group dynamics. We refer to it because it marked the first important shift away from static to dynamic explanations, from the "genetic" to the "telic" analysis of the social process. Further, it is the first explicit expression of the notion of directed, as contrasted with evolutionary, change in modern sociology.

The positive force in social dynamics, according to Ward, was intellect and foresight. In this view we can perceive a startling similarity between Ward's telic or intelligent social process and the "group wisdom" of recent group dynamics. The "wisdom of the group" refers to the group solution of a problem, a solution resulting from the combined resources which every member of a group is able to apply to it. Just as societal change directed by the telic process is effected by adjusting blind forces to surmount obstacles and secure future ends, so a group of interacting persons, bringing into the processes their individual resources, is often able to solve its problem more effectively. This is so because an individual, hampered by habitual learning "sets," is frequently

[3] Herbert Spencer, *First principles* (New York: Appleton–Century–Crofts, Inc., 1878).

[4] L. F. Ward, *Dynamic sociology* (2 vols.; New York: Appleton–Century–Crofts, Inc., 1893), Vol. I, p. 57. This work was first published in 1883.

less able to evaluate his own ideas and is often blinded by his own suggestions.[5]

Collective determinism: Émile Durkheim and others. Perhaps the most representative exponent of the group factor in human psychology is Émile Durkheim. Human behavior, according to him, can be explained only by knowing the collective structure of the group, particularly by its *répré-sentations collectives.* These collective representations are products of the union of individuals in group life. They represent the common experiences of men in groups, just as individual representations or ideas symbolize the experiences of individual men.[6] The union of individuals into a common association is not, however, an additive process. Durkheim is very emphatic about this.[7] The whole is not composed of the sum of its parts; it includes them but also differs from them. This fact is important in Durkheim's system, for it makes clear the relationship of the individual and the group. While collective representations are composed of individual representations, the collective representations are at the same time distinct from them. This is Durkheim's way of emphasizing the importance of the group factor in human behavior. It should be added, however, that in this emphasis he ascribes an independent existence to the collective representations, and thus returns, by a different route and without intending to do so, to something reminiscent of Hegel's Objective Spirit.

Some devoted followers of Durkheim expanded his general ideas and applied them to the study of specific psychological processes. Lucien Lévy-Bruhl studied the effect of the group on human thinking. There are no *inherent* ways of thinking, according to him; the ways differ with differ-

5 The evidence, both theoretical and experimental, in confirmation of this conclusion, is impressive. We shall have occasion to examine some of it in later chapters.

6 Émile Durkheim, Réprésentations individuelles et réprésentations collectives, *Rev. de Met. et de Mor.*, 6 (1898), 274–302.

7 *Les règles de la méthode sociologique* (Paris: F. Alcan, 1895), pp. 125–28. The student should compare this with recent field theory.

ences in the collective representations.[8] Charles Blondel applied Durkheim's principles to the study of the affective life. Feelings, he said, are not identical among human groups. They are products of group life. There are, accordingly, different ways of feeling in different groups. Grief at a funeral, for instance, is expressed differently in different groups, depending upon the affective ritual that prevails in each.[9] Maurice Halbwachs applied Durkheim's principles to the study of memory. Memory, he said, like thinking and feeling, is a collective phenomenon. It always presupposes some localization in a group. Outside a group a person could not remember; or at any rate, his memory would be unorganized and meaningless, for it would be devoid of a social context.[10]

Interactionism of Georg Simmel. No one in the history of sociology has made the concept of interaction as central as did Simmel. To him society *is* interaction. The proper study of the sociologist, he believed, is interactive social relationships (*Wechselwirkung*).[11]

Society, according to Simmel, is a pattern of all the functional relationships that bind individuals into an integral whole.[12] The concept of group belongingness (*Gruppenzugehörigkeit*), which plays a prominent part in current group dynamics, is basic in Simmel's analysis. It is fundamental to the understanding of such sociological facts as social contact and isolation. An individual with a low degree of group membership has few contacts, or few localizations in sociological space. The stranger, for example, is largely characterized by negative membership-character, or by isolation. In isolation an individual's life is segmented

[8] *Les fonctions mentales dans la sociétés inférieures* (Paris: F. Alcan, 1910).

[9] *Introduction à la psychologie collective* (Paris: A. Colin, 1928).

[10] *Les cadres sociaux de la mémoire* (Paris: 1925).

[11] This and other concepts which concern us here are found in his *Soziologie* (Leipzig: Duncker und Humblot, 1908).

[12] What follows is an adaptation of the present writer's article on the relation between Simmel's view and that of field theory. See H. Bonner, Field theory and sociology, *Sociol. Soc. Res.,* 33 (1949), 171–79.

and fragmentary, but as a functional or interactive unit in a group it becomes more unitary, for now it is part of the flowing stream of social events. Thus, while the individual's position appears superficially to be minimized, it actually gains in importance, for through participation it gains acceptance and approval.

The notion of conflict is very closely related to the group-dynamic concept of tension gradients. As conceived by both Simmel and group dynamicists, conflict is not necessarily negative. It is any restructuring of field organization. Simmel, indeed, defines it as a form of socialization.

> The seeming paradox is resolved once we introduce the dialectical notion of the relation of opposition between contraries. Opposition is a high tension state involving success or failure by a social group in transcending the barriers to freedom of locomotion. When the conflict ends in the transcendence of the barriers, equilibrium is restored. Thus, while it superficially appears to be an element of division in society, conflict is in actuality an integrating relationship: "the resolution of the tension between contraries."[13]

Leadership—to which more space is devoted in the literature of group dynamics than to any other concept—was already given a modern formulation by Simmel, free from mysticism and folk thinking. Conceived in terms of interaction, or reciprocity of relationship, the leader and the led are parts of a single whole. Influence takes place in both directions. The leader and the led influence each other, so that without the one the other cannot function. Leadership is not a mystical influence emanating from the personality of the leader. The leader's influence is always limited by the conditions of the total group structure.[14]

Underlying much current writing on group dynamics is the implicit notion of spatiality. The terms "social regions," "psychological space," "topological boundaries," and the like,

[13] Bonner, Field theory and sociology, p. 177. See also Simmel, *Soziologie,* p. 247.

[14] Simmel employed the term "superordination," rather than "leadership," for the most part. We suggest that his term is scientifically more neutral, and therefore preferable to, the folk-term "leadership."

were either foreshadowed or explicitly named in other terms in the writings of Simmel. In his chapter, "Die Kreuzung Sozialer Kreise," are found many contemporary ideas. The growth of an individual takes place in a social space, which can be designated by a circle. The circles frequently intersect, as when a person has membership in more than one group. He may belong, for instance, to a club, a church, and a college alumni association. The wider the area of social participation, the more numerous the intersections of the social circles.

Another spatial concept found in Simmel's work is "social boundary," a term used to describe the nature of social attitudes. Boundary separates one group from another, particularly the in-group from the out-group. Ethnocentrism and intergroup prejudice, which are vital problems in group dynamics, can be defined topologically, that is, spatially, as boundaries to which the behavior of a group can be ordered with respect to groups lying outside. Group life is replete with boundaries of circles that do not intersect, and which limit or prevent freedom of interaction. Within the in-group itself, these nonintersecting circles establish barriers to participation, in the form of mores, customs, laws, and institutions. Like present-day field theorists, furthermore, Simmel notes the existence of boundaries within the individual's own private personality—"that deeply isolated region of intimate experience the boundary of which no one can cross. It is the plane of reality of the individual's life-space to which the multitude of his unfulfilled drives and inarticulate longings may be ordered."[15]

The topological distribution of individual's in groups and of groups themselves presents us with a mechanism of individual and group differentiation. It explains the persistence as well as the change in social groups. According to Simmel, the concept of spatiality is thus an integrating element (*Beisammensein*) in the group process.[16]

[15] Bonner, Field theory and sociology, p. 175.
[16] Simmel, *Soziologie*, p. 616.

Social process and the primary group: Charles H. Cooley. It is difficult to understand the omission of Cooley's work on the primary group by those who attempt to attribute the origins of group dynamics to very recent researchers. His entire approach to both individual and social behavior was from the point of view of the concept of the primary group. Cooley believed that social process and social control, two fundamental factors of all group dynamics, have their being in the intimate and face-to-face interactions which are the mark of the primary group. In this group the individual is keenly sensitive to the opinions and actions of others. His very "human nature," that is, his self and his personality, is developed here. The individual learns to experience vicariously the experiences of other persons in the group, to view himself through the eyes, or to play the roles, of other persons. In this process sympathy is developed, and persons closely identify themselves with one another, so that what happens to one person is the intimate concern of all members of the group. The primary group is thus seen by Cooley to have a *psychological structure* as represented by this feeling of close identification, or intimacy.[17] An individual's behavior is thus determined not so much by his personality make-up as by the psychological structure of the group. This psychological structure is not to be conceived as existing separately and in its own right; rather it represents the fact that individuals exist psychologically for each other in some way, that they are responsive to one another's feelings, actions, and opinions.

When contemporary group dynamicists speak of the influence of the group on the individual's behavior, in which people of disparate personalities are led to the same opinions or behavior, they are but restating Cooley's basic and fruitful ideas. A statement by Krech and Crutchfield, typifies this similarity. They define a group as "two or more people

[17] This theme runs through Cooley's three important volumes, namely, *Human nature and the social order* (New York: Charles Scribner's Sons, 1902), *Social organization* (New York: Charles Scribner's Sons, 1909), and *Social process* (New York: Charles Scribner's Sons, 1918).

who bear an *explicit psychological relationship to one another*." They add that even though the individual's may differ, when they become members of a strongly knit group, when they "exist psychologically for each other in some significant way," they form a dynamic group.[18]

Group influence, group cohesion, group decision-making, while predominantly associated with recent group dynamics research, are concepts which abound in different terminology in Cooley's writings. In describing the primary group Cooley writes:

> The result of intimate association, psychologically, is a certain fusion of individualities in a common whole, so that one's very self, for many purposes at least, is the common life and purpose of the group. Perhaps the simplest way of describing this wholeness is by saying that it is a "we"; it involves the sort of sympathy and mutual identification for which "we" is the natural expression. One lives in the feeling of the whole and finds the chief aims of his will in that feeling.[19]

In summary, the primary group controls behavior, changes attitudes, and leads to common decisions. As in the primary group, so in the groups investigated by group dynamics, social order is achieved by role-playing, by sympathetic perception of another's ideas and sentiments, by consensus through collective problem-solving, and the like. Not formal instruments, but group processes, are used for social control and desired change.[20]

Early Developments Within Psychology. Until the end of the last century psychology had not concerned itself specifically with the behavior of groups. Its concern with the behavior of the individual, and with individual differ-

[18] D. Krech and R. S. Crutchfield, *Theory and problems of social psychology* (New York: McGraw-Hill Book Co., Inc., 1948), p. 18.

[19] Cooley, *Social organization*, p. 23.

[20] The professional sociologist who misses in this survey such important names as Tönnies, Ratzenhofer, A. F. Bentley, John Dewey, and G. H. Mead is reminded that this survey is not a history but an attempt to show that group dynamics is not as new as some enthusiastic followers of Lewin and of Moreno seem to believe.

ences, had left group psychology largely to sociologists.[21] Nevertheless psychologists eventually came to grips with the role of the group. We shall now examine this development briefly.

Effect of the group situation on performance. Since the establishment of the first psychological laboratory in Leipzig, in 1879, psychologists have been strongly motivated to put their hypotheses and generalizations to experimental test. Almost to the end of the nineteenth century, nevertheless, experimental work in psychology concentrated on the behavior of the individual. In 1897, however, Norman Triplett initiated the first experimental investigation of social influences on individual performance.[22] In a detailed exposition of the records of bicycle races and the performance of other motor tasks, and an evaluation and discussion of these records, Triplett demonstrated that a rider's speed was significantly increased when he was paced than when he was unpaced. The presence of another contestant, his data show, "serves to liberate latent energy not ordinarily available." The "dynamogenic" factor—how "modern" this sounds!—is an important item in the performance of an act, as compared with the performance of the same act in isolation from others.[23]

Triplett's investigation leaves no doubt in our minds that an awareness of the presence or absence of other human beings is an important factor in performance. It leaves no doubt in our minds, also, that the group differential was recognized and experimentally investigated in psychology four decades before the advent of the discipline of group

21 This is considerably true even of Freud who, despite his early interest in the psychology of the group, was interested in it to a great extent in so far as it might throw light upon the group origin of the human ego. See his *Group psychology and the analysis of the ego* (London: International Psychoanalytical Library, 1922).

22 See Norman Triplett, The dynamogenic factors in pacemaking and competition, *Amer. J. Psychol.*, 9 (1897), 507–33.

23 The present writer is indebted to W. H. Burnham for the citation of Triplett's article. See William H. Burnham, The group as a stimulus to mental activity, *Science, 31* (1910), 761–67.

dynamics. Triplett's investigation showed what recent group dynamics and social psychology in general have sufficiently demonstrated: a solitary individual and the same individual in a group are two different psychological structures.

Mayer, a German educator, designed an investigation in which he tested school children to determine whether, and if so under what conditions, the work of pupils in a group gives better results than pupils working alone.[24] The pupils were representative of different abilities and temperament, and the material on which they worked—mental arithmetic, memory tests, written arithmetic—was carefully chosen and was familiar to the pupils. The performance of the pupils in groups was, in general, superior to their work as isolates. This difference characterized not only the amount of time consumed in performing the task but the quality of the work performed.

During the same period other German psychologists and educators were investigating the problem. Meumann, a pioneer in intelligence testing in Germany, compared the retention of memorized materials of pupils when working alone and when working in a group. The difference, especially in children under twelve years of age, was strikingly in favor of group performance. In addition, he found that the majority of children preferred classroom work to individual work, and that most of those who preferred solitary work were children who, in the nomenclature of today, were somewhat maladjusted.[25]

Perhaps the most rigorously experimental work on the influence of the group on individual performance prior to 1914 was that of Moede. He investigated the role of the group in increasing or decreasing an individual's speed and vigor in the performance of muscular work. He found that competition tended to retard the speed of fast performers and accelerate the speed of slow ones. Intergroup rivalry increased

[24] See August Mayer, Über Einzel-und Gesamtleistung des Schulkindes, *Arch. f. d. Ges. Psychol., 1* (1903), 276–416.

[25] Ernst Meumann, *Arch. f. d. Ges. Psychol., 4* (1904). See also his *Haus-und Schularbeit* (Leipzig: Klinkhardt, 1914).

the individual's energy output, as contrasted with interindividual competition, which had no noticeable effect on the single individual's expenditure of energy.[26]

Effect of the group on cognitive behavior: F. H. Allport. Dissatisfied with the speculative theories of sociologists and social psychologists, Allport set himself the task of subjecting the "crude generalizations" of the past to experimental tests.[27] His experiments, which need not be described in detail, established some interesting and important results. He found that subjects produced *more* mental, that is, verbal, associations in groups than when isolated. The *speed* of associations in the group was also greater—especially in the early phase of the association process. Toward the end of the task, however, when the subjects were tired, being alone favored concentration, whereas group work contributed no benefit to the final and more difficult stages of the task.[28]

Allport next investigated experimentally the influence of the group upon the thought process, as typified in written arguments. He found that more ideas were produced in the group than by individuals working alone. When the ideas were compared for their quality, however, he found that those of superior quality occurred more frequently in the solitary worker than in the group. While more words were used in the arguments of the group—probably because the presence of others induced "a more conversational and expansive form of expression"—the ideas in the group were of a lower logical order. Intense logical thinking was much more characteristic of the individual working in solitude. "These results," Allport concludes, "appear to be related to the common observation that work requiring imagination

[26] W. Moede, Der Wetteifer, seine Struktur und sein Ausmass, Z. *f. pädag. Psychol.*, *15* (1914), 353–68. Moede also investigated experimentally the effect of the group on such standard individual performances as learning, forgetting, association, and attention. See further his *Experimentelle Massenpsychologie* (Leipzig: S. Hirzel, 1920).

[27] See F. H. Allport, The influence of the group upon association and thought, *J. exp. Psychol.*, *3* (1920), 159–82.

[28] *Ibid.*, pp. 166–67.

or more concentrated and original thought is best performed in seclusion."[29] Group influence, in short, was found to improve the quantity but not the quality of mental performance.

Burnham, on the basis of his review of several studies, came to the same conclusion. He adds, further, that there are undoubtedly great individual differences as regards the effect of the social environment, and suggests that there may be a type of individual that does his best work in solitude and another type that does his best work in a group. Finally, he observes—and here he is reminiscent of William James and Charles H. Cooley—that even in his solitude the thinker is not psychologically alone.

> The artist always works with the audience in his mind. The teacher also and the orator are apt to do much of their work with the class or audience in mind. . . . In fact this social stimulus colors everything. It is comparable only to the constant peripheral stimulation which is necessary to keep us awake; in like manner a social stimulus is necessary as an internal condition, as we may say, of consciousness.[30]

According to Dashiell, who also approached the problem of the effect of the group experimentally and investigated the effect of the *real* as compared with the *imagined* presence of others, there are two discernible trends regarding the problem. As participation in the group increases there is an increase in speed of performance and a decrease in its quality and accuracy. In most cases of group performance there is a leveling effect, so that the poorer individual workers improve in a group, while the superior ones perform less satisfactorily; that is, the group becomes more homogeneous.[31]

[29] *Ibid.*, p. 182. See further his *Social psychology* (Boston: Houghton Mifflin Co., 1924), chap. xi.

[30] Burnham, The group as a stimulus, pp. 765–66.

[31] See J. F. Dashiell, An experimental analysis of some group effects, *J. abnorm. soc. Psychol.*, *25* (1930), 190–99; Experimental studies of the influence of social situations on the behavior of individual human adults, in C. Murchison (ed.), *Handbook of social psychology* (Worcester, Mass.: Clark University Press, 1935), pp. 1097–1158; *Fundamentals of general psychology* (3d ed.; Boston: Houghton Mifflin Co., 1949), p. 484.

KURT LEWIN AND CONTEMPORARY GROUP DYNAMICS

To leap from the second and third decades of this century to current development may appear arbitrary and unwarranted. However, there are available studies that fill the gap. The important fact is that though Lewin's work on field dynamics, or the influence of group- or field-forces, was formulated and published in the late twenties, it was not until he settled in the United States that he began to apply his theoretical concepts to group behavior and to put them to crucial experimental tests.

The present writer has no desire to become a partisan in the current controversy over the priority of Lewin or Moreno in the establishment of group dynamics, for our survey leaves no doubt in our minds that neither one is the founder of the discipline. There is little historical justification for Toeman's assertion regarding the origin of action research (and hence of group dynamics), that "it was J. L. Moreno, author of *Who Shall Survive? A New Approach to the Problem of Human Inter-relations* (1934), who many years before them [Collier and Lewin] developed the theoretic foundations and instruments of action research."[32] We shall merely point out in passing that the Lewinians are more directly associated, both in their theoretical formulations and concrete applications, with the group-dynamics movement than is Moreno and sociometry. This observation in no way detracts, however, from the importance of Moreno's work.

Field Theory. The conceptual scheme and the basic theoretical formulations regarding human behavior, which has come to be known as field theory, was formulated by Lewin in Germany in the second and third decades of this century. In reviewing the growth of group dynamics and

[32] Z. Toeman, in a letter criticizing Laura Thompson's imputed claim, but denied by the latter, that Kurt Lewin is to be credited with the origin of action research. See *Sci. Monthly, 70* (1950), 345–46. See further, L. Thompson, Action research among American Indians, *Sci. Monthly, 70*, (1950), pp. 34–40.

comparing it with recent developments, it is easy to lose sight of the fact that the dynamical view of Lewin, or one very much like it, is a necessary condition for explaining the nature of human groups nonvitalistically. The dynamic group, from this point of view, is always a system—a complex of two or more individuals in symbolic or affective interaction. It cannot be accounted for only in terms of the preexisting characteristics of its individual members; it is to be explained more adequately in terms of the dynamic relations which the individuals bear to one another. The group constituted by this mutual or interactive relationship is not a "steady state" merely, nor a self-contained equilibrium, but a continuous process of adaptation of individuals to one another and to their mutual problems. The result of this mutual adaptation is a set or complex of differentiations, integrations, and ever more complex patterns of organization.

The basic concept in this view, whatever terminology is used, is *action in a field.* In nonsocial action, such as that of many animals, it may be called *simple behavior.* In the human individual, who always lives in a group, it is *symbolic interaction.* In group behavior it is an *intricate net of symbolic interactions.* When the group, finally, is complicated, as it usually is, by cultural demands or expectations, the behavior consists of *sanctioned forms of symbolic interaction.* Group dynamics as a science is thus an interdisciplinary investigation. It is the emphasis upon and exemplification of this interdisciplinary aspect which characterizes all of Lewin's psychological theories and researches.

One must point out, against persistent criticisms of the foregoing view, that in this mode of analysis the group is never reified. That reification has been characteristic of most earlier views of group structure cannot be denied. Because individuals act *as if* their groups were metaphysically real, we tend unwittingly to look upon them as objectively real.[33] In Lewin's view, however, the group is not the sum

[33] See F. H. Allport's telling criticism of the group-mind hypothesis in The group fallacy in relation to social science, *Amer. J. Sociol.,* 29 (1924), 668–706.

of its members. It is a structure that emerges from the interactions of individuals, a structure which itself produces changes in the individual members. Research has shown that it is difficult to predict the behavior of persons in a group from premeasures of personality variables. The clear fact emerges that "when individuals are put together a *system* is created [and this] is the critical fact which cannot be overlooked."[34]

Lewin resolved an old difficulty regarding the nature of the group and thereby bridged the gap between the group-oriented hypothesis and the individualistic approach. Much thinking and speculation regarding the group had defined it as a collective entity, or group mind. This view held that a group of people acts, feels, and thinks as a distinct being, for it *is* a distinct being.[35] The view of Le Bon was almost, but not quite, outgrown by McDougall. According to the latter, a group is an organized "system of forces," greater, more powerful, more comprehensive than any single individual, or any sum of individuals. It can think, will, and act in a manner similar to that of an individual who performs the same activities.[36] The chief merit of McDougall's view is his marked stress on groups as "unities" and "organic wholes."

The individualistic approach, on the other hand, as represented best by F. H. Allport, who helped us to break away from the vitalistic thinking of the past, runs the danger of reducing all group behavior to an elementaristic form. Group behavior, he held, is to be explained by the same mechanisms that explain the behavior of the individual.

[34] R. L. Solomon and T. N. Lemann, *Report for the first five years, 1946–1951* (Cambridge, Mass.: Laboratory of Social Relations, Harvard University, 1952). The above analysis runs throughout the works of Lewin, especially as expounded in the following: *Field theory and social science* (New York: Harper & Bros., 1951) and Group decision and social change, in G. E. Swanson, T. M. Newcomb, and E. L. Hartley (eds.), *Readings in social psychology* (2d ed.; New York: Henry Holt & Co., Inc., 1952), pp. 330–44.

[35] See G. Le Bon, *The crowd* (London: T. Fisher Unwin, 1917), originally published in Paris in 1895.

[36] W. McDougall, *The group mind* (New York: G. P. Putnam's Sons, Inc., 1920), pp. 9–16.

Thus, in contrast to most early psychologists and sociologists, who placed the group before the individual, Allport placed the individual before the group. His assertion that "if we take care of the individuals, psychologically speaking, the groups will be found to take care of themselves," is surprisingly uncritical in a psychologist who has shown more than ordinary scientific acumen. His view, instead of bringing the individual and the group together and stressing their inseparability, virtually eliminates the group altogether. It places group phenomena in the individual and by an additive process describes them as the sum total of the actions of each individual taken separately. This individualistic approach goes contrary to a generally accepted scientific proposition, namely, that a group possess properties which are different from those of the individuals taken separately. While Allport's view has made an important contribution in exorcising the "group mind" from psychology and arguing for the importance of the individual in group processes, he has failed to give us an adequate account of the crucial relation between the individual and the group.[37]

Properties of psychological groups. Until recently the focus in group dynamics, as we have shown, was not on such large and complex social forms as cultures, nations, and governments, but on smaller face-to-face groups, which might be called *psychological* groups. While it might be argued that there is no essential psychological difference between formal social organizations and psychological groups, this assertion rests on dubious premises. Whether or not the psychological factors that lead a small group, a committee, for instance, to a collective decision are in principle the same as those that impel a nation to engage in war, there is evidence that leads one to doubt the similarity of the two processes. This is, however, an open issue.

A psychological group exists only when at least two conditions prevail: (1) there must be at least two persons in

[37] Allport's systematic position is stated in his *Social psychology,* which has already been cited.

relation to each other, and (2) they must be interactive. The psychological "force" which holds them together and forms an elementary group is an *interact*. A psychological group is thus characterized by at least minimal awareness in which each individual responds at least minimally to the other. Maximally, each person perceives the others not only from his own perspective, but from the perspective of all of them. In terms of its dynamic properties, the psychological group is a structure of behaving individuals who are constantly undergoing a redistribution relative to one another. It forms a "field," not in the sense that it has an existence of its own, but in the sense that, while it differs from its members, the latter behave in such a way that the field, or the psychological structure as a whole, becomes the crucial and deciding factor in the behavior of each. As in any *Gestalt* or whole, the individuals are not obliterated, but they act now in accordance with the field of forces generated by the responses of each to all.

The upshot of the foregoing analysis is that neither the individual nor the psychological group structure has a separate existence. Each implies and functionally depends upon the other. The group's behavior always takes place between or among individual's; and the behavior of individuals is determined by the structure of their interrelationship. The study of the group, or the science of group dynamics, accordingly, is interdisciplinary. It accounts for group behavior by integrating relevant data from several disciplines, especially psychology, sociology, and cultural anthropology.[38]

Experiments with Groups. It was characteristic of Lewin, especially after he settled in America, to put his ideas to experimental test and to work out their practical implications. His pioneer research in this connection was carried on at the University of Iowa with the able assistance of Ronald Lippitt and R. K. White. This experimental study is now so well known, and its main results have been so com-

[38] See K. Lewin, *A dynamic theory of personality,* trans. by D. K. Adams and K. E. Zener (New York: McGraw-Hill Book Co., Inc., 1935), chap. i.

pletely assimilated in contemporary social psychology, that a detailed presentation here is unnecessary. However, the following summary may prove useful.

Study of "social climates." Lewin and his collaborators set out to investigate the effect on its members of small groups organized along "democratic," "authoritarian," and "laissez faire" patterns. The three groups were composed of ten-year-old boys. In the democratic group the leader did not order or direct and was "fact-minded" in his evaluation of the boys' activities. The boys for the most part worked out their own problems, but were free to consult the leader whenever they desired. In the authoritarian group, policies and activities were determined by the leader, and his evaluation of the boys' work was "personal." In the laissez faire group the leader neither participated nor voluntarily gave suggestions, and the boys were given complete freedom to solve their problems in their own way.

The results in behavior and work in these groups were strikingly different. These differences can be brought out by describing the authoritarian group only, for the other two varied from it in expected ways. The experiment clearly demonstrated that the authoritarian atmosphere impaired initiative and independence and bred hostility and aggressiveness. The boys were self-centered, frustrated, and hostile to a much larger degree than those of either the democratic or laissez faire group. They tended, furthermore, to be submissive, lifeless, and apathetic, and bodily tensions were frequently manifested.[39]

Action research in industry. When Lewin moved to the Massachusetts Institute of Technology, he began to apply his

[39] K. Lewin, R. Lippitt, and R. K. White, Patterns of aggressive behavior in experimentally created "Social Climates," *J. soc. Psychol., 10* (1939), 271–99. See also R. Lippitt, An experimental study of authoritarian and democratic group atmosphere, in *Studies in topological and vector psychology,* Vol. I (University of Iowa Studies in Child Welfare, No. 16, 1940); R. Lippitt and R. K. White, The "social climate" of children's groups, in R. Barker *et al., Child development and behavior* (New York: McGraw-Hill Book Co., Inc., 1943).

knowledge of group psychology to industry. In a controlled experiment which he performed before his untimely death, he was able to demonstrate that poor motivation, occasioned by the workers' resentment against authoritarian methods in a factory, was a very important factor in their failure and their unproductivity. The authoritarian management was found to be the frustrating agent in production efficiency. When the workers were permitted to air their own views and make suggestions, they felt that they were—as indeed they were—participants in the decision-making process, and their motivation improved and production exceeded previous levels.[40]

Group decision in changing attitudes. The effect of the group on the behavior of the individual was demonstrated by Lewin's experiment in changing people's food habits. During World War II, when meat for civilian consumption was scarce, Lewin and his collaborators were able, by means of group self-decision, to induce people to eat meats which are usually rejected by American homemakers. The investigators used six groups, consisting of thirteen to seventeen persons, in the experiment. Three groups were encouraged, by means of lectures, demonstrations, and patriotic appeals, to eat kidneys, sweetbreads, and beef hearts. The other three groups were given the same lectures, but they were also given opportunities to discuss the subject freely and at length. The results were clear cut. Of the women who listened to the lectures without participating in any discussion, only 3 per cent served any of the recommended foods. However, 32 per cent of the women who not only attended the lectures but also discussed the problem and arrived at their own decisions regarding the use of these meats served them to their families.

From this experiment Lewin concluded what subsequent researches and experiments have been confirming: When members of a group themselves have an opportunity to get

[40] See K. Lewin, *Resolving social conflicts* (New York: Harper & Bros., 1948), pp. 125–41; L. Coch and J. R. P. French, Jr., Overcoming resistance to change, *Hum. Relat., 1* (1948), 512–32.

the facts in a problem situation, they will solve it together and accept the solution because it is a product of their own deliberations. People will believe facts, in other words, because they themselves have discovered them and for the same reason that they believe in themselves.[41]

CONCLUDING REMARKS. It was pointed out before (p. 20) that premeasures of personality variables are not very helpful in predicting the behavior of persons in a group. This conclusion is in line with the field dynamic principle that the structure of the present situation determines an individual's behavior. This principle—the principle that only the contemporaneous field of forces or events affect an individual—has been the most controversial tenet in Lewin's systematic position. Whether it will be ultimately confirmed, we cannot here decide, but that it is logically necessary and methodologically useful in a systematic description of group behavior at present cannot be doubted. Unless we assume it as a premise, we cannot account for the crucial difference between individual and group behavior. Unless we use it as a working principle, we are baffled by the fact that, irrespective of an individual's psychological biography, he behaves in accordance with the properties of the group at a particular time.

In the interest of scientific objectivity we must make it clear that, contrary to widespread interpretations, the principle of the contemporaneity of causation does not deny the efficacy of the past nor the motivating force of the future. In meeting criticisms of his principle, Lewin carefully stated his view in terms of the perspective of time. The individual, he said, perceives not only the present situation but acts on the basis of his own past and his expectations of the future. The psychological past, present, and future are properties of a psychological field at a given time. The essence of scientific explanation and prediction of events in a certain area is

[41] For details of the above experiment see Lewin, Group decision and social change, in Swanson *et al.*, *Readings in social psychology*, pp. 330–44. The question might be raised whether the discussion group would have come to the same conclusion in the absence of the lectures.

the ordering of change to the conditions of the field at the time. This way of conceptualizing psychological causation makes it possible to account for individual and group behavior by means of a single principle, and promises to bridge the gap between individual and social psychology.[42]

MORENO AND SOCIOMETRY

While Moreno's work in sociometry is well known, its relevance to the developing field of group dynamics has not been widely recognized. Paradoxically, the Lewinians, who should have been quick to appreciate the relationship, have been less receptive to its importance than social scientists generally. His studies of role behavior, surely, should have been recognized as being directly related to group dynamics.[43]

ROLE THEORY. The subject of role-playing was extensively discussed in general and abstract form by Cooley and G. H. Mead. The merit of Moreno's work on the subject is that he used it at once as a mode of analyzing intragroup behavior and as a method of measuring social interaction. Taking the role of another is a mark of the socialized human being. Since one individual's role-taking presupposes the role-playing of another, role behavior gives people opportunities to accept and to be accepted by others. Role behavior is possible only in a group. The group presents numerous situations in which the individual can display his skills, exercise his abilities, and become recognized for whatever individual merits he may possess and the group is willing to recognize and reward. Group harmony depends in good measure on the ability and willingness of every individual to play his roles in such a way as to enable every other individual to play his own role successfully. Much of

42 For a comprehensive, though somewhat technical discussion of the concept of the present field, see Lewin, *Field theory in social science*, pp. 43–59.

43 For an early statement of role behavior and of sociometry, see J. L. Moreno, *Who shall survive? A new approach to the problem of human interrelations* (Washington, D.C.: Nervous and Mental Disease Publishing Co., 1934). Our survey has made clear, we hope, that the approach is not *new*.

the satisfaction that a person finds in belonging to a group is derived from his opportunities to play his role as one of its members.

Moreno described the interactive nature of role behavior in terms of attraction and repulsion. Mutual attraction, or positive sociometric choice, makes group interaction possible and fruitful; mutual repulsion, or negative sociometric choice, is inimical to interpersonal action. The attraction-repulsion valence is, in Moreno's system, the fundamental principle of social interaction and interindividual relations.

Sociometry. Moreno was not satisfied with a formal analysis and description of role behavior, but introduced a technique for measuring the attraction-repulsion dimension in human relationships. This technique he calls "sociometry." By this method attraction and repulsion of members of a group are represented by "sociograms," that is, diagrams indicating who is attracted by whom on the basis of spontaneous expressions of likes and dislikes by individuals for one another. The concepts of leadership and isolation have also been investigated by this technique, especially by Helen Jennings, a close collaborator of Moreno.[44]

Like field theory, sociometry is eminently an interdisciplinary investigation of group relations. It has, accordingly, been widely used by social psychology and sociology. In the interests of scientific objectivity, however, it should be added that the interdisciplinary character of both the theory and the method of sociometry has been adversely affected by the partisan nature of Moreno's influence. Neither psychologists nor sociologists have been as receptive to Moreno's work as they might have been because of the sectarian and almost cultist development of the field.

Group Therapy. While Moreno's work is not directly associated with group psychotherapy the kinship is very obvious. The concept of role-playing has been used by Moreno in his technique of "psychodrama." This consists in

[44] See Helen H. Jennings, *Leadership and isolation* (2d ed.; New York: Longmans, Green & Co., Inc., 1950).

the role-enactment of individuals in a group in more or less spontaneous expressions of emotional conflicts. Thus, a husband and wife with the aid, if necessary, of other individuals called "auxiliary egos," who represent important persons in the real-life situations of the married couple, have an opportunity to externalize their hostilities and thereby learn to see them and each other more objectively. The objectification of the conflicts through role-playing helps to resolve them. In this way the role-enacting group serves as an instrument of therapy for individual tensions and conflicts. Like all group therapy, psychodrama is a form of social re-education in which the individual is given an opportunity, through group participation and a permissive group expression, to acquire skill in role behavior and to increase individual security by learning the role-expectancy of others. The group is a form of social treatment in that group experiences of identification and acceptance are therapeutic realities.[45]

CONCLUSION

Our survey of the development of group dynamics has, we hope, established its multiple origin. It has, too, we trust, pointed up the futility and unfruitfulness of attempts to give priority to a single person or to a specific discipline. Sociologists, by the very nature of their interests, were without doubt pioneers in the study of group phenomena. Once they emancipated themselves from the static and metaphysical speculations of the precursors of scientific sociology, they concentrated largely on social change, social control, and collective behavior. In evaluating their contributions to the emerging science of group dynamics the most telling criticism is that their ideas were largely abstract and formal and inaccessible to objective and experimental investigation.

Psychologists, on the other hand, thanks to the established tradition of experimental attack on psychological

[45] See J. L. Moreno, *Psychodrama,* Vol. I (New York: Beacon House, Inc., 1946).

problems stemming from Weber, Fechner, and Wundt, were quick to subject group phenomena to experimental investigation. Thus, near the end of the nineteenth century, as we have seen, while sociologists were discussing social change and social control in the form of verbal analysis and empirical observation, psychologists were setting up experiments under controlled conditions.

Both sociologists and psychologists, nevertheless, made us aware of the importance of the presence or absence of other persons in the behavior of the individual. Both have stressed the fact that an isolate and a group have different psychological structures and that, accordingly, just as one can study the psychological structure of an individual, so one can investigate the psychological structure of a group. Sociologists and psychologists alike have recognized the potency of social stimulation in the form of encouragement, criticism, rivlary, and the like. They have surmised that the essential difference between the behavior of an individual and that of a group is that the isolated individual, if it is possible to discover a genuine isolate, has no established relationship with others, whereas a group of individuals always behaves in a social context.

If our survey has held fast to historical evidence, and if it has been relatively free from partisanship and personal bias—and we believe that it has done both—then it should be clear that group dynamics in its current form is *par excellence* an indisciplinary investigation. If we have failed to include the contributions of other social sciences, notably political science and anthropology to group dynamics, it is not due to a lack of appreciation of their share in bringing it to its developed form but to the limited scope of our investigation.[46]

[46] See for example, K. W. Deutsch, *Political community at the international level: problems of definition and measurement,* Organization Behavior Section, Foreign Policy Project, No. 2 (Princeton: Princeton University Press, 1953); E. D. Chapple, Quantitative analysis of the interaction of individuals, *Proc. Nat. Acad. Sci., 25* (1939), 58–67; E. D. Chapple and C. M. Arensberg, Measuring human relations, *Genet. Psychol. Monogr.,* Vol. 22, (1940). For political science ideas, see Chapter 11.

Our survey, finally, has suggested something of the slow process in which group psychology has emancipated itself from vitalistic descriptions of group phenomena and from the strong influence of the group-mind fallacy on the theoretical analysis of group properties. For significant work in this emancipation social psychology and group dynamics owe a signal debt to Floyd H. Allport and Kurt Lewin.

A word of caution should be interjected here, one that will be applicable throughout the exposition of every phase of group dynamics. There is a tendency in many present-day studies of group dynamics to overstress the influence of the group on the individual and to submerge the individual's role in the group. In some quarters this tendency has been carried to such lengths as to make the individual practically inconsequential. Existing data and experimental research *do not* support the confident claim that the group is almost always superior to the individual in solving problems, acquiring knowledge, and resolving social tensions. They *do not* justify the claims made for "leaderless" groups, or for the assertion that leadership to be justified in a democratic society must always be passed around from person to person, like a pipe of peace. It is historically unrealistic to minimize the role of ascendant individuals in the development of groups and the growth of human institutions. Group dynamics has *not* demonstrated that creativeness is largely, if not wholly, a group phenomenon. Just as it is a form of egotism to extol the individual beyond what the facts themselves permit, so it is a form of tyranny to worship the group as if it were the source of all excellence. The conception of group dynamics presented in this book, therefore, while reviewing as many facts as possible to show the effect—and even the frequent superiority—of the group over the individual, never implies that the studies here described are sufficient to corroborate the claims of extremists. Since our final chapter, however, deals in detail with this phenomenon, we merely voice our initial caveat here, hoping that the reader will bear it in mind as he surveys with us the many problems of group dynamics.

Part II

GROUP DEVELOPMENT: DYNAMIC FACTORS IN GROUP BEHAVIOR

CHAPTER 2

Psychological Structure of the Group

The study of the human group, which for a time was almost entirely the concern of the sociologist, is now an important problem in social psychology and a fundamental topic in group dynamics. Research on the nature of the group is an important convergence of several disciplines.

We gave initial descriptions of the group in Chapter 1, especially in our brief account of field theory and its analysis of the properties of psychological groups. The subject is so basic and important in the exposition of group dynamics that a more detailed treatment of it is essential. This is all the more evident in view of the fact that, as we have already stressed, earlier conceptions of the nature of the group were scarcely more than metaphysical fictions based either on common-sense observation or on vitalistic theories of the organization of parts into wholes. In this chapter, therefore, we shall present a social-psychological view of group structure that is at once consistent with the research discoveries of recent social science and the canons of a rigorous scientific analysis.

THEORETICAL ANALYSIS OF THE GROUP

The group, we have said, is not an aggregate or collection of individuals. Nor is the group, we have also argued, something which has an independent existence apart from the individuals who compose it. Concepts such as Le Bon's "collective mentality," Durkheim's "collective representations," and McDougall's "group-mind," to cite only the best known, are scientifically untenable. To argue as F. H. Allport does, on the other hand, that if we take care of the individual the group will take care of itself (see Chapter 1, p. 21) is not supported by the facts. Neither the individual nor the group, to reiterate once more, has an existence apart from the other. Isolated or completely independent behavior cannot be *meaningfully* defined, and as something occurring out of a social context, it is nonexistent.

Recent researches in biology, sociology, and anthropology disclose that the evolution of the individual has depended on the evolution of the group. What man might have become over the millennia of his evolution outside a group is idle speculation, but the evidence suggests that he is what he is in no small degree because he evolved, not merely as an individual, but in a group. The individual has survived only because he has from the beginning lived in a group, and groups themselves have evolved as socially fit organizations of individuals. Biological factors are not explanatory of survival and of present behavior. They have psychological meaning only in a social context. There is a growing conviction among biologists, based on experimental investigation, that all animals are social, and that the solitary individual is nonexistent.[1]

[1] There is a growing literature dealing with this problem. See especially B. W. Kunkel, Members one of another, *Sci. Monthly, 4* (1917), 534–43; W. C. Allee, *Animal Aggregations: A study of general sociology* (Chicago: The University of Chicago Press, 1931), *The social life of animals* (New York: W. W. Norton & Co., Inc., 1938, and *Cooperation among animals* (rev. ed.; New York: Abelard-Schuman, Ltd., 1951); J. P. Scott, Group formation determined by social behavior: a comparative study of two mammalian societies, *Sociometry, 8* (1945), 42–52; S. R. Slavson (ed.), *The practice of group therapy* (New York: International Universities Press, Inc., 1947).

FIELD DYNAMICS. At the basis of every study of organic relationship is the problem of organization. Philosophers, in seeking to understand the nature of truth, are invariably confronted with the problem of the relation between the particular and the general, with "internal" and "external" relations. Biologists, in investigating the nature of organic life, are faced with the problem of integrating the organ with the organism. Psychologists, in formulating a theory of group behavior, come up against the difficulty of relating the individual to the group. Each in his own way must sooner or later come to grips with the problem of the relationship of the part to the whole. Historically there have been three distinct philosophies of organization—the mechanistic, the vitalistic, and the field dynamic. The field dynamic, which alone concerns us here, affirms that, while we may theoretically isolate the individual from his context or milieu, the two are in reality inseparable and form a dynamic or organic unity. There are several factors that account for the organic unity.

Social interaction. This is a type of relationship between two or more persons in which the actions of one are affected by the actions of another. It takes place by means of communication, anticipation, role-perception-and-enactment, and significant symbols.

Interaction as such, while it mutually affects two or more people, may remain relatively static and unproductive of change in human relations. It is important in the study of individuals and groups because it takes place through *communication* whereby two or more individuals are enabled to reach common understandings and effect cooperative behavior. As interaction becomes more communicative, undifferentiated individuals and their behavior take on a clearer focus and meaning. Each can now more clearly articulate his relation to the others and adjust himself to them with greater skill. It is important furthermore because it is through communication that the individual experiences his initial feeling of belonging to the group, perceives its common culture, and discovers that he has a particular position in it. And finally, as will become clear later, group discussion, group decision, and collective problem-solving are impossible in the absence of communicative interaction.

The concept of anticipation or expectancy is well established in psychology, where it is often called "set," or a readiness to react to stimuli. All group behavior is characterized by anticipation or expectancy. When the infant cries, he "expects" the mother to come to him. While his mother is performing an accommodative act toward him, such as stimulating him with her breast when he is hungry, he is adjusting his behavior toward her in such a manner as to lead to the satisfaction of his hunger. His anticipation of nourishment is a step in the completion of the communicative act. An individual performing a group activity who is unskilled in anticipating the oncoming acts of others will be equally ineffective in modifying his behavior toward the group norm. In this case he never fully belongs to the group, for he fails to adjust himself to the expectation of others.

From anticipation to role-perception-and-enactment is but a small step. Man is a social animal, among other reasons, because he constantly views himself through another person's eyes, because he vicariously experiences the thoughts, feelings, and acts of another individual. Our acts are ways of behaving which we attribute to others because we perceive them in ourselves. Perceiving one's role is but one phase of the process. Man is also a role-playing animal. He *enacts* the perception which he has of his relation to other individuals. It is the enactment of another person's role that gives meaning to one's own role.

Communication, anticipation, and role behavior reach a high level of complexity when they take place by means of *significant symbolization.* Communication in a group proceeds through conventionalized language, through symbols which, while they frequently are no more than motor cues or gestures, have approximately the same meaning to everyone in the group. In complex interaction, such as that taking place in a dynamic group, the cue or gesture takes on a conscious or self-conscious meaning; it becomes a significant symbol. A significant symbol has the same effect on the individual using it that it has on the individual for whom it is intended.[2] By virtue of communication, anticipation, role behavior, and symbolic interaction people form common perceptions of one another and of the situation in which they interact. When they see the same object or event in very much the same way, they are able to work in unison toward the same goal. When they have no common perspective, they work at cross purposes, and their relationship is conflictual rather than consensual. Especially clear in this analysis is the role-perception-and-enactment function, in which each person assumes a clearly structured psychological activity toward the others.

C. *Role of the individual in the group.* The relation between the individual and the group has long been a vexing problem in social psychology. Although we have reiterated the proposition that the individual and the group are inseparable, the problem cannot be stated so simply. For too long it was thought—and the idea has been supported by common sense—that the group is a collection of individuals and that when there are no individuals there is no group. This interpretation gave rise to the equally untenable view that an individual remains unaffected by group membership, for the group consists only of the individuals acting individually. Recent researches have, however, dispelled this conclusion, along with the mystical notion of a group mind. While we cannot in the present state of our knowledge say with certainty that either view is correct, there is a growing consensus among social psychologists that individuals behave differently in groups than they do as solitary persons. There are psychological influences in a group which are different from those affecting a person in solitude. The group possesses properties unlike those that are

[2] See H. Bonner, *Social psychology: an interdisciplinary approach* (New York: American Book Co., 1953), pp. 42–46.

present in the single individual. The presence of other people elicits a different pattern of responses than those which characterize the behavior of an isolate. The co-ordinated behavior of group members is unlike the integrated behavior of a solitary person.

The experimental investigations reviewed in Chapter 1, as well as a large body of recent data, lend strong support to the foregoing observations. Particularly interesting and convincing is Sherif's well-known experiment on the "autokinetic" phenomenon. When an individual was exposed for a few seconds to a fixed point of light in a dark room, he saw it not only as a moving point but estimated its motion in terms of his own frame of reference, or "anchorage point." When several individuals, each with his own anchorage point, were permitted to compare their own range with those of others in a group, the individuals modified their frame of reference in the direction of the group's norm. They saw the light, in other words, as the group as a whole saw it, despite their prior individually established anchorage points.[3]

There is an aspect of the relation of the individual to the group, however, which is most unrealistically overlooked. Students of group dynamics, practical workers in the field more than researchers, have exaggerated the group-dependency needs of individuals. It is certain that individuals desire to belong and to be accepted by others. But all healthy individuals periodically get fed up with belonging and are motivated by a strong need for independence. Co-operation and agreement are not always a blessing, and independence, disagreement, and all-round self-expression are the source of individual creativeness and good will. If the extreme emphasis on group dependence becomes a norm, as some writers seem to think it is doing, the fear of expressing one's individuality will be an inescapable consequence. But in the eager desire to reach conformity and agreement among ourselves, we do not necessarily resolve

[3] M. Sherif, A study of some social factors in perception, *Arch. Psychol.*, *187* (1935).

our conflicts. On the contrary we conceal them, and in this way they do damage to the group in a manner analogous to the way repressed feelings injure the individual. In this manner the group can no more find out what troubles it than can the isolated individual. The fact is that conflict is an inescapable part of life. Dependence and independence need to be recognized as twin desires in all healthy individuals. The conflicts arising from the twin needs for dependence and independence in themselves may not be harmful, but the devious rationalizations which a denial of them generates can easily be detrimental.

Conclusion regarding the part-whole relationship. The problem of the relation of part to whole is an old one in science. It has plagued psychology in the form of the relation of the individual to the group. To most nineteenth-century sociologists the group was a reality and the individual an abstraction. To most psychologists of the same period only the individual was real, the group being an abstraction. Careful research in the past quarter-century, however, has demonstrated that the individual does not exist per se, but in mutual relationship with others; that the group likewise has no independent existence, but is a pattern of interacting persons, producing and produced by a situational context. The group is thus a *network of psychological relationships*, not a mystical entity. Using more conventional language, we might say that the group is the stimulus-situation, whereas the individual is the organism who is affected by and acts upon the stimulus-situation.

This way of stating an old problem has marked a turning point in the analysis of group structure. It denies autonomy to both psychology and sociology in the analysis and description of group behavior. The sociological concept of a group mind has been replaced by the social-psychological view of the group as a field of interacting and intercommunicating individuals. When then we speak in this book of collective problem-solving, group decision-making, and the like, we do not mean that the group as an autonomous being solves or discusses anything. It is but a way of stating that individuals, forming a psychological group structure, have solved a problem together. The solution, while a "product" in the sense that it can be denoted, is always a process of social interaction and cannot generate in a vacuum.

The old problem of priority—of which comes first, the individual or the group?—from our point of view is meaningless. Thus it seems to the present writer that neither the individualistic nor the collectivistic model is exclusively valid. To say, as F. H. Allport and J. F. Dashiell have done, that in group-cognitive activities the individual is the unit of behavior is to nullify their own demonstration that the individual's behavior is directed by the group. To assert, on the other hand, as Bales and Strodtbeck have done, that group problem-solving is the prototype of individual solutions is only a partial truth.[4] One can predict the solution of a common problem neither from the thinking of any single individual involved in it, nor from the group as a whole. The only satisfactory way of stating the problem is to assert that individual and group thinking take place in different field contexts. While individual thinking is no doubt to some extent an introjection of the thought processes of others—psychoanalysis would seem to confirm this in the development of thinking in a child—the essence of individual thinking is that the context is different. Group thinking occurs in a *real* social context; whereas individual thinking takes place in an imagined or remembered social context. A group solution represents the solution of a problem by individuals in interactive communication. It has no independent existence.

When we speak of the group, according to this approach, we think of it, not as a generalized entity, as sociologists do when they refer to an institution, but as an interaction system, as a dynamic and organized totality. This way of

[4] R. F. Bales and F. L. Strodtbeck, Phases in group problem-solving, *J. abnorm. soc. Psychol.*, *46* (1951), 485–95.

analyzing the problem exempts us from the charge of reification to which Lewin inadvertently exposed himself. Despite Lewin's misleading assertion concerning the "reality" of the group, however, the whole content and spirit of his researches and writings are a convincing refutation of the group-mind hypothesis. He has argued—and recent researches have confirmed his assertions—that the extremists on both sides have obscured rather than illuminated the problem of interindividual relationships. By stressing one factor to the exclusion of the other, writers on group psychology have concealed the most important fact, namely, that the two factors constitute a unity. To attribute priority to either the individual or the group is not only meaningless and unrealistic but is contrary to the evidence disclosed by competent research. A group product, whether it be a fact learned, a problem solved, or a tension removed is an interindividual property—something experienced by individuals but shared and agreed upon by them together.

Theoretical Constructs for Group Dynamics. Empirical explanations or descriptions of phenomena seldom probe beneath the surface. This is most frequently true when these phenomena are formulated statistically. Theoretical explanations, those that employ logical constructs, are designed to disclose the underlying dynamics of the phenomena being investigated. The history of science bears witness to the usefulness of theoretically sound constructs, for they have frequently led to the discovery of the interrelations between empirical or experimental variables. Their test lies in their fruitfulness, in their function of identifying the variables which are functionally connected with what can be empirically or experimentally observed. "A scientist may use any mathematics, a poet any language, and a philosopher any logic if it fits his needs."[5] The investigator in group dynamics, in seeking to find a "fit" to his conceptions, may use as Lewin has done, topological constructs and dy-

[5] H. Bonner, Field theory and sociology, *Sociol. Soc. Res.*, 33 (1949), 172.

namic analysis. We shall present the essential concepts in the present section.

Topological constructs. In presenting the interactionist position of Simmel we called attention to the concept of *social space* which characterizes his views on the human group (see Chapter 1, pp. 9–10). The spatial properties of human relationships may be described by means of topological constructs, of which the most important are those presented below.

A *region* is a segment of social space, an element of a social field. Regions differ in size, shape, and boundary. Irrespective of these differences they are topologically equivalent. A region can be divided into *subregions*, usually designated as subgroups, which frequently play important roles in making either for harmony or conflict in a group. Dissident elements, disruptive role behavior, minority groups are well-known examples. Subregions create important problems of group balance, group harmony, and the role of the leader in resolving group conflicts. The subregions represent social differentions, group imbalance, and collective reorganization.

A *barrier* represents the degree of resistance to inter-individual communication. It hinders group participation and group action. Examples are numerous. If a group, determined to resolve its own tensions regarding, say, race relations is dominated by prejudice, its attempt to reach its goal may be seriously impaired; or the group, unable to surmount the barrier, may cease to function altogether.

When a person surmounts a barrier, his behavior is ordered to a new social region. The new social region is instrumental in restructuring a person and changing his behavior. A person's behavior, as we have seen, is influenced by the region in which he has *membership*. To repeat a former assertion, when persons act together they give rise to a system of relationship, so that it is difficult to predict their behavior as a system or group from premeasures of personality variables (see Chapter 1, p. 20). Their membership in a group restructures their individual behavior.

Dynamic constructs. Spatial or topological constructs do not inform us regarding interaction, communication, and other behavioral manifestations. They do not account for change and activity. Activity and change require for their description constructs which indicate locomotion or mobility. For this purpose we need *dynamic* constructs.

While a *social field* is spatial or topological, its essential property is mobility. It is dynamic, that is, a changing pattern of interacting individuals. A social field is any acting or changing group to which the behavior of individuals, regions, and subregions may be ordered.

Tension is another dynamic construct. It refers to the excitation state of a field, a region, or an individual. It is not identical with the psychopathologist's notion of strain, anxiety, or emotional disturbance, but with set, expectancy, receptiveness. Abstractly, it is "a tendency for changes in the direction of equalization of the state of neighboring systems."[6] Thus, to cite Lewin's example, in studying morale in the army, it is important to know whether the loyalty of the individual soldier is directed to his squad, his platoon, his regiment, or to the whole army.[7]

The concept of *vector* has an important place in physics, where it is defined as a force having both direction and magnitude. If we define a "force" as a directed excitation state, we can use the concept of vector to describe the behavior of a group. Interacting individuals trying to solve a problem or directing their action toward a common goal are behaving vectorially; that is, they are moving in a certain direction with all the psychological energy which is available to them by the character of the field situation at the moment. A vector thus represents locomotions in a field, changes in field structure, the goal of individuals working together, etc. When strong barriers to interaction exist, the magnitude of

[6] K. Lewin, *Field theory in social science* (New York: Harper & Bros., 1951), p. 11.

[7] *Ibid.*, p. 162.

the vectors directed toward a goal will be greater than when the field is fluid or the barriers are few. Conversely, a field or group of interacting persons is the more fluid the smaller the forces which are necessary, other things being equal, to produce a given change in the situation.[8] The success of a group in solving a problem, for instance, will depend, among other things, upon the number and magnitude of the barriers which impede the free communication of ideas and feelings among the members. The situation as a whole is described by a psychological vector, by the striving of individuals for a specific goal.

The concept of *valence* represents the attraction or repulsion value of an object for an individual or a group. It describes cohesive and disruptive forces in group relationships, or cooperation and conflict. A *positive* valence designates membership-character, group belongingness, a vector directed toward the same region. A *negative* valence designates isolation, leaving the field (or group), a vector directed away from the same region.

The relation of the part to the whole, or of the individual to the group, may thus be analyzed topologically and dynamically. Topology is the general science of spatial relations. Dynamics is the general science of the motion of bodies. Topology and dynamics together give us a nonmetrical description of reality: the one, the positions of bodies in a field; the other, their motion through it.

Concluding Remarks. The value of the "constructive" analysis of group phenomena lies in its emphasis of dynamic relational concepts. A theory of group behavior, on the basis of this approach, relates concepts to one another, thus forming a system. In dealing with real group activities in concrete groups, it enables us to see the actions of individuals in their transactive relation with one another. Together, theory and practice give us a view of group behavior that takes cognizance of the individual case and of general laws

[8] See K. Lewin, *Principles of topological psychology* (New York: McGraw-Hill Book Co., Inc., 1936), p. 87.

at the same time. This is in substance the meaning of Lewin's important distinction between the Aristotelian notion of "substance" and the Galilean concept of "function."[9] The analysis of group structures is dynamic in proportion to the use of constructs by which empirical data are organized into a coherent system. Behavior itself, whether individual or collective, is dynamic if changes or adjustments in one "part" are followed by changes or adjustments in all the others. We need no longer worry, from this point of view, about the reality of the group. It is real, not in the sense that a substantive entity is real, but as a *dynamic whole*, as an *interdependence of parts*, as an identification of individuals with others in a transactive or cooperative relationship.

A dynamic group, then, is not a collection of interdependent individuals, merely, but a group of persons who are *psychologically* aware of their interindividual relationships and who are *moving toward a goal that they have agreed upon collectively*. The interaction of one person with others forms a web of relationships in which the action of each takes place more or less spontaneously. Their interactions are integrated in such a way that their psychological tensions are shared. The "togetherness" of the group as a dynamic structure is due to a "circular" reaction in which there is a high degree of self-intensification in each member of his own "excitement" as he finds it reflected in others. In this process shared feelings and tension, which in each member separately had no adequate outlet, are freely expressed. When a person's responses to others is shared by them, when these experiences become reciprocal or interactive, there exists the basic condition of group behavior.

[9] K. L. Lewin, The conflict between Aristotelian and Galilean modes of thought in psychology, *J. gen Psychol.,* 5 (1931), 141-77. This contrast is Lewin's application to psychology of a distinction made by Cassirer, who influenced Lewin, between substance and function in scientific and mathematical theory. See E. Cassirer, *Substanzbegriff und Funktionsbegriff* (Berlin: Verlag Cassirer, 1910); translated into English as *Substance and function* (Chicago: Open Court Publishing Co., 1923).

SOME OBSERVATIONS REGARDING GROUP DEVELOPMENT

On the basis of our analysis thus far, and as suggested by empirical studies of groups in process, some significant propositions emerge. These propositions, while involving concepts which have already been expounded, are not identical with them. We have, for example, discussed the concept or process of interaction on several occasions. Basic though it is to group formation, interaction helps to account for *any* kind of group process, from the casual greeting of two neighbors as they pass each other on the street to the complex involvement of persons in a decision-making group trying to solve a common problem.

MOTIVATION. It is a commonplace that human groups exist because in interacting with others in accommodative ways a person can better satisfy his own needs, desires, and wishes. His basic and derived needs can be satisfied only through the accommodation or cooperation of at least one other person. Survival, security, friendship, affection, and the like, can be gratified only in groups. Through concerted effort man can attain goals which he cannot reach in isolation.

Groups arise and function because of common motives. When men act at cross-purposes it is because they are impelled by individual, rather than common, motives, or by motives which are incompatible and irreconcilable. When a person's responses to others are shared by them, there exists the basic condition of group behavior. Modern psychological research has abundantly demonstrated that human behavior acquires meaning only in relation to a framework of factors operating in a social setting. This social setting consists, among other determinants, of human needs and the ways in which these needs are satisfied. On the basis of this research we can say categorically that most people, if not all, desire and enjoy belonging to a group. Because of the nature of early socialization, with its inescapable childhood dependence on others, all normal human beings are responsive to one another. From the early security of family relations other attitudes develop, such as loyalty, affection, and pride. These needs will differ from individual to individual, and the group does not satisfy them in he same way for all persons. Nevertheless, there are many recurrent strivings and modes of discharging them. Some of these we shall examine briefly.

Being a social animal, man derives satisfaction from *belongingness* as such. Isolation is a myth, whereas belongingness is a fact. There are various explanations of this pleasure of belonging, but chief among them is that it engenders general well-being. In associations like the family and friendship group, for instance, tension is reduced to a minimum. To the extent that members are enabled to take one another for granted, they create a relaxed atmosphere for themselves. Tension and insecurity are greatly reduced or eliminated altogether. The repertoire of defenses, concealments, and deceptions, which pervade so many of our daily relationships, can be dispensed with, and an atmosphere of mutual trust and acceptance is freely generated. We are not, of course, unmindful of the opposite conditions that prevail in some groups—of the conflicts, antipathies, and generally unhappy conditions that well-nigh destroy its members psychologically. Some of these conditions we shall describe later, especially in our discussion of intergroup tensions and conflicts. To the extent, however, that any group takes on face-to-face characteristics, as is true of a primary group, a committee, a discussion group, or a club, it provides its members with the conditions in which the need for self-defense and self-justification is greatly reduced.

Not all individuals, however, are satisfied with group belongingness as such. *Some desire not only to belong but even more to influence, persuade, or lead others.* In some people these motives exceed the need for acceptance. Belongingness as such is for them only a means whereby they may direct and influence others. When the need to dominate is all-powerful, authoritarian control becomes the central gratification. When it is softened by a consideration for the well-being of others, democratic leadership is a normal consequence. In the latter case, dominance loses its aggressive properties, and the individual finds satisfaction in being an instrument for the achievement of goals collectively.

Human beings are motivated to belong to a group because of the opportunity it affords them in playing the role of another. Taking the role of another is a mark of the socialized human being. Since one individual's role-taking presupposes the role-playing of another, role behavior gives people opportunities to accept and be accepted by others. Role behavior is possible only in a group. The group presents numerous situations in which the individual can display his skills, exercise his abilities, and become recognized for whatever individual merits he may possess and the group is willing to recognize and reward. Group cohesiveness depends in good measure on the ability and willingness of every individual to play his roles in such ways as to enable other individuals to play their own roles successfully. In short, much of the satisfaction that a person finds in belonging to a group is derived from his opportunities to play his role as one of its members.

Individuals participate in some group activities because there is no other way to perform these activities. Defending one's village or one's nation, discussing or debating an issue, singing in a chorus, playing a game, and the like are performances the satisfaction of which can be achieved only by group membership. Many activities give satisfaction purely through their collective properties, through the fact that they are performed in friendly concert with other people. Because these satisfactions are commonplace we must not ignore their importance, for they account for a large area of human behavior at every stage of individual and social development.

Individuals are motivated toward group belongingness, further, because *it gratifies their need for social status,* for recognition by others, especially by outsiders. Social status is a potent factor in the image which others form of us and in our image of ourselves. Not belonging can be a painful, even a terrifying, experience to most people, and some will go to extreme lengths to achieve group status. The writer recalls the case of an individual, while no doubt extreme, in whom status through belongingness reached pathological proportions. He conceived of his work as a new profession in need of a new name which would properly identify it. We shall call it *Artintecture.* Since he was the only Artintect in existence, he felt lonely and unrecognized. To end his feeling of isolation he printed a "Who's Who in Artintecture," composed of two hundred or more fictitious names, with his own inserted in the proper alphabetical locus. In moments of depression induced by the failure of his "school" to materialize, he turned to his "Who's Who" to find gratification in seeing his name listed with those of many others. While he knew that the directory was his own creation, he found pleasure in knowing that he "belonged."

People are motivated toward group belongingness, finally, because, as Gordon points out, *groups satisfy the desire for self-actualization.*[10] It is characteristic of every healthy individual to grow, and to desire a continuation of growth, of fulfillment and enhancement of the self. We have already remarked that the individual likes to belong to groups because they afford him opportunities to play roles, utilize skills, and gain recognition by others for such abilities as they are willing to recognize and reward. Self-actualization is the motive to realize these goals objectively, in the presence of others. The group thus provides the individual with a maximum degree of self-actualization, with the realization of potentialities, with the attainment of common goals. Stated in another way, the group serves as a matrix for self-direction and self-extension in that it elicits and demands loyalty and regard for the group and its interests and ideals. A mark of individual maturity may well be the degree of one's self-actualization in, identification with, and self-involvement in the goals and ideals of our group.

[10] T. Gordon, *Group-centered leadership* (Boston: Houghton Mifflin Co., 1955), pp. 54–55.

Group Norms. It is difficult to conceive the formation and preservation of a group in the absence of standard forms of behavior. While there may be no explicit standards present in the early interactive phases of group formation, a set of norms soon develops, giving the interactive structure a degree of stability without which it could not long function as a group. Just as society as a whole could not exist without codes or established rules of behavior, so a dynamic group would be impossible without standardized modes of interacting with one another. These standards, or norms, serve as frames of reference for the behavior of one individual in his relations to other individuals.[11] When an individual becomes a member of the group, his membership is determined by the fact that he accepts, at least provisionally, the reference frame of the group. He does not behave as he pleases, and he does not satisfy his motives arbitrarily. The dominant norms of the group give him a standardized interpretation of his own experiences, and as long as he remains a part of the group, he adheres to the meanings which its norms provide. One cannot explain the similarity of behavior of people in groups on any other ground. We have already called attention to the fact that one cannot explain the behavior of individuals in groups by their personal biographies only, and that one cannot predict group behavior from a knowledge of individual behavior alone. Early sociological studies of gangs, such as those of Thrasher, Shaw, and Landesco, established this fact at least thirty years ago.[12] The group norms of offending gangs, juvenile delinquent groups, for example, are in fact so binding upon their members that they constitute a challenge to the estab-

[11] For an important discussion of the whole psychology of norms the student should consult the writings of M. Sherif. See, for example, M. Sherif and H. Cantril, *The psychology of ego-involvements* (New York: John Wiley & Sons, Inc., 1947), *passim;* M. Sherif and C. W. Sherif, *An outline of social psychology* (rev. ed.; New York: Harper & Bros., 1956), chap. viii.

[12] F. M. Thrasher, *The gang* (Chicago: The University of Chicago Press, 1927); J. Landesco, *Organized crime in Chicago;* The Illinois Crime Survey, 1929; C. R. Shaw, *The natural history of a delinquent career* (Chicago: The University of Chicago Press), 1931.

lished codes of the larger community; in fact, they form a subgroup tradition, having its own internal structure, morale, *esprit de corps*, and strong solidarity.[13] They provide their members with a frame of reference, a pattern of behavior, in dealing with members of the in-group and with members of the out-group. The pattern of delinquent behavior is such that, although it may not be disorganizing of an individual as such, when expressed in the context of the gang's total subculture, it can make for a vicious criminal or delinquent. For the pattern consists of gambling, smoking, drinking, obscenity, promiscuous sexual relations, and the specific skills of pickpocketing, burglarizing, jack-rolling, and the like.[14]

Our primary task here, however, is not to diagnose antisocial behavior, but to demonstrate the effectiveness of group norms in determining the behavior of individuals as group members. Persons in groups regulate or control their behavior through the norms which they have collectively established. A person's status in the group, his acceptance or rejection by other members, is largely dependent on his adherence to its code. *Self-regulation* is an important property of dynamic groups. Rewards for adherence to, and punishments for deviations from, the group norms maintain and perpetuate the group. Some of the most crucial demonstrations of this fact have been made by studies of industrial and other working groups. If the group should, for instance, decide to perform only a specified amount of work, individual workers will generally abide by the group's wishes. A person who deviates from the expected norm is labeled a "rate-buster," is ignored as a person, is ridiculed, or may even receive physical punishment.[15] Those individuals, however, who deviate from the norms by performing insufficient work are also socially rejected. They are considered "chiselers" and are scorned as much as the "rate-busters."

13 Thrasher, *The gang*, p. 57.

14 *Ibid.*, p. 388.

15 See F. J. Roethlisberger and W. J. Dickson, *Management and the worker* (Cambridge, Mass.: Harvard University Press, 1941).

Studies like the above, of gangs and of factory workers, indicate the controlling force of social norms. Groups design or evolve explicit codes of expected behavior, and those who remain members behave in accordance with their dictates. Most members, even those who deviate from the group's demands, are aware of the norms and their binding force in the individual's behavior. These codes, or group norms, make for economy in interindividual behavior, for they are explicit indicators of how a person is expected to act in relation to other persons in a group context.

FUNCTIONAL HIERARCHY. Our discussion thus far has described intragroup relations as a structure of motives, roles, and norms. No group exists for a period of time, however, without organizing its interdependent members into a *functional hierarchy*. The roles which a person assumes in his group carry with them a specified function, such as that of a harmonizer, a dominator, and expediter, or a democratic leader. The position of each individual is determined by his specific contribution to the achievement of a collective goal. Differentiation, no less than integration, of function characterizes all interactive relations among individuals. Potentials for playing roles in a group, for solving common problems, for effective leadership, and the like are not equally distributed throughout a group. While it is true that in a democratic group, leadership may pass from one individual to another, there is a strong tendency for that important function to be discharged by those individuals only who are recognized by all others as capable of assuming the expected role; the role, that is, of *patterning* the behavior of a group, of *facilitating* action toward a goal.[16]

Some writers on group dynamics, in order to stress the democratic nature of group decision-making, have de-emphasized the hierarchical feature of intragroup relations. The two are not, however, incompatible, and the facts themselves compel us to recognize the existence of hierarchical

[16] See A. W. Gouldner (ed.), *Studies in leadership* (New York: Harper & Bros., 1950), pp. 17–18.

relationships. Social scientists, particularly anthropologists, have shown that both achieved and ascribed statuses in groups are contingent upon the group's response to an individual's capacities. The relation of one person to another is structured by the role and status of each. The role and status of every member are conditioned by the existing norms, or the members may generate new norms. This standardization of expected behavior toward others, this hierarchical grouping of individuals, points up the interrelation and interpenetration of motives, roles, norms, and differential function in accounting for the behavior of groups.[17] The objection to interpreting group behavior in terms of hierarchical dimensions rests, it seems to the present writer, not upon empirical evidence but upon the tendency to think of the hierarchical positions as stable and relatively permanent. Unless we assume that a group is a set of determinable relationships, however fleeting and tenuous, we cannot speak of a group at all. While not every member of the group may be *aware* of his position in relation to others, he can act as one of its members only by having such a position.[18]

Since in many small groups leadership is transmitted to various members, the illusion that no hierarchization exists is often developed. Although some writers on group dynamics speak of leaderless groups, the existence of the latter must be seriously questioned.[19] While in the initial phases of group formation no *discernible* structure of expectancies among members may exist, perceptual and intellectual jockeying does, nonetheless, take place. Gradually the expectancies become more specific, roles are more clearly defined, norms

[17] This hierarchical relationship of members one to another is interestingly brought out in W. F. Whyte's *Street corner society* (Chicago: The University of Chicago Press, 1943).

[18] For an early experimental treatment of this problem, see W. I. Newstetter, M. J. Feldstein, and T. M. Newcomb, *Group adjustment: a study in experimental sociology* (Cleveland: Western Reserve University Press, 1938).

[19] For a discussion of leaderless groups, see H. Ansbacher, The history of the leaderless group discussion, *Psychol. Bull., 48* (1951), 383–91; B. M. Bass, The leaderless group discussion, *Psychol. Bull., 51* (1954), 465–92.

are crystallized, and actions toward a goal are mutually fostered. A differentiation of function that was initially only incipient has become actualized.[20]

The functioning of the hierarchization principle can be seen especially in role conflicts. When faced with the conflict of roles, an individual will ascertain, consciously or unconsciously, a priority between them. Some things will then be viewed as more urgent than others. A foreman in a factory, for instance, is given orders by his boss. He will pass these orders in turn to the workers in his department. He cannot with impunity behave otherwise. A chain of communication operates in which each individual will enact the role expected of him. If the role which he enacts violates the norms of the group, he will be forced into line by its members. In a normal family, care of the children takes priority over the care of domestic animals. For students, attending classes has priority over the affairs of one's fraternity. The subject in each case must choose between alternative roles. Of course, we recognize the fact that role conflicts are handled or resolved by means other than hierarchization. For example, they are often resolved by enacting each role separately and at a different time. An individual may repudiate one role temporarily while he is enacting another. Another person may lead a double life, and so on. Our concern here, however, is with the enactment of conflicting roles in a single group through its temporal duration.[21]

A very interesting confirmation of the principle of hierarchical grouping is found in Munch's anthropological description of the interactions of three men on the island of Tristran da Cunha, off St. Helena. When they arrived on the island, they renounced any desire for or claim to hierarchical relationships, believing that they could live together effectively without the superordination-subordination rela-

[20] See M. E. Roseborough, Experimental studies of small groups, *Psychol. Bull., 50* (1953), 275–303.

[21] See S. A. Stouffer and J. Toby, Role conflict and personality, *Amer. J. Sociol., 56* (1951), 395–406; J. Toby, Some variables in role-conflict analysis, *Soc. Forces, 30* (1952), 324–27.

tionship to which they had been accustomed. Instead, complete equality was to govern their interactions. After a time, however, and despite their belief in the *ethical desirability* of the current arrangement, they soon found it unworkable. For the proper and efficient discharge of his duties, each person had assumed a certain role and status toward the others, and all of them recognized the necessity of their functional positions in the framework of the whole. Thus what avowedly started out as a "leaderless" group gradually took on a hierarchical structure in which each member was observed to perform a definable and necessary function.[22] Beginning as an undifferentiated and unstructured association of individuals, it developed into a psychological organization of distinct roles and expectations.

Further confirmation of the principle of hierarchization is found in an experimental investigation by O. J. Harvey.[23] In this experiment, which cannot be described and analyzed in detail here, adolescent clique members were asked to estimate the future performance of different individuals. Three members were chosen from each of ten cliques according to the sociometric position which each held in his group, namely, the leader, the individual occupying a middle rank, and the member with the lowest standing in the group. The level of aspiration of each member was also determined. Each clique member threw a dart, estimated his own performance on the next trial, and estimated the performance of the others.

The results revealed a statistically significant positive relationship between the individual's standing in his clique and the members' estimations of his performance. Members' estimates were highest for the leader, next for the member of middle ranking, and lowest for the member of lowest standing. Stating the results in the form of a generalization, we

[22] P. A. Munch, *Sociology of Tristran da Cunha* (Oslo, Norway: Jacob Dybwad, 1945). The above is confirmed in a study of a Japanese prison camp in the Philippine Islands. See E. H. Vaughan, *Community under stress* (Princeton: Princeton University Press, 1949).

[23] O. J. Harvey, An experimental approach to the study of status relations in informal groups, *Amer. sociol. Rev., 18* (1953), 357–67.

may say that "the level of aspiration of a member of an informal clique and the estimation of that member's future performance by other group members on a task of *significance to the group* bears a positive relationship to his relative position in the group hierarchy."[24]

The existence of a hierarchy in a group not only organizes its members in their interactive relations—and is thus conducive to cohesiveness—but is also the source of group tensions and imbalances. The flow of communication between persons of high and low status is often adversely affected. A person at the bottom of the hierarchy is less likely to influence one at the top, and his critical assessment of the latter's contribution to the group invariably suffers. The person at the bottom may perceive those at the top as a threat to his own position and freedom. On the other hand, high status enables an individual to indulge more freely and without apprehension in critical evaluation of the person below him. But Harold H. Kelley has shown in experimentally created hierarchies, there is also a general tendency for high-status individuals to restrict communication which would tend to lower their status or which would make them appear incompetent in the high-status position. Also, as he has shown, high-status persons inhibit their communication of criticism of their own performance to the groups below them.[25]

The adverse effects of hierarchical relations are further brought out in a study of power relations among group members. The results show that group members of *low* status "will perceive and behave toward high status members in an essentially ego-defensive manner, that is, in ways calculated to reduce the feeling of uneasiness experienced in their relations with *highs*."[26] Because of their ego-defensive-

[24] *Ibid.*, p. 367, italics in the original.

[25] H. H. Kelley, Communication in experimentally created hierarchies, *Hum. Relat.*, *4* (1951), 39–56.

[26] J. I. Hurwitz, A. F. Zander, and B. Hymovitch, Some effects of power on the relations among group members, in D. Cartwright and A. Zander, *Group dynamics: research and theory* (Evanston, Ill.: Row, Peterson & Co., 1953), p. 491.

ness, furthermore, the *lows* show positive reactions of liking the *highs*, tend to overrate the liking for themselves by the *highs*, and to communicate mainly with the latter. The authors sum up this relationship between *highs* and *lows* by saying that *lows* will be liked less than *highs* by both *lows* and *highs;* that all group members prefer less to be liked by *lows* than by *highs;* and that communnication with *lows* will be less desired by all members.[27]

The hierarchization process sharply points up the limitation, if not the error, of de-emphasizing the role of dominant individuals in group relationships. While it is true that in some groups, as they become increasingly self-directive, the leader is less necessary, there exist at the present time no crucial researches or experimental data to permit us to conclude that we can eliminate him altogether. The experiments at the National Training Laboratory in Group Development, at Bethel, Maine, while highly interesting, do not support some people's arguments for the "leaderless group." It would appear that these claims for the "leaderless group" may derive more from enthusiasm for a doctrine than from empirical evidence.

INTERGROUP RELATIONS

The psychology of group formation which we have expounded thus far has concentrated exclusively on *intra*group relations. An enormous amount of theoretical analysis and operational research in group dynamics in recent years has investigated the interdependence of individuals. It has studied the consensus and disharmony of the relations of individuals *within* a group. Group dynamics, however, is also the study of conflict and harmony *between* groups. *Inter*group antagonisms, such as ethnic and racial prejudice, religious and ideological conflicts, international tension and harmony, are also important problems, and they have been investigated since the inception of group psychology. The

[27] *Ibid.*, p. 492. For a sociometric analysis of the same relationships, see J. Thibaut, An experimental study of the cohesiveness of underprivileged groups, *Hum. Relat.*, 3 (1950), 251–78.

importance of intergroup relations has been vividly forced upon us by the realization, implicitly present for generations but only recently become the focus of scientific formulation, that just as no individual exists in isolation so no group functions by itself. No region of social space is a closed system but, as we pointed out in the discussion of topological and dynamic constructs, interacts with other regions. The intersection of social circles is a ubiquitous feature of human society. So great is the *interdependence of groups* today that events in one are almost invariably transmitted to others, producing either harmony or discord between them.

IN-GROUP AND OUT-GROUP RELATIONS. Although in-group and out-group relations are as old as man and have for centuries been recognized to exist, their conscious formulation into concepts was made, as far as one can determine, by William Graham Sumner.[28] This distinction is now so well known to the general reader that it is not necessary to give a detailed description of it. There are some features, however, which justify a brief elucidation.

Ethnocentrism describes the sentiment of acceptance by members of the in-group of one another and implies the attitude of rejection by the in-group of members of the out-group. While these attitudes are certainly pronounced in modern society, in some ancient and primitive societies they were carried to the point where "outsiders" were not even classified as human beings. Sumner describes this situation vividly. He writes:

> When Caribs were asked whence they came, they answered, "We alone are people." The meaning of the name Kiowa is "real or principal people." The Lapps call themselves "men," or "human beings." The Greenland Eskimo think that Europeans have been sent to Greenland to learn virtue and good manners from the Greenlanders. Their highest form of praise for a European is that he is, or soon will be, as good as a Greenlander. . . . As a rule it is found that nature peoples call themselves "men." Others are something else—perhaps not defined—but not real men. In myths the origin of their own tribe is that of the real human race. They do not account for the others.[29]

[28] W. G. Sumner, *Folkways* (Boston: Ginn & Co., 1906).
[29] *Ibid.*, p. 14.

Our concern is, of course, with ethnocentrism in contemporary groups. Although in contemporary groups, it does not usually involve the almost total rejection of the out-group, ethnocentrism is nevertheless pronounced. Lines of cleavage exist between a variety of groups, especially between nations, classes, races, and ethnic and religious subcultures. Antipathy, prejudice, and other attitudes of exclusion characterize all these groups to some extent, coupled with preferential sentiments for members of their own group. Dynamically speaking, the in-group is a social field or region in which members are fairly homogeneous in attitudes and feelings; the out-group is a social field or region with reference to which the social and psychological boundaries of the in-group are relatively impermeable. They are social circles whose boundaries do not intersect.

In-group and out-group relations have also been described by the degree of *social distance* obtaining between one group and another. This concept "measures" the extent of acceptance or rejection of persons in group relationships.[30] It is also used to designate cleavages between groups, and therefore serves well to describe intergroup relations. Thus those groups between which conflict is at a minimum are described by less social distance than those between which sympathy and acceptance are relatively absent. Generally, there is more social distance, for example, between labor and management than between groups of workers themselves.

In-group and out-group relations, as measured by social distance, are always determined by *social norms*. Whether two groups will accept or reject each other is dependent on whether or not they agree on a standard of behavior or common norms. They accommodate themselves to each other and produce harmony between themselves when they either sympathetically respect each others' values or evolve a pattern of interaction based upon mutually accepted standards of behavior. In the absence of reciprocal norms, disharmony

30 Bonner, *Social psychology*, p. 30.

and conflict easily arise. Numerous studies of social distance and ethnic attitudes in particular confirm this view.[31] They especially bring out the appalling extent of intergroup hostility in American life. Scientifically it is unrewarding to merely call attention to this fact and condemn it. Before intergroup hostility can be dealt with effectively, it is necessary to understand its nature and its source. Economic status, parental influence, education, and similar factors, play significant roles in its origin and propagation. Basic to all these, however, is the fact that a group lives in accordance with its dominant mores. In-group and out-group relations, whether manifested in ethnocentrism, social distance, or outright conflict, are, accordingly, products of the clash of social norms, not of the perversity of human nature. Conformity is a universal social pressure, and in their attitudes of exclusiveness toward one another men are simply bowing to its sovereign influence.

Role of Personality Variables. On several occasions we asserted that one cannot dependably predict the behavior of members of a group from a knowledge of their personalities. Personality variables cannot, however, be safely ignored. The problem faces us again when we consider the character of intergroup relations. While the results are inconsistent, there is some evidence to justify the hypothesis that harmony and hostility between groups are facilitated, even if they are not generated, by personality factors. This is especially true in intergroup prejudice. Although the investigations of Adorno, Frenkel-Brunswik, and others on the "authoritarian personality" have recently been subjected to severe criticism, their conclusions agree with the findings of other investigators. These conclusions assert that a prejudiced person is excessively rigid both affectively and intellectually. Cognitively the prejudiced person tends to be "intolerant of ambiguity"; that is, he cannot accept propo-

[31] For the beginner a good review of this whole subject will be found in E. L. Hartley, *Problems in prejudice* (New York: King's Crown Press, 1946), and G. W. Allport, *The nature of prejudice* (Reading, Mass.: Addison-Wesley Publishing Co., Inc., 1954).

sitions that are not clearly structured and properly categorized and pigeonholed. Affectively, he rigidly represses his hostility toward figures in authority, such as his parents. The hostility is displaced, eventually finding its expression in antagonism toward the out-group. The ambivalence which results from his submission to authority, and the "repression and externalization of the negative side of this ambivalence," lead him to an uncritical acceptance of the in-group and a violent rejection of the out-group.[32] Moreover, the expression of his superego is directed for the most part toward condemnation, punishment, and rejection of others. He is oriented toward power over others rather than affection for them. He judges people less on the basis of their intrinsic worth than on the basis of their social conformity. His fear of punishment and retaliation, generated by the negative and threatening interpersonal relations which characterized his early home life, impels him to approach others, especially those who do not conform to his own standards, with categoric and hostile attitudes. He deals with them not primarily as persons but as representatives of a group. He categorizes them as "Dagos," "Niggers," or "Kikes."[33]

We stated that intergroup attitudes are facilitated, even if not aroused by, personality variables. Their origin lies, as we have shown in passing, in the group, either the family or some other social structure, such as the school, church, or reference group. Children growing up in an atmosphere of rejection and moralistic condemnation are unable to establish close personal contacts with those who differ from themselves. Having received little or no affection from their family group they cannot as adults give affection to other

[32] T. W. Adorno, E. Frenkel-Brunswik *et al.*, *The authoritarian personality* (New York: Harper & Bros., 1950), p. 482. An important study antedating this is A. H. Maslow, The authoritarian character structure, *J. soc. Psychol.*, *18* (1943), 401–11.

[33] This observation is hardly new. What many psychologists have only recently begun to investigate systematically and experimentally was well known to sociologists and anthropologists at least sixty years ago. See F. H. Giddings, *The principles of sociology* (New York: The Macmillan Co., 1896).

groups. They can relate themselves acceptingly only to members of their own clique which, being more like than unlike themselves, constitute no serious threat to their own safety. This is the psychological dynamics of the in-group-out-group dichotomy.

EXPERIMENTAL INVESTIGATION. Until recently, the study of intergroup relations has tended to be either arm-chair or naïvely empirical. The empirical work consisted of analyses of the nature of prejudice, descriptions of in-group *vs.* out-group relations, "measurements" of social distance, ascertainment of the factors in attitude change, and so forth. If these investigations appear to be "experimental" in character, it is because they have been cast into an *ex post facto* experimental mold. On the other hand, some of the experimental investigations impress one as being inconsequential. The study of group behavior by reproducing social situations in the laboratory is unquestionably desirable; but it is a fair question to ask to what degree the laboratory and real-life situations are, if not identical, at least very similar. Since group phenomena are seldom as simple as those produced in the laboratory, one is often left with the uneasy feeling that too many conditions in the latter situation are not adequately controlled. Nevertheless, and when due precautions are exercised, the experimental study of small groups has decided advantages over the empirical methods by means of which many generalizations have traditionally been formulated. Since an exhaustive analysis of methodology and the variety of experimental investigations of intergroup relations is not here contemplated, we shall select only one instance to illustrate the experimental approach.

In an experiment designed by Sherif, the process of in-group and out-group formation, and particularly of inter-group hostility, is nicely illustrated and objectively confirmed.[34] Sherif selected 24 well-adjusted boys, twelve years of age, with similar economic and educational backgrounds,

[34] See M. Sherif and C. W. Sherif, *Groups in harmony and tension* (New York: Harper & Bros., 1953).

and placed them in a sumer camp in northern Connecticut. Conditions were further controlled by prohibiting visitors, keeping the boys ignorant of the experimental nature of the camp, and by preventing other external influences from affecting the experimental conditions. While our interest here is in the intergroup relations, it is necessary to point out that the boys first developed into informal groups and took on definite in-group attitudes. The group formations were made more explicit by one of them naming itself the "Bull Dogs" and the other "Red Devils." Among the many activities in which they engaged were competitive games. As in-group and out-group attitudes crystallized, the boys described themselves and each other by familiar stereotypes. Members of the in-group were described as "playing fair," whereas those in the out-group were perceived as "dirty players." As the competition between the two groups increased, friction and hostility also increased. The winning "Bull Dogs" players developed strong identification with one another and a noticeable pride in their superiority. The losing "Red Devils" members suffered noticeable frustration, which expressed itself in recrimination and mutual blame; their vindictiveness was directed particularly against their own in-group members who held lower positions in the status hierarchy. Hostility was now directed by them not only to the out-group but to members of their own group. Aggression was channelized into other activities, including eating, when a great amount of overt hostility was expressed by the "Red Devils" against the "Bull Dogs." A general pandemonium prevailed as the two groups threw food and eating utensils at each other, interlarded with catcalls and uncomplimentary epithets.

The experiment confirms the hypothesis that when two groups are in interactive competition with each other, or in situations which are frustrating to one group or the other, they tend to develop hostility and conflict in their relation to each other. This is true even when the members are, as in the foregoing experiment, "normal" or well-adjusted persons. As before, we find it necessary to consider both the individuals and the structure of their interrelationship in the group to account for intergroup relations.

CONCLUSION

In this chapter we have dissected the group in order to determine the nature of its organization and functioning and to indicate the chief social psychological forces that operate in intergroup relations. Our analysis has shown that when two or more people are confronted by the same problem but have no established ways of dealing with it they tend to evolve or construct more or less effective means of solving it. The ways of dealing with the situation do not take place in a vacuum, and even if they are novel, they rest to some extent upon existing standards. Within this substructure of existing standards new norms and regulations emerge, roles are assumed by or ascribed to the members, hierarchical relations involving some differentiation of status arise, and members begin to perceive themselves in relation to others and to their own common problem. Each person brings to the collective situation not only his own psychological being, but his society as a structure of norms and standards. When he enters into reciprocal relationship with others, he does not completely unlearn what he has already acquired, but modifies it in accordance with the expectations that arise in the new situation.

The psychology of intergroup relations does not involve a different set of principles from that of intragroup relations. Theoretical and experimental evidence supports the conclusion that intergroup relations are not independent of intragroup attitudes and behaviors. This does not imply that one cannot account for intergroup relations by concentrating his attention solely upon relations within a group. The field-dynamic view which we have described does not permit such a conclusion. Human relations, we have said, are holistic not additive. The forces at work in group relations are influenced and modified by personal, cultural, and collective trends within groups and between them. The properties of groups are transferred to intergroup contacts, where they are integrated, modified, or rejected variously according to how effectively they promote intergroup conflict or harmony.

The structure and functioning of groups have been studied for a long time, but the studies have been speculative and crudely empirical. Today the study of groups comprises an area of interest intensively cultivated by scientific psychologists and other social scientists. In their efforts to understand group behavior, social psychologists in particular have studied groups under carefully controlled conditions in the laboratory and in their natural setting. As a consequence they have been able to isolate specific group properties, to define the nature of the relation between group members, and to organize a body of fairly reliable knowledge of group behavior in general. These properties, relations, and behaviors seem to be universal, and they strengthen the conviction that group psychology is developing into a reliable science with important theoretical and practical implications for science and for society as a whole.

CHAPTER 3

Cohesive and Disruptive Forces in Group Behavior

Although our aim in Chapter 2 was not to analyze the nature of group cohesiveness, we nevertheless discussed it indirectly in describing the psychological structure of the group. By group cohesiveness we mean the totality of forces which induce members to remain in a group. Group cohesiveness takes place in part because groups satisfy needs and motives which cannot be realized in isolation. Cohesiveness is a function, furthermore, as we saw, of the operation of established rules of behavior called norms. Social sanctions in the form of rewards for conforming to the standards of the group and punishments for their violation are well-known and well-established sources of group solidarity. If we analyze group cohesiveness, as we shall do at length, in terms of a group's attractiveness for its members, we are confronted by the obvious fact that without at least a minimal attraction of members to each other a group cannot exist at all.

Since cohesiveness is related to many problems of group dynamics, its conceptualization takes on an increasing importance. The influence of the group in changing the behavior of its members is closely related to their attractiveness to each other. The changes which the group can induce can never exceed the degree of attractiveness to each other of its constituent members.[1] The group's attractiveness to its members affects the operation of its norms and creates pressures toward uniformity in their behavior. The pressure toward uniformity, however, is countered by forces making for disruption and dissolution of groups. These forces impair or destroy the lines of communication within or between groups, damage mutual trust and attractiveness, and distort the perceptions of members to the point where hostility rather than acceptance displaces the expectations of all. Cohesiveness, in short, suggests that there is also disharmony in human relationships, so that it is unrealistic to discuss group cohesion without carefully conceptualizing group disruption. This is the task that we set for ourselves in the present chapter.

NATURE OF GROUP COHESIVENESS

Consensus, group solidarity, *esprit de corps,* and the like are well-known characteristics of "healthy" group life and have been investigated by social scientists for many decades. Group cohesiveness or group solidarity presupposes that members of a group have something in common. Differences tend to generate insecurity and impair concerted action. It is apparent that people who have had common or at least similar experiences tend to be more cohesive. If this circular mode of arguing is unpalatable, it is not a case of bad logic but an organic necessity, for it stresses a well-known fact—namely, that the forces making for cohesiveness are themselves reinforced by cohesiveness. People who have shared common or similar norms or values are already, by definition, more cohesive than people who differ widely from one another. This calls attention to the first condition of group cohesiveness.

Shared Norms. In the preceding chapter we stressed the importance of role behavior in group formation. It is neces-

[1] See L. Festinger, S. Schachter, and K. Back, *Social pressures in informal groups* (New York: Harper & Bros., 1950).

sary now to indicate that the perception and enactment of roles are defined by the norms which members of a group share in common. Playing a required role presupposes a knowledge of the group norms which define it. In playing his role in the group, a person must be able to anticipate another's response to his own role. He can do this only if he already knows the values and standards which motivate others to play *their* roles. The tension, anxiety, and clumsiness with which new and marginal members play their roles is further confirmation of this principle. Other things being equal, then, the more norms and standards are mutually shared, the greater will be the resulting cohesiveness of the group. On the other hand, the more people diverge in their perceptions of life and of their relationship to one another, the less communication takes place between them, and the less will they be able to respond positively or acceptingly to one another. Thus, there can be no group cohesiveness in the absence of shared values and a dependable anticipation by each member that others will accommodate themselves to him.

However, this is scarcely a novel discovery, or one to be associated exclusively with the researches in group dynamics. For example, De Tocqueville, writing on American society in 1830, was keenly aware of its importance. He observed that a society can survive only when there are common understandings, or when people view a great number of things from the same perspective.[2] In short, it has long been obvious to thoughtful men that social organization cannot exist and continue without consensus, so that cohesiveness is a fundamental characteristic of any continuous organized social life. In its absence, social disorganization is an inevitable consequence.

Furthermore, when defined by social norms, cohesiveness is not enacted or effected by fiat or compulsion. While a group may be held together as a physical entity by force, as in a dictatorship, it is not the kind of group which we are

[2] A. De Tocqueville, *Democracy in America* (2 vols.; Cambridge, Mass.: Sever and Francis, 1862).

here describing. Cohesiveness as it is here defined is a system of interlocking roles initiated and sustained by standards either already existing or evolved by members of a group in the course of striving for a common goal. Even if not every member's behavior coincides with the norms of the group, it must to some degree adhere to them. Sharing of group norms is, accordingly, an important index of group cohesiveness.

The force of group norms in the interactions of individuals is made particularly vivid when persons deviate from them. Deviations are not readily countenanced. When deviations exist, their range and degree are themselves defined by the group. Permissive behavior is itself "designed" to preserve the norms and maintain the stability of the group. No group is absolutely inflexible. Thus, for instance, although in theory all members of a Zuñi household are expected to live amicably together, there are many cases of conflict. Although in Manus society everyone is expected to assume economic responsibility, exception is made in the case of *independents,* whose irresponsibility is socially tolerated. Many examples of such permissive behavior are found in different groups in our own society.[3]

Particularly significant for the study of group dynamics are the deviations and their effects in miniature social situations.[4] Thrasher's study of the gang and Whyte's description of the street-corner boys, to which we have already referred, are cases in point. The controlling force of shared norms has been very well established in the codes of criminals and the underworld in general. Incarcerated criminals erect codes of conduct to govern their life in prison. In this situation most inmates conform to their own established norms, and those who ignore or reject them not only are rejected by the

[3] See H. Bonner, *Social psychology: an interdisciplinary approach* (New York: American Book Co., 1953), pp. 236–41.

[4] We are using the term "miniature social situation" in a broader sense than that suggested by Vinacke. See W. Edgar Vinacke, *The miniature social situation* (Honolulu: University of Hawaii, Psychological Laboratory, February, 1954).

others but they usually suffer psychological disorders as well.[5]

In his discerning analysis of secret societies Simmel showed, at least fifty years ago, that the same ruling force of group norms dominates them. Secrets of the group, or activities which challenge established norms, must be carefully guarded, and those who violate its expectations are severely punished or even killed.[6] The demand for secrecy is spreading to other areas of group behavior in contemporary society, and reveals the same claim to conformity that is found in the groups already described. Bureaucracy in its various forms is a good example. Indeed, as Max Weber pointed out, the concept of the "official secret" governs many aspects of bureaucratic life, from commercial policy to constitutional government; and its intolerance of deviation is equally fanatical.[7]

B. Morale. It is paradoxical but nevertheless true that, despite the voluminous publications on this subject, the nature of morale is still difficult to understand. This situation is comprehensible when we consider it in the light of early speculative and analytical attempts to disclose the nature of morale. Such clarity and certainty regarding it as we now possess, small though they may be, have been made possible largely by the efforts of scientifically minded investigators, especially in the field of industrial relations. Nobody doubts its existence, and every student of the subject is impressed by its importance for group cohesiveness.

Morale and esprit de corps. Traditionally morale has been discussed on the background of the feeling of rapport known as *esprit de corps.* This is an example of defining *ignotum per ignotius,* for our understanding of *esprit de corps* is as vague as our understanding of morale. We know

[5] See D. Clemmer, *The prison community* (Boston: Christopher Publishing House, 1940).

[6] G. Simmel, The sociology of secret societies, *Amer. J. Sociol., 11* (1906), 441–98 (translated by A. W. Small). See also N. P. Gist, *Secret societies: a cultural study of fraternalism in the United States* (University of Missouri Studies, Vol. XV, No. 4, 1940).

[7] M. Weber, *Essays in sociology,* edited by H. H. Gerth and C. W. Mills (New York: Oxford University Press, 1946), pp. 233–35.

only that this feeling of belonging together, of identifying one's self with others, is a prerequisite of group participation. In its absence the initial step toward group cohesiveness cannot be taken, for in this condition people are marked by reserve, unfamiliarity, even alienation. When the reserve is broken down, an opportunity for attraction to one another arises, some identification takes place, and a perception of themselves in relation to one another begins to crystallize. What this really means is that *esprit de corps* is both a cause and a consequence of an initially existing structure, however vague and elementary it may be. The forces, as we have said before, making for solidarity are reinforced by the feeling of solidarity. Morale serves as a catalyzer and reinforcer of *esprit de corps,* an agent making for persistence and group self-maintenance in the face of difficulties and disruptive tensions. It fosters in-group organization and uniformity of behavior. It is universally characterized by attraction to and liking among members of a group.

Morale and group atmosphere. In our description of democratic, authoritarian, and laissez faire "social climates," attention was called to the greater social solidarity of the democratic group. The morale of the democratic group, the greater acceptance of the members of one another, including the leader, was higher than the morale of the other groups. Morale, however, characterizes any group possessed of solidarity, even the most authoritarian. This is clearly revealed in a well-known study made during World War II by the Morale Division of the U.S. Strategic Bombing Survey. This survey was an attempt to determine the effect of bombing on the civilian population of Germany. The survey disclosed a correlation between morale, or its absence, as measured by willingness to surrender unconditionally, and the ability of urban populations to endure the widespread destruction of public utilities, especially transportation. For the ability to tolerate the destruction of transportation faciliies, the correlation was +.81.[8]

[8] U.S. Strategic Bombing Survey, *The effects of strategic bombing on German morale,* Vol. II (Washington, D.C.: Government Printing Office, 1946).

Particularly important in supporting our claim for the role of group atmosphere in morale and cohesiveness was the finding in this same survey as to the differential effect of the bombing upon the Nazi and non-Nazi populations. The Nazis displayed stronger morale than the non-Nazis, as shown in the attitude of each toward the Allied bombers. Sixty-eight per cent of the Nazis condemned the Allies, whereas only 26 per cent of the non-Nazis condemned them. The Nazis, in other words, showed more in-group solidarity or cohesiveness that the non-Nazis.[9] Their higher morale sustained the Nazis in the face of calamities that were heaped upon Nazis and non-Nazis alike. Differences in group identification between the two groups made for differences in the meaning of the raids for each, and in the differences of their reactions to adversity.

Studies of the relation between morale and productivity yield similar results. Katz and Hyman, in their study of this problem in five shipyards, found that divergent attitudes existed among the workers in the different yards toward such aspects of their work as the attitudes and conduct of the managers, wages, production records, and the like. Investigation revealed that the men in Yard C had good morale, while those in Yard E had poor morale. Eighty-three per cent of the workers in Yard C were satisfied with their wages, 67 per cent had confidence in the management, and 16 per cent were dissatisfied with their production record. In Yard E, on the other hand, 47 per cent of the workers were satisfied with their wages, 54 per cent felt dissatisfied with their production record, and only 20 per cent had confidence in the management—despite the fact that both were under the same management![10]

Morale and self-involvement. Morale and its relationship to group cohesiveness cannot be understood wholly as a

[9] H. Peak, Observations on the characteristics and distribution of German Nazis, *Psychol. Monogr.*, 59, No. 6 (1945).

[10] D. Katz and H. Hyman, Morale in war industries, in T. M. Newcomb and E. L. Hartley, *Readings in social psychology* (New York: Henry Holt & Co., 1947), pp. 437–47.

group phenomenon, although it is basically so described. A fact that has stood out in our discussion of group structure, especially the place of norms in group formation, is that people participate in common action because the norms of the group have become internalized as properties of the self. If people do not feel the norms of the group as entirely peremptory and externally imposed, it is because they have identified them with their own needs and aspirations. The group's norms are *their* norms. The norms are *shared,* not merely endured; they have become *personal* and are not felt wholly as external pressures. This personal aspect of morale, this involvement of the ego in the group's values and activities, is a very important property of good morale. People fight for their team, feel pride in their school, or are intensely loyal to their country not because of social constraints only, but because of interest in, attachment for, or allegiance to, something which they cherish as *persons.* Criticism of or attack on any of them arouses personal as well as collective responses. This fact but demonstrates once more the validity of our claim that the individual and the collective, the person and the group, are inseparable elements in a field of social relationships.

Esprit de corps, morale, and self-involvement in the group's activities are thus prerequisites of group cohesiveness. *Esprit de corps* refers to the feeling of group identification—a kind of "team spirit"; *morale* sustains the members long enough to make coacting with one another possible and enduring; and *self-involvement* transforms the collective into intensely personal values and activities. Without them a group might arise and even function, but could not long endure.

LEADERSHIP. Inasmuch as we shall devote an entire later chapter to the study of leadership, our comments here shall be brief. This is the more true because our objective in this section is not to describe leadership as such but only to disclose its place in the development of group cohesiveness.

There is a tendency in some quarters to de-emphasize the role of the leader in democratic group development. It is unrealistic, however, not to recognize that people in all groups, whether democratic, authoritarian, or laissez faire, depend, at least *initially*, upon either an informal or an established leadership. This is true, not because one person is necessarily endowed with greater superiority than others in a group, nor because of any inherent or inevitable need for some to lead and others to follow, but because a group cannot function as such without a center of potential, without a sense of direction. The leadership may be expressed in the behavior of a single person, or as a chain of command, or as a productive activity transmitted to several or all persons in the group during its life history. It does not necessarily imply any power relationship between the leader and the led, not a helpless dependence of the latter upon the former. A person is the leader of a group when he invests his emotions and energies in such a way as to contribute to the group's maintenance and enhancement. A group is the more cohesive the more effectively the leader is able through participation to guide the members' perceptions toward a common goal. Group cohesiveness—or solidarity, integration, group morale—is demonstrably influenced by the group's leader. Although Cattell's analysis of leadership cannot be taken as conclusive, his conception of it, especially as it applies to group cohesiveness, or to use his own term, "group syntality," is important and highly relevant. He has shown that the leader has much to do with developing group syntality; and he has measured the effectiveness of the leader in influencing group syntality by "*the magnitude of the syntality change* (*from the mean*) *produced by that person*, i.e., by the difference in syntality under his leadership and the syntality under the leadership of the average or modal leader."[11]

Research has shown that group cohesiveness depends enormously on member satisfaction. Member satisfaction,

[11] R. B. Cattell, New concepts for measuring leadership in terms of group syntality, *Hum. Relat.*, *4* (1951), 161–84.

in turn, is hindered or enhanced by the quality of leadership which is present in the group. The results of numerous investigations show that member satisfaction, and hence group cohesiveness, is greatly facilitated by participatory, or group-centered, leadership, beginning with the classic study by Lewin, Lippitt, and White, which we have already cited, to very recent researches. Preston and Heintz found that, not only were changes in group opinion more easily effected by means of participatory than by supervisory or dominating leadership, but that the group members were more satisfied with the changes resulting from member-leader deliberations. The "followers" were also less satisfied with the supervisory leader and more satisfied with the participatory leader. Although both the participatory and supervisory groups rated their discussions as generally friendly, enjoyable, and productive, the participatory subjects, both leaders and followers, rated their discussions as being *more* friendly, enjoyable, interesting, and productive. Also the participatory leaders found the group atmosphere more enjoyable than their followers, while supervisory followers found the atmosphere more enjoyable than did their leaders.[12]

The results of the Preston and Heintz study were later confirmed by an investigation by Hare with several troops of Boy Scouts. The boys, whose average age was thirteen years, were asked to rank ten items of camping equipment in the order of their importance for a hypothetical camping trip. They were next divided into groups of five followers and a leader for a twenty-minute discussion period. Without going into further detail regarding the design of the investigation, the results show not only that participatory leadership was more effective than supervisory leadership in changing the boys' opinions, but that the boys in the participatory group were generally more satisfied with the

[12] M. G. Preston and R. K. Heintz, Effects of participatory *vs.* supervisory leadership on group judgment, *J. abnorm. soc. Psychol., 44* (1949), 345–55.

group decision than were the boys in the supervisory groups.[13]

Although we have briefly described a few telling researches and experiments on group cohesiveness, our description has been on the whole more empirical than operational, more analytical than behavioral. As a first approximation this approach has shown that cohesiveness is a feeling of "we-ness," of friendliness of members toward one another, and of loyalty to the group. A cohesive group is one in which members act in concert toward an agreed-upon goal, in which everyone assumes a position of responsibility with respect to its achievement. These characteristics are reflected in and reinforced by the existence of shared norms, morale, and its interrelated properties of *esprit de corps*, group atmosphere, self-involvement, and an effective leadership.

There is a condition of group cohesiveness, however, which we have not yet described, but which has been extensively explored operationally. To this we now turn our attention.

INTERPERSONAL AND GROUP ATTRACTIVENESS

The concept of valence has already been defined as the attraction or repulsion value of an object for an individual or a group. It may be used to describe the cohesive and disruptive forces in group behavior. A positive valence, we said, represents group belongingness, or group cohesiveness; whereas a negative valence designates isolation, or a diminution or destruction of cohesiveness (see Chapter 2, pp. 44–45). Since our concern in this section is wholly with group cohesiveness, the concept of positive valence may be used to describe it. Since, however, the bulk of research on group cohesiveness has been performed by investigation and

13 A. P. Hare, Small group discussion with participatory and supervisory leadership, *J. abnorm. soc. Psychol.*, *48* (1953), 273–75. It should be remarked, however, that unlike the results of Preston and Heintz regarding member satisfaction, Hare's differences were not statistically significant.

measurement of *group attractiveness,* we shall employ this concept rather than its equivalent term, positive valence.

The organic character of the science of group dynamics is again demonstrated by the fact that group attraction was logically presupposed in the preceding chapter. There we listed and described briefly some of the reasons why people join or belong to groups. We stressed the factors of belongingness as such, the need to persuade or to lead others, to play roles, to belong because there is no other way to perform certain functions except in groups, the gratification of the need for social status, and the desire for self-actualization. While these underlie as powerful motive forces the attractiveness of groups, we shall not discuss them further here. Instead we shall examine group attraction as a psychological concept and relationship, describe important experiments on the subject, and indicate the possibility of its measurement. In so doing we are moving away from the formalistic discussion of cohesiveness as "morale," "spirit," or "group atmosphere" which has characterized most writings on the subject, toward conceiving it as the field of forces which impel members to remain in the group.

CONCEPT OF GROUP ATTRACTIVENESS. The attractiveness of the group may be considered in two different but related ways. One refers to the group's members, the other to its goals. The first describes interpersonal attraction; the second, the attractive power of the group as such to its members.

Interpersonal attraction.[14] In his very excellent book, *The Human Group,* Homans describes this attractiveness by means of the concept of interaction. Men have, to be sure, known the force of interaction in group relations intuitively and pragmatically for a very long time. Homans, on the basis of a study of workers in an industrial plant, stated this observation in the form of an explicit hypothesis. He noted

[14] This term was originated by Newcomb; see T. H. Newcomb, The prediction of interpersonal attraction, *Amer. Psychologist, 11* (1956), 575–86.

that when persons interact frequently with one another they tend to form positive responses of liking, friendship, acceptance, or rapport with reference to one another.[15]

It is well to note in the foregoing hypothesis—and Homans duly cautions the reader to do so—that liking and friendship, as well as their opposites are to be understood as continuous gradations, as relative and not absolute values. The degree of the liking which individuals bear toward one another will increase or decrease according to the frequency of their interaction. Moreover, as the positive valence toward their own group members increases, the greater, on the whole, is their negative valence toward members of the out-group. The liking of one another within a group carries with it some rejection or dislike of members outside the group. This is seen in the case of the Bank Wiremen in Homan's study, who after some time in the Observation Room developed antagonism toward the men remaining on their regular jobs; and who, moreover, expressed their hostility by accusing the men on the regular jobs of discriminating against them.[16]

Again, Homans' data on the Bank Wiremen makes it possible to elaborate the hypothesis to mean that as the interactions of members increase they tend to lead to *participation* in a common activity. Thus, generally speaking, and "other things being equal," the more people interact, the more they share one another's feelings, sentiments, and attitudes, and the more are they likely to behave as a group working toward the same end.

What happens to interaction and mutual liking, however, when other things are not equal? Homans believes that interaction and mutual acceptance are affected by the presence of intrusive factors, such as irritants, authority, and failure to achieve the group's goals. Interacting persons like one another only if the activities which each performs are not

15 G. C. Homans, *The human group* (New York: Harcourt, Brace & Co., Inc., 1950), p. 111.

16 *Ibid.*, p. 113.

mutually irritating. Irrelevant behavior, such as horseplay on the job, is another intrusive factor that may cause antagonism. Personality factors, such as dominance or laziness, may affect the relationship. Positive interaction, or liking, takes place, furthermore, when inhibiting authority does not enter the relationship. If when two persons are working together one has authority over the other, liking may be inhibited because of the relation of inequality, or a felt need by the subordinate of respect for or even fear of the superior. A superior and a subordinate are less likely to generate friendliness than if the two persons had the same status. The relationship, according to Homans, is likely to be ambivalent, for there are two influences at work—one of friendliness and one of constraint. The relationship of an officer to his men is a good example.[17] Another intrusive factor, finally, is the failure to achieve the group's goals. If the group fails in its purpose, mutual antagonisms and recriminations arise which may not only destroy friendships but result in the disintegration of the group. We have said before that when people as a group face a common problem or danger, and especially when they succeed in solving one or overcoming the other, their feelings for one another become positively toned, warm, and friendly.[18]

There are numerous studies besides that of Homans that support the foregoing observations. They range from the work of Roethlisberger and Dickson, on which Homans' generalizations are largely based, through Whyte's street-corner groups, to the researches of Festinger, Schachter, and Back, and the more recent investigations of Sherif on the sociometric choices of youngsters in a boys' camp. All of them show clearly that interaction and participation increase the degree of interpersonal attraction. It is interesting to note in this connection, however, that in at least one study liking for one another, or friendship, led to increased interaction, thus making liking or friendship, rather than interaction, the

[17] *Ibid.*, p. 116.
[18] *Ibid.*, p. 117.

determining variable.[19] While this study is open to criticism, it at least calls attention to the great probability that the two variables, interaction and liking of one another, are interdependent, mutually supporting, and mutually modifying.

The nature of group attraction has thus far been described as the positive valence of group members to one another. It is found to be embedded primarily, though not exclusively, in the individual. The descriptive unit of group attractiveness, and hence of cohesiveness, is the individual member in his interactions with other members. The psychological properties of liking or friendship, acceptance or rejection, are "located" in the individual in his interactions with other individuals. This analysis, however, is one-sided, for it takes into account only what is personally or individually meaningful. Since the person and the group are interdependent, we must also take into account the object toward which the mutual likings are ultimately directed, namely, the group. Attractiveness to the group and group cohesiveness cannot be defined exclusively in terms of interpersonal attraction nor in terms of attraction to the group conceived as an organization of two or more individuals seeking a common goal. We shall, accordingly, examine next the nature of group attractiveness in terms of the relation of the individual to the group.

Group attractiveness. Group cohesiveness is enhanced by a type of attraction which is not directed toward individuals primarily, but toward the group. It is due to the valent properties of the group itself. If we define group cohesiveness, as we have done, as the resultant of forces acting on the members to remain in the group, we find that common perceptions, expectations, and shared norms play a vital part in the process. How strong the forces acting on the members to remain in the group are, however, will de-

19 See R. Potashin, A sociometric study of children's friendships, *Sociometry, 13* (1946), 48–70. The works of Roethlisberger and Dickson, of Whyte, and of Festinger, Schachter, and Back have already been cited. M. Sherif's study is found in J. H. Rohrer and M. Sherif (eds.), *Social psychology at the crossroads* (New York: Harper & Bros., 1951), pp. 388–424.

pend in large measure upon the need-satisfying power of the group.

What are some of the more important forces acting on members to stay in the group? We shall consider this problem in the present section.

Conformity to group standards or norms as a factor in cohesiveness stands out in bold relief. Group standards make it possible to effect uniformity, and hence "agreeableness," among group members. As conformity to standards increases, cohesiveness increases also, and vice versa. As an element of group cohesiveness, attraction to one another, or friendship, may in turn enhance conformity. Friendship, or liking of one another, furthers communication between members, and thus also enhances conformity and group cohesiveness. In the study by Festinger, Schachter, and Back, already cited, the relationship between cohesiveness and conformity is clearly demonstrated. In this study two housing projects for married war veterans were used to determine the effect of group standards. One group or project evolved standards regarding mutual attitudes and behavior, whereas the other did not. The investigators were able to predict that a positive relationship between friendship behavior and conformity to the group standard would hold, whereas no significant relationship would arise in the project where no group standard existed. In the former project a rank-order correlation of +.74 at the .02 level of significance was obtained, whereas a rank order of only +.27 was obtained in the latter. The study shows, in fine, that group cohesiveness and group conformity are positively related, and in a significant way.

The attractive power of the group is further demonstrated in the social support or security which friendship relations generate in its members. In a study of the emotional aspects of group relations Cartwright asserts that personal security is dependent upon an individual's awareness of his own power, his knowledge of the friendliness of others, his acceptance of the norms of his group, and his perception of the enmity of others against him.[20] Since it is beyond the centrality of our subject matter to stress individual power, and since we shall give due attention to the role of hostility later, we emphasize the importance of group norms, with its conduciveness to friendliness, as an indispensable generator of group attraction. Most of the ideas and data which we have discussed thus far in this book give decisive if not eloquent testimony to the supportive power of group standards for its individual members. Groups which are high in the attraction variable are those which support the individual member, influence his behavior toward increasing conformity to its standards, and nullify the effect of those variables which generate hostility and avoidance.

Experimental Investigation of Group Attraction. The experimental manipulation of group phenomena has received much attention in the last decade. Much of the work expounded thus far has been analytical, descriptive, and systematic observation. We shall now examine some laboratory research investigations of group cohesiveness, with particular attention to the attractiveness of the group.

In a study of the effect of social communication on individual members, Back designed a laboratory experiment in which attraction of members to each other and attraction to the group were both investigated.[21] Using volunteers to participate in two-person discussion groups, Back submitted questions designed to produce strong and weak valences between the members. To the "strong" group he stressed the fictitious information that they were greatly attracted to each other, and to the "weak" group he gave the impression that they were not unusually attracted to each other. He further assigned to the "strong" group the task of interpreting a set of pictures, stressed the importance of the task as a test of their imaginative capacity, and in addition offered

[20] D. Cartwright, Emotional dimensions of group life, in M. L. Reymert (ed.), *Feelings and emotions* (New York: McGraw-Hill Book Co., Inc., 1950), pp. 439–47.

[21] K. W. Back, Influence through social communication, *J. abnorm. soc. Psychol., 46* (1951), 9–23.

a cash reward for the best solution. He assigned the same task to the "weak" group, stressed the measure of imaginative capacity, but offered it no cash award. He found that the members of the "strong" group were more influenced by mutual discussion and strove harder to reach agreement than the members of the "weaker" group. Attraction to the group, in short, is affected not only by the members' knowledge of how much they liked each other, but by the importance of good performance on a task and by the status of the group as measured by the subjects' liking it because of its prestige-value—in other words, by the attractiveness of the group itself.

In an experimental investigation of the effects of leader-centered and group-centered techniques on interpersonal affect, Bovard gives further support to our description of group attraction.[22] He devised a rating scale for measuring the anonymously expressed feelings of members for one another on an 11-point scale, ranging from −5 for strong disliking to +5 for strong liking. The reliability and validity of the scale were adequately established. The scale was administered to six "stable" groups with a population of 55 that had met together for an average of 231 hours, and seven "temporary" groups with a population of 53 that had met for an average of only 2.47 hours. Omitting the details of the design of the experiment and concentrating only on the results, we can say that Bovard established, among other things, the hypothesis that "members of the group-centered population would rate each other higher on an affect scale than members of a comparable leader-centered population would rate each other." He also found in both populations that the group was rated significantly higher than were the separate individuals forming it.[23]

[22] E. W. Bovard, Jr., The experimental production of interpersonal affect, *J. abnorm. soc. Psychol.*, *46* (1951), 521–33. Although Bovard was not investigating group attractiveness specifically, his findings are fully relevant to our problem.

[23] *Ibid.*, p. 524. Bovard's experiment supports not only the hypothesis that persons are attracted to the group for the reasons already stated, but that the group as a whole is an identifiable perceptual object.

An extensive and rigorous use of experimental techniques for the study of group attractiveness was recently made by Libo.[24] It is unnecessary to give more than a very brief review of it here. After a brief discussion of the experimental setting Libo presents a detailed description of two measures of attraction, namely, the Attraction Questionnaire and the Group-Picture-Impressions technique (G-P-I). The questionnaire contained three items referring to the individual's wish to remain in the group, how often he would like to come to its meetings, and, should the group break up and someone tried to revive it, whether he would want to rejoin it. The G-P-I is a projective technique consisting of a booklet containing three pictures, concerning which short stories were to be written by each subject. Both the Attraction Questionnaire and the Group-Picture-Impressions technique discriminated significantly between the high-attractiveness condition and the low-attractiveness condition.

Libo's findings may be summed up briefly. The experimental manipulation of group attractiveness was found to be valid, as shown by the fact that those in the high-attractiveness condition tended on the whole to remain in their groups, whereas those in the low-attractiveness condition tended to leave their groups. The Attractiveness Questionnaire not only discriminated significantly between the two sets of conditions but was found to be a valid predictor of whether a member would leave or remain in his group. The Group-Picture-Impressions test yielded significantly higher scores for the high attractiveness than for the low attractiveness conditions, for those who remained than for those who left their groups. Since both the Questionnaire and the G-P-I were valid measures of group attractiveness, a significant relationship between them was predicted. The correlation between them was found to be +.23 for males, +.38 for females, and +.34 for the combined sample, each highly significant ($P < .01$).[25]

[24] L. M. Libo, *Measuring group cohesiveness* (Ann Arbor, Mich.: Research Center for Group Dynamics, University of Michigan, 1953).

[25] *Ibid.*, pp. 47–48.

The reader is aware, no doubt, of a telling weakness of the various measures of group attractiveness. We have already called attention to this weakness by emphasizing the *continuous gradation* of liking, friendship, and other positive valences in commenting on Homans' discussion of the role of interaction in cohesiveness (see Chapter 3, p. 77 f). Since we have defined group attractiveness as a consequence of the forces impelling a person to remain in or to leave his group, the resulting classification of behavior is dichotomous. It seems to leave no room for what on the basis of other evidence we know to be true: the fact that behavior takes place on a continuum, involving a gradual transition from one end of a scale to the other. Both attraction to and repulsion from group membership as distinct criteria of measurement violate the principle of continuity. While this failure to provide for continuity of attraction to the group need not and will not be permanent, it must be recognized as a serious limitation.

Concluding Remarks. In the preceding pages of this chapter we have reviewed the cohesive factors in group behavior. We have found that cohesiveness, defined as the product of the forces acting upon individuals to remain in the group, is a complex phenomenon. While a knowledge of the factors of shared norms, morale, and leadership tells us much concerning the nature of cohesiveness, the concept of group attractiveness is more incisive. Group attractiveness has been subjected to intensive study and experimentation in the last decade. Investigations have shown that the most fruitful way to study the phenomenon is through the measurement of interpersonal attraction and the valent character of the group itself. Neither one nor the other alone, but the two as interrelated phenomena, yield a more complete as well as a conceptually more refined analysis of the nature of group cohesiveness. The operational test of group cohesiveness which has emerged from the experimental investigation of the subject is that, given a choice, an individual will remain in the group. The member who remains in the group is one who has a stronger force acting upon him to remain than one who withdraws from it.

There are other conclusions suggested by the researches which we have described, only some of which are stated here. It has been found that in highly cohesive groups members are more receptive to interpersonal influence than individuals in noncohesive groups. With the increase in influence goes an increase in conformity—or better, uniformity—of attitudes and opinions. There is greater uniformity in participation also and, paradoxical though it may seem, a greater amount of change in members, than in less cohesive groups. In short, the more attractive the group is to its members, the greater is its power to produce changes in its individual members, such as solutions of problems, increasingly effective discussion, productivity on a task, and the like. The amount of change, however, it should be added, which a group can effect in its members, can never be greater than the force acting upon them to remain in the group.[26]

On several occasions we asserted that acceptance, liking, and friendship are conducive to group cohesiveness. While this is generally true, some investigators have shown that interpersonal liking may also impair and disrupt the cohesiveness of group behavior. Homans' study of the Bank Wiremen (see above, pp. 78 f.), has shown this to be true. Some forms of group activity are adversely affected by close friendship. Problem-solving can be impaired by the inattention generated by excessive social communication between mutually attracted individuals. Horsfall and Arensberg, for example, found that work groups which engaged in an excessive amount of social activity were least productive.[27] This is but one more confirmation of the belief that group phenomena are variable—that we cannot speak with complete assurance regarding the behavior of persons in groups.

[26] Festinger, Schachter, and Back, *Social pressures in informal groups.*

[27] A. B. Horsfall and C. M. Arensberg, Teamwork and productivity in a shoe factory, *Hum. Organization, 8* (1949), 13–25.

DISRUPTION OF GROUP BEHAVIOR

In view of the existence of intrusive factors, irritants, and other impairments of cohesiveness, it is necessary to examine the other side of the group process, namely, the disruptive factors in group behavior. To this we now turn.

A superficial observation of contemporary life leads to the widespread belief that life is composed largely of conflicts and disharmonies. If this were true, it would be difficult to understand how groups could survive at all. On the other hand, many studies which we have thus far reviewed lead one to the equally distorted view that cooperation and cohesiveness are the most adequate and efficient ways for groups to discharge their functions. There is an implicit bias in many studies, especially those dealing with industrial problems, in favor of the view (which probably has an ethical motivation) that cooperation is the most desirable way for groups to function. The truth probably lies somewhere in between the two extremes. Cohesiveness is no doubt necessary for group functioning and survival, but competition, hostility, and disruption are also inescapable aspects of group behavior. Competition and conflict are not always negative or destructive; they can also be stimulating and constructive. The very fact of interaction and interdependence of group members, which is basic to group behavior, suggests competition and conflict with and frustration by members of the group. Group disruption is implied by group cohesiveness as long as members are dependent upon one another. There is good reason to believe, moreover, that the greater the self-involvement of members in group activities, the greater the potential for group disruption as well as for group cohesion. An individual whose interest in the group's goals and activities is only lukewarm, or whose self is only partly involved in its aspirations, is not likely to be acutely aroused by its collective efforts nor deeply frustrated by its failures. Disruption results, finally, from differences in individual and collective goals and the conflicts they generate. All members of a group are not likely to agree on all issues nor strive for the same goal at all times. Group disruption, in fine, is a potential consequence of social living.

Types of Group Disruption. Since our knowledge of this subject is far from complete, we shall describe only those forms of group disruption which have been disclosed by careful research, particularly by experimental investigation.

In an experimental study of the subject, French divided group disruption into two main categories.[28] One class consisted of "a real splitting of the group" by the formation of opposing factions, a relative absence of leadership, little *esprit de corps,* and the permanent withdrawal of some members. The other class was characterized by "minor disruptions" in which temporary escape from the field, interpersonal aggressions, and a general disorganization of group activities were the outstanding features.[29]

French's experiment was performed on sixteen groups, of which eight were organized and eight unorganized. Each group contained six members. In the organized groups some were members of athletic teams and some of clubs engaged in athletic activities. The members of the unorganized groups were unacquainted with one another at the beginning of the experiment. All the groups were deliberately frustrated by being required to solve unsolvable problems, namely, a mathematical puzzle, the Hindu pyramid of discs problem, and a motor-skill puzzle.

Summed up, the results are clearly differentiating. While aggression, consequent upon frustration, mounted in the organized groups and hostility was openly expressed by its members, they still remained closely knit groups and wished to continue working on the problems at the end of the experiment. The outstanding feature of the unorganized groups, on the other hand, was the rapid cleavage of members into opposing factions. Interdependence was minimal,

[28] J. R. P. French, Jr., The disruption and cohesion of groups, *J. abnorm. soc. Psychol., 36* (1941), 361–77. This study, although primarily concerned with the emotional behavior of small groups, nonetheless throws valuable light on the problem of group disruption.

[29] *Ibid.,* p. 366.

leadership was weak and ineffectual, the feeling of group belongingness was absent, and frustration was very low. On this latter point it appears that frustration is generated more readily and intensely in groups that are working hard to achieve a collective goal. This is consistent with what we know about the relation between self-involvement and frustration. A person whose self is only peripherally involved in group activities is at once less desirous of working for a collective goal and less adversely affected by the group's failure to achieve it.

With this background, we can turn next to a more detailed consideration of these forms of group disruption, namely, group cleavage and minor disorganization of activity.

Group cleavage. As already noted, group cleavage, the splitting of the group into factions or more or less uncoordinated individual activities is an expected consequence of deficient we-feeling and lack of organization. In the experiment we are describing this fragmentation is seen in the emergence of an in-group and an out-group. The in-group worked rapidly and cooperatively with little or no help from the others, most of whom by now constituted the out-group. The in-group, moreover, rejected proffers of help from the out-group, especially from one member who chronically complained and saw nothing but failure in the task ahead. As the cleavage became sharper, frustration increased, and hostility between the factions became more overt. Members of the in-group charged the members of the out-group with lack of perseverance and accused its most disgruntled member of sabotaging the group's efforts. The cleavage into opposing factions was, moreover, largely responsible for the failure of the group as a whole to shift its efforts to the solution of all three problems. The split-off group, finally, rejected many more suggestions for solving the problems than the intact group.[30]

[30] *Ibid.*, p. 364. The author rightly injects a note of caution here. We must not confuse the factions working independently of each other with cooperating subgroups characterized by a division of labor. Sociological

2. *Minor disorganization.* Unlike group cleavage, minor disorganization does not eventuate in any permanent division of the group. This form of disruption is much more frequent in the organized than in the unorganized groups. This conforms to the frequent observation that a cohesive group, characterized by a high degree of self-involvement and we-feeling, engages in constructive opposition and conflict without endangering its structure. Hostilities and aggressions openly expressed are thereby more readily controlled or channelized into motivations for solving mutual problems.

Minor disruptions are of three kinds: (1) interpersonal aggression, (2) temporary escape from the field, and (3) general disorganization.

1. *Interpersonal aggressions* consist of such forms of behavior as individual hostility, domination of others, blaming others, sarcasm, recrimination, and the like. An important feature of interpersonal aggression is that it is usually accompanied by the members' insight into their own behavior. The insight enables them to view their failures as being no one individual's fault, to avoid looking for scapegoats, and stop blaming one another. In the experiment described, for example, some individuals, much to the chagrin of others, laughed at their failures and thereby reduced their own tensions.

The maintenance of the group is the more remarkable when we consider the large number of interpersonal aggressions that were recorded in the experiment. The average number for the unorganized groups was 6 and for the organized groups 45. The author remarks that the actual number of aggressions was much larger for the organized groups than could be recorded. Estimates ran as high as 600 in one organized group.[31]

2. *Temporary escape from the field* is another form of minor disruption. Having defined group cohesiveness as the

---

studies abound, indeed, with evidence showing that differentiation of function goes hand in hand with interdependence and cohesiveness of the group as a whole.

[31] *Ibid.,* p. 366.

product of the forces acting upon individuals to remain in the group, it is not difficult to see that withdrawal from the field, or group, should result in disruption. Since the withdrawal is only temporary, there is no permanent disorganization or disruption of the group. The temporary escape in the experiment consisted of withdrawal from the problem, attempts to change problems, substitute behavior, cheating, and the like. In the face of repeated failure, some members tried to escape the blame and criticism of others by appealing to the good will of the experimenter, others blamed scapegoats. One scapegoat withdrew from the group in protesting anger, returning only after being mollified by an appeal to his personal pride. Quantitatively expressed, the average number of escapes from the field was twelve for the unorganized and sixteen for the organized groups.

3. *General disorganization* of the group's activity is a third form of minor disruption. It is manifested most clearly in uncooperative, and especially uncoordinated, behavior in which every member freely blames every other member for his own failures. Every serious failure is followed by complete, but temporary, disorganization. Lasting disorganization of the groups in the experiment was probably averted by the ability of the members to talk to and encourage one another, and by their decision at the crucial point of stress to stop blaming one another, for they were aware that failure was no one person's fault. While the author did not record general disorganization quantitatively, he reported that it was more frequent in the organized than in the unorganized groups.[32]

FACTORS IN GROUP DISRUPTION. *Restriction and breakdown of communication.* Recent researches have made abundantly clear that group solidarity and cohesion depend on effective communication. When communication between individuals is restricted, or when it breaks down altogether, persons form stereotyped attitudes toward others. Since they do not or cannot check their own observations of others,

[32] *Ibid.*, pp. 366–67.

they develop private opinions of them. While not all restricted communication inevitably leads to stereotyped attitudes, much of it does result in the type of distortion of the intention of others that is characteristic of the isolated person. This distortion often breeds hostility toward other members of the group. The "autistic hostility," as Newcomb calls it, is encouraged by restrictions or barriers to communication.[33] Adequate communication (that is, communication which entails no threat to the members), on the other hand, reduces hostility between them, for it encourages comparisons and modifies members' attitudes toward each other.

It is important not to confuse an individual's isolation from others with the socially "shared autism" which develops in a group. Shared autism, and the shared hostility to which it may give rise, derive their potency and capacity for producing mischief from being socially reinforced. There is some communication here, but it is restricted; and the meanings, which are shared, are correspondingly distorted. Each member of the group perceives the other in a framework of threat and responds to him defensively. Defensiveness breeds hostility and hostility provokes defensiveness. The situation as it applies to the group is similar to the vicious circle of the individual neurotic in whom hostility and anxiety mutually reinforce each other. Just as an individual who does not adequately communicate with himself (that is, one who represses his hostility) is blind to his own ill feeling toward others, so individuals who do not communicate their ill will toward others are seldom aware of their hostility toward them. The difficulty in both cases lies in the area of communication.

An interesting case of this form of misunderstanding in group relationships, leading to perceptual distortion and potential alienation, is the condition of "pluralistic ignorance." In this condition no one believes, but everyone believes that everyone believes. Schank describes an example of such a contradiction between private views and public attitudes.

[33] T. M. Newcomb, Autistic hostility and social reality, *Hum. Relat.*, *1* (1947), 69–86.

Each member of a Methodist church in a small town believed that everyone in the church disapproved of card-playing, despite the fact that each member played cards himself. There was no testing of attitudes against reality in this situation, for communication on this matter was entirely absent. One person could not affect another person because no common ground for awareness or agreement existed between them.[34]

Studies of the behavior of industrial groups are rich sources of evidence of the deficient functioning and disruption of groups caused by breakdown in the channels of communication. When communication between a worker and his superior breaks down, there is not only serious misunderstanding between them, but the worker's effectiveness on the job is also jeopardized. The worker's resentment over not being consulted regarding matters that affect him on the job not only militates against cordial relationships between himself and the foreman but affects his efficiency and production even more. Resentment and inefficiency are also generated in the foremen when communication between them and top management is impaired or breaks down. When the foreman is conscious of the fact that his ideas and wishes are not taken into account in the decisions of top-policy levels, it is practically impossible for him to identify himself with the interests of his employer. Poor performance may be largely due to the breakdown of communication between organizational levels.[35]

Communication leads to group disruption not only under circumstances of restriction and breakdown but very frequently under conditions of *selective transmission.* One person may tell another only what he thinks the latter should or would want to hear. This is seen in all those relationships where no one wishes to "stick his neck out." The subordinate

[34] R. L. Shank, A study of a community and its groups and institutions conceived as behaviors of individuals, *Psychol. Monogr.*, *43*, No. 2 (1932).

[35] The literature dealing with this problem in industry is enormous. A good source for the beginner is B. B. Gardner, *Human relations in industry* (Chicago: R. D. Irwin, 1946). See especially pp. 45–67.

who is dependent on his superior for desired rewards will communicate only information to the latter that will protect or advance his own interests. This condition is particularly encouraged in complex and formal organizations, like modern industrial plants, where the channels of communication between subordinates and superordinates are continually lengthened and multiplied. Under these circumstances, as Homans and Roethlisberger have shown, each channel transmits only part of the information, and no one is responsible for the whole message. Every new channel "may increase the insecurity of men located on the other channel, for it by-passes these men and transmits information that, in the hands of a leader inadequately skilled, may bring criticism back down upon them."[36]

An important factor in selective transmission is *the image which each has of the other* in the communication process. The content of messages transmitted by a subordinate to a superordinate is different from that of messages going in the opposite direction. Facts are slanted, modified, or distorted in accordance with the image that the subordinate has of his superior, and in accordance with his notion of what the boss wants to hear. If the boss is conceived as a threatening tyrant, he is almost sure to get only such information as will protect the worker from his wrath. If in turn the boss sees the worker as a person too easily upset by critical information, he might convey to him only such facts as will tend to encourage him.

An interesting illustration of the role of one's image of the other is furnished by the Hartleys. One of them describes a nursery school child regarding whose behavior the teachers sought help and advice. While the consultant had traveled six hundred miles to meet with the teachers, the latter brought only such minor behavior problems to his attention as they could easily have handled themselves. Not until after the conference did he discover the reason for the

[36] Homans, *The human group*, p. 461; F. J. Roethlisberger, The foreman: master and victim of double-talk, *Harvard Business Rev.*, 23 (1945), 283–98.

teachers' disturbance over the child's behavior, and why they had called on him for help. The perturbing element in the child's behavior was frequent masturbation, but as the consultant remarked, "no teacher had mentioned this because the supervisor was a man, and all the teachers were women! The teachers' 'image' of a male apparently precluded discussing sexual activity with him, and the supervisor's 'image' of the teachers had not included such an element of reticence."[37]

The importance of communication, of some mutual agreement among individuals, is obviously essential to group functioning. Outside mere casual association, which characterizes fluid crowds or aggregations of people, a frame of references composed of common perceptions and fundamental ideas of the nature of social reality, is essential for group existence. In the absence of communication, common perceptions, and the sharing of values, a group would probably not arise; or if it did, it could not long endure. Accordingly, anything which interferes with the communication process eventually brings about a disruption in human relationships.

Intergroup hostility. Intra- and intergroup relations, we have said, are based on similar psychological principles. Because intergroup conflicts and hostilities loom large in contemporary society, and because they have significant practical implications, we must investigate them separately.

In the preceding section we established the fact that adequate communication is essential to organized group-functioning. Good communication brings and holds people together. On the other hand, as we have also shown, poor or impaired communication disrupts or destroys human relationships. It breeds distorted images of one another, creates misunderstandings between people, and gives rise to intergroup hostility. But here, as in many other group phenomena, we observe a familiar psychological circularity.

[37] E. L. Hartley and R. E. Hartley, *Fundamentals of social psychology* (New York: Alfred A. Knopf, Inc., 1952), p. 52.

Hostility in turn impairs communication. When two groups do not operate within the same frame of reference, do not share the same norms, words and concepts have divergent meanings. In this situation two groups impute negative values to each other and see each other as potential "enemies" or aggressors. In this "frame of mind" neither can see the other objectively and each interprets the other's behavior as hostile. As the negative perceptions are multiplied and intensified, the communication between them is correspondingly reduced or eliminated. As the communication diminishes, the groups become more withdrawn and different from each other and their social frames of reference increasingly more distinct. As the frames of reference diverge, misunderstandings arise and hostile reactions to each other multiply. The only way out of this circle is the replacement of one behavior pattern by another. This calls attention to a very important fact concerning intergroup hostility, namely, the role of learning.

There is enough experimental evidence to permit us to say, with considerable confidence, that *hostility in actual situations is learned.* We have the emotional capacity to dislike or feel hostile toward other people, but a feeling or display of hostility toward them is acquired or learned. As in all learning we *select* the individuals or groups toward whom we react in certain ways. We learn to communicate with some groups and not with others. Those whom we select are persons or groups who do not differ too much from ourselves, who in a broad sense speak the same language, and whose locomotions take place in the same reference frames of shared norms. We learn to select the persons or groups in childhood through conditioning, example, and deliberate inculcation by adults, such as parents and teachers. Repetition of the early conditioning reinforces the hostility which in turn is transferred to other persons or situations. The attitude of hostility, in other words, is *generalized* to include any person or group which presents similar characteristics.

Since hostility is learned, it can also be eliminated. The elimination is not a process of "forgetting" in the popular sense. It consists of replacing one kind of learning with another kind. It is largely, but not entirely, a process of *unlearning*. But unlearning attitudes like learning them can take place only when there is interaction or communication between members or between groups. Intergroup hostility, accordingly, may be best eliminated if the hostile groups are brought into contact with each other. We observed the functioning of this learning principle in our description of the hostilities and conflicts of the in-group and the out-group. We shall describe it in more detail later when we discuss the reduction of hostility and intergroup tensions in interracial housing experiments. For the present it is sufficient merely to call attention to the fact that people cannot learn to like or accept one another if they have no opportunity to unlearn their hostility through the mechanisms of contact and interaction.

Hostility within and between groups can be explained, finally, by *hypercompetitiveness*. The present writer is keenly aware that the negative effects of competition on behavior have been exaggerated by some investigators. He believes that competition within controlled limits may have salutary effects. The harm comes not from competition itself, but from excess, or from an all-embracing ramification of it in group life. In the latter situation man's failure in the competitive struggle is attributed too exclusively to the individual without recognizing that the real cause of his failure may be in social conditions beyond his control. In group relations competition may be so pronounced that rapport between members or between groups cannot be established. In this situation every individual or every group is working against all others, thereby precluding friendly relations among them. It goes without saying that under these conditions participation, sharing, and cooperation are impossible. The experiments of M. Sherif which we described in the last chapter illustrate and support these observations.

A note of caution needs to be injected here. While we have stressed the importance of communication and the reduction of excessive competitiveness in the resolution of intergroup tensions and hostilities, contact and interaction in themselves are no guaranty for the elimination of intergroup frictions. Hostile attitudes between in-groups and out-groups may continue despite interaction between them. Sherif's experiment with the "Bull Dogs" and "Red Devils" showed a persistence of name-calling and derogatory stereotypes between the two groups despite their mutual participation in shared athletic events, birthday parties, campfires, and the like.[38]

CONCLUSION

The processes of group cohesiveness and group disruption have both theoretical and practical significance. A knowledge of each broadens and deepens our understanding of the psychology of groups and aids us in the construction of techniques for effective communication and for resolving tensions and conflicts in human relationships. In this chapter we have concentrated almost wholly on the nature of cohesiveness and disruption of groups. The resolution of conflicts will be examined in detail in Part III.

We have reviewed empirical, theoretical, and experimental data in this chapter. While we have marshaled only a small amount of the prodigious research that has been done in this area, we have presented enough to acquaint the reader with the essential properties of both cohesiveness and disruption in group behavior. An encouraging trend in research is the increasing emphasis on empirical and experimental studies. Out of this research there has emerged a not inconsiderable amount of dependable and operational description of the conditions that influence group cohesiveness and group disruption.

[38] For a fuller acquaintance with the problem under consideration, the reader should consult the researches of M. Sherif that have been cited, and M. Sherif and C. W. Sherif, *An outline of social psychology* (rev. ed.; New York: Harper & Bros., 1956), pp. 301–32.

While our interest in this chapter is concentrated on cohesiveness and disruption, we have by implication suggested the forces which are at work in the entire field of group behavior. In one way or another the remainder of this book inevitably touches upon the subject expounded in the present chapter. Cohesiveness and disruption affect or are affected by other variables in group behavior. In proportion to the extent and degree that we formulate these variables operationally, group dynamics is moving away from philosophical and intuitive explanations to scientific descriptions. This transition is most clearly evident when we compare the formulation of cohesiveness as *esprit de corps* with descriptions of it in terms of the attractiveness of members to each other and to the group; and when we compare the analysis of group disruption as breakdown in morale with descriptions of it in terms of interpersonal aggressions and distortions in communication. This is not to say that concepts like *esprit de corps* and morale are to be discarded. They no doubt refer to real conditions or processes. Certainly, when conceived as forces acting against conditions frustrating the efforts of a group to achieve a goal, these concepts have a meaningful status. But until they are defined more rigorously than as *feelings* of group identification or as group *will,* they will not in the long run add significantly to the science of group behavior. Indeed, our study shows that *esprit de corps* and morale gain in specificity of meaning to the degree that they are understood as problems of group cohesion and disruption. *Esprit de corps* and morale, from our point of view, both refer to the forces acting upon individuals to remain in the group, including the degree of coordination of members' efforts to do so. In this way we are able to describe the cohesiveness and disruption of groups by means of a single unifying concept.

CHAPTER 4

Group Learning

For centuries it has been uncritically believed that thinking, learning, and other cognitive processes are wholly individual phenomena, and that productive learning and thinking are the result of individual effort. A widespread prejudice exists to the effect that committees and other groupings never produce significant results, for creative and productive activities are individual phenomena. If solutions of problems emerge from groups, it is because a leader or other exceptional person puts his talents to work and influences others to agree with his decision.

Stuart Chase describes two instances of this deep-rooted bias. He cites first the case of a psychologist who put three students to work as a team on a Ph.D. dissertation. They produced an excellent study which the psychologist rated better than one which anyone of them alone could have written. But since the institution had no formally recognized way of giving Ph.D.'s to groups, the project produced only consternation.[1]

[1] S. Chase, *Roads to agreement* (New York: Harper & Bros., 1951), pp. 60–61. In a footnote the author adds that New York University has announced group theses for Masters' degrees. The present writer can add to this the information that he was recently a member of a dissertation committee at Columbia University which supervised a doctoral dissertation written by two individuals. The product was of a high order.

The other instance of this old bias relates to another university professor, teaching a class by the group-dynamics method, who graded the whole class rather than the individual members. However, the dismayed and angry dean ordered the professor to stop this unorthodox method, "no matter how much better the students learned the subject."[2]

These instances call attention to the extreme misconceptions of the nature of group learning. The evidence clearly shows that in some circumstances and regarding some problems group learning is superior to individual learning, while in other situations the reverse is true. The consensus of individuals in a group is not a necessary criterion of truth; there are other factors to be considered, chief among which is the demand for validity. The adherents to the view of the superiority of individual learning need not fear, for the exponents of group superiority in learning and problem-solving will never be able to eliminate the individual from the learning process. The dichotomization of the individual and the group is as unrealistic and false as the by-now-discredited division between the person and his environment. It is in this spirit and with the confirming evidence of contemporary research that we approach the problem in this chapter.

NATURE OF LEARNING

Our brief review in Chapter 1 of the effect of the group upon human performance has made it clear that interest in and research upon this problem is not as recent as the present enthusiasm over group dynamics seems to suggest. Nevertheless, the bulk of research in this area and the rigorous standards of observation and experimentation which characterize numerous studies during the past twenty-five years have placed the psychology of group learning and group problem-solving at or near the center of the scientific study of group relations.

An underlying assumption in our view of learning, supported by ample evidence, is that our perceptions of the

[2] *Ibid.*, p. 61.

world around us, of other people, and our relations to them are acquired or *learned.* This is true whether we are dealing with simple responses to physical stimuli, complex reactions by means of interpretation and meaning, or highly organized social perceptions involving group norms and expectations.

Analysis of the Problem. No topic in psychology has been subjected to greater scrutiny and rigorous experimental investigation than learning. Although the results of classical conditioning experiments were greatly oversimplified and subsequently mostly outgrown, the bias in favor of the animal model in learning theory has become deeply entrenched. We do not question the use of experimental animals in the study of learning, nor do we seriously challenge the validity of cautious extrapolation from animal to human learning. There is no doubt that all learning is characterized by a few elementary principles. Too often, however, the extrapolations have afforded us insufficient understanding of individual human learning, and in the area of group learning they have rarely offered the social psychologist any usable insights. The value of the universal elementary principles is diminished because they are too frequently devoid of cultural or group content. Reinforcement, which looms large in contemporary learning experiments, has been confined too narrowly to the laboratory situation, with the consequence that the learning psychologist is rarely able to predict human behavior outside it. Human, in contrast to most animal, learning is often circuitous and deflective, and it is not wholly governed by need reduction—even supposing that this is so in lower animals, which is doubtful. Human beings are not, except in hypothetical or fictitious cases, isolated. Their learning is affected by other human beings who act as reinforcing agents. While we must therefore conclude that learning goes on inside the individual, the kind of learning which we are investigating is operationally meaningful only when we consider it in the external context of the group. We begin, not with the classical learning process, but with learning as it takes place in social interaction. From a social-psychological point of view it is no more mysterious to "explain" human learning as an interactional process than to account for it wholly in terms of the behavior of the individual organism. The charge of mysticism applies to earlier group-mind speculations, but is without foundation when directed against recent inquiries into social learning and collective problem-solving. The reinforcing agent in group learning is not need satisfaction, which is always—and questionably—assumed in individual learning, but a stimulus situation of two or more individuals modifying one another's behavior. Evidence of this is found all the way from the early interactions of parent and child in the socializing process in the home to the latest unlearning of racial prejudice or the resolution of a conflict between management and the worker in an industrial situation.

Again, in a group situation, in contrast to that of the formal laboratory, where the animal is usually half-starved and where the apparatus unduly limits its possible behavior, the individuals are free to choose among many possible alternatives. The choice of alternatives is determined by the norms and expectancies of the group, by its cohesiveness, by the "force" of its leadership, the nature of the group goal, and the like. The difference is not one of complexity, as is sometimes assumed, although this may play a part in some forms of group learning, but of the structure or organization of the group. Accordingly, just as the sophisticated laboratory investigator of animal learning in a controlled experiment is conscious of the limitation imposed upon the results by the apparatus which he is using, so the student of group learning is certain that the interaction which he is investigating is affected by the pattern of the group membership. Just as individual learning is affected by the maze or the puzzle box, so group learning conforms to the "demands" of the group. The common ground of both types of learning consists of the interaction of individuals with specific events.[3]

[3] This mode of analysis rejects the classical, oversimplified S-R connections, and the fractionation of learning to which it leads. From our point

Perceptual learning. A view firmly entrenched in much psychology is that the perceptual like the cognitive field is inherently organized. This would mean that our very earliest perceptions of objects are predetermined. While it is difficult to test early perceptual organization in a very young child, recent evidence points to the conclusion that perception, too, is learned.[4] Animals without experience of certain visual objects the latter as vague or unorganized, rather than well-defined patterns. Objects are not meaningful as such; meaning is imputed to them through repeated contact with them. The reason why the mother in our culture is a "significant other" lies not in her being a structured object-person, but in the fact that she channelizes the child's perceptions and thereby structures his image of her as a person. His perception of his mother as a provider of pleasure is learned. Meaning is thus an act of interpreting event-structures, or the perceiving of an event in a total situation—in more conventional psychological terms, an interpretation of stimuli. Through perceptual contact, an object or event becomes different. If the object or event should be a person—say a Negro, we perceive him in a new way, so that he takes on a positive instead of a negative value for us. It is in this fashion, for example, that prejudice is removed.

Self-involvement. Group learning is enhanced—indeed, made possible—by the identification of one person with other persons in an interactive relationship. While the beginnings of this process, as we pointed out, are found in the family, it soon extends to the community and to a large variety of groups—from the peer group of childhood to the self-involvements with class, professional groups, and one's nation. The satisfaction which members get from group-belongingness reinforces the need or desire to interact with others. Morale,

---

of view, group learning is not a kind of total of individual learning, but a molar behavior in which the learning of each member of a group is modified by that of others. The stimuli are interpreted as *events* and the responses as *interacts*.

[4] See, for example, A. H. Riesen, Arrested vision, *Scientific American* (July, 1950), 16–19.

esprit de corps, and group cohesiveness, which have traditionally been explained in semi-mystical ways, are learned modes of group behavior. When the learner has identified himself with a group the satisfaction which he derives from participating in its activities is reinforced in the same manner as other satisfactions. Conforming to its pressures and expectations, like adjusting to any set of norms, is a mode of learning. When we learn in a group we learn to perceive others and our relations with them in the same manner as they perceive and relate themselves to others.

Role behavior. The psychology of role behavior is treated at length in Chapter 12. Here we wish only to relate it to the process of group learning. Roles are learned modes of behavior. Because the group "rewards" the individual for enacting some roles and withholds satisfaction from him for playing other roles, he learns to perform those roles which bring satisfaction and to avoid those that bring dissatisfaction. This is but another way of stating what we already said in the foregoing paragraph, namely, that people in groups tend to act in conformity with the expectations of others. It follows that the more a person learns to perform his roles skillfully, the more (other things being equal) the group functions cooperatively and achieves its goal in concert. The more clumsily he enacts his roles, the more difficult it is for all others in the group to play their roles adequately, with the consequence that group action becomes difficult or impossible. Learning to play one's roles is thus an important feature of group behavior.

Group learning vs. individual learning. A problem of first importance in group dynamics is the relative merit and efficacy of group learning and individual learning. While we shall discuss this problem in detail later in this chapter, it will be helpful to state it briefly in this section.

We do not subscribe to the extreme view—a view for which the reason has never been made fully clear—that the group is almost always superior to the individual. In reviewing the research and experimental work in group dynamics of the past 15 years, the writer gains the impression that in the minds of certain enthusiasts for "group dynamics," the group, like the king of old, can do no wrong. Although this is patently untrue, nevertheless, there is a substantial body of evidence supporting the proposition that, in large measure, men learn some things easier in groups than in isolation. Long before the advent of group dynamics it was known that learning is aided by mutual discussion. Dynamic groups furnish their members with unusual opportunity for interaction, discussion, and effective communication. Group discussions are effective learning experiences, for they entail praise and criticism, which are forms of reward and punishment. Just as learning one's role is facilitated when performed as a mode of adjustment to other peoples' roles, so learning "intellectual" material may be made easier when one's performance is subjected to the careful evaluation of others.

A recent awareness of the effectiveness of group learning was forced upon us by necessity. As a consequence of the shortage of dons at Oxford and Cambridge during World War II, it was discovered that students in groups of five or six learned more and faster than as single individuals by the traditional tutorial method. In his book, *Roads to Agreement,* Stuart Chase reports that students, writing themes for their class instead of their instructor, acquired more effective habits of communication. Group instruction in music has been found to produce better results than individual teaching. Ski instruction works in the same way. These are just a few examples.

Human learning under normal circumstances is social learning. Social psychologists have, of course, known for a long time that socialization, or social learning in its broadest sense, never takes place in isolation. Socialization is the process of learning the ways of a group—its attitudes, values, beliefs, and prejudices. If our attitudes persist, it is not because they are in themselves inclined to be long-lived or permanent, but because the group is constantly reinforcing them and thereby making them resistant to extinction. By the same token attitudes are most effectively changed when the group sets up a new learning process whereby the old is caused to drop out or be forgotten. There is a widespread fallacy that "learning about" a race or a minority people will eliminate hostile attitudes against it. The fallacy is based on a one-sided conception of the nature of learning and largely ignores the differential effect of the group on learning. The one-sided conception of learning results from exclusive concentration on the learner and neglect of the circumstances in which the learning takes place. In saying this we are not, as should be clear in view of what we have already said, minimizing the importance of the learner's personality, motivation, aptitudes, and the like, but only emphasizing again that these traits take on a different configuration when the individual interacts with other individuals in a group. The growth characteristics of the learner are not obliterated in the group; they are modified and redirected. Consequently, the results of learning are often different in a group from what they might have been in the solitary individual. Learning is a unitary process, but it takes different forms, depending on individual or collective circumstances. In the group, individuals experience a set of events, or a stimulus-situation, in a new way, because every member contributes his own perceptions and learnings to form a new totality. A growing amount of research data corroborates the hypothesis that working together in a learning situation, especially under conditions of high rapport, results in increased effort, remaining with the task longer, and retaining more than does individual learning. Some of the data we shall present in this chapter.

SCIENTIFIC STUDIES OF GROUP LEARNING

Having analyzed the nature of learning, particularly as it takes place in groups, we can now examine some of the experimental attempts to investigate the problem. Simply stated, the problem is this: How does the interaction of one person with another influence the learning of both?

We must admit at the very outset that, although this problem has interested workers in group dynamics for at least a quarter of a century, it has not been extensively investigated on an experimental basis. The studies dealing with learning in groups have been largely concerned with the individual's learning within the group, not with an examination of the learnings of the group as a whole. This neglect has been due in part to a lack of adequate technique, on the one hand, and to the traditional aversion to conceiving the social group as a structure or entity in its own right, on the other. Since we have already discussed this problem and have described experiments on groups and not merely on individuals in groups, we need not be further detained by it. Since, however, each kind of investigation is important and has yielded significant results, we shall describe both.

LEARNING IN THE CLASSROOM. The writer is acutely aware of the fact that learning in the classroom is not a simple process. It involves many and interrelated variables, such as motivation and need, success and failure, reward and punishment, the role of the teacher, the character of the relationship between the teacher, the student, other individuals in the classroom, and the parents, and so forth. Our task is to examine the relative efficiency of the individual effort and the group technique of learning academic material.[5]

Classes in English. Some thirty years ago, Theodora M. Thie conducted an experiment "to ascertain which teaching method was better, the group or the regular class method," in improving English composition. Although this experiment was not concerned with learning as such, it helps to throw light on our problem. For insofar as improvement involves change of behavior and change or adjustment of behavior is a form of learning, efficiency and improvement in English composition is a problem of learning.

The experiment was performed on two groups of equal ability as measured by the Thorndike-McCall Test, Form I,

[5] We are not, of course, oblivious to the fact that the purpose of classroom instruction is not academic achievement alone, but many other important values.

and by a written descriptive paragraph. The classes were divided into two groups, one working together and the other "in the usual manner." The class that was to employ the group method was divided into six sections of five pupils each. The groups were kept as similar as possible in ability. They were prepared for writing and wrote their paragraphs in the same manner. After the paragraphs were completed, a summary of the characteristics of a good paragraph was made, and each pupil was given a list of questions to ask himself in correcting the work.

Each child read his paragraph to his group and received its criticism. In this way six compositions were being read or discussed, one in each group, at the same time. After each pupil read his paragraph to his group, the members of the class returned to their regular seats, and each child, with the aid of his group's criticism, corrected his own paper.

In order to hold the interest of the children the procedure was occasionally varied. Each group, for example, selected the best part of the paragraph of every member, combining the fragments to make a "group composition." Each of these group compositions was read to the class, criticized by it, and the best of them selected by the group.

In the regular classes no group correction was performed. The compositions were read before the class, and the criticisms were made by the entire class. While the competition was as keen in the class as in the groups, it was individual, rather than group, rivalry.

At the end of the semester the classes were retested by standard procedures, and each pupil was asked to write a paragraph, without group help or group criticism. The results of the experiment show that the children using the group method improved more in composition work than did those using the regular method. The class using the regular method gained 35.4 points; whereas the class using the group method gained 57.1 points.[6]

[6] T. M. Thie, Testing the efficiency of the group method, *English J.*, *14* (1925), 134–37. Commenting on the superiority of the group in learning to write, the author notes that in group work children have a chance for

Learning science. In principle, what is true regarding the learning of one kind of knowledge holds for all other kinds. A cohesive group, marked as it is by cooperation and good morale, exerts a strong positive influence upon effort and achievement. This holds in groups learning to play tennis, to ski, to write English composition, or to acquire a knowledge of chemistry.

In an experimental group in high school chemistry, Ward found that the factor of group, as contrasted with individual, *interest* was a crucial factor. The students learned more chemistry, as measured by the amount of subject matter retained, when it was functionally adapted to the interests and needs of the members as a group. Here, as in other forms of learning, sharing and exchange among members of the group arouses more interest, and with increased interest and attention more learning is acquired and retained.[7]

In another experimental study, Thelen gives additional corroboration of the effectiveness of learning in cohesive groups. He gave members of an experimental group the opportunity to participate in developing a college course in chemistry. This participation consisted, in addition to merely taking part in the chemical experimentation, of the opportunity of deciding the objectives, planning the experiments, choosing the techniques for the solution of problems, and evaluating the results. The results showed that the performance of members of the experimental group, when compared with those of a conventional class, were superior in several ways. They acquired and retained more knowledge of chemistry, showed keener interest in their work, thought more critically about chemical concepts, and showed more positive and friendly attitudes toward one another.[8]

---

more activity, show a greater spirit of cooperation, manage their own activities better, and enjoy the course more than the children in the regular sections.

[7] See W. E. Ward, An experimental study of two methods of teaching chemistry in senior high school, *J. exp. Educ.*, *11* (1942), 69–80.

[8] H. A. Thelen, A methodological study of the learning of chemical concepts and of certain abilities to think critically in Freshman chemistry, *J. exp. Educ.*, *13* (1944), 53–75.

A large amount of research, some of which is reported in this book, testifies to the positive effect of the group cohesiveness on learning and thinking.

The foregoing experiment is valuable, not only in demonstrating that people in groups learn more, but even more in showing that learning is facilitated and enhanced in a group because the latter furnishes the occasion for cooperation, for the exchange and evaluation of ideas, and for the reinforcing properties of interstimulation to operate freely.[9]

As our survey in Chapter 1 has demonstrated, experimental investigation of the influence of the group on the learning process has interested psychologists and educators for several decades. The researches of Mayer, Meumann, Moede, and others, like more recent investigations, point unequivocally to the conclusion that the group has a facilitating influence upon learning, as well as upon other intellectual activities, such as thinking, reasoning, and judgment. The proximity of other individuals and the sharing of their ideas which is made possible by interaction and participation stimulate members of a group in discernible ways. Since most groups are composed of individuals of varied knowledge and abilities, the suggestions of others, particularly of the superior ones, tend to stimulate others toward greater productiveness than they would display in isolation. Quite frequently the slower and poorer learners profit more from the mutual give and take than the faster and superior ones, and not infrequently the superior learners are retarded in their productiveness by the poorer members. In either case, as the data show, the learning of persons in groups is different in quality and quantity from that of solitary individuals. The mental activities performed by others who are engaged in working on the same task as ourselves accelerate —or retard—our own performance. The tendency of a group

[9] This conclusion, while generally true, cannot go wholly unchallenged. Forlano, in a study of cooperative behavior in children, found a tendency for the average child to work with greater zeal and efficiency for personal gain than for the sake of helping his group. See G. Forlano, An experiment in cooperation, *J. educ. Res.*, *25* (1932), 128–31.

is, accordingly, to reach a common level of performance, which we describe as the *group's* achievement.

Learning through participation both depends upon and induces group cohesiveness. When individuals are aware that they are sharing in the learning process, when they interact positively with their classmates and teachers, and when they are cognizant of the importance of their own roles in contributing to the group's learning experience, they are more positively motivated to learn, and their learning is correspondingly accelerated.

LEARNING ON THE JOB. Learning is conventionally conceived by psychologists as a change in behavior. While this is an elementary fact concerning learning, it is not, as we have pointed out, broad enough to encompass the forms of learning that interest the social psychologist. This is not a weakness of the definition itself, but characterizes the types of change which learning theorists usually have in mind when they deal with the process. From our point of view, learning is not confined to the memorizing of academic subjects or the acquisition of various skills. We are also concerned with the learning and change of attitudes, values, and prejudices, and with the whole interactional complex of individuals working in groups. It is only through this extended meaning of learning that we can understand the changes that take place when people in a plant or an office acquire skills, transfer from one type of work to another, change their mode of operation, or relearn acquired skills in a new situation.

Learning to work together. At the risk of stating a platitude, we affirm that cooperation is a learned form of behavior. Working together is an activity which takes place when individuals are stimulated by a common objective and when they respond positively to the efforts of others working toward the same goal. We shall see in a later chapter that working together on a job is not determined solely by such consideration as wages, hours, and working conditions. Equally important is the satisfaction of psychological needs, such as respect for one's personality and recognition of one's own role in the productive process. The attitudes of fellow-workers, managers, and supervisors establish a mental set in the worker which is carried over to influence the individual on his own particular job. The worker learns his job and improves his production rate to the extent to which his positive attitudes or his acquired "set" is reinforced by the rewards of wages, satisfying work-relations, and awareness of his own place in the industrial scheme of things. We know with a good deal of certainty that how a person behaves in any learning situation, be it in an academic setting or an industrial plant, depends upon his previous experience and behavior, as well as upon present circumstances. Consequently the reinforcement of the learned behavior of co-operation, sustained or increased production, enthusiasm for the job, and the like is as important in the factory as it is in the classroom and in the laboratory.

By the same token, unproductive behavior is eliminated through negative reinforcement, or nonreinforcement. Positive and negative reinforcement, however, are exercised not only on existing norms but are enlisted in the cause of creating new ones. Improvement of human relations in industry depends on the acquisition of new habits and new attitudes, not merely on reinforcing the ways of doing things which proved to be effective in the past. When individuals in a working group are confronted by problems for which there is no ready-made solution, the transfer of old habits to new situations can be fatal. Changes in established modes of behavior entail the formation of new norms, perceptions, and attitudes, not merely the discarding of old ones. Given the opportunity, men in groups form new ways of behaving because the process of interaction itself produces changed relationships. When the lines of communication between individuals and groups are free and open, the establishment of new ways of doing things is almost inevitable. When the lines of communication are closed (as often happens, for example, in the relations of the manager and the worker), the learned stereotype that each has of the other, and the burden of negative value judgments which are bound up with it, impair or destroy the effectiveness of the group as a whole.

Learning to adjust to change. A habit may be defined as the persistence of learned behavior. Once we have acquired a set of responses that enables us effectively to adjust to our surroundings or to achieve our goal, we tend to persevere in the direction of previous responses. Resistance to change is stamped in because established habits are comfortable, lead to the reduction of tension, and restore equilibrium. The resistance to change, which habits induce, creates serious problems in those productive relations where new techniques of performance are constantly in demand. New techniques are usually introduced because American industry is recurrently changing its products and invariably finding it necessary to devise new methods to meet the changed conditions of production. People, also, are moving from job to job and factory to factory. Occupational mobility is pronounced and turnover is a chronic defect of American industrial life. These changes, in turn, demand corresponding changes in the working habits of the American worker. New learnings must be initiated and different skills cultivated. The psychology of learning has abundantly shown that this is not an altogether easy accomplishment. The acquisition of habits or skills is not a simple process of conditioning, of a simple connection between a stimulus and a response. As in all learning, the total individual is involved. A change in habits, skills, or performances is, accordingly, not a simple unlinking of the two ends of the total act, but a process in which the total individual must change his attitudes and not only his mechanical activities. Changing from one job to another is not merely a change in the individual's repertoire of habitual acts but a change in the individual himself.

An investigation by Coch and French, while not concerned specifically with learning as such, but rather with the problem of resistance to change, nicely describes the learning process in job performance.[10] The study focused on the resistance of workers to the necessary changes in jobs and methods of work at the Harwood Manufacturing Corporation, in Marion, Virginia. Past efforts in dealing with the problem by means of monetary allowances for transfers, enlisting the help of the union, making layoffs on the basis of efficiency, and the like were ineffective in dealing with the problem. The research tried to find answers to two questions:"(1) Why do people resist change so strongly? and (2) What can be done to overcome this resistance?"[11] Without going into the background details of the company's policies, it is important to note that whenever it is necessary to transfer a person from one type of work to another, he is given a "transfer bonus." The bonus is so designed, the authors point out, that the changed operator who learns at an average rate will not lose any earnings after the change has been made. Despite this attractive feature, however, workers usually resist job changes.

An examination of the learning curves of several hundred changed operators throws light upon the nature of learning in groups. Thirty-eight per cent of the changed operators returned to the standard unit rating of 60 units per hour, or better. (A unit is equal to one minute of standard work, so that 60 units per hour equal the standard efficiency rating.) The remaining workers either became permanently substandard operators or quit during the transfer period. The average relearning curve of those who regained or bettered the standard production rate required eight weeks. Recovery to the standard unit rating was slow for the first two or three weeks, although it improved noticeably to about 50 units an hour, with an increase of 15 units in two weeks. This was followed by another slow progress period, the operators improving only 3 units in two weeks, but ended with a spurt of 10 units in one week.[12]

[10] L. Coch and J. R. P. French, Jr., Overcoming resistance to change, *Hum. Relat.*, *1* (1948), 512–32.

[11] *Ibid.*, p. 512.

[12] The reader is cautioned to observe that these learning curves are averages of individual productivity. Group productivity is the standard agreed upon by the whole group as a basis for group action.

The authors call attention to an important characteristic of the relearning period. The relearning period of an experienced worker is longer than that of a new operator. This is true, they point out, even though the failures who never return to standard performance are dropped from the curve. On the whole, however, changed operators make few false movements after the first week of change. From the evidence before them, the investigators conclude that "proactive inhibition or the interference of previous habits in learning the new skill is either non-existent or very slight after the first two weeks of change."[13]

Other experiments, however, challenge the foregoing results. Describing an unpublished investigation by Alex Bavelas in the same plant and on the same kind of transferred operation, Lewin points out that transferred workers performed less satisfactorily on the new job. For a transferred worker, he says, the new operation is more difficult than the previous one. Transfer, furthermore, is accompanied by a lowered work morale, in the sense that the drive for higher production is decreased. Learning is astonishingly slow. Accordingly, although the operators are familiar with the machines, their production rises so slowly that "it is more profitable for the factory to hire new workers than to change the job of experienced workers."[14]

There are several factors which explain the slow learning of a transferred worker, chief of which are the lowering of working morale and a drop in the level of aspiration. Morale drops because the worker on the new job, being unable to maintain, let alone surpass, his previous level experiences a drop in status. Level of aspiration is lowered because the worker sees his job in the light of standards which are too high for him to attain.

A practical consequence of experiments on transfer of jobs is the attention it calls to the learning process in work efficiency. Again citing the unpublished experiments of Bavelas, Lewin calls attention to the role of special training

13 Coch and French, Overcoming resistance to change, p. 515.

14 K. Lewin, Frontiers in group dynamics, *Hum. Relat., 1* (1947), 29.

in job transfer and its role in learning. Bavelas gave special training to an individual who was then put in charge of training beginners in a factory. This training resulted in a marked rise of the learning curves of the beginners. When a few week later the specially trained man was withdrawn and replaced by the regular trainer, the learning curve promptly dropped to "the level it would have had without the training of the trainer." This fact suggests the probability that a learning curve may serve as a base line, or the line of "equal level," for determining the production learning of persons in a working situation. This would eliminate the use of such absolute standards as the amount of productivity in the determination of a worker's achievement, which are probably valid only in groups whose capacities do not change.[15]

THE EFFECTS OF COOPERATION AND COMPETITION ON LEARNING. We have already called attention to the biased and evaluative view held by people, especially in the United States, regarding the relative merits of cooperation and competition in various activities. We have asserted, what reliable observation and research have corroborated, that cooperation is not inevitably good and competition is not ineluctably bad. The effect of each depends on the goals we try to reach and the consequences each brings about. Nevertheless, in view of the extensive bias regarding these phenomena, we must call attention to the fact that there is some evidence proving that learning, like many other social processes, is favorably affected by cooperation and impaired by "intense" or "excessive" competition. This is clearly disclosed in Deutsch's investigation of the effect of these forces upon the group process.[16]

Deutsch presents thirty-four carefully stated hypotheses regarding the effect of competition and cooperation on social

[15] *Ibid.*, p. 30.

[16] M. Deutsch, The effects of cooperation and competition upon group process, in D. Cartwright and A. Zander (eds.), *Group dynamics: research and theory* (Evanston, Ill.: Row, Peterson & Co., 1953), pp. 319–53. Unsupported theory and speculation abound in this area, and Deutsch's study is one of the few in which hypotheses are tested by experimental procedure.

process, and he designs an experiment for testing them. The hypothesis regarding learning in competitive and/or cooperative activities is stated as follows: "*Indiv. coop.* will learn more from one another than will *Indiv. comp.*"[17] In order to test the hypotheses, Deutsch set up an experiment in which ten groups of students, each group consisting of five members, were instructed to act as a board of human relations experts. Their task was to analyze and discuss, as groups, puzzle problems and human relations problems. The puzzle problems were such as to permit individual work without group consensus. The human relations problems presented "no clearly discernible objective criteria of locomotion," that is, tasks in which the group itself, by agreement, provided the criteria for work performed.

The results regarding most of the activities were found to favor cooperative behavior. With reference to learning, the outcome was less striking. Deutsch states the matter by indicating that "the cooperative group members in three of the five pairs rated themselves as learning more from discussion of the human relations problem than did the competitive members rate themselves."[18] The differences, however, it must be pointed out, were not statistically significant. The best that can be said about the learning process in the experiment is that the trend is in favor of individual cooperation. The author also states, parenthetically, what we have already asserted in another context—namely, that the members with more knowledge and experience will learn less in a cooperative group than those less experienced and not so well informed.

The foregoing conclusions are in line with the important observations and the experimentally supported generalizations that have frequently appeared thus far in the pages of this book. Cooperative interactions generally result in greater productivity, whether motor, mechanical, or cognitive, than is the case when members are in competition

[17] *Ibid.*, p. 328. The italicized abbreviations designate individual cooperators and individual competitors.

[18] *Ibid.*, p. 347.

with one another. As we saw in Chapters 2 and 3, cohesiveness, mutual acceptance, and high morale engendered by cooperativeness and friendliness open the line of communication which results in increased motivation and greater productiveness. Some research evidence, furthermore, strongly suggests that competitiveness arouses fear and anxiety, and especially generates hostility which cannot be readily channelized into permissible forms of expression. Psychologists have known for a long time that too much anxiety and fear disorganize learning. While a certain strain of expectancy is conducive to preparing the individual for the learning situation, the disequilibrium resulting from an overmobilization and dispersion of emotional energies generally impairs the acquisition and retention of new knowledge.

In light of the foregoing results and conclusions Deutsch fittingly calls to our attention one of their implications for education. One may well ask, he asserts, whether the competitive grading system in general use in our educational institutions does not impair the "task-centeredness" and individual security which, one would believe, should be important objectives of our educational system. We cannot, of course, answer the question with confidence, but a thorough investigation of the problem is long overdue.

The psychology underlying the impairment of learning in competitive situations is relatively simple. Excessive competition puts most people on the defensive. Thus competition is a two-way process. It puts every member of a learning or deliberating group into a position of defending his own ideas more tenaciously; this threat to the individual, in turn arouses defensiveness and the need for retaliation. Since the best, and sometimes the only, way of handling this situation lies in achieving personal security, the preservation of the individual's ideas and opinions tends to become a goal in itself. Learning always consists in change and readjustment in the individual, but normally it is adversely affected by a threatening situation. The individual will, in fact, more likely revert to an earlier form of adjustment, such as negativism or withdrawal. The more threatening the situation is to the members of the group, the greater is the tendency to become aggressive or to leave the field altogether. This mode of behavior, the reader will recall, was very apparent in our discussion of the cleavages within unorganized groups, as described by French (see Chapter 3, pp. 88–91). Constructive participation in a group and the changing of attitudes, which is in reality an act of learning, is usually impaired by a feeling of personal inadequacy generated by too much competition. While individuals differ in this matter, of course, it is not too much to say that probably everyone, in some competitive group situations, is negatively affected by them. The fear of rejection is the negative side of the need of belonging.

The fear of rejection, on the other hand, not only impairs the learning process but discourages individual thinking and creativeness and places a premium on conformity. Cooperation may thus be bought at the price of destroying novelty and individuality. In this instance an exclusive emphasis on teamwork, cohesiveness, and agreement is inhibitive rather than creative; thus we are led once more to an earlier contention that the group can be wrong as well as right. What the researches on learning in cooperative as against competitive groups reveal in the final analysis is *not necessarily* that group participation is more conducive to learning than is individual effort; rather they show that learning is less efficient in groups in which participation is limited than in groups where it is specifically encouraged.

Contemporary studies of learning in competitive or cooperative groups, furthermore, fail to take sufficient account of the fact that, although resistance may be overcome, the attempt to change it may cause disturbance and thereby impair the process of learning for which the group was initially organized. Little cognizance is taken of the ambivalent nature of the learners in a learning situation involving the acceptance of change. This ambivalence exists in learners as individuals and in learners as members of a group. An effective leader of groups is one who recognizes the dual or ambivalent nature of the individuals in whom change is desired. He recognizes the inevitability of conflict and makes of it an ally instead of a barrier to the acquisition of new attitudes. He places the conflict where it truly belongs, namely, in the need of the person to accept the ways of others—to conform—because of his desire to belong, and in his need to resist the ways of others because of an equally strong desire to remain free of their influence. When change does take place, therefore, it is not because members of the group learn under any group compulsion; rather there has been an intelligent recognition of their polar needs to belong and to remain independent. They learn to understand their function in the group instead of pitting themselves against its members.

The present writer, with clinical rather than group-dynamic evidence, would even go farther and assert that all learning, even the most group-centered, is fundamentally self-imposed. The group learner assimilates his experience by making the group's goals his own. Only in this way can he escape the tyranny of group-imposed norms.

The reports of many observations of the relative effectiveness of competitive and cooperative groups, finally, have not been carefully evaluated. What is particularly wanting is systematic study to check the results against a well-defined and, if possible, measurable criterion. Their chief value consists in calling attention to the fact that the group experience serves as an opportunity for tapping hidden resources. While this is no small achievement, it is insufficient to serve as a basis for reliable scientific generalizations. This conclusion holds with almost equal force regarding other group activities which we have described thus far.

Learning Unstructured Materials. Since the days of Ebbinghaus' study of the learning of nonsense syllables, psychologists have sporadically investigated the learning process by the use of "meaningless" or unstructured materials. While this technique has thrown little light upon the study of human behavior, it has the sure advantage (or so it has been thought) of presenting the experimenter with a stable or constant unit of experimental investigation.[19] The technique has been used in an experimental study of "the properties of group-qua-group learned products" by Perlmutter and de Montmollin.[20]

The chief merit of this experiment is that, first, it makes explicit the differential conditions of group "thinking" and individual thinking; and, second, group phenomena are adequately conceptualized. The investigators, by using such nonsense syllables as *Zevut* and *Zuvat,* examined and compared the learning curves of the group and those of individuals, compared the errors of each, and noted the time required in both situations, in order to determine "under what conditions and along what dimensions groups differ from individuals on 'learning.'"

The subjects in the experiment were students at the Sorbonne, most of them first-year students of psychology. Most of them were French, the remainder being Belgians, Egyptians, Italians, Moroccans, and Swiss. The experiment lasted two hours. Two statistically equivalent lists of 19 two-syllable nonsense words were used. The experiment was divided into two parts, with a 15-minute rest period between them. In one part the subjects were required to learn the words as a group; in the other they worked separately but in the presence of one another on an equivalent but different list of words. Without going into further detail on the method of the experiment, we may report the results and make some brief comments.

The subjects working as groups were found superior to individuals working individually but in the presence of others. Especially interesting and significant is the report that the group was superior in total score to the average individual score, but not significant statistically from the average of the best individuals in the groups, provided the

[19] For a report of the original learning experiment using nonsense syllables, see H. Ebbinghaus, *Memory,* trans. by H. A. Ruger and C. E. Bussenius (New York: Columbia University Press, 1913).

[20] H. V. Perlmutter and G. de Montmollin, Group learning of nonsense syllables, *J. abnorm. soc. Psychol., 47* (1952), 762–69.

best individuals had previously worked in a group on a similar task. Moreover, in seven out of twenty instances there were individuals who surpassed or equaled the performance of the group. Again, it was found that groups require more time for recall during the early stages of the experiment but have a higher over-all recall rate than individuals in the group. Under certain conditions, furthermore, a group commits more errors than individuals by repeating more words, whereas individuals tend to deform or invent more words than groups. All in all, according to the authors, the conditional superiority of a group is indicated along all dimensions.

The experiment points up the importance of a current problem in group dynamics: Is a group more "intelligent" and "wise" than single individuals, including those who perform in the presence of others? The fact that the group-learned product curve is often identical with the learned product curve of a poorer member of another group, suggests that there are "low intelligence" groups as well as "high intelligence" individuals. "One adult," the writers point out, "can solve a problem that thirty children could not even comprehend. Within the adult groups as well, it would be difficult to derive the group 'intelligence' from the summation of individual intelligence scores."[21] The conclusion is, of course, an artifact of the experimental design, and does not necessarily prove the conclusiveness of the results. The authors, accordingly, suggest the necessity of a group intelligence test, and point out that until this is done "we are not certain that a group performs well because it is inefficient but very intelligent as a group, or because it is quite unintelligent but very efficient in employing its potentialities."[22]

We made some critical remarks heretofore regarding the concept of "group wisdom"; yet, much of the evidence presented thus far is a partial support of its superiority to the learning and wisdom of the individual. Therefore, perhaps

[21] *Ibid.*, p. 769.
[22] *Ibid.*

a word or two of clarification is in order. We do not subscribe to the supercilious belief that group members, because they are not necessarily experts or, worse yet, because they may be less educated than the group leader, are incapable of making productive contributions to group knowledge and decision. We do, however, assert that the evidence in favor of group learning and "group wisdom" is not yet decisive. The fact is that there is insufficient evidence to prove the superiority of either the individual or the group. Whether a group or an individual learns better or makes wiser decisions frequently depends on specific circumstances. In a group where the resources of every member are freely accessible to all, the group is more likely to prove itself superior to the individual. In an individual in whom habitual "sets," or expectancies, are barriers to productiveness, the group, as we have shown in an earlier chapter, is in a better position to eliminate them and work productively. On the other hand, in a group where (for whatever reason) all the available resources of its members are not sufficiently tapped, or where the leader alone (again, for whatever reason) possesses all the relevant facts in the learning of an attitude or the solution of a problem, the group is more likely than not to be no better and possibly worse than the individual. Yet, it is true that in some groups only the resources of an individual or two are accessible to all, but the results are adequate and useful.

However, this last observation does not commit us to the unsupported conclusion that an individual "gatekeeper" is necessarily sufficient for effective group activity. We wish merely to stress the *fact* that those who stress the primacy of the "wisdom of the group" (sometimes motivated by partisan zeal) often base their claims not on objective evidence, but on their notion of an *ideal* group. Scientifically, there is no objection to hypothecating this group as an *ideal construct;* but this is not what the exponents of the notion of group superiority have in mind. Only a very few of the groups reported in the literature even approximate the ideal group whose superiority to the individual has been uncritically exalted.[23]

Although the existing evidence affirms the proposition that group learning may sometimes be more effective than individual learning and wisdom, the data and the criticisms presented here show clearly that it is not justified to contend that the group is always superior to the individual in learning. In order to counteract the common and ancient belief in the superiority of individual learning, the evidence presented here has stressed the advantages of group learning and group wisdom. But this is not to claim, as enthusiasts for group dynamics sometimes have, that the group is always superior.

CONCLUSION

At the beginning of this chapter we asserted that in view of the extensive interest of group dynamicists in the study of changing attitudes and in collective problem-solving, the psychology of group learning has come to occupy an important place in our discipline. Individual learning has, of course, long held an honorable and dominant position in psychology. While we recognize this fact, we need not slavishly ape the individual psychologist. The important factors of group behavior have precluded this and have impelled us to examine the nature and conditions of group learning. It is, as a matter of fact, precisely because we have not uncritically imitated the laboratory psychologist that we have escaped the atomistic-mechanistic descriptions of learning which characterize a considerable segment of modern learning theory. The individual psychologist observes learning under conditions that are too circumscribing and inhibiting. In this situation he cannot be blamed if he views learning as largely a collection of discrete items. Nor can

[23] One of these, interestingly enough, concerns clinical insight in the group, as reported by Bovard, and another reported by Paluev. See E. W. Bovard, Jr., Clinical insight as a function of group process, *J. abnorm. soc. Psychol.*, *47* (1952), 534–39; K. K. Paluev, How collective genius contributes to industrial progress, *General Electric Rev.* (May, 1941), 254–61.

this mode of procedure be effectively criticized if the psychologist's primary interest is measurement based on statistical predictability. But in social learning and group dynamics, where we take the whole situation into account, try to "measure" the learnings or changes of an integrated set of individuals, and aim to predict the behavior not of discrete individuals but of organized totalities, statistical probabilities are of no great consequence.[24] The learning theorist seldom observes one learning subject in the presence of other learning subjects, and practically never examines learning as a group product. We have therefore tried to place before the reader examples of learnings under both sets of conditions.

Our exposition has critically tackled the problem of the superiority of the one type of learning over the other. The results are far less conclusive than the respective claimants have alleged. But even though the results are not as conclusive as one would wish, generally speaking they favor group learning over individual learning. That they do so is largely due to the effectiveness of the group in dissolving the rigid "sets" of individuals, eliminating false starts, encouraging change, and facilitating the process of acquiring new habits under socially rewarding conditions. While there is the constant risk of replacing old "sets" by new ones in the form of excessive uniformity, there is also the sure knowledge that many forms of change are greatly facilitated by group acceptance and collective stimulation.

[24] It is only fair to add that psychologists of learning do not *in toto* subscribe to the atomistic view. More and more of them are coming to consider learning as a unitary process, and are especially recognizing emotional, motivational, and other properties as aspects of the total learning situation.

Part III

RESOLUTION OF GROUP TENSIONS: CONFLICT AND ADJUSTMENT OF GROUPS

CHAPTER 5

Intergroup Relations

In a provisional analysis of intergroup relations in Chapter 3, we described intergroup hostility as an aspect of the larger problem of group disruption. No attempt was made, however, to narrow the problem as we will in this chapter to what has come to be its standard concern, namely, the conflicts and adjustments of ethnic, racial, and religious groups. The standard conception of intergroup relations, unfortunately, has not always encompassed the vital problem of religious differences. We shall attempt to do this in the present chapter.

A systematic study of intergroup relations suggests two avenues of approach. We may, on the one hand, conceptualize group relations by considering them as the resultant of the efforts of certain members to leave a group because of some unattractive features; or, on the other, as the consequence of the members' expulsion from the more inclusive group. In either case, the new formation, or "splinter group," as it is sometimes designated, can be described on the basis of a subgroup's failure to be attracted by the group. Group attractiveness, we have seen, implies group unattractiveness, or the desire of individuals to leave or to be excluded from the social field. When a group fails to provide enough permissiveness to its members to enable them to actualize their "deviant" interests or potentialities, they are motivated to detach themselves from the parent group and form a new association of individuals. When members, because of their separate interests, hamper the group in achieving its goals or maintaining its stability, they are frequently expelled from it. Since the need to belong is a strong social motive, and since some interests can be satisfied only in coacting relationships, the rejected individuals, given a free choice, will form a new group of like-minded individuals. The stronger the needs and convictions of the dissident elements are, the greater will be the probability, generally speaking, that they will form new groupings. This observation automatically excludes from our survey the perennial joiners, for they seldom leave one group when joining another. They are not—shall we say?—an issue in group dynamics but a problem in the psychology of personality.

FORMATION OF SUBGROUPS

Among the vital problems in group dynamics pressing for solution are the origin and nature of group conflicts and the setting up of practical means for resolving them. Conflicts are frequently resolved when groups attain a new equilibrium, when new groups arise in response to dissatisfaction with the old, or when dissident elements are eliminated from the social field and form a new set of interactive persons. When these changes occur, the central problem of group dynamics becomes the task of investigating the balanced relationship of the function and responsibility of the new subgroups, and to understand the role of the leader in the changed relationship.

There are many examples of the foregoing changes, some of which we shall describe in detail. Harmony within a group is often achieved when recalcitrant individuals or groups organize their discontent in new formations. Groups of individuals in the form of scapegoats afford opportunities for dominant groups to direct their aggressions toward them; while at the same time the rejected subgroup of scapegoats erects powerful defenses against the dominant group and thereby achieves a new equilibrium. The leadership structure may also be radically altered, wherein the established leaders are forced from the group, or have their function and position drastically changed, or new leaders may emerge to take the position of those who have been deposed.

Subgroup formation depends, finally, upon the size of the parent group. The problem of group size is a difficult one, and despite a considerable amount of discussion of the issue in the literature, we are not yet in a strong position to designate an optimum number. There are some data, nevertheless, which permit us to say that, on the whole, the larger the parent group, other things being equal, the greater the possibility of the formation of subgroups. Since satisfaction with and continuation in the group is a consequence of group attractiveness, the more opportunity a member has of participating in the group's activities the greater will be the chances of his staying in the group. As the size of the group increases, the chances of participating diminishes and dissatisfaction increases. Individual members come to feel that they do not count and that the leader's skill becomes disproportionately influential. In this situation factional disputes arise which frequently end in the development of independent groups.[1]

In all this we do not mean to suggest that the subgroups formed by dissociation from the parent group necessarily affect the latter adversely, although often conflict and dis-

[1] For an extensive investigation of this problem, see A. P. Hare, A study of interaction and consensus in different sized groups, *Amer. Sociol. Rev.*, *17* (1952), 261–67. According to Hare, whose investigation pertains only to discussion groups, when the size of the group exceeds a dozen members, dissatisfaction with it becomes noticeable. A carefully designed study by Bales and Borgatta, dealing with groups of different sizes, throws further interesting light upon this problem. See R. F. Bales and E. F. Borgatta, Size of group as a factor in the interaction profile, in P. Hare, E. F. Borgatta, and R. F. Bales (eds.), *Small groups: studies in social interaction* (New York: Alfred A. Knopf, Inc., 1955), pp. 396–413. Since we are concerned in this chapter with a variety of subgroups, the problems of group size is of no great importance. Discussion groups will be examined in a later chapter.

equilibrium are its serious consequences. The process may, as a matter of fact, increase the parent group's valent power, its attractiveness to other individuals. This is seen when subgroups function positively to enhance the attractiveness of the whole. Fraternities on a college campus, while absorbing some of the individuals' loyalties to the school, will also enhance the school's attractiveness. Some people go to college and show devotion to its ideals because they have, or hope to have, the opportunity to join a Greek letter society. Conflict and disruption of group life would normally take place only if the goals and ideals of the two should be totally at variance with each other.

Preadult Subgroups. Long before an individual becomes an active and effective member of those subgroups which are responsible for the graver cleavages and conflicts of the human community, he is attracted to associations that satisfy his early needs. Chief among them are peer groups and adolescent cliques.

Peer groups. Although most children acquire some knowledge and experience of group relations in their own family life, these interactions first become truly social in the reciprocal relations they have with others in their peer groups. The norms of the family, which govern the child's early behavior, are followed for the most part mechanically, or with a kind of "literal realism," and are conceived largely as external impositions. Frequently he acts counter to them because he does not feel them to be his own. Much of the "disobedience" of a young child is a negative reaction to standards which he has not internalized into his own reaction system. He has not yet developed what Piaget so aptly calls "moral realism"—that is, an objective conception of responsibility.[2] Piaget has also noted the egocentric character of a child's linguistic habits. During the first six or seven years of life, the child shows little social collaboration in speech. In his conversation with others he does not at-

[2] J. Piaget, *The moral judgment of the child,* trans. by M. Gabain (Glencoe, Ill.: The Free Press, n.d.), p. 106.

tempt particularly to use words appropriate to the person addressed, but engages in a repetitious monologue mostly to please himself. His language is permeated by egocentric expressions.[3]

The child reaches a period, however—normally by the age of seven—when both his language and other behaviors take on the character of reciprocity and become truly social. For example, he passes from the more or less unstructured playing with others to participation in games. The game, as G. H. Mead has shown with fine discernment, "represents the passage in the life of the child from taking the role of others in play to the organized part that is essential to self-consciousness in the full sense of the term."[4] His attitudes are thus formed through interaction not only with his parents but also—and often more directly and permanently—with his peer group. The norms of the latter are more sharply experienced because the youth plays a more active role in forming them than he does in those prevailing in his home, and he is more ready to accept these norms as his own because of this. It is in his peer group more than in his home that the young person learns to understand and to engage in reciprocal relationships. It has been pretty well established that the development of the self, especially in its social aspects, is greatly enhanced by the child's participation in a group consisting of children roughly his own age and motivated by the same needs of independence and autonomy. Skill in relating himself to others and success in taking their roles is made easier, in our culture at least, in the youth's unhampered participation in the varied activities of the group.

The basic and compelling reasons for the ease of participation in the peer group, and the youth's overpowering preference for and loyalty to it, are not difficult to understand. In the home the child's roles are defined by his

[3] See J. Piaget, *The language and thought of the child,* trans. by M. Warden (New York: Harcourt, Brace & Co., Inc. 1926), pp. 99 ff.

[4] G. H. Mead, *Mind, self and society* (Chicago: The University of Chicago Press, 1934), p. 152.

parents, obedience to their demands is felt as binding and often "oppressive," and the parents too frequently fail to understand the child's need for independence. He evaluates his parents' demands not realistically in the light of their own sense of duty as they see it, but in the light of his expected freedom in the associations with his fellows. The parents at the same time may be unable or unwilling to acknowledge the pull of loyalty of the subgroup in enlisting the interests and emotions of the young person. A frequent consequence of this divided loyalty is that the child is even more strongly drawn to the peer group, thus making the separation and conflict between the parental and the peer groups rapidly more intense. The widespread complaints of contemporary adults that our young people are "going to the dogs," and the adolescents' retort that parents are "out of touch with life," and old-fashioned besides, are thus based upon a misunderstanding on the part of both groups.[5]

This conflict of the peer group and the family group is not present in all societies. In many primitive cultures, while differentiation into age-mate groups is common, their formation is in line with the mores of the culture. They are sanctioned and their status is supported by the society as a whole in the form of explicit indications of their boundaries by ceremonies and "rites of passage." In this situation the adolescent is never confused regarding his place in the community and the role behavior expected of him. In these circumstances it is not necessary for him to rebel against or withdraw from the family group, for there is nothing against which he needs seriously to rebel. Accordingly, while many discontinuities exist in primitive life, as in every culture, they are usually more clearly defined by the customs of the group than is true in our own society. The result usually is an easier transition in primitive culture from one group to another, or from one set of expectations to another.

[5] It is hardly "news" to assert, as many do, that the present generation is worse than the preceding one. This attitude is perhaps as old as man. Recall Cicero's plaintive cry: "*O tempora! O mores!*"

The need to withdraw or rebel, in our society, is not only directed against the family but against any group or institution whose norms the young person finds it difficult to accept and endure. The school, for example, is not an uncommon object of his dissatisfactions and aggressions. Much of the "hooliganism" in our public schools, which the daily press constantly belabors, reflects the same need for finding satisfactions in peer groups that the school does not adequately fulfill. Despite the marvelous improvements in our educational systems, too many schools are still operating on authoritarian principles. Since the adolescent has little or nothing to say regarding those school policies which directly touch his emotional needs, he becomes either indifferent, negative, or aggressive. His main thought is of the dismissal bell and the expectant satisfactions accorded to him by his peer group. This is a rich area of investigation which group dynamics has scarcely begun to tap.

Adolescent cliques. The differention of peer groups and adolescent cliques may well be challenged. Many adolescent cliques, it might be argued, are peer groups, and vice versa. The distinction is justified, however, if we bear in mind that peer groups tend to form on the basis of age, and are frequently designated as age-mate groups. Adolescent cliques are usually characterized by a sharper awareness of common emotional ties, division of function within the group, and the sovereign demand of loyalty to it. This is outstandingly true of adolescent gangs which, in order to maintain their autonomy, may even move against the larger society in the form of delinquent behavior.

The rejected and disowned youth, whether he achieved this status by the absence of family ties or by the indifference of his community or school, finds in a clique or a gang the acceptance which he eagerly seeks. The new subgroup becomes the center of orientation and presents the youth with the possibility of gaining status and even distinction among his peers. Belonging to any group is better than belonging to none at all; and while the individual may "buy" his membership at the price of conformity greater than that against which he originally rebelled, the standards which he is asked to accept in the subgroup correspond more naturally to his own. Thus, while the new standards may be more severely binding than those of his home, psychologically they do not carry the flavor of tyranny and arbitrariness which the individual imputes to older people. Since he is interacting with persons who are more like himself, he more readily adopts the ways of his clique than those of a group in whose formation he played no part.

Shaw's descriptions of such individuals in the slums of Chicago are incisive and lay bare the powerful need for group belongingness, with which even the home could not compete. Describing the cheap movies and flophouses which abound in the neighborhood, one individual finds them a refuge more strengthening than the home. "When blue and broken-up," he says, "I would always find an old pal there to tell my troubles to and receive the sympathy that comes through mutual understanding." The bums and other derelicts made up his "family." "We all ate at the same table and enjoyed ourselves at the same theaters," he observes. He perceives the whole group as "a brotherhood whose object was mutual pity and sympathy."[6]

It is a serious mistake to characterize all gangs and cliques as antisocial or delinquent. The fulfillment of needs, which draws members to various groups, may be realized in either a wholesome or a destructive way. There are many factors making for one or the other type of association. Cliques and gangs normally form only when a group of young people fails to have its major needs satisfied by other institutions. Gang-formation is a normal social process, and when the gang's activities are directed into constructive channels, it often becomes an important socializing agency for the maturing adolescent.

Again, the goal-direction of the clique, or the gang, will be largely determined by the aspirations of its members, by

[6] C. Shaw (ed.), *Brothers in crime* (Chicago: The University of Chicago Press, 1938), p. 79. See Chapter 2, pp. 50–51.

the kinds of deprivations which its members acutely suffer, and the degree of exclusion from group membership that they feel. Individuals who engage in stealing, for example, are more likely to be recruited from economically deprived families. Boys from well-to-do homes may have need satisfactions quite at variance with those of boys from the slums. Their greatest need might be to excell, to surpass, or to perform feats that will prove their daring and manhood. Others may find their needs satisfied best in groups performing sexual orgies or in the perverted pleasures of narcotic sprees. In brief, the growing child will seek membership in those groups that enable him to gratify the wishes and emotions which are left unfulfilled by other groups.

No single institution can satisfy the child's every need; and for those needs which are not gratified, he will seek other associations. The normal child will find basic satisfactions in the home; and where there is a conflict between the standards of his home and those of his clique, the values of the parents will usually take precedence. Conflict between the generations is, however, inescapable, particularly in a highly mobile society like our own, where interests are varied and where many groups exist to gratify the child's need to emancipate himself from his home. The character of American society is such that its adolescents are unavoidably placed into a "minority" group where they soon find or evolve their own standards of behavior. Their peer groups, cliques, or gangs, accordingly, provide them with gratifications that are too frequently neglected by the formal and sanctioned institutions of the larger society. The growth of subgroups and the conflicts which they generate are therefore important areas of investigation for group dynamics.

ETHNIC AND RACIAL CONFLICTS

Historians, sociologists, and politicians have for generations fondly called our nation a "melting pot." The extraordinary heterogeneity of our people is a fact, and the fact is most impressive. The concept of the melting pot has, however, been considerably distorted. While people from various countries and of different racial origin have been amalgamated, they have not always become integrated. "Assimilation" has too often been external accommodation, rather than genuine cultural identification. The process of absorption, furthermore, has often been achieved at the cost of widespread and intense intergroup conflict.

America was conceived and developed in violence. The history of the labor movement in this country, to cite but one example, is a chronicle of intergroup disturbances. World War I left in its path a nationalism frought with suppressions and conflicts alien to the principles of the democracy we have professed. Following World War II this trend became intensified, and while large-scale immigration from foreign countries ceased, intergroup hostilities were not correspondingly reduced.

Friendly intercourse between differing groups has not—group dynamics and action programs to the contrary notwithstanding—reduced intergroup tensions as much as had been hoped. A summer spent in friendly contact of different races has sometimes effected gratifying results, but there is no sure indication that the change is permanently transferred to the home community. To some extent our slow progress in dealing with intergroup tensions can be traced to a singular failure to realize that learning is not wholly an intellectual phenomenon but is strongly tied up with motives and feelings, and especially with strong self-involvements, which brief interracial contacts often leave untouched. (See Chapter 4, p. 104.) There is no dependable evidence in support of the belief that learnings and other behaviors are transferred from one group situation to another. What is true in an academic learning situation may be quite untrue in a context whose emotional character is very different. In their zeal to describe group relations solely in collective terms, furthermore, many workers in this field have, as we have already shown, overlooked the role of personality. Regardless of their contacts with different racial groups some individuals find in their hatred of them convenient channels for the expression of deeply rooted aggressions. Some of these hatreds can be resolved perhaps only by means of individual or group therapy.

Race prejudice, furthermore, is seldom based on racial characteristics exclusively. One need only consider the widespread prejudice against "foreigners" whose appearance is identical with that of the prejudiced individual. Even at the other extreme, a Negro or an Oriental is disliked not only for his color but for the alien culture which he represents.[7]

Minority Groups. Collective discrimination against minority groups is widespread in the United States. Because of their physical or cultural traits certain groups of people are singled out by the dominant group and accorded unequal treatment. Specifically, the minority group is denied full participation in the social, economic, political, and religious life of the nation. Interpreted in the light of our democratic ethic—the doctrine of the rights of man—which avowedly treats every individual and group equally, minority peoples are deprived of the status which they possess as human beings. As a consequence of this separation both the dominant and the minority groups experience important psychological changes. The minority group develops a sense of isolation, inferiority, and insecurity, not to mention an accompanying hostility which develops as a mode of defense. The dominant group, whose change is more subtle and hence usually unrecognized, suffers too in the face of their discrimination. No society can be said to be healthy which stunts the growth of its minority groups. Cohesiveness is bound to be injured by discrimination, and where poverty and substandard communities are by-products of this differentiation, the total economy inevitably suffers.

The discussion of minority groups could be simplified were it not for the fact that human prejudice distinguishes between ethnic and racial groups. The presence of such

[7] While the culture of the American Negro is largely identical with that of the white, the prejudiced person invariably attributes cultural characteristics to him which he then violently rejects. Such imputed cultural characteristics are low class status, cheap religiosity, inferior moral standards, and the like.

physical characteristics as color of skin complicates the problem. The problem is further complicated by the fact that differences among people consist, when all is said and done, of the *perceptions* which one group has of another. Whether there are any visible marks of separateness of minority group members is unimportant if the dominant group believes that they possess certain physical and psychological characteristics. The *beliefs* which the dominant group has regarding minority peoples will in the final analysis determine the ethnic or racial status of the latter. Since it is a widely accepted practice to classify both ethnic and racial minorities under the single category of *ethnic groups*, for purposes of simplification we shall follow this practice in the present discussion.

Group relations and attitudes, we have shown, are learned. The evidence for this statement is so preponderous that we may consider it an established fact.[8] Statements to the contrary are invariably based on ethnocentric perceptions, distorted observations, and anecdotal descriptions. Researches too numerous to document here have demonstrated that ethnic attitudes rarely appear in children before their third year.[9]

The learned character of ethnic attitudes is further demonstrated by the fact that they are both variable and inconsistent. Blake and Dennis found that, while Southern grade

[8] See, however, G. W. Allport's view that we possess a predisposition to prejudice in the form of a "constitutional bent toward rigidity" which is the source of favorable or unfavorable attitudes toward ethnic groups. Allport speaks of this bent as a *possibility* and offers no evidence in its support. On the contrary, he asserts that "concerning this important matter we know absolutely nothing." See G. W. Allport, Prejudice: a problem in psychological and social causation, *J. soc. Issues*, Supplement Series, No. 4 (1950), 14.

[9] The reader may sample the investigations by examining the following references: E. L. Horowitz and R. E. Horowitz, Development of social attitudes in children, *Sociometry, 1* (1938), 301–8; K. B. Clark and M. P. Clark, Racial identification and preference in Negro children, in T. M. Newcomb and E. L. Hartley (eds.), *Readings in social psychology* (rev. ed.; New York: Henry Holt & Co., Inc., 1947), pp. 169–78; M. E. Goodman, *Race awareness in young children* (Reading, Mass.: Addison-Wesley Publishing Co., Inc., 1952).

school and junior high school children held the conventional stereotype of the Negro, as they moved up in the grades they began to see a few favorable traits in him. This is in contrast to the wholly negative attitudes of the children in the lower grades.[10] It is only fair to add, however, that the difference was so small that the careless or ethnocentric observer might easily perceive the difference as no change at all.

The degree and extent of ethnic attitudes differs also by locality. This can easily be seen in anti-Negro attitudes. The social atmosphere of New York City, for example, is less characterized by ethnic hostility than that of most large cities in the Middle West. Differentiation is also made along class lines. According to one good study students in the upper classes in Tennessee were found to be considerably more prejudiced against Negroes than those in the lower classes.[11] Inconsistency in ethnic attitudes, especially in young children, also demonstrates their acquired nature. While prejudice develops gradually, it seldom follows a straight course. In the study by Goodman cited above, this inconsistency is clearly brought out. Since children have not had sufficient time for the conventional stereotypes to be reinforced, their attitudes toward ethnic groups tend to fluctuate. Most studies show that the process of internalizing the prevalent ethnic attitudes in childhood tends to increase, although not steadily, with age.

Sources of ethnic attitudes. An enumeration and full discussion of the determinants of ethnic attitudes is obviously beyond the limits of the present chapter. The available data are so abundant that only a full-length monograph could do them justice. We shall, accordingly, select for brief discussion only those which in our judgment are most salient.

[10] R. Blake and W. Dennis, The development of stereotypes concerning the Negro, *J. abnorm. soc. Psychol.*, 38 (1943), 525–31.

[11] P. L. Boynton and G. D. Mayo, A comparison of certain attitudinal responses of white and Negro high school students, *J. Negro Educ.*, 11 (1942), 487–94.

If the whole determines the behavior of the parts, as we argued in Chapters 1 and 2, then we must begin with the influence of the *cultural norms* in the formation of attitudes. Too much energy is often expended on the issue of whether the family or the cultural community is more influential in forming our attitudes. The truth is that parents are too readily credited for the behavioral characteristics of their children. In this we sometimes act as if the world external to the family had only a minor influence in the socialization of the child. The present writer cannot agree with such an assumption, for he has observed too many instances where children integrate not the attitudes of their parents but the prevailing prejudices of the community. Parents themselves, moreover, live largely in accordance with the mores of the community. If the child internalizes the ways of life which he finds in his home, they are the ways of the community as they are transmitted to him by his parents. It is true of course, that parents interpret the norms in the light of their own motives and personalities, sometimes even to the point of idiosyncrasy; and the children, in order to escape parental disapproval, will conform and make their parents' attitude their own. Thus by a process of continuous reinforcement the children's attitudes take on the coloration of the family norms. Most families, however, tend to be conventional and to accept the norms of their group without serious distortion. This conformity is but one aspect of the more inclusive tendency of the members of a group to think and act in accordance with the established norms.

The sharing of a common body of values and sentiments invariably strengthens group cohesion; and anyone who does not share them, either by virtue of exclusion or because of a preference for his own norms, is "different" and therefore an outsider. As an outsider he is often perceived as a threat to in-group solidarity, and consequently feared or despised. Thus the American Negro, for example, because of his high social visibility tends to disturb the relationship of familiarity between in-group members. He is, accordingly, denied the participation which the white man accords only to his "own kind."

The *family*, of course, because it is a strategic socializing agent is an important instrumentality for the transmission of ethnic attitudes to children. Although it reflects the prejudices of the culture in which it exists, the family has its own way, often quite directly through verbal inculcation, of influencing the growing child to be unfavorably disposed to ethnic groups. A score of excellent studies document parental influence in the rise of prejudice. Meltzer, in a study of children in the eight- to thirteen-year-age group, clearly found the influence of parents on the ethnic attitudes of their children. Frenkel-Brunswik and Sanford found an unmistakable relation between the prejudices of parents and those of their children. Allport and Kramer found that almost 70 per cent of a large group of college students traced their negative attitude toward ethnic groups to their parents. Radke and Trager found the same influence in their study, and the volume by Goodman which we have already cited corroborates the findings of the others.[12]

The ethnocentric family, judging by a study by Frenkel-Brunswik, is characterized by certain traits which undoubtedly play an important role in forming incipient antiethnic attitudes. It is overconcerned with status. The need to separate itself from others who are perceived as socially inferior is easily transmitted to the child who thus learns to avoid them in his social relations. The parents frequently use harsh discipline which the child interprets as capricious and as indicative of rejection and absence of genuine love. The child, accordingly, is deprived of the opportunity of relating himself positively and warmly to others, especially those who are already negatively pigeonholed by virtue of

[12] For the above results, see H. Meltzer, The development of children's nationality preferences, concepts, and attitudes, *J. Psychol.*, *11* (1941), 343–58; E. Frenkel-Brunswik and R. N. Sanford, Some personality correlates of Anti-Semitism, *J. Psychol.*, *20* (1945), 271–91; G. W. Allport and B. M. Kramer, Some roots of prejudice, *J. Psychol.*, *22* (1946), 9–39; M. Radke and H. Trager, Children's perceptions of the social roles of Negroes and whites, *J. Psychol.*, *29* (1950), 3–33.

their status, nationality, or color. He fails, above all, to judge people by their intrinsic worth, and too easily submits to the acquired habit of evaluating them by superficial but socially perceptible and culturally significant traits.[13]

In view of the prejudiced family's concern with status and the close relation of status to economic position, it is unnecessary, in a brief review, to show the relation of ethnic attitudes to economic status. This is all the more advisable in view of the fact that it is very difficult if not impossible in the present stage of our knowledge to disentangle the influence of the multiplicity of factors in the determination of ethnic attitudes. We do not miss the mark appreciably if we merely affirm that class attitudes are transmitted to the child by adult members of the family.

We have already stressed the view that in group dynamics the *personalities of group members* must not be ignored. Prejudice is learned and reinforced because it satisfies important personality needs. An adult who was rejected as a child and deprived of the love which he wanted and needed, is generally less able to integrate his balked wishes in a wholesome and constructive way. For such a person hostility and aggression toward others, especially if the latter are at the same time widely recognized scapegoats, are ready compensations. This is all the more true because scapegoating, being a rationalized form of aggression, frees the aggressor from the haunting sense of guilt which would deeply trouble the less vindictive individual. It is true also —and this factor is what makes scapegoating at once so attractive and insidious—because the target of prejudice and aggression is helpless to retaliate. The person who hates his father, or any symbol of authority which he associates with his personal frustrations, does not need the support of his group to justify his hatred. The mere existence of others who dare to be different from himself is sufficient to arouse his pent-up hatreds.

13 See E. Frenkel-Brunswik, A study of prejudice in children, *Hum. Relat.*, *1* (1948), 295–306.

The foregoing observations once more point up the role of the family in the learning of intergroup prejudice. The personality variables which we have been describing are products of interpersonal relations in the family. Operationally, nevertheless, they are personality traits rather than family characteristics. A child reared in a home where a negative and constricting socialization prevails may become prejudiced even when the parents themselves show no noticeable ethnic hostility and do not directly indoctrinate the child with negative ethnic attitudes. The parents' role may be indirect and devious, in that through their inept handling of the growing child they give rise to personality needs which he can satisfy only in hatred for those who differ from himself.

Concluding Remarks. The literature on cultural and racial conflicts is enormous. For this very reason we have made no attempt at an exhaustive exposition of the subject. We have, however, presented the facts and generalizations which are essential to a group-dynamic study of the problem. We have left wholly untouched the ethical issues which are involved. The facts unequivocally point to the conclusion that the common value-system on which as civilized people we profess to agree is too often disregarded in the interest of sectarian, national, racial, and religious dogmas. To the last of these we now turn.

INTERRELIGIOUS CONFLICT

There is no social scientist who is not sharply aware of the existence of interreligious conflicts in the United States. Yet, while we have a prodigious amount of historical research dealing with the warring religious ideologies, we have very little reliable scientific knowledge of the social-psychological character of this conflict. Student of intergroup prejudice have analyzed religious conflicts in terms of ethnic attitudes. This has been notably true of anti-Semitism. We do not wish to detract even in a minor way from the importance of the superior research done within this framework. Interreligious conflicts are not fundamentally, however, symptoms of ethnic attitudes. The Jew in the United States, for example, is rejected by the dominant group not only because he is alleged to belong to a different "race," but because his religious beliefs are perceived as a threat to the established religious values. It is perhaps safe to assume that, because of the growing interest in—though not necessarily increasing devotion to—religion in our society, the conflict will probably increase until such a time as practical means are designed to eliminate it. Although optimists may foresee such a possibility in the near future, there is little evidence of it to encourage the skeptic. At any rate, one must be blind indeed not to recognize the fact that, while religious conflicts may not be altogether eliminated, there exist at the present time few persons or religious organizations that are trying to make the conflicts socially productive. It is a historical commonplace that religious differences have been the cause of some of our most ignominious conflicts.[14]

Every close observer of the religious scene, provided he is himself free of distorting religious attitudes, can report the existence of religious prejudice in people who may exhibit no noticeable hostilities to ethnic groups. Sectarian college students frequently betray this apparent inconsistency. They are ready to accept differences in race, culture, and political ideology, and glow with pride over their "broad-mindedness," yet show a fierce intolerance of individuals or groups which differ from them in religious outlook. Denominational colleges may have Negroes and Jews on their faculties, but they will not knowingly tolerate an "atheist" in their midst. A striking instance of this bigotry is a recent arbitrary dismissal of an "atheist" from the faculty of a university in our nation's capital, followed up by the dire edict that henceforth no "atheist" will be appointed to its faculty.[15] Ethnic conflicts and religious antagonisms cannot

[14] A good source for the general reader is E. K. Nottingham, *Religion and society* (Garden City, N.Y.: Doubleday & Co., Inc., 1954), especially chap. i.

[15] Reported by B. Blake in an article entitled Must college professors believe in God? in *The Christian Register* (March, 1957), 8.

always, in short, be explained by the same social-psychological mechanisms.

CHRISTIAN-JEWISH ANTAGONISMS. The foregoing inconsistencies call for explanations on other than conventionally ethnic grounds, though the latter are often present to complicate an already perplexing problem.

The inconsistency is partially based, we believe, on the Christian doctrine of love or compassion. Christianity admonishes its believers to love all men irrespective of racial differences, but in the same breath, so to speak, asserts that religious truth is found only in its own doctrine. Accordingly, the Jew is hated or disliked in many instances, not because he belongs to a different "race," as this word is popularly interpreted, but because he believes in a different kind of God.

There is, furthermore, an implicit antagonism between Judaism and Christianity which accentuates the religious conflict between Christian and Jew. Adorno ascribes to this difference not only the incompatibility of two disparate cultures, but the Christian's rationalization of his anti-Semitic attitudes and feelings as well.[16] The evidence on which he bases his argument is partly historical and partly empirical. In this instance we can do no better than to quote Adorno at length. He writes,

> . . . Christianity as the religion of the "Son" contains an implicit antagonism against the religion of the "Father" and its surviving witnesses, the Jews. This antagonism, continuous since St. Paul, is enhanced by the fact that the Jews, by clinging to their own religious culture, rejected the religion of the Son and by the fact that the New Testament puts upon them the blame for Christ's death. It has been pointed out again and again by great theologians . . . that the acceptance of Christianity by the Christians themselves contains a problematic and ambiguous element, engendered by the paradoxical nature of the doctrine of God becoming man, the Infinite finite. Unless this element is consciously put into the center of the religious conception, it tends to promote hostility against the outgroup.

[16] T. W. Adorno, E. Frenkel-Brunswik, *et al., The authoritarian personality* (New York: Harper & Bros., 1950), chap. xviii.

Then, following Samuel, Adorno continues,

> . . . the "weak" Christians resent bitterly the openly negative attitude of the Jews toward the religion of the Son, since they feel within themselves traces of this negative attitude based upon the paradoxical, irrational nature of their creed—an attitude which they do not dare to admit and which they must therefore put under a heavy taboo in others.[17]

The Christian rationalizations of anti-Semitism cannot be well understood on the basis of conventional ethnic attitudes. The Christian's antagonism against the Jew, Adorno holds, is an expression of the conflict between the "Redeemer and the Christian Devil." Citing Trachtenberg, Adorno shows that the Christian's image of the Jew is a "secularization of the medieval imagery of the Devil." The well-known image of the Jewish banker flows from the tale of Jesus driving the userers from the Temple. The Jewish traitor who betrays his country is the image of Judas.[18]

Years of effort on the part of individuals and organizations to eradicate Christian-Jewish religious antagonisms have not on the whole been very successful. While people may shed their ethnic prejudices as a consequence of increased interaction between cultural and racial groups, a like increase in interreligious contacts seldom produces similar results. On the contrary, the friendly contacts of people from the warring religious groups, where an easy ventilation of differing views may take place, reinforce and often intensify the antagonism which heretofore was only incipient or even nonexistent. The writer has observed this state of affairs so often, especially between Roman Catholics and Protestants, that he is tempted to generalize it into an important dynamic principle. What is needed to confirm it, of course, is not only theoretical argument and careful

[17] T. W. Adorno, E. Frenkel-Brunswik, *et al.*, *The authoritarian personality* (New York: Harper & Bros., 1950), p. 728. See further, M. Samuel, *The great hatred* (New York: Alfred A. Knopf, Inc., 1940).

[18] Adorno, Frenkel-Brunswik, *et al.*, *The authoritarian personality,* pp. 728–29. See also J. Trachtenberg, *The devil and the Jews* (New Haven: Yale University Press, 1943); M. Horkheimer and T. W. Adorno, Elemente des Antisemitismus, in *Dialektik der Aufklärung* (Amsterdam: Querido Verlag, N.V., 1947).

observation but systematic objective research. This kind of research is notably lacking at the present time.

Roman Catholic–Protestant Antagonisms. While Roman Catholic–Protestant conflicts are no less complex than other religious prejudices, the basic source from which they spring is the Roman Catholic belief in the exclusive rightness of the Roman Catholic church. This is not a proposition about which devout Roman Catholics argue; it is the absolute truth which they never question. This Roman Catholic claim to absolute truth is not peculiar in the history of Christianity. The Greek Orthodox church has made a similar claim. It affirms its priority to the Roman Catholic church, claiming that it is the only Catholic and Apostolic church. Protestants have indulged in the same practice by refusing to recognize as Christian such religious institutions as the Unitarian church or the Humanist Society. Every dependable observer of the religious scene can report the existence of many ethnically unbiased Roman Catholics and Protestants who portray each other in unflattering terms. Each imputes to the other characteristics which betray well-entrenched stereotypes. The socially harmful aspects of this antagonism is not the divergent theological views on which it is based but the practical consequence to which it leads. Some of them merit serious examination.

Field of education. The Roman Catholic church in the United States has been outspoken during the past decade in requesting public moneys for the aid of its parochial schools. The Protestants in every community interpret this request as a conflict between the historical separation of church and state and oppose it on many fronts. While this opposition, in view of the Protestants' efforts to circumvent the Supreme Court's ruling regarding religious education in the public schools, is neither logical nor gracious, it has aroused additional ill-feeling between the two groups.[19] Roman Catho-

[19] It is a credit to American Jews that they have not only not sought public funds for the support of Jewish education, but they have been consistently opposed to the use of such funds for any religious education.

lics, indeed, deeply resent their exclusion from the benefits of public expenditure on education. The cry of "double taxation" by American Roman Catholics represents their conviction of the grave injustice of the established practice.

Currently the antagonism is in a state of unstable equilibrium. While their dissatisfaction has not diminished, Roman Catholics have for the time being resigned themselves to accepting secondary, but nonetheless valuable, benefits. Chief among them are school luncheons and public transportation for parochial school children.

The distribution of secondary benefits is, however, very uneven, and in some communities where it is given the antagonisms have not subsided. An instance which can be duplicated in other communities is presented by the city of Stamford, Connecticut. By a vote of five to four, the Board of Education of that city denied the application of the Parents Association of St. Cecilia's School for transportation for their children. The chief argument of the opposition was that the Connecticut statutes forbade the granting of public funds for the use of private schools. Meanwhile the State Legislature is preparing to clarify the legal rights of communities to provide transportation for all pupils, and the losers in the controversy are preparing to appeal the decision of the board.[20]

There is a possibility that the conflict may appreciably subside as a consequence of some predicted changes in the complexion of public school enrollments. Joseph H. Fichter, an authority on Roman Catholic parish sociology, recently predicted that in the next decade two out of every three Roman Catholic elementary school-age children will be enrolled in public schools. In an address on the "Parochial School and the Community," delivered in San Francisco, he remarked that the parochial school building program cannot keep pace with the increase in the number of Roman Catholic children. As a consequence, the public schools are faced with the entrance of large numbers of Roman Catholic children.

[20] Reported in *The New York Times,* March 24, 1957.

Fichter also states, what many would be ready to challenge, that "*the public's attitude has changed from criticism to admiration, gratitude and even support of the parochial school.*" Presumably this change of attitude is due to the public's recognition that Roman Catholic schools "save the taxpayers money." In support of the latter claim Fichter describes a situation in a Midwestern city. Here the parochial schools, with a population of 6,611 children, are contributing to that city $1,871,839 annually which would have to be raised through community taxes if these children attended city schools. The 150 classrooms in the parochial schools of that city would cost the taxpayers $4,500,000 to replace.

The spirit of giving seems to be somewhat diluted, however, by Fichter's observation that the Roman Catholic parents believe that they deserve a rebate on school taxes, and that assistance should be forthcoming to them, "not as a privilege but as a right, from the larger community.[21]

The home. No religious group in America has more jealousy guarded the sacredness of the home than the Roman Catholic church. This concern with family relations is, of course, commendable, and no thoughtful Protestant or Jew opposes it. Conflict with other religious groups arises, however, when the edicts and prescriptions of the Roman Catholic church are militantly universalized. It is one thing for the Roman Catholic church to condemn birth control for its members, but it becomes interference with the rights of non-Roman Catholics when it fiercely combats legislation to legalize it for others. It is fitting and proper, in the framework of Roman Catholic dogma, to pronounce divorce as sinful and deny it to its believers, but it is a cause of serious intergroup antagonism and an obstruction of the rights of others when organized Roman Catholic pressure induces legislators to evade the issue.

Our interest in these matters is not, we are sure, with the religious character of the antagonisms, but only with

[21] Reported in *The New York Times,* March 24, 1957. Italics ours.

the antagonisms themselves. A society is socially and psychologically disturbed when these conflicts exist. Disturbed relations are an important area of research in group dynamics, the area of intergroup prejudice.

Concluding Remarks. If our diagnosis of intergroup prejudice is substantially correct, then we must exercise more caution in the use of this term than is generally the case. It does not necessarily denote a unitary process. Prejudice varies somewhat with the character of the groups which are in conflict. A decade ago Williams had the perspicacity to challenge the belief that prejudice was necessarily the same in all groups.[22] Our own study challenges the claim further, especially as it applies to interreligious prejudices, which do not completely conform to the traditional descriptions of ethnic attitudes. Interpreted in terms of learning, the same divergence is suggested. A number of studies show that transference of learnings from one group to another varies with the group. A prejudice toward one minority group is not always transferred toward other minority groups.[23]

REDUCTION OF INTERGROUP HOSTILITY

Group dynamics has greatly increased our knowledge and understanding of intergroup antagonisms, and "action research" based on group-dynamic principles has offered us better tools for reducing them than exhortations and good will. While these developments are positive contributions, they do not yet form a sufficient body of reliable skills to enable us either to control or eliminate with certainty the conflicts that plague every community. This is not a criticism of what has been accomplished but an honest recognition of the limitations of both our knowledge and our instruments. Yet viewed in the perspective of a quarter-century, we have come a long way. Viewed in the light of

22 R. M. Williams, Jr., *The reduction of intergroup tensions,* Social Science Research Council, Bulletin No. 57 (New York: 1947), chap. iii.

23 See A. M. Rose, *Studies in reduction of prejudice* (New York: American Council of Race Relations, 1947). Mimeographed.

its potentials, the promises the study of group dynamics holds are encouraging.

The self-styled "hard-headed" scientist might well challenge the propriety of our concern with the reduction of intergroup hostility in a volume descriptive of group-dynamic principles. He is logically bound to expose the ethical premises on which it rests. We recognize this fact. But this criticism can be met by pointing out that our interest is not, however, in the *advocacy* of plans of action but in an objective description of the psychological nature of the resolution of intergroup tensions. Williams states the social scientist's position correctly when he says that the "only necessary assumption is that under *some* circumstances certain individuals and groups find it desirable to attempt to reduce hostility or conflict or both." There is accordingly, he adds, "a social raison d'être for scientific study directed toward testing the results of various means used in these attempts."[24]

It is necessary, however, that we recognize the difficulty confronting any efforts to achieve intergroup harmony, especially the all-important one, corroborated by both history and scientific research, that intergroup conflicts are generally more difficult to resolve than those that arise in intragroup relations. In perplexed moments that at once suggest hope and discouragement, one is tempted to follow the field-dynamic view of the part-whole relationship to its logical conclusion and suggest that intergroup conflicts can be eliminated only when a world community has been established. At the present time this world community is as remote as it is desirable. Our review of intergroup conflicts in this chapter starkly suggests the difficulties we face. Deviant members and dissident subgroups, as we have shown, either leave the group voluntarily or are rejected by it. Although there is a powerful tendency for individuals to modify their perception and thinking in the direction of the group's norms, not all individuals and groups are uniformly

[24] Williams, *The reduction of intergroup tensions*, p. 5.

influenced. This is especially true when the individuals are self-involved and the groups are ethnocentrically oriented.

Role of Education. It has been frequently said that Americans have a boundless faith in the possibilities of education. If this is true, the fault, if such it be, is a good one. As scientific students of group life, however, it is of the utmost importance that we recognize both the merits and the limitations of education. The results as reported in the literature, moreover, are not infrequently inconsistent and even contradictory. Generally speaking, education in our schools neither substantially reduces prejudice nor effectively immunizes children against it. Since intergroup attitudes are rooted in the folkways of the group and in the emotions of the individual, rational arguments leave them largely untouched.

Education is not, however, confined to formal instruction in the school. It includes any intelligent effort to change people's attitudes. Lectures, exhortations, appeals to character and nobility—these, too, are instruments of education. In this connection it is instructive to note the ineffectiveness of a "pledge" taken by citizens of Minneapolis, as reported by A. J. Marrow. The Governor's Interracial Commission in that city urged Minnesotans to take the following pledge:

> I will never by rumor or careless conversation indict a whole race or religious group by reason of the delinquency of a few members. I will daily deal with every man in business, social or political relations solely on the basis of his individual work.

Nevertheless, as Marrow points out, no Jew had at the time of the study (1951), been admitted to luncheon clubs or civic boards in that city, and its local Auto Club had informed Jewish prospects that there were no new memberships open.[25] Whether these things are still true today, we do not know.

If we consider advertising as a potentially effective medium for changing attitudes, as it has indeed been in many areas of human motivation, it too, like education, has

[25] A. J. Marrow, *Living without hate* (New York: Harper & Bros., 1951), p. 16.

largely failed to reduce prejudice. Despite intensive campaigns of advertising the evils of prejudice, no very tangible results have yet taken place. Psychologically speaking, this should have been expected. One does not "sell" an idea like democratic ethics as one does tooth paste or the latest breakfast food. Ideas, especially those touching human conduct, are deeply embedded in irrational emotions. As Marrow points out, man will give up a prejudice only when something else is substituted for it that will serve the same vital need as well if not better.[26]

The foregoing statement points up the fact that most of our education for "tolerance" fails because it does not produce an understanding of other people as human beings like ourselves. Insight in intergroup relations is best achieved by means of the free participation of peoples of different racial and ideological backgrounds in common activities. We shall consider this factor later when we describe the effect on attitudes of interracial housing.

Process of Re-Education. We have been proceeding in this book on the assumption that learning prejudice and distorted perceptions of other people and acquiring veridical ones are fundamentally the same. Changes in behavior, whether cognitive, perceptual, or emotional, do not take place independently of one another. They involve, on the contrary, as field dynamics shows, a change in the person's total life in the group. A change in the individual is preceded by, or is concomitant with, a change in the cultural milieu. The individual can stabilize his changed views only if, as Lewin pointed out, his conduct is anchored in the culture of his group. A logical step-by-step argument may put the prejudiced individual on the defensive—and a defensive individual will usually find some way, no matter how illogical or irrational, to retain his beliefs. He will surrender them only when he has also changed from hostility toward alien beliefs to an emotional readiness to accept them.[27]

[26] *Ibid.*, p. 18.

[27] See K. Lewin, *Resolving social conflicts* (New York: Harper & Bros., 1948), p. 66.

The possibility of re-education is increased when the prejudiced individual develops a feeling of group belongingness with reference to the out-group. Accepting new beliefs is equivalent to accepting group belongingness with others. The person is learning new values by feeling accepted by others. The process is similar, according to Lewin, to that of the delinquent or of the alcoholic who changes because he feels that everyone is in the same boat. Group identification prepares the individual to accept the group's values, because in this situation the group's values are the individual's values. Lewin states this with discernment when he says, to repeat, that an individual will believe facts he himself has discovered in the same way that he believes in himself.

Change of attitudes, then, takes place most readily when the values to be accepted by the prejudiced individual control his perception of those which he formerly rejected. His acceptance of the new beliefs and values is linked with a specific group. This linkage between acceptance of new values and new groups is very close. It explains the great difficulty, says Lewin, of changing attitudes and values in an atomistic, item-by-item fashion, and adds that this linkage is "a main factor behind resistance to re-education, but can also be made a powerful means for successful re-education."[28]

Legal Methods. It has frequently been pointed out as if it were self-evident that society cannot legislate prejudice out of existence but only pass laws against public discrimination. There is, of course, considerable truth in this statement, but it is not wholly true. Law and public policy have enormously altered the structure of discrimination in American life in the past decade. The New York State law against discrimination in employment, while by no means completely successful, has nevertheless reduced discrimination in this area. A survey of 504 residents of New York City who were questioned whether they were discriminated

[28] *Ibid.*, p. 68.

against after the law was put into effect, shows that only about 19 per cent of the respondents claimed that they were discriminated against in relation to their jobs.[29] Even if the discrimination was much larger, as one may not unreasonably assume, the survey supports the belief that discrimination is reduced by legal action.

An important consequence of legal action, and one not sufficiently appreciated, is that laws against discrimination help to create a social atmosphere of greater tolerance. If the law makes it possible for enough people of different ethnic background to be thrown together, the community can challenge the attitudes of indifference and acquiescence which so often prevail. On the job, where frequent contacts are necessary, people learn to accept one another more readily. These contacts, as the writer has remarked elsewhere, lead to other, less job-related, interactions, such as eating together and visiting together.[30]

On the basis of historical evidence, in short, it is reasonable to assume that law and public policy, while themselves alone incapable of dissipating prejudice, not only reduce discrimination but also in the long run create a social atmosphere which is conducive to greater acceptance of ethnic differences. In a very imperfect social order this is a significant gain.

EQUAL-STATUS INTERACTION. The potentiality of law for creating sentiments of racial acceptance is nicely demonstrated by a well-known investigation of attitude change resulting from contacts in an interracial housing project.[31] Our interest in it is not as a legal weapon but as a psychological tool for destroying ethnic prejudice.

[29] See G. Saenger and N. S. Gordon, The influence of discrimination on minority group members, *J. soc. Psychol., 31* (1950), 95–120.

[30] H. Bonner, *Social psychology: an interdisciplinary approach* (New York: American Book Co., 1953), p. 374. See also B. Mackenzie, The importance of contact in determining attitudes toward Negroes, *J. abnorm. soc. Psychol., 43* (1948), 417–41.

[31] See M. Deutsch and M. E. Collins, The effect of public policy in housing projects upon interracial attitudes, in G. E. Swanson, T. M. Newcomb, and E. L. Hartley (eds.), *Readings in social psychology* (rev. ed.; New York: Henry Holt & Co., Inc., 1952), pp. 582–93.

Deutsch and Collins proceeded on the assumption, supported by social-science evidence, that the most important factor in race relations in housing projects is the *occupancy pattern.* To ascertain the influence on attitudes of different occupancy patterns, the investigators chose to study race relations in two types of housing projects, namely, the *integrated interracial* project, in which families are assigned to apartments without consideration of race, and the *segregated biracial* project, where Negro and white families are assigned to apartments in different buildings. An example of the first project was found in New York City and of the second in Newark, New Jersey. For comparative purposes the authors were careful to select the projects in the two cities that had approximately the same ratio of Negroes to whites. Their information regarding the attitudes of members of the two groups was obtained by means of intensive interviews lasting on the average for an hour and a half. The interviews elicited information in five major social and psychological areas: (1) the attitudes of the housewives toward living in the project, (2) their attitudes toward members of the other race, (3) the amount of intimate contact between the races, (4) the extent of support the white women received from members of their own race, and (5) the social characteristics of the housewives.[32]

The results of the Deutsch-Collins survey imply that "official policy, executed without equivocation, can result in large changes in behavior and attitudes despite initial resistance to that policy." [33] The projects show, in brief, that if persons of different ethnic groups have equal-status contacts prejudice between them is effectively diminished. Referring specifically to the two projects which they investigated, the authors inform us that *"the net gain resulting from the integrated projects is considerable; from the same point of view, the gain created by the segregated bi-racial projects is slight."*[34]

[32] *Ibid.,* pp. 584–85.
[33] *Ibid.,* p. 592.
[34] *Ibid.,* p. 592. Italics in the original.

It is important to inject a note of caution here. This study, like a few others dealing with equal-status contacts, shows that the latter result in attitude change only when they fulfill certain conditions. These may be described briefly as follows:

1. The behavior of the members of the minority group must be such as not to conform with the common stereotypes. The Negroes with whom the prejudiced individual interacts must not exhibit the traits of "laziness," "ignorance," "delinquency," etc., which he had associated with them.
2. The interactions of the prejudiced person with the target of his hostility must be strong enough to resist any tendency to cognitive distortions—that is, the interactions must be such as to enable the prejudiced person to check his perceptions with reality.
3. The interactions must occur "under conditions which make the nonconforming behavior seem relevant to the basis on which the objects of prejudice are grouped together." If, for example, a Negro attendant is clean and honest in a situation where cleanliness and honesty are expected or required, this fact may have very little influence in changing the prejudiced person's attitudes. He must be seen clean and honest in relations other than those of a Negro attendant.
4. The prejudiced person must have values, such as democratic equality, or be exposed to social influences, such as public policies, that will "strongly conflict with the unabashed retention of unrationalized prejudices."[35]

Concluding Remarks. The foregoing ways of reducing ethnic prejudices and other intergroup hostilities are only a few. We have omitted propaganda, for instance, because it is, on the one hand, impossible to discuss it in a single chapter and, on the other, because its effects have never been carefully determined. This is not even to mention the fact that the results of a number of investigations are contradictory. Moreover, while we do not wish to minimize the influence of propaganda on attitudes, especially in people

[35] *Ibid.*, pp. 592–93.

who already have an unconscious predisposition to accept certain beliefs, there is some danger that its effectiveness might be overestimated. The evidence suggests that, generally speaking, propaganda is most successful when unrest and collective fears abound, and not in all situations.

We are also omitting any consideration of so-called action programs and interest groups to reduce racial tensions and discriminations. A description and evaluation of these would require an undesirable extension of the present chapter. We suggest that the reader consult original sources, of which there are several good ones.[36]

CONCLUSION

The formation of subgroups is a normal social process. In some cases the subgroups, by breaking away from the larger or parent group, effect a new equilibrium by satisfying their needs and interest in a different setting. Children and adolescents in our society are potentially in conflict with the older generation, and the formation of peer groups, adolescent cliques, and gangs is a way of achieving the autonomy which growing children both want and need. In this way the break in the family ties aids at once in reducing tensions and facilitating the process of socialization, particularly in the form of emancipating the child from the exclusive dependence on the home. To repeat an earlier observation, these independent formations are harmful only when they manifest themselves in such antisocial and destructive behavior as juvenile delinquency and gang wars.

The problem of intergroup prejudice and its dissipation constitutes one of the most challenging theoretical and

[36] We suggest the following: On propaganda: C. I. Hovland, A. A. Lumsdaine, and F. D. Sheffield, *Experiments on mass communication* (Studies in Social Psychology in World War II, Vol. III [Princeton: Princeton University Press, 1949]); J. Harding, A. F. Citron, and E. King, An experimental study of answers to anti-Negro remarks, *J. soc. Psychol.*, 37 (1953), 3–17. On action programs, see L. A. Cook (ed.), *College programs in intergroup relations* (Washington, D.C.: American Council on Education, 1950); M. H. Wormser and C. Selltiz, *How to conduct a community self-survey of civil rights* (New York: Association Press, 1951).

practical issues of contemporary life. Everyone is somewhat conditioned early in life to behave in accordance with the dominant stereotypes of his family or community. The problem is complicated by the fact that when preconceptions are eliminated in one area of life they are not eradicated in all of them. Probably the attitudinal life of most adults is characterized by conflicts and contradictions. When they are confronted by such conflicts they characteristically ignore them or stop thinking about them altogether. When faced by contradictions between religious beliefs and scientific conclusions not a few scientists will either rationalize them or refrain from thinking about them. A Roman Catholic may be loyal to democratic ideals and at the same time submit to the authoritarian dogmas of his church. A socially minded individual may be appalled by the injustice of racial segregation but cringe from taking any action against it. Too often the prejudices are not even recognized, for, as we said before, they are part of the folkways of our society.

Education must be constantly encouraged and strongly supported, but education, even when it is partially successful, is not enough. Education for ethnic understanding is a community problem, not the task of formal education only. In any event, the claims for the success of education in intergroup relations have yet to be validated.

Law and public policy have been successfully used to diminish discrimination in certain areas of intergroup living. Even if they do not wholly succeed in destroying prejudice, there is some reason to believe that they are effective in creating a social climate of opinion which may bear fruit in the long run.

As far as research is concerned, the data accumulated thus far give considerable support to the conclusion that, under certain defined circumstances, equal-status contacts are the most effective means of destroying interracial prejudice. While everyone familiar with the contemporary scene must feel heartened by the progress made, both research and practice indicate that the promise is far greater than the achievement. This is dismaying or discouraging only if we expect too much from both. The social scientist, who is familiar with the complexity of the problem, is not defeatist. He knows only too well that there is no single formula for eliminating conflicts from human relationships. The problem, he is convinced, must be studied from as many sides as human capacity permits. Only through the collaboration of several disciplines will it be ultimately understood and, one ventures to believe, at least largely erased from the world.[37]

[37] For a confirmation of our viewpoint here, see Religious conflict in the United States, *J. soc. Issues, 12,* No. 3 (1956). This entire number is devoted to interreligious conflict.

CHAPTER 6

Group Leadership

Despite a number of excellent objective studies of leadership, and despite the fact that no other subject in group dynamics has been more thoroughly investigated, it is still controversial. It has been distorted during its history by excessive romanticism and hampered by too much plausible mythology. Descriptions of the leader by trait attribution has been mostly a sterile exercise.

Writing at a time when group dynamics had neither formed into a special discipline nor become the focus of zealous extremists, Pigors argued for the inseparability of the leader and his followers. Like Simmel thirty years before him, he conceived leadership not as something residing in the individual, but as a way of behaving derived from the leader's relationship with others.[1] This is the theoretical position of most present-day investigators of the nature of group leadership. From the vantage point of this position the leader is not endowed with mystical power, and he is not independent of the group of which he is a part. While he "controls" the group to which he belongs, it also "con-

[1] P. Pigors, *Leadership or domination* (Boston: Houghton Mifflin Co., 1935). For Simmel's view, see his *Soziologie* (Leipzig: Duncker und Humblot, 1908). See also Chapter 1, p. 10.

trols" him. "Leadership is then conceived as the product of the interaction between the total personality of the leader and the dynamic social situation in which he has his being."[2]

There is almost no adequate research evidence in support of the view adhered to by a few *advocates* of "leaderless groups," that in a democratic society people object to a firm leadership. On the contrary, people often welcome the initiative of those who, by the happy congruence of individuals qualified to play certain roles effectively and the field conditions prevailing in a group at a certain moment, are able to help the group achieve its goals. In a democratic group the individual who is able to integrate his own role with those of others has the moral responsibility to lead, especially if without his initiative desirable goals are not achieved or confusion results from needless hesitation.[3]

DEFINITIONS OF LEADERSHIP. A cursory review of the literature on leadership quickly discloses that it has many definitions. They run the gamut of anecdotal, common sense, "literary," and scientific conceptualizations. They abound, even today, with preconceived notions, and attempts to establish the validity of the "scientific" view by means of semi-empirical evidence are not uncommon. It is an ancient belief that in every group individuals exist who will try to dominate over others. Those who triumph over others are acknowledged as leaders. Genetic studies of lower animals confirm the existence of dominant and submissive behavior among them. The "pecking order" of hens is a popular illustration of this phenomenon. However, such an order of dominance in the human species has not been empirically corroborated. Moreover, as a human trait dominance has been beclouded by confusing it with self-esteem and self-assurance. Dominance may conceivably be a genetic trait, but there is no reliable evidence to support the belief that self-esteem is other than a social-psychological characteristic. If Hitler

[2] H. Bonner, *Social psychology: an interdisciplinary approach* (New York: American Book Co., 1953), p. 399.

[3] See G. C. Homans, *The human group* (New York: Harcourt, Brace & Co., 1950), pp. 423 ff.

was able to beat the German people into abject submission, it was not because he possessed any outstanding qualities of leadership but, among other reasons, because of his sordid life he compensated for his lack of self-assurance and self-esteem by means of a ruthless dominance.

Again, every leader, be he a dictator or an elected official, must appeal to men's interests and needs. Elsewhere, the present writer has described this relationship for a specific leader-and-group as follows:

> Hitler, with all the help of a colossal machinery of propaganda and mass persuasion, could not have swayed the German nation to his cause had he not voiced the frustration, anger, humiliation, and hope of millions of its population. Hitler played his role superbly. He succeeded because he embodied their aspirations; they followed him because they sensed in his vibrant, though distorted, personality the power that would restore for them their national self-respect. That in the end he destroyed them but confirms the theory we are espousing: having released certain forces in his environment he was finally engulfed by them. As he gained control over the world around him, the world in turn enslaved and destroyed him.[4]

The above description calls attention to the view of the leader, which we shall develop at length in this chapter—namely, that the leader does not alone bring about changes in the group or in its members, but that these changes are the resultant of the relation of the leader to the dynamic processes of the total social field. But, before analyzing the group-dynamic view, we shall examine other explanations.

Great Man Theory. This is the oldest explanation, other than "primitive" or mystical views, of the nature of the leader. According to this view, changes in social or group life are effected by men of uncommon talents or abilities. The most respectable and influential modern proponent of this view was Sir Francis Galton. He presented a great deal of genetic and statistical data in support of his position.[5]

[4] H. Bonner, *Social psychology: an interdisciplinary approach* (New York: American Book Co., 1953), p. 399–400.

[5] F. Galton, *Hereditary genius* (London: Macmillan & Co., Ltd., 1914). This book was originally published in 1869. See also his book, *Inquiries into human faculty and its development* (London: Macmillan & Co., Ltd., 1883).

Whether the evidence established his theory depends a great deal on how it is evaluated. Without going into this complex question it is sufficient to point out that this approach endows certain individuals, who by virtue of their achievements are called leaders, with specific inherited characteristics. Social changes allegedly are brought about by the concrete decisions which these individuals make. Our popular views of national heroes, especially, largely reflect this mode of explanation. In our own generation the average citizen's "mental image" of President Eisenhower has conformed to the foregoing description. Certainly no "ordinary" individual, it is nonetheless a biased view to regard him as an exceptionally endowed person.

Like many inadequate explanations of human nature, the great man theory possesses enough elements of truth to make it plausible to uncritical minds. Under some kinds of conditions a leader may effect changes which he could not bring about under others. Since from the standpoint of field dynamics the degree of change which an individual may induce depends upon the structure or organization of the group as a whole and his position in it, he may affect the group in certain ways when it is "ready" for them. While this point may be argued, it seems that President Eisenhower was less able to effect change in his second than he did in his first administration. Although his physical health and the second-term amendment may have been influencing factors, they did not markedly change him as a person. Social conditions, however, had changed, and along with it the "honeymoon" atmosphere had disappeared, so that he was a less effective leader in his second term.

The attribution of specific traits to persons who are, or eventually become, leaders is not to be dismissed. Extensive research during the past quarter-century has isolated specific leadership traits in individuals all the way from nursery-school children to graduate students and business executives. We cannot, of course, detail these studies and their conclusions in the present chapter. A few traits, however, should be mentioned.

Physical factors inevitably crop up in studies of leadership. A number of investigations suggest a positive relationship between leadership and such traits as height, weight, and energy output. Leaders tend to be taller, heavier, and more energetic than nonleaders. Group-dynamic studies would suggest, however, that the relation of these traits to leadership probably varies with the type of leadership activity performed. It is certainly possible that tall, heavy, and energetic persons impress people more than short, slight, and sluggish individuals; and yet it is a fact that some world-famous leaders were conspicuously devoid of the former characteristics.

Certain important *psychological* variables have also been singled out. Intelligence, initiative, and self-confidence are found to be positively related to leadership in numerous investigations. It would be rash to deny the importance of general intelligence in leadership, for there are reliable studies indicating its importance. The argument in favor of this relationship, however, is sometimes pushed too far. If the difference between leader and followers is excessive, the leadership relation is adversely affected. This is so because, if the discrepancy is too great, each forms a distorted image of the other and neither one can play his role or perform his function adequately. The evidence points to the sure conclusion that persons of exceptionally superior intelligence are less likely to become leaders than individuals who, while more intelligent than their followers, are not too greatly removed from them. This relationship has been "measured" in a study of leadership among children, and was revealed by Terman's study of the intelligence of geniuses many years earlier.[6]

At the risk of being tedious it is important, therefore, to point out, what group-dynamic investigations suggest; that it is not intelligence as such that makes leaders, but its rela-

[6] On children, see L. S. Hollingworth, *Children above 180 I.Q.* (New York: World Book Co., 1942). On adult geniuses, see L. M. Terman, A preliminary study in the psychology and pedagogy of leadership, *Pedag. Semin., 11* (1904), 413–51.

tion to the totality of conditions which describe the social field or group structure at a particular segment of time. If Cattell is right, moreover, then intelligence is a factor in leadership insofar as it is linked up, as it tends to be, with other psychological variables, such as independence, emotional maturity, conscientiousness, and "wisdom."[7]

Since we have called attention to the trait of dominance, we might well examine its place as a psychological variable in leadership. In doing so we permit the reader to get a further glimpse of the difficulty in studying leadership, for the evidence is far from consistent. One study finds a positive relationship in both college students and mature adults between dominance and leadership.[8] In a well-known sociometric study, on the other hand, Jennings reveals that dominant individuals are not chosen for leadership roles, but are rejected instead.[9] Cattell and Stice, finally, found no significant relation between leadership and dominance.[10]

"Situational" Theory. The great man theory of leadership stresses largely, if not exclusively, the possession of genetic and psychological traits by the leader. It is thus largely a "hereditarian" view. The situational theory, on the other hand, is an "environmentalist" approach. More specifically, it attributes leadership to a specific historical period. A leader, from this point of view, can emerge only if "the times" are such as to permit him to use whatever skills and ambitions he might possess. In the great man theory the leader is independent of or superior to the group which he heads. In the situational theory he is dependent on or in the grip of external social forces over which he has little or no effective control.

[7] R. B. Cattell, *Description and measurement of personality* (Yonkers, N.Y.: World Book Co., 1946).

[8] H. M. Richardson and N. G. Hanawalt, Leadership as related to the Bernreuter personality measures, *J. soc. Psychol., 17* (1943), 237–67.

[9] H. H. Jennings, *Leadership and isolation* (2d ed.; New York: Longmans, Green & Co., Inc., 1950).

[10] R. B. Cattel and G. F. Stice, *The psychodynamics of small groups* (Urbana, Ill.: University of Illinois, 1953).

Adherents to this view delight in pointing out examples of "displaced" geniuses, of men who were born either too soon or too late to actualize whatever talents they might have possessed. "Full many a flower is born to blush unseen." Had Edison and Ford, with all their individual genius, lived in the seventeenth century they could not have invented the phonograph or the motor-car, respectively. While the times would have been psychologically ready for its people to enjoy the pleasures yielded by their inventions, the world of science and technology lacked the requisite knowledge to make them possible. Were Christ living today, it is doubtful that he would have the same hypnotic effect upon the masses that he had in his own time—and especially the degree of effect he had a few centuries after his death. From the standpoint of early history he was born too soon; but from the standpoint of contemporary life, he would have been born too late.

In contrast to the great man theory, then, which places the origin of events within the leader, the situational theory locates it in the social and historical events outside him. While this latter view is also one-sided, it more nearly approximates the field-dynamic explanations in stressing the effect of historical conditions upon the behavior of the leader. Its fatal weakness is that it imputes to the environmental field alone a generating property which it does not possess. Rather, it is the leader and the group of which he is a member, considered as a totality, we shall see, which are the origin of social change.

Sociometric Approach. In harmony with its principle of sociometric choice, sociometry accounts for leadership by the frequency with which an individual in a group is identified as one who influences others within it. Sociometric choice, as we pointed out in Chapter 1, refers to the attractions and repulsions of group members to one another. From this standpoint a leader is that individual who is regarded by members of his group as having "influence" over their behavior, or who is "chosen" by them appreciably more often than other members of the group are "chosen."

The sociometric technique, while a rather restricted instrument, has been extensively used for determining group leadership in community projects, classrooms, industrial plants, and military service. Its success in identifying leaders has been impressive, and its validity and reliability, both of which have been extensively investigated, invite a considerable measure of confidence.[11] Several good studies show that members of small groups are able reliably to identify those individuals who are centers of influence, and that this identification corresponds closely to that obtained by other criteria. To cite only one example, Gibb found a correlation of nearly 0.80 between leadership as indicated by sociometric choice and by the ratings of competent external observers.[12]

In the preceding paragraph we described the sociometric technique as a rather restricted instrument. Leadership is defined exclusively in terms of choice, or of a recognized influence of the leader upon others. Group dynamics, however, consistently stresses group goals and group self-direction. Sociometry does not place shared values, group goals, or group self-direction at the center of its conception of leadership. Without minimizing the importance of sociometric choice and an awareness of the leader's influence, the central fact concerning the leader as he is conceptualized in this book—namely, his role of helping group members to attain a common or collective goal—is insufficiently stressed.

Along with the great man theory and other views which place emphasis on the character or personality traits of the

[11] For the reader who might not be altogether clear regarding the meanings of these terms, we propose a brief definition of each. *Validity* refers to the extent to which a device or instrument measures what it purports to measure. An intelligence test, for example, must measure intelligence and not some other factor, such as the effect of schooling. *Reliability* refers to the consistency with which it measures a purported trait. It must give similar results every time it makes a measurement of the same trait.

[12] C. A. Gibb, The sociometry of leadership in temporary groups, *Sociometry, 13* (1950), 226–43.

leader, sociometry has the weakness of being basically a static interpretation. Sociometric choice is based in this view, implicitly if not explicitly, on the notion of status: the leader is chosen because he possesses traits which call attention to himself. The works of Moreno and Jennings, which have been already cited, depict the leader as a person who is most frequently chosen by others, and that he is chosen by others because he possesses characteristics which make him popular or attractive to them. Sociometry does not explicitly take account of the fact that being *chosen* as a leader, or being assigned the *position* of leadership, does not necessarily result in leadership *behavior* by the person selected. The chosen leader may very well be no more than what Cowley some years ago called a "headman." "Headship," or the designation of a position, is not a dependable criterion of leadership.[13] In fairness to Jennings, however, it must be pointed out that she was cognizant of the fact that leadership is a role in which many individuals share. This position has recently been emphasized by Gardner, who modestly and correctly points out that the approach is not new.[14] Thus conceived leadership, he holds, "is a continuous distribution . . . from the extreme leader (who leads all the time) to the extreme follower (who follows all the time and never influences another member of the group)." Gardner follows the logic of his observation to include as leader even that individual whose behavior is negative, in that his influence impels people to act in a manner which is opposite to his intentions.[15]

Leadership as "Attempted Leadership Acts." As at once a rigorous research tool and a view of the nature of leadership the definition of leadership as *attempted leadership acts* is an advance over the others which we have expounded. Attempted leadership acts are "acts accompanied

[13] See W. H. Cowley, Three distinctions in the study of leaders, *J. abnorm. soc. Psychol.*, 23 (1928), 144–57.

[14] G. Gardner, Functional leadership and popularity in small groups, *Hum. Relat.*, 9 (1956), 491–509.

[15] *Ibid.*, p. 493.

by an intent to initiate structure-in-interaction during the process of solving a mutual problem."[16] In this framework a leader is any person who engages in leadership acts. This view also has the merit, more explicitly seen in Hemphill's earlier formulation, of stressing the fact that leadership acts are directed toward a *shared goal.*[17] This element—this pursuit of a common goal—is the essence of leadership and is confirmed by a large amount of contemporary research.

Leadership as Defined by Group Performance. This view is similar to but more inclusive than Hemphill's, and like the latter's, it "measures" leadership not in terms of sociometric choice, popularity, or "influence," but on the basis of the group's performance under the leader's guidance. Leadership is then defined by the effect which an individual has upon group behavior and can be measured, as we pointed out before, by the performance of the group considered as a totality. Cattell, the leading exponent of this view, speaks of this group performance as *syntality,* and of leadership as "the magnitude of the syntality change (from the mean) produced by" the leader.[18] This has the added advantage of defining and measuring leadership in terms of the "increase or decrease of particular syntality dimensions," instead of using questionable valuative concepts, such as "good" leadership and "bad" leadership.

Cattell's approach is in line with the most recent and most advanced researches into the nature of leadership. It challenges the old stereotype of "a single leader and a mass of followers," for it stresses the fact, borne out by many investigations, that there are different kinds of leaders as determined by the character of the situation. While Cattell

[16] J. K. Hemphill, P. N. Pepinsky, R. N. Shevitz, W. E. Jaynes, and C. A. Christner, The relation between possession of task-relevant information and attempts to lead, *Psychol. Monogr. 70,* No. 7 (1956), 1.

[17] J. K. Hemphill, *Leader behavior description* (Columbus, Ohio: Personnel Research Board, The Ohio State University, n.d.). Mimeographed.

[18] R. B. Cattell, New concepts for measuring leadership in terms of group syntality, *Hum. Relat., 4* (1951), 161-84. See above, Chapter 3, p. 74.

as a scientist is not concerned with establishing the "superiority" of democratic group leadership, his data, as he himself points out, favor a democratic viewpoint. They imply that "every member of the group is more or less a leader," since in any complete measurement of syntality each affects the total result. At the same time the syntalic definition does not, theoretically, deny that one individual may be a center of greater potential than others, nor that he initiate more group changes than the rest. On the contrary it may well be that when the syntal effects for all members are plotted the scores for total group changes may form a J-shaped curve, indicating that a disproportionate share of leadership falls to one individual.[19]

In introducing Cattell's approach we said that it does not account for leadership in terms of the *influence* of the leader upon others. The reader may rightly be puzzled by this assertion, since the definition by way of group syntality strongly suggests it. Cattell has not been sufficiently careful in this connection, and, in fact, his view is open to this objection. It is much more in the spirit, if not in the explicit intent, of Cattell's study of leadership to describe the syntal relationship of the leader and other members of the group as the *effect* of the leader upon others. Couched in this term the concept of leadership is more naturalistically defined.

Again, the term "influence" frequently connotes a *power* relationship between the leader and other members of a group, and suggests *control* over them. While it would be utterly unrealistic, especially in view of our stress on hierarchical groupings, to deny the roles of power and control, they are not central in group leadership. The group leader does not primarily control others, but initiates acts that cause others to perform certain acts that result in satisfactions to the group as a whole. He leads others in the sense that, in playing his roles, he enables others to play theirs, so that together they achieve a common goal. If people follow a leader, it is not primarily because he has power

19 See Cattell, New concepts, p. 184.

over them, but because he facilitates the achievement of their ends, or because they approve his ideas and sanction his behavior. The followers in this situation are aware, perhaps only dimly but nonetheless truly, that in exercising his initiative the leader enables them to realize their own aims. By following the suggestions of the leader, they develop initiative by thinking for themselves. Leadership is thus always directed toward an end desired by both the leader and the led, and "control" is exercised by all. Under any other condition leadership becomes domination.

In this connection Pigors' distinction is a helpful and, we believe, a fundamental one. Challenging Jacobsen's distinction between coercive government and "genuine" leadership, Pigors astutely observes that there is a very great difference between "a *common cause* which is fully shared by all participants and an *objective aim* visualized by one man, which happens to include the partial satisfaction of other people's interests."[20]

The partisan views, which at one extreme define leadership in terms of power, and at the other define it out of existence, are both one-sided. If one clear fact emerges from the prodigious research on leadership and from the enormous state of confusion which exists in its wake, it is that leadership and power, like leadership and followership, are interdependent. Human behavior, whether individual or collective, takes place on a continuum. Leadership is no exception. If people single out the opposite poles of the continuum, it is largely because extremes are more dramatic. Even autocrats and dictators do not achieve their personal ends without the help of those whose interests are identified with their own. History bears this out so convincingly that to object is to cavil.

Returning now to Cattell's formulation of leadership, we can see that a leader is not merely one who occupies a lead-

[20] Pigors, *Leadership or domination,* p. 21, n. 1. See also W. Jacobsen, Fuehren und Fuehrertum, *Koeln. Vierteljahrshft. f. Soziol., 11* (1933), 326–49. Cited by Pigors.

er's position or office.[21] To call the President of the United States a leader merely because he holds the office is to be naïve, even though in some cases the occupant has been recognized as an outstanding person. Occupying an office to which leadership has been traditionally assigned does not make a man a leader. Leadership behavior must be "located empirically, by examining coefficients of association, to detect 'that behavior which is found empirically to be more frequent in men who have greater measured effects on syntality.' "[22]

Concluding Remarks. The conception of leadership in terms of its effect on syntality, expressed in a variety of different ways by different writers, seems to be the most recurring one. It defines leadership by a fundamental social-psychological concept, the process of interaction. It highlights the essential quality of leadership, namely, the leader's act of relating himself to others in such a way as to effect integrated behavior among them. The leader is an integral member of the group whose goals he shares and the realization of which he hopes to facilitate. He "stimulates" others, or adjusts himself to them, in such a way as to help them to do what they already wish to do.[23] Whether or not he assumes a leadership function will depend, then, upon the structure or kind of group in which he functions and in many cases upon the nature of the task which it is performing. He differs from other members of the group which he leads, at least according to one carefully designed investigation, in two respects: (1) he analyzes the problem situation in order to get insight into it, and (2) he initiates more actions than

[21] The assumption that it is, is essentially the view of Shartle and Stogdill. See C. L. Shartle and R. M. Stogdill, *Studies in naval leadership* (Columbus, Ohio: Ohio State University Research Foundation, 1952), pp. 5–7. Their definition refers to headship rather than leadership.

[22] Cattell, New concepts, p. 184.

[23] See T. N. Whitehead, *Leadership in a free society* (Cambridge, Mass.: Harvard University Press, 1936). Whitehead employs the term "chosen" by the group, which we have already questioned. People do not always choose their leaders. They relate themselves to others in ways that cause the latter to respond to them in an accepting manner.

anyone else in a given task. Leaders show a statistically significant difference in these two categories from other members of the group.[24]

The great bulk of recent analysis of and research on group leadership points to the conclusion that, while individual traits cannot be ignored, a knowledge of the individual leader yields a very imperfect understanding of leadership itself. Personality variables, intelligence, physical characteristics, and the like, which have played a very prominent role in studies of leadership in the past, do not by themselves account for leadership. These characteristics induce desired behavior in others only if the individual who possesses them shares the values of the group and coacts with the group in ways that promise the fulfillment of the interests of all. Apart from the group situation an individual may possess "leadership traits," but operationally they are meaningless, since in themselves they do not inevitably lead to leadership acts. An individual possessing these traits who becomes an acknowledged leader today may lose his leadership tomorrow. While we still need to know much concerning the persistence of leadership through time, much recent research shows that it depends on the adaptability of the leader and the stability of the group. Generally speaking, the more stable the group, the more persistent the leadership of a specific person. If leadership in democratic groups is highly changeable and goes from one member to another, it is not because such a sharing is ethically desirable—as indeed it is—but because the groups themselves do not persist. Authoritarian leadership, on the other hand, is not shared but persists in the leader as long as he maintains the group's stability or changes it in accordance with his own design. It is a well-known historical fact that authoritarian leaders like Hitler and Mussolini tried to maintain the *status quo* of their own power and that innovators became leaders in periods of rapid change. These things being true, we

[24] L. Carter, W. Haythorn, B. Shriver, and J. Lanzetta, The behavior of leaders and other group members, *J. abnorm. soc. Psychol.*, *46* (1951), 589–95.

should expect to find what recent research has discovered: that leadership, as contrasted with domination, is a shared social activity.

Gouldner, who has reviewed the defects of the trait theory of leadership and emphasized the saliency of shared activity, suggests a plausible integration of the two approaches. While Gouldner does not explicitly recognize it, his idea is based on a view of human nature and society that was expounded by C. H. Cooley many years ago. It assumes that all human groups might conceivably possess some traits in common. This universal similarity Cooley attributed to the primary group—a *psychological structure* representing a feeling of close sympathy. To the extent that such common elements exist in all groups, we should expect, believes Gouldner, that there would be some leadership traits common to all leaders. Accordingly, "some leadership traits should be unique, specific to the concrete groups and situations, while some could be common to all leaders."[25]

Gouldner's description corresponds to our own, defined earlier in this chapter in terms of stimulation, interaction, and role behavior. The leader, we have suggested, "stimulates" others in such a way as to enable them to do what they wish to do. He plays his roles in ways that will enable others to play their own roles more effectively. Insofar as he perceives what the group wishes to do, he is also dependent upon it, which is to say that the leader is also led by the group.[26] The group will or will not respond to a leadership situation depending on its receptiveness to it. It may respond because members perceive the leader as specially endowed, or because he is an expert, or because the formal organization of the social systems leaves little or no choice but to select him, or because leader and led perceive a problem situation in the same light, or for still other

[25] A. W. Gouldner (ed.), *Studies in leadership* (New York: Harper & Bros., 1950), p. 35. For a review of the defects of the trait theory and the possible uniqueness of some leadership traits, see *ibid.*, pp. 17–45.

[26] As G. Simmel, quoting a German parliamentarian addressing his party, put it, "I am your leader, therefore I must follow you." See Superiority and subordination, trans. by A. W. Small, *Amer. J. Sociol.*, 2 (1896-97), p. 171.

reasons. In any case, the field dynamical view describes the leader as a center of high potential in a social field at a particular period of time. To repeat an earlier statement, an individual leads a group when he is able to invest his emotions and energies in such a way as to contribute to its maintenance and enhancement. He patterns group behavior, in short, neither wholly because of any special endowments that he might possess, nor entirely because the group determines its own destiny, but because, by a happy congruence of the qualities of each, his behavior stimulates the group to engage in self-directing activities. From our point of view, then, both the *leader as a person* and the *group as a potentially self-directing structure* are indispensable in describing the nature of leadership.

TYPES OF LEADERSHIP

The problem of "typing" psychological phenomena is often considered as either falsely conceived, unnecessary, or unrewarding. Since behavioral characteristics are distributed on a continuum, many psychologists hold that it is arbitrary to divide them into specific types. Objection to the "typing" of behavioral processes is based on the misconception by some psychologists that a type is an enduring psychological organization, a more or less permanent structure.[27] Typologies may, however, also be based on the assumption that traits are not distributed in a random and disorderly fashion. On the contrary, they tend to cluster into larger organizations or structures. The relatively orderly arrangement of the parts into wholes is what we have in mind by the concept of types.

The claim that the ordering of psychological phenomena into types is unprofitable depends on one's view of the objectives of science. One of these objectives—and not the least important either—especially in the early phases of a science, is classification. Typing is a form of classification, and classification has an important economic function in

27 See D. W. MacKinnon, in J. McV. Hunt (ed.), *Personality and the behavior disorders* (New York: The Ronald Press Co., 1944), Vol. I, p. 24.

science. The danger of typing behavioral traits inheres not in the typological approach but in the ineptitude of the typologist.[28] A typology is a heuristic device whose value and adequacy must be judged by its economy, by the extent to which it is able to reduce a proliferation of traits to a workable scheme. If we think of a psychological type, not as an actual entity, nor even as the average of many instances, but as a hypothetically pure case, then the process of typing individuals or groups becomes a valid enterprise. So conceived a type, say an authoritarian leader, is an ideal or pure case toward which concrete instances discovered by means of empirical research approximate in varying degrees. "Typing" then is more than a process of pigeonholing; it is a form of psychological analysis which can lead to dependable and illuminating insights into human behavior.

Authoritarian Leadership. While all leadership, as we have pointed out before, is characterized by some degree of power and domination, these traits are fundamental and conspicuous in authoritarian leadership. When we describe such leadership in terms of the psychological variables of the person who leads, we find that the authoritarian leader is extraversive, dominating, and aggressive. In his relation to others he stresses the value of discipline, deference to authority, and the outward symbols of status and power, such as the military officer's uniform and the policeman's badge. He has little or no confidence in those whom he leads, implying that he does not tolerate human errors, for these are an expression of human weakness. His leadership relies not on persuasion or group consensus but on various instruments of power which are inherent in his position or office, or in punishment, reward, and denial. In this way he is able to reinforce and perpetuate his leadership position; for when the group is not permitted to set up its own goals and can initiate action only, if at all, with the permission of the leader, its members are not motivated to act independently.

[28] See I. Chein, Personality and typology, *J. soc. Psychol., 18* (1943), 89–109.

Interpersonal acts and communication between members are discouraged if not restricted by the authoritarian leader. In this way the leader strengthens his own position and further assures his power over them. Since his followers communicate largely through him and not through one another, he becomes indispensable to them. The fear that he generates in them is a resultant not only of his power position but also of the followers' own dim awareness that without him the group not only cannot function but may disintegrate as well. To this fear is added their constant anxiety regarding future action. Since every consequential act is predetermined by the leader and information is not passed on to his followers, any future course of action must in the nature of the situation be problematic and uncertain. He rules through fear, therefore, not necessarily because he threatens to punish his followers—he may, indeed, be a "benevolent despot"—but because they cannot with any assurance anticipate a clear course of action. From the standpoint of the leader this condition has the added advantage of assuring that the followers will continue to be dependent on him and submissive in their attitudes toward him. From the standpoint of group considerations, however, the condition is largely negative; for where one almost entirely controls the other—the leader the led—there is no longer any constructive socialization, and the group is held together largely by intimidation, fear, or brute force.

This brief analysis of authoritarian leadership points up once again the role of the personality in group relations. The individual who employs authoritarian techniques in dealing with other people tends to be an "authoritarian personality." According to the investigations of Adorno and his collaborators, which we have already briefly described, the authoritarian personality is rigid and stereotypical in his cognitive organization. This rigidity predisposes him to a dogmatic and intolerant view of people and social reality. He orders his life, and imposes the same expectations upon others, by means of a conventionalized set of rules. A consequence of this is that he distorts reality to make it fit his preconceived, and often autistic, view of life and people. In order to truly convince himself of the correctness of his perceptions, he indulges in self-glorification. Since his ego, however, is essentially weak, often hidden behind a flimsy façade, and is characterized by a high degree of dependence, he develops what Frenkel-Brunswik has described as an *ego-alien self-contempt*—an attitude of profound doubt concerning himself. This doubt is made bearable only by means of distortion. Thus he will disclaim any responsibility for his own failures, blaming other people instead, or holding "external circumstances, uncontrollable forces within oneself, or heredity," responsible for them.[29]

The foregoing description should help to make clear why the authoritarian leader fears and distrusts individual and social change, and why, in the light of his absolutistic conception of himself and others, and his relation to them, he should hold on to his power position as a guaranty of his own safety.

Equally interesting and important is the fact that the followers in an authoritarian leadership relation are of the same type. The dependence and helplessness of the led predisposes them to unquestioningly follow the dictates of the leader. Both are characterized by the ego-alien self-contempt which we have cited, and both, therefore, are in need of dominating and of being dominated. While it would be unwise, in the absence of crucial empirical evidence, to generalize about all such groups, it was most true of Germany during the dictatorship of Hitler, when submission was the only way of avoiding anxiety.[30] At any rate, the evidence strongly supports, what the field-dynamic view of leadership affirms, namely, that the authoritarian leader functions effectively only in an authoritarian social situation.

[29] E. Frenkel-Brunswik, in T. W. Adorno *et al.*, *The authoritarian personality* (New York: Harper & Bros., 1950), chap. xi, especially pp. 423–28.

[30] See E. Fromm, *Escape from freedom* (New York: Farrar, Straus & Cudahy, Inc., 1941), especially chap. i, where he describes the authoritarianism and sado-masochistic mechanisms of escape.

Democratic Leadership. It should be made clear, first of all, that we do not use the word "democratic" in a complimentary or evaluative sense, but descriptively. That is, we are concerned only with the quality of the interaction between the leader and those whom he affects, and to a lesser extent with the personality variables that seem to describe him best.

The characteristic of democratic leadership that stands out sharply and consistently is that the leader is not interested in the possession of power over others but in stimulating members to participate in group activities and working as one of them in trying to achieve a collective goal. He corresponds to our previous description of the leader as an individual who enacts his role in such a way as to facilitate effective role behavior in others. He substitutes for power over others the distribution of responsibilities to every member. If he stands out from others in the group, it is not because of his possession of certain traits only, but more truly because he may serve as a resource person possessed of knowledge or wisdom, or because he has certain needed skills, or because he encourages communication and interpersonal contacts among members, or because he puts the interests of the group above personal considerations.

Ideally, the democratic leader shows all the foregoing characteristics in his behavior. If it is possible to sum up these aspects of his behavior, then perhaps we can describe him best as a person with confidence in and respect for human beings. In this he personifies an old and revered conception of democracy at its best. If in his relationship with others he acquires "power," *it is power which he shares with others.* It is power flowing from an integration of many and often conflicting interests. Clearly, in this relationship the leader, while a center of high potential, is not necessarily the focal point of the group's behavior. He leads by facilitating others to lead in the attainment of ends.

In describing the authoritarian leader, we cited his most striking personal characteristics. In order to further contrast authoritarian and democratic leadership, we shall also single out the most important traits of the democratic personality. In this description we shall again draw heavily upon the researches of Frenkel-Brunswik. Although she does not present the democratic person as such we can get a good view of him from his low scores on the various prejudice-testing instruments and interviews.

The democratic personality accepts himself and is thus relatively free of ego-contempt. In his relation to others he is primarily "love-oriented," that is, he is mild toward them and accepts them as they are. His ego is relatively strong, and while he does not have a fully integrated personality—this is an ideal in any case—he does not repress his impulses unduly but is able to intellectualize them and thereby integrate them within himself by understanding them and their role in his total psychic economy. Unlike the authoritarian person, the democratic individual is relatively flexible, and what rigidity he shows is usually distributed differentially over only some areas of his behavior. He tends to expose himself extensively to cognitive, perceptual, and emotional experiences, even if this compels him to change his preconceived notions of persons and social reality. He is *realistic-objective* regarding the world generally. Since he is, on the whole, on good terms with himself, he tends to be on good terms with others. This may well be due to the fact, as Frenkel-Brunswik remarks, that he was sufficiently loved and accepted as a child by his parents.[31]

It is these positive and "healthy" personality traits that help the democratic leader to generate and to sustain a "democratic group atmosphere." Because he is able to relate himself to others acceptingly, he encourages interpersonal contacts between them. Because he is relatively free of crippling or destructive tensions and conflicts, he becomes an effective agent for reducing such forces in others.

[31] See Frenkel-Brunswik, in Adorno *et al., The authoritarian personality,* chap. xi, *passim.*

We can sum up the qualities of democratic leadership by quoting the present writer's previous comments:

> The democratic leader is fundamentally motivated . . . by persuasion, conciliation, and a tolerance for human weakness. He is conspicuously less concerned with discipline, and his relation with his followers is friendly rather than distant and authoritarian. He tends to trust people's good sense and to believe that, with adequate guidance, they can attain their own ends. His effect on his followers is seldom dramatic, for they sense in him only a common man like themselves. He need not use propaganda in the opprobrious sense, for, having faith in people's intelligence, he relies mostly on facts and logical argument.[32]

Laissez Faire Leadership. If in the light of our position regarding the compatibility of behavior typology and behavior continuum we place the democratic and authoritarian leaderships at roughly opposite poles, then the laissez faire type falls somewhere between the two extremes, but on the democratic side of the leadership dimension. The well-known study of Lewin, Lippitt, and White, by contrasting the polar forms of leadership more sharply than the facts permit, has put the laissez faire leader in a somewhat odious light. They give the impression that this type of leader does little or nothing, that he is fundamentally a passive and unproductive individual. Every observant participant in laissez faire groups, however, must have been impressed with the fact that not infrequently this leader is more than a passive figure. While he unquestionably initiates fewer leadership acts than either the authoritarian or democratic leader, the "good" laissez faire leader is an active listener who intelligently reflects back to the group members their own thoughts sympathetically and lucidly. In our view he facilitates the process of communication among the members and helps to increase group cohesiveness and group "thinking." This interpretation is a far cry from the view which makes the laissez faire groups anarchic—a description which was introduced into the early literature of group dynamics twenty years ago by Lewin and others.

[32] H. Bonner, *Social psychology: an interdisciplinary approach* (New York: American Book Co., 1953), p. 400.

Again, some alleged laissez faire leaders are potentially authoritarian. They are concerned neither with aiding the group to solve its problems nor with intelligently reflecting its wishes but, by subtly ignoring its aims, surreptiously imposing their own wishes upon it. Being largely uninterested in the wishes of the group, these leaders can neither understand nor sympathize with it.

Some leaders, finally, are diagnosed as laissez faire individuals because the latter's behavior is consistently nonevaluative. This refraining from passing judgment on others' contributions is interpreted to be indifference. The very critics of this type of leadership, while giving high acclaim to the democratic form, fail to see that a truly democratic group can function best only when it is as free as possible from dependence on a formal leader. It might well be that instead of being a "do nothing" leader the laissez faire individual, through his own self-control and self-discipline, induces the group to engage in self-generating behavior. Should this be so, the laissez faire leader may be highly democratic and may well be an excellent demonstration of a truly sociocentric leadership. In that case the strictures of Lewin and his associates, and the criticism of those who have been aping them, must be re-examined and amended.

Bureaucratic Leadership. It is odd that very few discussions of leadership make room for the bureaucratic individual. One's perplexity is increased in view of the ubiquity of bureaucracy in contemporary life. Modern industry, business, government, religion, and the armed services are all structured on a bureaucratic organization. Since the image of the business executive looms large in our society, it has generated one of the most popular views of leadership. Then, too, an active concern of industry is the training of executives who will become leaders of the business and industrial world. The perplexity is minimized, however, when we take note of the fact that most studies dealing with the problem view it not primarily as a study of leadership but of an individual in an office. A leader from this point of view is one who holds a leader's office.[33] A general, for example, is a military leader because he occupies a leader's office. In view of the superior researches on the nature of bureaucracy, especially by certain sociologists, the foregoing definition is too simple. What we wish to know is what bureaucracy is as a social phenomenon and what role the bureaucrat plays in it as a psychological being.

Nature of bureaucracy. All roads to the understanding of bureaucracy lead to Max Weber.[34] He described it with fine discernment, and his observations are highly informative. He thus deserves a great share of the credit for making the study of bureaucracy an important problem in social science.

A bureaucracy is characterized by a number of clearly discernible traits. The controls which operate in a bureaucratic group are inherent in the office; that is, the regulations which control the behavior of the bureaucrat and his subordinates make the bureau what it is. The controls themselves are rigid, standardized, and impersonal. While individual competence plays an important role in the selection of bureaucratic leaders, the latter's decisions are determined by the formal criteria or rules which inhere in the organization. This is designed to assure objectivity in judgment and to discourage nonrational evaluations. A universal consequence of this rigid formalization is that adherence to the rules tends to become an end in itself, and like all absolutes generates results which work against the avowed interests of the group itself. The efficiency that it was designed to achieve is rendered ineffectual by hamstringing the bureaucrat and immobilizing the group itself. In this way both the bureaucrat and the bureau for which he is responsible become unadaptable and often incapable of achieving the desired ends.

[33] See Shartle and Stogdill, *Studies in naval leadership,* pp. 5–6. See further, E. C. Hughes, Institutional office and the person, *Amer. J. Sociol.,* *43* (1937), 404–13.

[34] See M. Weber, *Wirtschaft und Gesellschaft* (Tubingen: J. C. Mohr Verlag, 1922), Pt. III, chap. vi.

Bureaucratic leader. The individual who is most readily selected for bureaucratic leadership is one who potentially exhibits traits and forms of behavior conducive to bureaucratic functioning. As he persists in his office, these traits are reinforced and thus become progressively more exaggerated. An individual already very rigid becomes more inflexible as he continues in his office. He exhibits in his attitudes and behavior the characteristics already cited, and discipline which was once only a means to an end is transformed into a rigid way of life. The realization of collective ends is sacrificed to adherence to inflexible rules. A flagrant but instructive example of this incapacitating process is found in military red tape.

Since impersonality is an important characteristic of bureaucratic structure, the individual who is responsible for the affairs of a bureaucratic office is invariably impersonal. He cannot discharge his responsibilities unless he divests himself of those personal traits which we associate with affection, hostility, and other dispositions. The expectations of his office will eventually depersonalize the bureaucratic leader to the point where most of his actions are determined by an automaton conformity with his official role. Thus, characteristics which are inherent in his office eventually become attributes of his person.

While we have no empirical evidence to confirm our view, the psychological "damage" of this depersonalized role must be considerable. Being aware that his competence bestows upon him his bureaucratic status, he must nonetheless confront the fact that his authority results, not from his responsibility and skill, but almost wholly from the nature of his office. Although he has feelings and attitudes toward others in the bureaucratic hierarchy, he cannot normally express them. While this protects him from arbitrary decisions and actions, it deprives him of a sense of autonomy as a person. Unlike the relationship of leader and followers in a democratic or in a laissez faire group, the relation of a bureaucrat to his organization consists of his subservience to the domination by his office. Unlike the situation in an authoritarian group where the leader may easily become the victim of his *own* commands (Hitler, for example), the bureaucrat is subservient to an *impersonal organization.*

Followership in a bureaucratic group is similarly affected. Although members of bureaucratic organizations have a degree of security stemming from the tenure of their office, they also feel the constricting influence of the group. Since hierarchization is rigidly established, climbing the ladder of success depends largely on the subordinate's readiness to submit to the will of the bureaucrat immediately above him. Sycophancy thus becomes a desirable, if not a necessary, behavioral attribute. It should not be surprising if the foregoing traits are transmitted to other areas of behavior. Recent studies of role behavior strongly suggest a positive relation between the self and the roles which one enacts in daily life. In his excellent review of role theory Sarbin states this relation as an hypothesis to be tested. The effects of a prolonged occupation of a bureaucratic office on the self, he points out, "are such that rigidity and depersonalization become qualities that can be inferred from behavior in other (nonoccupational) roles." Citing Waller's well-known observation on what "teaching does to the teacher," Sarbin suggests that the same hypothesis may be stated about other positions in the group.[35]

Bureaucratic leadership demonstrates, but in a somewhat different way, the dependence of the leader upon others. Unlike the dyadic relationships thus far described, the relationship of the bureaucrat to others is pluralistic. He depends not alone on the members of his group but also, as Gibb has shown, on "an administrative staff (or bureaucracy), and a group of relatively inactive members"—that is, members such as those of the clerical staff with whom he has no functional relations.[36]

[35] T. R. Sarbin, Role theory, being chap. vi in G. Lindzey (ed.), *Handbook of social psychology* (Reading, Mass.: Addison-Wesley Publishing Co., Inc., 1954), Vol. I, p. 249. See also W. W. Waller, *The sociology of teaching* (New York: John Wiley & Sons, Inc., 1932).

[36] C. A. Gibb, Leadership, being chap. xxiv in Lindzey (ed.), *Handbook of social psychology,* Vol. II, p. 897.

Bureaucratic leadership, finally, by virtue of its rigidity and impersonality, provides an element of escape not so readily found in other forms. The all-pervasive force of the categoric rules which govern the bureaucrat's behavior in his office free him within definable limits from responsibility and from taking initiative, and in case of failure he can often blame the inflexible "system."

Charismatic Leadership. This type of leadership seems not to have caught the sustained interest of group psychologists. This is due in part no doubt to the fact that charismatic leadership is generally not found in small groups and to the more important reason that it arises and functions most naturally in periods of great distress. It cannot be in any way likened to other forms of leadership, for the charismatic leader is neither chosen in the sociometric sense nor imposed upon others by coercion. He does not "emerge" as a consequence of the free participation of individuals in a group, nor is he appointed as a bureaucrat of a formal organization. He is rather, as Weber who knows him well has described him, a man of "specific gifts of the body and spirit."[37] These gifts are believed to be supernatural and are not possessed by anyone else. For this very reason also group psychologists have understandably left him out of their investigations. Since there are many famous examples of this type of leadership, and because we wish to be as exhaustive as the spatial limits of this chapter permit us to be, we shall examine it briefly.

The supernatural qualities of the charismatic leader are imputed to him by his followers. The qualities are, however, reinforced by reason of his claim to an indisputable mission. Unless his followers "recognize" the traits which they attribute to him and identify themselves with the mission which he single-mindedly pursues, he will have no appreciable influence on their actions. When these conditions are present, the charismatic leader usually has an "hypnotic" effect on others. He inspires blind devotion in that his

[37] Weber, *Wirtschaft,* Pt. III, chap. ix, p. 753.

followers feel it to be their duty to recognize him as their charismatic leader.[38] Well-known examples of this form of leadership are found in Jesus, Joan of Arc, and probably Gandhi.

From a nonvaluative point of view, charismatic leadership is more a problem in mass psychology than in group dynamics. Scientifically speaking, neither Jesus nor Joan of Arc could have been completely what each was described to be by his devoted followers. Each was endowed with traits that were undoubtedly present in each in varying degrees, but which were distorted and unconsciously exaggerated by their simple and uncritical followers to satisfy a felt need in themselves. In this as in other forms of leadership the leader and his followers are mutually dependent. To hold that the charismatic leader follows only his own "inner force," as Weber holds, is to use language carelessly, for it suggests that the leader needs no one else in order to exist. That he depends upon followers is seen in explicit assertions by Weber himself. Whatever the leader's end in view may be, Weber notes, he must always *prove* his capacity to those who surrender themselves to his will, by performances which will enhance their well-being. Thus, a prophet must perform miracles, and a warrior brave deeds. The charismatic leader, in short, is always responsible to those whom he rules, and he must be able to demonstrate by deeds that he is in fact their master.[39]

LEADERSHIP SHARING

The direction of our discussion of the nature of leadership unequivocally points to shared leadership, by whatever term we describe it. While we have used evaluative terms like "democratic" or laissez faire to describe it, the leadership which we have in mind in this book is fundamentally group-oriented. Although, as we have repeatedly remarked, the personality of the leader is an element in the leadership relation, the most important consideration is the performance

[38] *Ibid.*, p. 754.
[39] *Ibid.*, p. 755.

of the group as a whole. This was stressed when we quoted Cattell as saying that "every member of the group is more or less a leader."[40] It also stems from the view, consistently stressed in the pages of this book, that in a dynamic group every member affects the behavior of the whole, even though some individuals are centers of higher potentials than others, and are therefore more likely to lead, and to lead more often, than the rest.

In view of the fact, furthermore, that in several chapters of this book we concentrate on the topics of collective problem-solving and group decision-making, a discussion of shared leadership is indispensable. But this emphasis does not imply the rejection of other approaches to the study of leadership. On the contrary, most of them are compatible with our own, and some of them are integral parts of it. We described the leader, the reader will recall, in terms of personality traits, sociometric choice, occupation of an office, group syntality, goal direction, and leadership acts. These facts are meaningful only in the context of the leader's group. From this point of view leadership is truly group-oriented only when many, if not all, members share in its expression. The stress on leadership sharing is based on empirical evidence showing that a great deal of imagination and leadership lies fallow because conventional groups do not permit it to become actualized. This has been dramatically exposed in employer-worker relationships, where the workers are given opportunities to participate in decision-making at important policy levels.

Nothing bears out so well the character of group structure as shared leadership. If the essential feature of the group is the interdependence of its members in such a way that they psychologically affect one another, then the leader is an important stimulating agent in the interactive process. Again, members are the more interdependent, the more varied the roles, including the leadership roles, are in a given group. Sharing involves not only the assumption of a single role,

[40] See above, page 173.

but as many as a given situation demands or permits. This obviously includes the role of the leader. Shared leadership is thus an important problem in group dynamics; hence, a careful study of leadership-sharing increases our understanding of group leadership.

Sharing Leadership Functions. A number of interesting and well-conceived investigations deal with this problem. We shall briefly describe only one of these, namely a field observation of 72 governmental and industrial conferences in being.[41] Of the chairmen, who were the initial leaders of the groups, 63 were above the mean of the group in organization status, and only 9 were at or below it. The measures in this study were obtained largely from the records of an observer or coder, who coded the participants' remarks from the time each began to participate until the next person spoke. After every meeting each participant was given a five-item questionnaire in order to assess his satisfaction with its various phases. Some of these ratings, all of which were highly intercorrelated, were averaged to form a measure of the group's satisfactions with the conference. Without going into more detail regarding the methods of collecting the data, we shall simply call attention to the fact that the entire procedure was meticulous and in accordance with the best canons of social science research.

The results can also be stated briefly, and they may surprise the advocate of leaderless groups. The more the chairman discharges his function of leading the group, the more satisfied the latter is with its conference. Satisfaction increases, the author points out, as "the chairman controls the group's process." Moreover "the more functionally differentiated he is, and the greater the proportion of functional units addressed to him," the greater is the satisfaction. "Satisfaction also increased the less the members participate relative to all the participating done in the group, and the

[41] L. Berkowitz, Sharing leadership in small, decision-making groups, *J. abnorm. soc. Psychol., 48* (1953), 231–38.

less they do of all the solution proposing done in the group."[42]

While satisfaction is negatively affected by shared leadership, productivity, however, is not, as seen in the fact that the proportion of agenda items completed was high. Group cohesion is also negatively affected by leadership-sharing. Cohesiveness diminishes as the designated leader, or chairman, shares his leadership with other members. Leadership-sharing is most readily accepted by the entire group when the problems with which it is dealing are urgent.

All in all, the chairman of conference groups—and we must stress that these were problem-solving groups—is expected to be the "sole major behavioral leader." Other group members in this situation who assume leadership functions are, apparently, reacted to negatively if their behavior is perceived as challenging the position of the chairman. This attitude seems to reflect the familiar negative attitude toward the nonconformist.[43]

The study by Berkowitz confirms a repeated observation in this book, namely, that people not only do not object to "strong" leadership, *provided that they know that they can participate and take the initiative if they wish;* but in certain kinds of groups, particularly problem-solving groups, they welcome it if the leader proves his competence in action. "It may be," Berkowitz states in closing, "that the group's motivation to reach an adequate problem solution as quickly as possible lessens the importance of the hypothesized group tradition."[44]

Participatory vs. Supervisory Leadership. A common condition in social science research is an inconsistency in many of its results. In a study preceding that of Berkowitz, Preston and Heintz, dealing with group cohesiveness and member satisfaction, it was shown that participatory or

[42] *Ibid.*, p. 233.

[43] *Ibid.*, p. 236. For a detailed analysis of leadership in conference groups, see H. Guetzkow (ed.), *Groups, leadership, and men* (Pittsburgh: Carnegie Press, 1951), pp. 55–67.

[44] Berkowitz, Sharing leadership, p. 238.

group-oriented leadership is much more conducive to effective group-functioning than supervisory, or leader-centered behavior. In this they confirmed the still earlier study of Lewin, Lippitt, and White, to which we have made frequent reference. Reported in the same publication as Berkowitz's study is an investigation by Hare confirming the "superiority" of leadership-sharing to formally designated leadership.[45] The reader will recall that in the latter studies changes in opinion, increase of membership satisfaction, and enlargement of cohesiveness were effected by participatory or shared leadership.

Viewed from our standpoint regarding both group formation and group leadership, these inconsistencies may only be apparent. Nevertheless, they tend to support our frequent contention that group phenomena, including group leadership, are neither simple nor uniform. Much depends upon the structure of the group, the composition of its membership, the task which it is trying to perform, the goals which it is striving to achieve, and the psychological character of its most active members. There may well exist what may be somewhat paradoxically described as a kind of *individuality of the group.*

"LEADERLESS" GROUPS. No survey of the problem of group leadership is complete that does not give at least a brief account of this controversial problem. The study and use of leaderless discussion techniques was initiated—surprisingly, in view of the simplified stereotype of the "German mind"— in Germany, according to Ansbacher.[46] The technique Ansbacher reports was used by the German navy during World War II. This fact contradicts the impressions of many American psychologists who, influenced by their somewhat distorted view of German culture, could see noth-

[45] See Chapter 3, pp. 75–76. The studies of Preston and Heintz and of Hare are cited on pp. 75–76.

[46] See H. L. Ansbacher, The history of the leaderless group discussion technique, *Psychol. Bull.,* *48* (1951), 383–91. The technique was introduced by J. B. Rieffert around 1925.

ing but complete control of German intellectual life, including its psychological research.

A leaderless group is one in which several individuals are confronted by a problem that requires cooperation among its members for its solution, and in which no single individual becomes a focal person. The subject is comprehensively discussed in various sources, and we need not go into details here.[47] In a leaderless group members are asked to carry on a discussion for a given period of time without a designated leader. The purpose is to assess leadership tendencies among its members as they participate in a free discussion. While our objective is not to evaluate the technique as a measuring device, it seems, on the whole, to have some validity in the assessment of potential leadership.[48] What the various studies confirm with relative consistency is an observation we have frequently made, that leader and follower do not function in isolation. The leadership position, as was shown in our discussion of leadership-sharing, is distributed among different members of the group in accordance with their needs or interests. It requires no special astuteness to observe that in discussion groups a discussant may be verbally active at one period and relatively quiet at another. At the risk of repetition we say again that leadership depends upon the congruence of leadership characteristics and a specific group situation.[49]

A final point, critical in tone, concerns leadership-training as it is advocated and applied by some exponents of the leaderless group *philosophy*. It is impractical for those who espouse this view to devise techniques for developing group leadership if it naturally emerges in certain interactive

[47] See B. M. Bass, The leaderless group discussion, *Psychol. Bull.*, 51 (1954), 465–92.

[48] *Ibid.*, p. 488.

[49] For a partial confirmation of this conclusion, see O.S.S. Assessment Staff, *Assessment of men* (New York: Rinehart & Co., Inc., 1948); H. H. Jennings, *Leadership and isolation* (2d ed.; New York: Longmans, Green & Co., 1950); L. F. Carter, Leadership and small group behavior, in M. Sherif and M. O. Wilson (eds.), *Group relations at the crossroads* (New York: Harper & Bros., 1953).

situations. What the advocates are, in effect, saying is not that there are leaderless groups but that leadership is shared or transmitted to different members. Leadership, in short, is "group-centered."[50]

The above remarks are not made in disparagement of programs in leadership-training, but to call attention to the inconsistency of training leaders by persons who exalt leaderless groups uncritically. Such training groups as the National Training Laboratory for Group Development and its associated centers like those in Chicago and Denver and at the University of Illinois are recognized for their superior performance. They show that leadership, like other skills, can be learned.

CONCLUSION

No one is more distressingly aware than the present writer of the shortcomings of this chapter on leadership. In its introductory paragraphs we called attention to the existence of a prodigious amount of research, both theoretical and operational, on the subject. Perhaps the very abundance of the literature dealing with it is an effective deterrent to its systematic conceptualization. Indeed, it has multiplied our views of the nature of leader, leadership, and follower, and the richness of this variety is in a way a pleasure to behold. Investigators are so busy studying the problem that they have little time and perhaps even less inclination to formulate a systematic view of the nature of leadership. Expositors like the present one are frustrated and baffled in their attempts to see the woods instead of the trees. Whatever they come up with in the way of a consistent description and formulation is bound to disappoint many readers and to invite the critical shafts of those who have their own theory to defend.

[50] This term naturally suggests itself to anyone dealing with group-sharing, but it was first used formally by Bovard, and later by Gordon, who deals with it in book-length detail. See E. W. Bovard, Group structure and perception, *J. abnorm. soc. Psychol.*, *46* (1951), 398–405; T. Gordon, *Group-centered leadership* (Boston: Houghton Mifflin Co., 1955).

What, in effect, has emerged from the foregoing pages, which, while in need of confirmation by further testing and more testing still, gives us a clear and plausible image of group leadership? We shall describe it briefly in the remaining part of this chapter.

The nature of leadership is dependent upon the nature of social groups. A social group we have defined at different places in this book as a complex, or system, or social field which arises whenever two or more people enter into an interdependent relationship. The behavior of each is affected and modified by *the relationship involved in being a member*, or more concretely, by the behavior of the other. Group behavior, accordingly, can be described wholly neither in terms of the psychological variables of the individual members nor the collective structure of the group, but only by their interdependence. Since groups differ, moreover, we cannot assign unitary traits to them. The members who are interactive parts therefore also cannot be described by means of unitary traits. This fact is true of the leader as well: he is not characterized by the possession of permanent and unitary traits, but differs with changes in group organization and group goals. The basic concept of the *interact*, which we employed in Chapter 1 (see p. 22), explains the behavior of the individuals, including the leader and the followers. This interactional nature of individual-group relations, then, takes account of all the leadership factors which we have already described, namely, personality variables, the organization of the group, the goals and tasks with which the leader and the group are faced, the nature and needs of the followers, group performance, and the perceptions which leader and followers have of one another. None of these attributes taken separately, however, accounts for leadership. They, too, form an interactive relationship in which they mutually affect and modify one another. No matter how superior the qualities of a potential leader, he will not become a center of high potential unless he is perceived as such by others, unless he satisfies their needs and aids them in reaching their goals. A leader who conforms to this description need be neither superior as an individual nor "normal" as a person. The effect of Hitler upon the German masses is a supreme example. In their perception of him as a man who promised to fulfill their needs, they followed him uncritically. While the structure of democratic groups is such as to encourage leadership-sharing and while the blind obedience to the leader's role is completely absent, the interactive, interdependent, mutually perceptive attributes are what differentiate it from authoritarian domination. Leadership as an interactive process, in short, consists of the free communication between the individual who for the time being is designated as a leader and the followers who depend on his initiating behavior.

CHAPTER 7

Collective Problem-Solving

Thus far we have discussed group tensions and their resolution by considering intergroup conflicts and adjustments and the role of the leader in facilitating the production of consensus and harmony among group members. The present chapter continues this mode of group analysis by considering the process of problem-solving.

Psychologically, when a group, like an individual, is faced with a problem or difficulty, its condition may be described as a state of disequilibrium or tension. Since a group in disequilibrium "seeks" to reach an optimum steady state, to overcome the barrier which it faces, or to resolve the tensions produced by indecision, the question of collective problem-solving or group decision-making takes on central importance.[1] Solving its collective problem aids a group in achieving integration, whereas failure to do so generates tensions and conflicts within it.

[1] Lest we convey the impression that we are arguing for a static theory of homeostasis and thereby contradicting all that we have asserted regarding the nature of dynamic groups, we must add that the steady state we have in mind is von Bertalanffy's "steady state in open systems," in which there is constant adaptation to other states outside itself and an endless differentiation and integration on higher levels of organization. See L. von Bertalanffy, *Problems of life* (New York: John Wiley & Sons, Inc., 1952).

In Chapter 1 we reviewed some of the early investigations concerning the effect of the presence of others in learning and problem-solving situations. The researches of F. H. Allport and J. F. Dashiell, we said, found that social situations have, on the whole, a facilitating effect on "group thinking." The investigations of Mayer, Meumann, and others before them, we found, were similar and set the stage for later studies of group effects upon individual performance. During the past twenty-five years an increasing number of studies have been carried on in this area, and in the past decade in particular the subject of collective problem-solving or group decision-making has become a topic of major interest in group dynamics.[2]

STUDIES IN COLLECTIVE PROBLEM-SOLVING

The sense of much of what we have said in this book is that people are more ready to accept and to put into action changes in which they themselves had a free opportunity to play a part. Much empirical evidence is now available, furthermore, to show that in this process of group self-decision both the amount and quality of productiveness is positively affected by member participation. This is not to mention the probability that when collective problem-solving takes place the participants are often more independent and yet more free of hostile attitudes toward one another.

In view of the importance of decision-making in group dynamics today, a better understanding can be obtained if we analyze the nature of the problem and cite a few well-known—and probably influential—studies dealing with it.

A number of careful studies, including controlled laboratory investigations, on the relative superiority of individual and group performances in problem-solving have been pub-

[2] See for example the following references: K. Gordon, A study of aesthetic judgments, *J. exp. Psychol.*, *6* (1923), 36–42; W. A. Barton, Jr., Group activity versus individual activity in developing ability to solve problems in first-year algebra, *J. educ. admin. Supervis.*, *12* (1926), 512–18; E. B. South, Some psychological aspects of committee work, *J. appl. Psychol.*, *11* (1927), 348–68, 437–64; G. B. Watson, Do groups think more efficiently than individuals? *J. abnorm. soc. Psychol.*, *23* (1928), 328–36.

lished during the past quarter-century. All are studies of groups in which the resources of their members are utilized to adjust themselves to one another or to effect changes in attitudes or behavior or to reach decisions regarding a course of action that would result in satisfying the needs of all. The researches, furthermore, are either based on the *assumption* that every member is a potential resource person, that is, one who possesses knowledge or skill, or they discover that most if not all members in reality *are* sources on which the group can draw.

Much has been made by these studies of the "superiority" of the group to the individuals composing it in the solution of complex problems. It always smacks of personification to impute cognitive attributes to group behavior. Instead of describing the group's behavior in problem-solving as superior (or inferior), it is better to say that it *differs* from the solutions of its individual members. A group solution is always the *resultant* of the ideas, knowledges, and ratiocinative skills of some or all its interactive members. When it is "superior" to the solution by separate individuals, it is characterized by more solutions, more correct answers, fewer errors, and the like.

The questions facing us are, broadly speaking, the following: When is a group solution better than an individual solution? Why, when it is better, *is* it better? What group conditions inhibit the communication of individual resources? Do group solutions tap the resources of every member?

We shall discuss the issue with these questions in mind, not in this order but by the bearing of their importance on the total problem.

THINKING IN COOPERATING GROUPS. An early, and by now a model, investigation under controlled conditions of the collective problem-solving process was made by Marjorie Shaw.[3] She compared the ability of individuals and cooperating groups of four members in solving given problems. In

[3] M. E. Shaw, A comparison of individual and small groups in the rational solution of complex problems, *Amer. J. Psychol.*, *44* (1932), 491–504.

contrast to earlier researches, which we have already described, in which an individual learned or solved problems merely in the *presence* of other individuals, Shaw's subjects worked as *cooperative* groups. While the problems upon which the subjects worked were not yet the kind faced in real-life situations, they had certain distinct advantages for controlled experimentation. The problems had only one answer, they permitted only one type of best solution, and they were relatively free of the emotional bias which often characterizes problem-solving in real-life situations.

The subjects in the experiment were largely graduate students in a class in Social Psychology at Columbia University. The experiment was divided into two halves, with three problems in the first half and three in the second given two weeks later. The first half was composed of two groups of four women each and three groups of four men each. At the same time nine men and twelve women were working on the same problems individually in the same room. The second half was composed of two groups of four men each and three groups of four women each, while ten men and seven women worked individually in the same room. No rationale for the segregation of the sexes was offered other than that, in general, this arrangement would make for "better cooperation and more smoothly running groups."[4]

It would require more space than we can permit to describe the reasoning problems in this experiment. A well-known example will be sufficient. On one side of a river are three wives and their husbands. All the men but none of the women can row a boat. No man will allow his wife to be in the presence of another man unless he is also in the boat. The problem is to get them to the other side of the river in a boat carrying only three persons at a time.

The results in Shaw's experiment are impressive. Individual subjects made only 5 correct solutions out of a possible 63, whereas groups made 8 correct solutions out of a

[4] *Ibid.*, p. 492. This explanation may only reflect a culturally induced bias, and is probably, therefore, the mechanism of disregarding any evidence which might disturb an original attitude.

possible 15. In percentage this means that only 7.9 per cent of individual solutions were correct, whereas 53 per cent of group solutions were correct. Again, although both individuals and groups obviously give erroneous solutions, the individuals were found to make errors sooner on the average than the groups. The groups also check errors more frequently and reject more incorrect suggestions than individuals do. This conclusion is in line with studies of individual learning and problem-solving. It has been reasonably established that learning and cognitive "sets," or established habits, often prevent an individual from seeing new suggestions or act as impediments to discovering errors. The "superiority" of the group in problem-solving must then be in part attributed to the fact that individual "expectancies" do not have an opportunity to express themselves, and to the fact that errors are more frequently eliminated. In contrast to an individual a group has no *habitual way* of solving a problem and is not, accordingly, blind to new suggestions and solutions.

Although Shaw's study supports the view that groups are relatively superior to individuals in problem-solving, it is fair to ask whether the statistical significance is not made spuriously high. Inasmuch as the same number of individuals are working on problems in groups and individually, it would seem that the comparison should be made not between the average of groups and the average for individuals, but rather between the number of solutions gotten from this particular number of subjects in the group situation as compared with the individual situation. Certainly, when individuals are grouped, the problem-solving capacity may still function. Thus, one able individual in a group of five less able individuals may well raise the number of solutions in this group of five as compared with the average number of solutions obtained from each of the five working separately, but this hardly means that the group situation improved the problem-solving performance of these five individuals.

Shaw's conclusion should not be generalized to include *all* groups. While we have no experimental evidence in our support, anthropological and sociological studies of stable and semipermanent groups strongly suggest that the more permanent a group is, the more likely it will view problems from an established perspective. Certain simple groups and communities seem to learn little or nothing from group cooperation. They continue in the same direction and do the same things in the same way, with the benefit of close interaction, without substantial changes, even when the established ways are detrimental. A glaring example of the place of rigidity in group observation, though not in group thinking, is the child's resemblance to his father in Trobriand society. The mores impose the view on everyone that a child cannot resemble anyone but the father, even though to an impartial outsider it is obvious that it looks like the mother, or some other blood relative.

It appears, then, that small, dynamic, and somewhat impermanent groups benefit most from collective efforts to solve problems. In such groups latent attitudes, or habituated ways of thinking, have not been established, thus making room for novelty and new cognitive directions. They have no characteristic method of approaching a problem, no precedents to rely upon, and therefore obvious and simple solutions are not so readily overlooked. Cognitive sets and group inertia inhibit communication and exchange, thereby impairing the effectiveness of thinking in some types of groups.

The fourth question, concerning the extent of the contribution of group members to the solution of problems is also answered by Shaw's study. She found that all members do not participate equally in the solution of problems. This is compatible with what we saw in our discussion of leadership—namely, that, although not all individuals participate in group discussion, members feel satisfied with the group if they know that, should they want to participate, they are free to do so.

Our discussion, summarized, shows that (1) the group is superior to the individual *when* it carefully and critically assesses the contributions of its members; (2) it is superior *because* it destroys habitual sets and eliminates false starts; (3) it does not function efficiently when it is so formalized that free communication is inhibited; and (4) group solutions do not tap the resources of every member. In an ideal group, where every individual contributes his own productive capacity, collective solutions should generally be superior to individual efforts. No one individual, we must assume, possesses the required skills, ideas, and knowledges to answer every question with which he is faced. Participation in cooperative solutions in which the creative potential of every member is tapped promises to compensate for the limitations of the individual. In any case some researches reveal that under the conditions which we have briefly specified, groups perform better than individuals working on the same tasks in isolation.

ROLE OF LEADERSHIP IN GROUP THINKING. Group thinking or problem-solving is also facilitated by effective leader-participation. Maier has demonstrated that a leader can raise the level of group thinking by asking good questions and influencing members to engage in effective thinking.[5] To accompish this the leader has to possess skill, a grasp of the group-creative process, and be able to produce a permissive atmosphere. Maier also found that group members will not accept suggestions from a leader which have little or no merit and which are contrary to their interests. The improvement in group thinking by the leader's participation, according to Maier, was due to the fact that the leader created opportunities for the expression of minority views. If a minority view has merit, Maier held, it should be able to influence the quality of the group's thinking.

To test these ideas, Maier made an experiment which we shall outline very briefly. He was careful, it should be stressed, to prevent other contributions of the leader than

[5] N. R. F. Maier and A. R. Solem, The contribution of a discussion leader to the quality of group thinking: the effective use of minority opinions, *Hum. Relat.*, 5 (1952), 277–88.

the ones to be examined from affecting the results, and to set up a control group in which a similar discussion took place without a formal discussion leader. A total of 353 students of both sexes participated. They were divided into 67 groups, 34 of which had a discussion leader and 33 an observer who did not lead the discussion. Results were recorded for the groups before and after discussion. The problem on which all the groups worked was briefly as follows: A man bought a horse for $60, sold it for $70, bought it back for $80 and sold it again for $90. What was his profit?

The results supported the hypothesis that group thinking can be improved by the leader's influence. Prior to the discussion the correct answer was given by 45.8 per cent of the 177 persons in the "leader" groups and 44.3 per cent of the 176 members in the "observer" groups. In other words, the memberships of the two types of discussion groups were similar in their performance prior to discussion. Following the group discussions, however, the correct answers of the "leader" groups rose to 83.6 per cent (an improvement of 82.5 per cent), while the observer groups rose to only 71.6 per cent (an improvement of 61.6 per cent). A *chi* square test showed, furthermore, that the difference was significant at less than the 1 per cent level.[6]

Maier's interpretation of the results is worth noting. As we have already pointed out, the leader created a permissive atmosphere in which minority opinions had a constructive effect upon other members. In typical discussion or deliberative groups the majority view exerts great pressure on the opinions of the rest of the members. If the majority opinion is wrong, its influence on the outcome of the discussion is undesirable. In the "leader" group, however, the social pressure of the majority is reduced and the minority opinions have an opportunity to exert their influence. "In protecting a minority opinion from the social pressure of the majority, the leader allows the minority to have enough influence to make a possible contribution to the quality of a group's

[6] *Ibid.*, pp. 280–81.

thinking."[7] In short, the democratic leadership technique not only aids in effecting cooperation but is also effective in improving the quality of a problem solution.

EFFECT OF LEADERSHIP TRAINING ON PROBLEM-SOLVING. In the experiments of Maier which we have cited important light is thrown on what goes on when a group is trying to solve problems collectively. In a later study Maier explores still another aspect, namely, the effect of training leaders to use a permissive approach.[8] There are two questions bound up in this problem, namely, whether training affects the leader's behavior and whether it facilitates the solving of problems in a group.

To answer the questions Maier conducted an experiment in which trained and untrained groups were given the same problems to solve. Both groups were industrial personnel consisting mostly of first-line supervisors and intermediate management. The experiment was set up as a multiple role-playing situation. The uncontrolled variable of personality differences was neutralized by using a large number of groups. The experimental variable was the training in group decision which was given to the experimental groups but not to the control groups. (Although we shall discuss *group decision-making* later, we wish to inform the reader that group decision-making is not different from collective problem-solving, but is an integral stage or step in the complete process.)

Forty-four groups (the experimental group) were exposed to eight hours of presentation on the method of group decision-making and how it could be adapted to dealing with job problems. They had impressed upon them that employees will collaborate upon and accept a solution if they are given the opportunity to participate in their own decision-making. The foremen's functions, they were informed, are

[7] *Ibid.*, p. 285. See also an earlier study: N. R. F. Maier, The quality of group decisions as influenced by the discussion leader, *Hum. Relat.*, 3 (1950), 155–74.

[8] N. R. F. Maier, An experimental test of the effect of training on discussion leadership, *Hum. Relat.*, 6 (1953), 161–73.

to furnish the group with facts and to carry on a permissive discussion. The groups were also given four hours of discussion which permitted a free expression of the participants' attitudes, to ask questions, and to air personal views. The presentation and discussion periods were combined in three training periods of 2½ hours each. The role-playing problem was an integral part of the training program.

Thirty-six other groups (the control group) received no training except for a lecture which introduced the role-playing problem. The lecture dealt with resistance to change, with particular reference to the importance of differences in employee attitudes, the importance of accepting exchanges of jobs in order to facilitate the changes, the need for recognizing motivational differences in employees, and the importance of listening to the employees in order the better to understand them.

Role-playing was introduced into both the control and experimental sets of groups. Both were told that they were going to participate in solving a lifelike job problem. The latter, they were told, would involve a foreman who must discuss a job situation with three employees, and it was explained that this task would give them "a firsthand experience with the types of influence which operate." They were further informed that they would be divided into groups of four and given instruction regarding the part each was to play in the situation.

All subjects, finally, were divided into groups of four. Each group was given a set of instructions, one page for each member, and the member who took the set from the assistant was made the foreman. He kept the top page and passed a page with a role to each of the other three persons.

The role-playing situation dealt with resistance to change. The men work in teams on an assembly job. To reduce boredom they change jobs. The skills of the men would be more effectively used, however, if each man continued to perform the same operation. This desire to change gave the foreman an opportunity to introduce the problem of change and to initiate discussion of the problem under consideration.

The results may be briefly stated. The untrained groups had a greater variety of failures. Failures were results in which the groups either refused to change their method of working, reached no decisions in the allotted time, or in which the foreman imposed his own solutions, against which the workers rebelled. Successes were results in which employees were willing to change their work methods in conformity with the time-study man's figures. There were also compromise solutions but for the sake of simplification we omit them here. In the trained leader groups 4.5 per cent were failures and 59.1 per cent were successes.

The results of this investigation show that resistance to change can be markedly reduced by a leader who has been trained in group-decision techniques. The untrained, in contrast to the trained, leader tries to motivate a group to change its work methods by stressing that the workers can make more money and by refuting objections which only create hostility in them. The trained discussion leader, on the other hand, presents the situation as a problem to be solved and encourages suggestions and criticism on the part of the workers. In short, leaders trained in group-decision techniques can favorably influence discussion procedures in the direction of the successful solution of a group's problems.

Role of Opposition in Problem-Solving. In our discussion of the place of competition and conflict in group learning we stressed the fact that these psychological forces tend to affect cognitive processes adversely. Some studies show that consensus is difficult to attain under conditions of intense rivalry and competition. Nevertheless, since these factors are bound to exist in democratic groups, they must be understood in the light of their final effects and of the nature of the problem to be solved. To repeat an earlier observation, competition and conflict are not in themselves destructive of group functioning, and may even be a means to consensus and collective problem-solving. They may result in a restructuring of field organization. As Simmel pointedly observed many years ago, conflict itself is a form of socialization. The paradox—if such it is—is resolved if we use the dialectical notion of the relation between contraries. Employing this concept, opposition may be described as "a high tension state involving success or failure by a social group in transcending the barriers to freedom of locomotion. When the conflict ends in the transcendence of the barriers, equilibrium is restored." While therefore it appears to be a divisive element, conflict may have integrative effects—a "resolution of the tensions between the contraries."[9]

A theoretical formulation of this problem, however, is insufficient. We must look for empirical or experimental data to confirm or infirm it. There are a number of good studies dealing with the issue; we shall select one by Guetzkow and Gyr, as one of the better ones.[10]

The data of the Guetzkow-Gyr study were obtained by observing business and governmental decision-making conferences involving about seven hundred individuals. The participants were divided into groups from five to twenty persons for the purpose of making policy and staff decisions. The purpose of the research on these groups was to answer the question: Are there "conditions under which tension or conflict within a conference terminates in agreement or consensus among the participants, as contrasted with other conditions under which conflict ends in disagreement?"[11]

Conflict in this study was defined by important differences of opinion among the members regarding suggestions, interpretations, solutions, and so forth, which were given during the conferences. Consensus was defined by agreements with and support and approval of suggestions or solutions. Expressions of conflict and consensus were recorded by an observer throughout the conferences. Observations were also made by another observer to determine if the behavior of the participants was intellectually or affectively moti-

[9] H. Bonner, Field theory and sociology, *Sociol. Soc. Res.*, 33 (1949), 171–79. See G. Simmel, *Soziologie* (Leipzig: Duncker und Humblot, 1908), p. 247.

[10] H. Guetzkow and J. Gyr, An analysis of conflict in decision-making groups, *Hum. Relat.*, 7 (1954), 367–82.

[11] *Ibid.*, p. 368.

vated. Conflicts were of two kinds, namely, substantive and affective. Substantive conflicts were rooted in the nature of the task performed, that is, in the suggestions or solutions proposed; affective conflicts were those derived from the personal and emotional phases of the members' interpersonal relations.

Since a full statement regarding the empirical findings would be both long and complex, we can do no better than to reproduce the investigators' own summary. They write,

> There are a number of conditions under which both types of conflict—substantive and affective—result in consensus. There are also striking and significant differences between groups in conflict in the factors associated with consensus. A group in substantive conflict tends to achieve consensus by emphasizing those factors which positively promote consensus. A group in affective conflict tends to achieve consensus by reducing those forces which hinder the achievement of consensus. This reduction is largely achieved by withdrawing from a situation in which these forces are present.[12]

The results of the investigation confirm, in short, one of our frequent reiterations, namely, that reaching decisions or solving problems in groups may be either inhibited or promoted, depending on different conditions. There are no data and no theoretical reasons which would justify the generalization that conflict and competition are necessarily detrimental to productive group deliberation. It has been known for a long time that rivalry for a shared goal may be more or less productive, depending on the structure of the group in which it is taking place.[13]

Effect of Group Size. The problem of group size is a recurring one in group dynamics, and a knowledge of the optimum size of a group engaged in problem-solving is of considerable practical value. Simmel, who formulated numerous theoretical problems concerning social interaction, was a pioneer in this as in so many other phases of group

[12] *Ibid.*, p. 373.

[13] See J. B. Maller, Cooperation and competition: an experimental study in motivation, *Contrib. Educ.*, No. 384. New York: Teachers College, Columbia University, 1929.

processes, and was early cognizant of the importance of group size as a determinant of interindividual relations. In his discussion of the dyad and the triad he demonstrated that small groups have qualities which disappear when they become larger. He observed, on the basis of theory rather than empirical research, that certain group characteristics appear only in structures above or below a certain number of interactive individuals.

The small amount of dependable evidence which we possess leads to the conclusion that dynamic or interactive groups tend to be small. One investigator has found that they range in size from two to seven, with an average size of three.[14] He adds that larger groups are "molecular arrangements of small groups."

While a number of investigators agree on one size, others hold different views. On the basis of existing knowledge of group learning and group thinking it is clear that in problem-solving and decision-making enough persons must exist in interaction with one another to initiate suggestions; yet not so many as to bog down the free communication of ideas. The problem, we shall see later, is particularly important in the area of group psychotherapy. Groups consisting of six to ten persons offer maximum conditions for interaction in group problem-solving.

One of the most rigorous tests of group size has been made by Bales and his associates.[15] Most of the groups studied by them were, in the widest sense, problem-solving groups. Two of them were therapy groups, which, by our definition, are also problem-solving in character. While the investigators were concerned primarily with acts of communication, their study throws light upon the importance of group size. It is to be noted that the groups which they

[14] J. James, A preliminary study of the size determinant in small group interaction, *Amer. sociol. Rev., 16* (1951), 474–77. For an excellent analysis of the problem of group size, see H. A. Thelen, Principle of least group size, *The School Rev., 57* (1949), 141–47.

[15] R. F. Bales, F. L. Strodtbeck, T. M. Mills, and M. E. Roseborough, Channels of communication in small groups, *Amer. sociol. Rev., 16* (1951), 461–68.

studied were all small, their size ranging from three to ten persons. Groups of this size were found to be highly interactive, affording a maximum number of initiating and receiving acts by every member.

Hare's investigation throws further light on our problem.[16] He demonstrated, by means of a series of tested hypotheses, that the pattern of interaction differs in different groups, and that these patterns afford less satisfaction and agreement as the size of the group increased.

It will help the reader to get a sharper idea of the importance of group size if we summarize the seven major and the three minor hypotheses, of which all but three were substantiated. These hypotheses are set forth in the following paragraphs.

Consensus in group discussion decreases as the size of the group is increased from five to twelve. For groups of five the average amount of agreement after discussion increases to 0.88; for the groups of twelve, 0.67. The average amount of change in consensus for the small groups is significantly larger than the average amount of change in the large groups. Also, members in a group of five individuals change their opinion more toward agreement than those in a group of twelve.

Again, the leader's skill affects the amount of change in consensus in all groups of the same size. Although this hypothesis is only partially verified, it conforms to our earlier conclusion that the role of the leader is important in group problem-solving (see pp. 205–7). The leader in the group of five, furthermore, tends to have a greater influence in group decision-making than the leader in a group of twelve. This confirms the hypothesis that leaders in small groups have a more positive effect on group discussion and group problem-solving. Hare's study, moreover, was that nonleaders have more influence on the group when the group is large. This was not, however, substantiated significantly.

16 A. P. Hare, A study of interaction and consensus in different sized groups, *Amer. sociol. Rev.*, *17* (1952), 261–67.

Another hypothesis which the study confirmed was that, given a limited period of time—an average of about fifteen minutes—a group of five feels that it has enough time for discussion, while a group of twelve feels that this is insufficient time for the same purpose. Both leaders and followers voice approximately the same opinion regarding sufficiency of time in the two different-sized groups.

If members are not given sufficient opportunities to participate, because of the time factor, they express dissatisfaction with the group. There also are more dissatisfied members in the large groups. The followers, particularly, show a significant increase in dissatisfaction as the group is increased from five to twelve.

In larger groups, members tend not to participate as frequently as in smaller ones, because they feel that the group's size renders their contributions unimportant. Since the difference among the leaders in the different-sized groups in this regard is not significant, even though it tends in the expected direction, the hypothesis is only partially verified.

All in all, this study, like a number of others, shows that as the size of the group is increased the degree of consensus and satisfaction with it decreases when the time for discussion is limited; and that with the increase in size above a certain number (in this study twelve) factionalism is a frequent outcome.

One more study of the effect of group size which we shall briefly relate is that of Taylor and Faust.[17] Using as their subjects 105 students from the introductory course in psychology, the investigators divided them into fifteen individual respondents, fifteen groups of two members, and fifteen groups of four members. All were given four problems a day for four successive days. The problems were of the type popularized on radio and television programs, in which various objects were to be identified as animal, vegetable, or

[17] D. W. Taylor and W. L. Faust, Twenty questions: efficiency in problem solving as a function of size of group, *J. exp. Psychol., 44* (1952), 360–68.

mineral. While the experiment was designed to answer other questions as well, the question of importance here concerns the relative efficiency in problem-solving as determined by the size of the group.

The results were generally similar to those of other studies. Group performance was superior to individual performance in the number of questions answered, the number of failures, and elapsed time for each problem. The performance of groups of four was not superior to that of groups of two, except that the groups of four had fewer failures. In terms of the time required for the solution of problems, the performance of individuals was superior to that of groups; but the performance of groups of two was superior to that of groups of four.

The authors suggest that the fact that there were negligible differences between groups of two and four may mean that the optimum-size group is not larger than four. This is, of course, only an inference, and its substantiation will require much more careful research than has been done to date. Since optimum size is still a controversial issue, we may logically assume that the "ideal" size would be a group in which every member has an opportunity to contribute according to his maximum ability to the solution of a group's problem. As we have stressed it on several occasions, and as Taylor and Faust themselves point out, increasing the size of the group within "efficient" limits reduces the persistence of wrong "sets" which may have been present in a smaller group, very much in the way that wrong "sets" which tend to persist in the individual problem-solvers are eliminated by exposure to a diversity of suggestions and ideas. Finally, to reiterate still another prior statement, in a group that is small, but not too small, the abilities of every or most members can be readily tapped. In a group that is too large the permissiveness and freedom of communication, which we have found to be exceedingly important in problem-solving, become an obstacle; for in this situation there is a tendency for a few dominant individuals to monopolize the time, and thus deprive others of the opportunity to express themselves.[18]

Effect of the Problem in Problem-Solving. It has long been suspected that the nature of the task facing a group has something to do with its performance. The results in a free-response situation may be different from those in a highly structured one or from one in which the problem is such as to permit only fixed alternatives. Thorndike found that the superiority of group solutions is sometimes due to the wide range of responses afforded by a task situation. In four tasks which he presented for solution, each was designed in two forms, the two differing from each other in the range of alternative responses. For this purpose he administered two forms of the CAVD Sentence Completion Test and the CAVD Vocabulary Test. One form permitted unrestricted completions and the other permitted only multiple-choice answers. A third instrument was a Limericks test, again in two forms, one requiring the addition of three lines, the other of only one. A fourth task was the *free construction* of a cross-word puzzle and the *solving* of one already devised. Thorndike found that, not only were the performances of the group on all four problems generally superior to those of individuals, but the group was superior on the unstructured or "free" forms particularly. His experiment established what has been amply confirmed in more recent investigations, namely, that the wider the range of alternatives, the better a group performs the task.[19]

But quite different results were reported in a more recent study by McCurdy and Lambert, thus confronting us with

[18] A few other good studies on the effect of group size are suggested: L. Carter, W. Haythorn, B. Meirowitz, and J. Lanzetta, The relation of categorization and ratings in the observation of group behavior, *Hum. Relat.*, *4* (1951), 239–54; J. R. Gibb, The effects of group size and of threat reduction in a problem-solving situation, *Amer. Psychologist, 6* (1951), 324; F. F. Stephan and E. G. Mishler, The distribution of participation in small groups: an exponential approximation, *Amer sociol. Rev., 17* (1952), 598–608.

[19] R. L. Thorndike, On what type of task will a group do well? *J. abnorm. soc. Psychol., 33* (1938), 409–13.

the not infrequent inconsistencies of results in group-dynamic investigations.[20] In their experiment thirteen groups of three persons each and eleven individuals separately were given a complex task to perform. This task consisted of changing the positions of from one to six switches which were wired in such a way that a light flashed on when the pattern of switch positions tallied with that on a master control board. The subjects were scored according to the number of correct patterns completed within a specified time period. In the three-person groups each subject was responsible for two switches, whereas individual subjects had six switches. The three-person groups' progress depended on the quality of each individual's performance on the task.

The authors found that individual scores were markedly superior to those of the three-person groups. They explained this difference by suggesting that a group is very likely composed of at least one or two members who were sufficiently careless concerning the experimental instruction to make errors in their performance. The importance of the results lies, of course, in the demonstration that the nature of the task or problem affects the quality of group performance.

Role of Individual Motivation in Group Performance. At the risk of being tedious we must remind the reader once more that individual psychological characteristics must not be excluded from the study of group behavior. The interdependence of the individual and the group is a stubborn fact.

The problem of motivation has already been examined in the studies cited in this book of competition and rivalry in group behavior. The studies on ego-involvements highlight the importance of motivation in both individual and group performance. If an individual knows that he can perform a task or achieve a goal only by cooperating with others, his determination to work with a group increases markedly.

[20] H. G. McCurdy and W. E. Lambert, The efficiency of small human groups in the solution of problems requiring genuine cooperation, *J. Pers.*, *20* (1952), 478–94.

Horwitz convincingly demonstrated this fact in an effective recent experiment.[21] Horwitz's problem was the following: "Can the motivational concepts which have been developed for individuals who are acting for their *own goals* be applied to individuals who are acting so that a group will achieve *group goals?*"

The measurement device employed in this experiment is an adaptation of Zeigarnik's now well-known method of recall of interrupted tasks. It was applied to the group situation within the conceptual framework of Lewin's topological and vector psychology which we discussed in Chapters 1 and 2. The experiment is complex and ingenious and as such difficult to summarize and still convey the necessary information, let alone the meticulous care taken by the investigator in designing it. The subjects of the experiment were sorority women placed into eighteen groups, each group consisting of five members, and assigned the task of working together on jigsaw puzzles. At a point approximately midway through each task the subjects voted on whether or not the group should complete it. After the votes were taken, work on the problems was either halted, partly completed, or fully completed.

The principal, although obvious, findings of Horwitz's study are these: (1) when the group agrees to complete a task, the members become motivated to reach the group's goal; (2) when the group does not wish to continue working on the task, motivation to work toward a goal is not generated; (3) the individual's motives to strive for the group's goal is not affected by whether he does or does not participate in deciding upon the group's continuation with the task. If he accepts the consensus of the group, he will behave as if he had participated in its decisions; that is, he will desire for the group to continue with and to complete its task. Group productivity in problem-solving is thus seen to be affected, not primarily by the goals of the individual

21 M. Horwitz, The recall of interrupted group tasks: an experimental study of individual motivation in relation to group goals, *Hum. Relat.*, 7 (1954), 3–38.

members, but by their desire to see the group as a whole achieve its collective ends.[22]

NATURE OF GROUP DECISION-MAKING

On a preceding page of this chapter (p. 207), we referred to decision-making as an integral phase of the process of group problem-solving. In his book on *Group-centered Leadership,* which we have already cited, Gordon divides the group problem-solving process into four interrelated stages. These stages consist of (1) facing a problem; (2) diagnosing it, in order to determine cause-and-effect relationships; (3) making decisions regarding how the problem is to be solved; and (4) carrying out the decision in action.[23]

Decision-making, which alone concerns us at the moment, is a very important step in the process of collective problem-solving. In "democratic" groups of the type we have been describing problems are solved by the constructive participation of most members. In the "traditional" group, which is still abundantly found in most areas of problem-solving, the decisions are made by a designated leader who holds a commanding position in the power structure. In education, business, industry, and other vital areas of societal life decisions pertaining to the functioning of groups are still largely the province of "experts" or of peremptory authority. Theirs is the right to settle issues, to determine and adjudicate disputes. The more important the issue or dispute is, the less is it delegated for consideration by the group whom it vitally concerns. An important consequence of authoritarian decision-making has been that it has, first, prevented the development of group self-direction and, second, used the failures of

[22] See further, N. T. Fouriezos, M. L. Hutt, and H. Guetzkow, Measurement of self-oriented needs in discussion groups, *J. abnorm. soc. Psychol.,* *45* (1950), 682–90; D. G. Marquis, H. Guetzkow, and R. W. Heyns, A social psychological study of the decision-making conference, in H. Guetzkow (ed.), *Groups, leadership, and men* (Pittsburgh: Carnegie Press, 1951); S. Schachter and R. Hall, Group-derived restraints and audience persuasion, *Hum. Relat.,* *5* (1952), 397–406.

[23] T. Gordon, *Group-centered leadership* (Boston: Houghton Mifflin Co., 1955), p. 61.

the group as an argument for the latter's incompetence. Little or no thought was given by persons in authority to the fact that others, especially a group of coacting individuals, could hardly be expected to develop skill in decision-making if they had no opportunity to assume responsibility. When given an opportunity to reach its own decisions, a group tends initially to confirm an authority's conviction by the uncertainty and ineffectiveness of its own actions. Decision-making is a skill, and like all skills has to be learned or acquired. It will repay the reader, therefore, if he will briefly examine with us the difficult and complex problem of acquiring decision-making skill.

Persistence of Attitudes. Habitual and traditional attitudes are invariably imposed upon the early phases of group decision-making. People are accustomed to depending upon a leader, or other designated authority figure, to initiate discussions or to suggest a course of action. In the face of a problem demanding group participation, every member approaches it in a characteristic manner. He will look to the leader of the group, appeal to the good will of the members, or recoil in silence rather than risk the rejection of his ideas by the group. Others, while stressing the importance of consensus will, as Gordon points out, rely too much upon the status of a leading individual to suggest a solution. Still others, according to him, will do scarcely more than make frantic appeals to do something and not waste everybody's time. In the absence of experience and the persistence of habits people are impatient and "pushing for decisions." There is an urgency "to end the confusion and frustration" generated by indecision, but the urgency only intensifies the dissatisfaction with the group's progress. "Let's move ahead, let's get some of this stuff out of the way," is a common expression of this attitude.[24]

Increased Understanding of the Decision-Making Process. The urgency of getting ahead with the solution is, as a consequence of the impatient groping, generally followed

[24] *Ibid.*, pp. 266–67.

by a better understanding and increased acceptance of the group decision-making process. Especially important in this phase is the discovery that group decision-making is a time-consuming process. The recognition of this fact prepares the members to accept the necessity of giving every individual time and opportunity to make his contribution to the solution of the problem facing the group. Respect for the opinion of others describes the process most simply.

Why does the initial urgency and impatience give way to sensitivity to the views of others? The evidence, while not giving us a sure answer, suggests practical reasons. It is quite possible that the members become cognizant of the likelihood that, first, better decisions are made when most or all suggestions are considered, and second, that decisions achieved through maximum participation are more likely to be carried out.[25]

Decision-Making Methods. As a psychological process group decision-making is similar to individual problem-solving. Some of the most striking similarities are false starts, trial-and-error, unwitting experimentation, and variety of techniques employed. In his "Workshop Experiment" Gordon found four types of decision-making procedures. We shall describe them briefly.

1. *Voting.* This technique is so common and natural in a democratic group that members readily resort to its use. Since, however, the method of voting is usually employed in a traditional leadership situation, it creates problems in group-centered decision-making. Disagreement about the timing of the vote is inescapable. Since there is no designated leader to call for the vote, no vote is called. If someone volunteers to call for a vote, his action may be resented and ignored. Frequently, discussion of the issue continues even after the group has voted. Sometimes a single dissenting vote will disturb the group sufficiently to cause it to postpone action until the dissenter's reasons have been exam-

[25] *Ibid.*, p. 269.

ined, or until it is reassured that his feelings have not been hurt.

Gordon has made some interesting observations on the voting technique in the Workshop project to which we have referred. He found that group members, because of the foregoing characteristics of the voting process, lost faith in its efficacy. They used it only when the issue involved very little controversy. On important and controversial issues, he observes, the group apparently did not dare employ the vote. Rather it was used primarily as a "straw vote" to give the group "a preliminary clue to the amount of discussion that would be required to arrive at a consensus." While more research on this problem is needed, and while the experience of Gordon in his Workshop should not be overgeneralized, it suggests that self-directing groups do not find voting a reliable method of reaching group decisions.

2. *Consensus.* The typical process of reaching consensus in Gordon's Workshop involved suggestions made by a few members and followed by evaluations by others. The evaluations stimulated group-wide discussion until someone sensed that the group was reaching a decision. Questions were asked, the usual silences took place, and verbal expressions of consensus were made. "Thus, in a very informal and flexible manner, the group would sensitively 'feel out itself' with regard to its readiness for a decision. In a very real sense, the group, not a leader, kept control over the decision-making process."[26]

3. *Postponing decisions.* As Gordon points out, this is a method by means of which a group can "agree to disagree." It serves to protect a minority—even a very small minority—from the will of the majority. It makes it unnecessary for some members to violate their deepest convictions, and thereby avoids the dissolution of the group itself. Gordon cites an example of this technique in his "Workshop Experiment." An important issue, whether the group should have a formal worship period, sharply divided the membership.

[26] *Ibid.*, p. 271.

The objection was not toward the worship itself but was directed against the efforts of those who advocated it as a shared experience. The issue was discussed at several meetings but no decision was reached, and the problem was deferred several times. No *formal* decision was ever made, but the group one day spontaneously agreed to the suggestion of one of its members that a period of silence be observed at the beginning of a discussion period. The suggestion was accepted because it required no one to worship publicly and still permitted those who wished to worship to do so on their own initiative.[27]

4. *Delegation of decision-making authority.* Democratic groups are frequently criticized for being slow-moving, inefficient, and time-wasting. While this criticism is often justified, it is not fatal. These groups may, and frequently do, delegate the power of decision-making to individuals or small committees, who in some cases are able to make quicker decisions than groups. In Gordon's Workshop decision-making was delegated under certain conditions, namely, when time could be saved, when certain individuals were known to have the facts upon which decisions could be based, and when the group had sufficient confidence in individuals or committees to feel that their decisions would not be harmful to itself.[28]

GROUP SUPERIORITY: FACT OR ARTIFACT?

Since the inception of rigid and experimental investigation of group learning and group problem-solving, students of group dynamics have debated the question of group superiority *vs.* individual superiority in collective deliberation. A number of the studies in group learning and collective problem-solving which we have described favor the view that the group tends to be superior to the individual. Some of these studies, as we have noted, particularly those of Shaw and Perlmutter and de Montmollin, attribute the group's

[27] *Ibid.*, p. 271.
[28] *Ibid.*, p. 272.

superiority to specific underlying social processes, notably the evaluation of solutions by many individuals and the rejection of the solutions if they are incorrect. Again, several studies suggest that superior group performance is not due to improved individual solutions under favorable group conditions; most individuals do not equal their group performance; and none surpass them.

On the other hand, the claim that individuals are usually if not always intellectually more efficient and productive than groups has been challenged by empirical evidence. Critics of group productiveness magnify the waste, distraction, irrelevant and interminable discussion by groups, and stress the conflicts which invariably accompany group discussions.

An early investigation of the relative superiority of groups and individuals was made by Watson.[29] Using 108 graduate education students divided into twenty groups whose size varied from three to ten members, the subjects were asked to construct words from letters deposited in envelopes. In one session the subjects were asked to make words each by himself; in another session the groups made words and announced them aloud to a recording secretary.

While Watson was aware of the limitations of his study, particularly as it pertained to the simplicity of the task, the selective character of his subjects, and the like, he was able to support his hypothesis that the "group thinks more efficiently" than separate individuals. More specifically, he found that, not only is group thinking distinctly superior to that of the *average* member, but it is superior to the *best* member of the group. Also, the larger the group, within the range from three to ten, the more superior the group product tends to become. Finally, Watson enthusiastically claims, with insufficient evidence from his own data, group performance is a matter "so different from individual production in the same field that one is practically no index of the other. Most of the factors that make for efficient work

[29] G. B. Watson, Do groups think more efficiently than individuals? *J. abnorm. soc. Psychol.*, 23 (1928), 328–36.

as a member of the group, lie outside the range of the things we are doing in education to equip individuals to do the tasks by themselves."[30]

STATISTICAL POOLING. In the course of dealing with the problem of group superiority in problem-solving, the question has been frequently raised whether the alleged superiority of the group is a "real" one attributable to some special or unique property of "group thinking," or whether it is a consequence of an artifact, such as would be present in statistical pooling. To date we have no clear-cut answer. Since the subject is a crucial one, however, we shall examine it briefly.

In an early experimental study of this problem Gurnee made the claim that the "major reason for the group superiority was pooling of individual judgments," although he admitted that "social influences" and not pooling alone also accounted for the results.[31]

In this experiment Gurnee submitted statements about facts to five different groups, varying in size from 18 to 66 subjects in three experimental situations. In each experimental situation the subjects were to give first individual answers and later group answers. The individual judgments were obtained by means of true-false tests. The group answers were made by majority vote. The nature of the experiment was such that there was no verbal interstimulation, thereby eliminating the complicating factor of social stimulation.

The results of the experiment showed that the groups "not only excelled the average individual performance in number of correct judgments, but equaled or approximated the performance of the best member." Gurnee explained the superiority of group judgment by the pooling of individual judgments. A marked feature of individual responses was a distribution of individual errors. On the basis of statistical

[30] *Ibid.*, p. 336. The reader should review Lewin's study of the superiority of group decisions in changing food habits.

[31] H. Gurnee, A comparison of collective and individual judgments of fact, *J. exp. Psychol.*, *21* (1937), p. 112.

analysis of group performance in terms of sigma distance from the average performance of the individual members, Gurnee found that by collective action "the frequency of correct judgments of a group of persons will be increased approximately plus two sigmas over the average of their individual responses."[32] It should be noted, further, that a superiority of +2 sigma distances indicate that only approximately one out of forty subjects could be expected to equal or surpass the group performance.

Gurnee admits that pooling alone cannot account for all the group superiority, but may be partly explained by social influences in the group. An example of this condition was the tendency of doubtful subjects to delay their response in order to observe the reactions of the "dominant" side, and then to cast their votes with it.

There is an element of equivocation in Gurnee's conclusion. He tells us that "the increase of right responses was chiefly, if not wholly, a result of social influences in the collective situation." He also asserts, however, that the "major reason for group superiority was pooling of individual judgments." While these statements do not contradict each other, they leave us in doubt as to which factor was more important. The chief weakness of the experiment is that it does not take explicit account of the discrepancies between implicit and expressed opinions. In the absence of evidence for or against a proposition people are known to be influenced by the prevailing opinion. The less articulate and the less self-assured people are, the more they lean upon the views of the articulate and aggressive individuals of the group, and the more they will accept the opinions of the latter. There is no satisfactory proof, however, that compliance with the dominant view necessarily results in a genuine acceptance of it. If the more timid members expressed their views overtly, they might conceivably change the complexion of the group consensus. These considerations gain support from an observation already made, namely, that

[32] *Ibid.*, p. 109.

truly self-directing groups do not find voting a reliable method of reaching group decisions.[33]

A telling experiment dealing with the problem of pooling group consensus is that of Timmons.[34] The problem was to decide whether and how a state parole system should be changed. The subjects of the experiment were required to read prepared literature on the subject. The material was first read by the subjects individually, and then ranked by them. Sixty-seven experimental, four-member groups were paired with equal-number and equal-size control groups. After some discussion of the problem the experimental group ranked a given five solutions. This procedure was followed by individual ranking by the same experimental group, of five alternative solutions. The members of the control group individually restudied the literature, but without benefit of discussion, and individually ranked the alternative solutions. The correct answer, it should be added, was the ranking made by several experts on parole systems.

Considering only the bare summary of the results, Timmons' experiment leaves little if any doubt that group problem-solving, while subject to the influence of a statistical pooling effect, cannot be explained by means of it. Neither acclamation nor simple averaging is sufficient to account for the difference between individual and collective problem-solving.[35]

Limitations of the Problem-Solving Situation. In the earlier chapters of this book we called attention to the very strong tendency of individuals to conform to the standards and pressures of the group. This fact was strongly emphasized in our discussion of cohesiveness, as defined by the attraction of the group. The pressure to conform to group norms is now so well known, thanks to many investigations

[33] See above, pp. 221–22.

[34] W. M. Timmons, Can the product superiority of discussers be attributed to averaging or majority influences? *J. soc. Psychol., 15* (1942), 23–32.

[35] See further the Perlmutter and de Montmollin study, already cited, regarding group learning, in Chapter 5.

dating from the experimental work of Sherif, that it needs no further discussion. Its role in group judgments and collective problem-solving has also been demonstrated in several excellent researches. Asch's well-known investigation deserves attention.[36]

Asch discovered that when individuals were faced by majority opinions many of them changed their own to conform with those of the group, even though the majority opinions were contrary to fact. These reactions—independence and yielding to the majority—he ascribes to several factors. The first such factor was the "character of the stimulus situation." He found that, on the whole, as the stimulus-conditions diminished in clarity the majority effect grows stronger. As we indicated before, especially in our discussion of leadership, many people yield their independence of thinking and judgment to others when the situation facing them is not clearly defined or in situations where expectancies are divergent or inconsistent. Second, individuals were highly sensitive to group opposition, especially when it resulted in a loss of group support. The greater the unanimity of the group, all in all, the more likely the individual will yield to its pressure to conform. The same pressure to conform, Asch points out, is not present when the dissenter meets group members individually. A third factor in yielding to the pressures of the group was the "character of the individual." This factor supports our emphasis on several occasions upon the personality variables of the individuals in the group. Such variables are confidence in one's experience, independence, the felt obligation to deal adequately with the problem, and the like. The differences were hypothesized by Asch to be dependent on "relatively enduring character differences."

Furthermore, as Thorndike has shown, when individuals communicate or expose their opinions to others, especially in a group, they are usually both more circumspect in their thinking and cautious in presenting them to the group. If

36 S. E. Asch, Effects of group pressures upon the modification and distortion of judgments, in Guetzkow (ed.), *Groups, leadership, and men.*

the group decision therefore is superior to—or at least different from—that of separate individuals, this fact is partly explained by the effect of the social context upon individual effort.[37]

The upshot of the foregoing brief analysis is that the nature of the social situation, or group structure, has something to do with the group's solution of a problem. The *fact of interaction and communication* makes a difference, so that the same individuals who are interacting as a group might have different solutions as individuals. Since we have already written on communication at length, the force of the preceding statement should be obvious.

The foregoing studies, as well as some others not cited in the present context, while showing that group problem-solving is generally superior to the solutions made by individuals, do not settle the issue with certainty. The results of investigations show the existence of discrepancies, and evidence exists that the group's solution is not always superior. All the conditions making for group superiority have not been discovered, nor has their role been fully assessed. The superiority of the group, when it exists, is not only a function of various social conditions but is an *artifact of the experimental situation.* Some of the factors of this situation are the size of the group, the nature of the group task, the quantity and quality of the available information bearing upon the problem, and the leadership skills of some of the subjects. It might not be an overstatement to say that comparisons of individual and group problem-solving are theoretically and practically valuable, not because of the need to prove that one or the other is superior, but because comparisons might shed a great deal of light on both. This is all the more true in the face of the fact that, despite the publication of a number of excellent studies of collective problem-solving, the nature of this process is not yet clear because of our still relative ignorance concerning the nature

[37] See R. L. Thorndike, The effect of discussion upon the correctness of group decisions, when the factor of majority influence is allowed for, *J. soc. Psychol.*, 9 (1938), 343–62.

of the group process. While experimentation should be continually encouraged, the construction of systematic theories of group behavior must not be neglected. It is systematic theory construction that will, in the long run, give us more reliable knowledge of group-functioning and of collective problem-solving. We must take seriously Lewin's well-known assertion that nothing is more practical than a good theory. On the whole, a good theory is seldom, if ever, destroyed by additional facts; it is usually vanquished only by a better theory.

CONCLUSION

Whatever the enormous quantity of research on collective problem-solving may eventually disclose regarding its superiority, one thing is surely clear. In the face of many convincing data, the traditional attitude of contempt for the ability of a group to direct its own activities and solve its problems collectively is wholly unjustified. The question has been decided, not by preferential attitudes, such as an admiration for the democratic process, but by numerous incontestable facts. If the group often yields a superior performance, it is not because it is "better" than the individual, or preferable to him, but because the structure of the group situation is such that it challenges more available resources than are possessed by the individual, utilizes more suggestions, and rejects more bad ideas. This is generally true whether we consider discussion groups, decision-making committees, or therapeutic sessions. Since in many problem-situations an individual cannot bring to them a large variety of skills and does not possess sufficient knowledge and wisdom to face every task productively, the integration of the ideas of several individuals in interaction with one another increases the probability of producing a correct or adequate solution.

Other things being equal, the more individual resources are brought to bear on a problem, the greater the likelihood that the group will solve it correctly. Consequently, that group is superior to separate individuals in problem-solving, which is able to utilize the creative potential of as many individuals as can be effectively brought into interaction with another. All researches on group size have shown that the productive interactions diminish as the group becomes either too small or too large. While there is no agreement at the present regarding optimum size, the greatest success in collective problem-solving is found in small face-to-face groups. There is nothing in this conclusion, however, to preclude effectiveness in larger groups. From a practical standpoint, indeed, it is important to investigate larger groups, such as communities, political bodies, and international groupings.

In due time we shall critically examine the main features of group dynamics. For the present we shall merely call attention to a possible danger of overextended generalizations regarding group superiority in problem-solving. Overemphasis on agreement can act as an effective barrier to the expression of bold and imaginative ideas. The stress on consensus and the strong tendency to conform to group standards may discourage originality. The hazard in overstressing group conformity is that it encourages agreement on matters which may be of no great consequence. By their very nature original ideas are often disturbing, and the demand for conformity may discourage their acceptance. The individual, always sensitive to the criticism of others, may give way to a feeble compromise. In this situation novel ideas are either emasculated or prematurely nipped in the bud. When this happens, creative democracy gives way to uniformity at any price, and mediocrity is an inescapable consequence.

CHAPTER 8

Group Dynamics in Education

Most investigators in group dynamics have shown an interest and deep concern for the implications of their findings for different areas of human interest and social action. Education has received a large share of this interest; and while enthusiasm has committed some educationists to doubtful and exaggerated claims regarding the role of group dynamics in educational policy and planning, the effect has been largely positive. Particularly significant in this connection is the fact that group dynamics has helped to move educational theory from fruitless discussion to collective action. The teaching-learning process has begun to move away from formalism and authoritarian practices to group participation and democratic leadership. At the same time, the concern for the individual learner has been giving ground to the development of the child in a group situation. If one does not press the historical sequence too far, it may be described as the process of change away from teacher-oriented and child-oriented to group-oriented education. The influence of the group upon the learning situation has never been denied in modern educational theory and practice, but it is only recently that group relations have explicitly been recognized as basic and integral factors in the educational process.

While some of the claims and practices of the National Training Laboratory in Group Development cannot be unqualifiedly approved, the latter has been an important agency in the integration of group dynamics and educational practice. Its procedures in training individuals for skillful group participation are generally recognized to be highly effective not only in educational situations but in many self-directing group activities, such as industry, labor, government, adult education, and community relations.

Perhaps the greatest stress in applying group dynamics to education is on the development of democratic teaching in the public schools. The most sustained criticism by sponsors of group dynamics in education is that our schools give lip-service to the democratic ideal, but largely ignore it in practice. The purpose of education, say the group-minded educators, is to educate youth to become skillful in democratic living. This skill, they hold, can be acquired only by means of democratic teaching. To this end they utilize the findings of group dynamic research concerning the psychological structure of groups, the process of group change, decision-making, group leadership, learning and thinking in groups, teaching as guidance through self-directing groups, and so forth.

In contrast to the traditional philosophy of education, which implicitly separated the individual and the group, the group-dynamic approach stresses their inseparability. We do not wish to give the impression, however, that traditional education ignored the group. It recognized the obvious fact that every individual is inescapably a group member. From the group-dynamic point of view the most important function of the school is to enable the child, by free participation in the group's activities, to find his place in the group. Thus instead of feeling a sense of oppression by the group, the growing child, through the help of others, learns to understand it. Since through participation he develops a sense of belongingness, the ways of the group become his own. To achieve this condition, group-centered educators would reorganize the school in such a way as to help every child to gain a better understanding of the role of the group in his education and growth. This reorganization would consist of a series of effective goals, such as teacher-pupil planning, socialized recitation in which group discussion was the chief technique of teaching and learning, the opportunity for each child to actualize his potentialities, and so on. "Discipline," which has been a consuming problem in education, thus becomes *self-discipline*—a reflection, as we have said, of the individual's integration of behavior which the group defines as desirable.

The most marked characteristic of the group-dynamic approach to education is the radical changes in the educational program which it demands. The profoundness of the changes which it seeks are so deceptively familiar that, at first blush, they hardly evoke surprise. At the bottom of the whole group-dynamic movement in education, however the idea may be couched, is the first consistent and thoroughgoing emphasis on the *human factor* in the educative process —the view that education must be concerned with human relations.[1]

VALUE PREMISES OF GROUP-CENTERED EDUCATION

Although we have not explicitly stressed the underlying philosophy of group dynamics, it has been an unstated premise in the foregoing pages. This philosophy, while in no way incompatible with a scientific investigation of human relations, has nevertheless posed the problems and influenced the course of research in group dynamics. Scientists, like other citizens, have a social conscience, and their goal in group dynamics has been the attainment of a reliable knowledge of the conditions under which living together can best be realized. The ethical motive, in other words, has guided the great bulk of research in group dynamics as

[1] There is not enough evidence, however, to reassure one that those who espouse this view are always aware of the baffling questions which it raises and the paucity of experimental data to confirm their hypothesis.

it has in some other sciences. Whether this motive has overshadowed critical intelligence is a fair question; on the whole, it is equally fair to answer that they have been eminently successful in maintaining an objective position.

Nowhere more than in education has the problem of the underlying ethics of group dynamics so consciously and persistently obtruded itself. This is understandable; for in no other area of life, except religion, is the concern for the welfare of the growing child and youth more paramount than in the school and college. Nowhere else more than in the educational process is there the same determination to aid the child to gain an understanding of the group and his functional place in it. In the face of these facts it is necessary for us to examine briefly the value premises which either implicitly or explicitly guide the use of group-dynamic techniques in our schools.

Basic Premise: The Democratic Way of Life. The meaning of democracy is characterized by an illusive simplicity. Because we take democracy for granted and seldom ask questions about it, we are not aware of how difficult it is to define. There are wide differences concerning its meaning, and many divergent actions and attitudes are defended in its name. One need only participate in groups where philosophers, social scientists, natural scientists, and historians attempt to define it to become aware of the conflicting views which men of intelligence and good will hold concerning it. Without involving ourselves in the niceties of definition, we shall present that view of democracy which has most direct relevance to the issues of group dynamics in education. If this minimizes the popular overemphasis of political organization, it is not that the latter is unimportant, but that it is too narrowly conceived.

Democracy as a way of life. This is the view most consistently espoused by certain modern philosophers, especially John Dewey. It goes beyond the widespread but narrow view in which democracy is regarded as the rule of the majority or a political tool in the hands of elected officials.

As a way of life, democracy is a means of rendering life more free. It consists of the sharing of power and interests—a process of working together, striving together, suffering, and enjoying together. In this sharing of interests with others the individual can contribute his part to the sum total of human freedom. As Bode put it, "Liberty grows as the area of common interests is widened."[2]

The democratic view of human nature. As a way of life democracy is deeply concerned with the socialization of the individual and with his realizaton of his constructive potentials. The existence of a democratic society does not alone guarantee self-actualization. It does not require extensive documentation to establish the fact that when democracy is scarcely more than a political ideology or institution its view of the nature of man may be no better than that of an autocracy. And it follows that under such circumstances it becomes a temptation for those who are responsible for the education of children to foist their own set of habits upon the plastic and growing child. Yet the democratic way of life, as such, stresses the dignity of human personality. It respects the worth of every individual. It defines development and growth in terms of affording every individual an opportunity for the full development of his competence, and the achievement of mature self-direction.

Education in a democracy. Group dynamics in education rests on the assumption that one of the chief aims of education is to safeguard the democratic way of life. An important educational technique for the realization of this end is group-sharing and collective-learning. Traditional teaching method has been teacher-oriented, rather than group-centered. Its task has been conceived to be the imparting of information to a docile child and the imposition of ways of behaving demanded by an authority. John Dewey long ago exposed the undemocratic nature of the process. Writing in 1922, he said sharply:

[2] B. Bode, *Democracy as a way of life* (New York: The Macmillan Co., 1937), p. 32.

When we think of the docility of the young we first think of the stocks of information adults wish to impose and the ways of acting they want to reproduce. Then we think of the insolent coercions, the insinuating briberies, the pedagogic solemnities by which the freshness of youth can be faded and its vivid curiosities dulled. Education becomes the art of taking advantage of the helplessness of the young; the forming of habits becomes a guarantee for the maintenance of hedges of custom.[3]

Group-centered education, as we shall see, has different aims. Basing itself firmly on the tenets of the democratic way of life, it aims to develop individuality and originality through group participation. Conceiving men as free individuals, rather than as depersonalized entities, it proceeds on the assumption that they prefer to work together rather than against one another. In this way democratic freedom is not only an ethical ideal but a reasonable tool: it brings agreement into human relationships which are too frequently characterized by opposition and hostility.

Democratic teaching. No tenet of group-centered education is more often reiterated than that the chief goal of education is the production of democratic citizens. Democratic citizens, however, can develop only in those groups where democratic leadership is free to originate and equally free to be widely distributed. From this standpoint a democratic, group-centered teacher is one who stimulates or enables every child to contribute whatever he can to the total effort of the group to become productive and self-directing.

Democratic teaching, then, is a technique of guidance instead of a process of compulsion. It is a means whereby teachers and pupils create a milieu in which stimulation to learning, thinking, self-expression, and group harmony are important outcomes. The stress on harmony and consensus does not mean a blindness to individual differences. On the contrary, democratic teaching unfailingly recognizes differences in interests, aspirations, and abilities and respects them more consistently than any other method. The recognition

[3] J. Dewey, *Human nature and conduct* (New York: Henry Holt & Co., 1922), p. 64.

of leadership in teaching does not argue for teacher-domination but for intelligent efforts by the teacher to facilitate the process of learning, thinking, and democratic living. In this process no single individual—not even the teacher—is indispensable. Teaching is, in short, a way of stimulating and guiding the learning and thinking of a group—and that of the teacher as a member of the group—along such lines of change as organized society deems necessary or desirable.

This is probably nowhere more true than in the area traditionally described as "discipline." Group-centered teaching rejects the traditional identification of discipline with punishment. It posits, on the contrary, the need for *self-discipline*. A self-disciplined individual, as we have already said, is one who has internalized the norms of the group in such a way that he considers them to be his own, rather than as impositions by others. He acts in a group-approved way even though the group may not be present to reward or punish him. Discipline is thus fundamentally a group problem, and the object toward which the discipline is directed is not only the individual but also the group. The individualism emerging from this form of discipline is not "rugged"; it is not rebellion, but autonomy within a collective framework.

THE RATIONALE: AN AFFIRMATION OF ENDS. The sociology of knowledge has made many scientists conscious of the role of ends or values in shaping their observations and conclusions. No individual can escape from the necessity of positing or setting up ends. Whenever a scientist selects and classifies data, chooses a method of attacking a problem, formulates an hypothesis, and draws a conclusion, he is assuming a set of values in the light of which his activities take on meaning. A scheme of values is a system of ends or purposes.

Group character of human ends. Traditional value theory usually places ends or values outside the situation in which they are alleged to operate—in the individual or in God, for example. From the group-dynamic point of view a goal is not something external to activity itself; it is a habit arising out of the need of the individual to adjust himself to his group. Ends in this view are not "striven for," as tradition would have it, but are terms or events in a dynamic relationship. As an event in a dynamic relationship, an end cannot be isolated; it is nothing apart from the relationship. The goal "seeks" the individual as much as the individual seeks the goal. It is similar to the habit of walking as described by Dewey, namely, that walking is an affair of the ground as much as of the legs.

Social nature of intelligence. A democratic objective of education is the development of an effective social intelligence. A superb example of this intelligence is to be found in scientific efforts to control the forces of nature to human ends. Like the cooperative intelligence of scientists, which recognizes no barriers of race or nationality in disseminating discoveries, so group-centered education aims to organize intelligence in the interest of the common good. This is education conceived not as a preparation for life but as living. Its aim is to produce habits of thinking and behavior that are consonant with the actual life in which men live. Thus, we do not say of a man that he has acquired a democratic education, for education, as a part of group life, is not achieved, but lived. Democratic education does not reside outside the group, nor in tomorrow's reward for today's deed. It is a continuous process of growth and development going on here and now.

CONCLUDING REMARKS. The democratic ethic underlying group-centered education, we have said, is implicitly assumed or explicitly stressed by most group-minded educators. In view of the effectiveness of group performance the stress on collective effort is fully justified.

There is some tendency toward excess in this direction, however, which is not justified by the subjective nature of the value preferences of its devotees. Group education will not necessarily release creative potentials under all circumstances. It is not a panacea, but only one method among others, better than many but not as good as some others.

The elevation of the democratic ethic to exaggerated heights is particularly dangerous, first, because it sanctions group dependence out of proportion to its known value and, second, because it forgets its own stress on the social nature of knowledge by giving us a moral justification for what may be only a cultural trend. It affirms as a scientific reality what may, in fact, be merely the latest fashion. It makes group consensus or harmony the only valid measure of one's loyalty to and integration with society, when, in fact, there are other tests of one's social obligations, a point which group-centered education seems to overlook. In short, the too zealous exponents of group dynamics inflate the value of group techniques and unwittingly distort the truth which they have themselves helped to establish.

It should be noted that our criticism is directed, not against the assumption of a value system, but against confusing it with the whole of a person's social obligation. Having stressed the importance of a fundamental agreement on a set of values several times in the pages of this book, this distinction should be very clear. Almost everything we have written thus far points up the necessity of agreement on common norms or standards for reaching group decisions and making common action possible. It makes no sense to speak of group belongingness, or of subordinating one's own wishes to the demands of the group, unless one recognizes the power of a value system in controlling the actions of both individuals and groups. In a very real sense belonging to a democratic group means accepting its norms—but consciously and critically, rather than blindly. An individual who, as a member of a group, is free to disengage himself from its pressure for conformity, is more likely to participate creatively in its deliberations and actions than one who feels he has been "stampeded" into agreement by the "power" of the majority. Anything short of this violates a cardinal principle of collective agreement, namely, that even if not every individual actively participates, he has the assurance that the group's decisions are based on consensus rather than on majority opinion.

Educational leadership, finally, has not competently wrestled with what may be the most important question of all concerning democratic education—the ethics of attitude change. What moral justification does educational leadership have for trying to change the people who are deeply involved in the educational process: pupils, teachers, parents, administrators, and community groups? Deliberate change is justified only when the widest human experience is brought to bear on educational decisions and when the decisions themselves are accepted by the group as consequences of its own deliberations. We agree wholeheartedly with those individuals who warn us that educational change must not be a commodity to be "sold" to the public. Exploitation in education is ethically outrageous and methodologically wasteful. Only that educational change is ethical which furthers the welfare of the democratic community.

CONSTRUCTIVE CHANGE IN EDUCATIONAL PRACTICE

The most persistent problems of educational change concern educational leadership and curriculum change. There is a growing dissatisfaction with the traditional practice of leadership in the school and an increasing awareness of the fact that changes in the curriculum do not exclusively concern modification of its content, but even more specifically involve changes in the people engaged in its development. It is coming to be realized that curriculum change, like any other social change, is a problem in human relations.

In no other area are the foregoing observations more true than in the field of adult education. Here the traditional methods of rewarding and punishing by credits and grades are not very effective. Lectures and recitations do not meet the enthusiastic response of adults who are bent on achieving an understanding of the world they live in, rather than accumulating a large body of more or less related facts. Conditions like these demand a re-examination of the psychology of motivation, particularly as it applies to classroom instruction and curriculum changes. They also require an intelligent attack on administrative functions in our educational structure. This is no easy task, for in education, as in religion and politics, changes are not only unwelcome but vigorously combated. The task is made more difficult by the fact that changes in the school program are not merely changes in an institutional structure but, from our point of view, a *change in the behavior of people in groups.* To effect this change we must understand, and apply our understanding to, the dynamics of group formation and collective action. Group dynamics, with its stress on the group process and group leadership conceived as a democratic "change agent," can thus be effectively enlisted in the cause of educational advancement. Educational group dynamics is thus defined as "a method of social engineering whose operating procedures incorporate both democratic ideas and values and the knowledge and skills relevant to initiating and controlling the change process."[4]

ADMINISTRATION AND SUPERVISION. The administrative function of the American educational system has traditionally kept criticisms of its performance beyond the pale of the teachers and the public. Preservation of the status quo has been one of its offending practices. Like other "vested" interests, school administrations resist the probing minds of critics lest they discover conditions that demand reform. While many have had little respect for social scientists, they have paradoxically attacked them for exposing administrative weakness. Like managers in industry, who are quick to recommend changes in the workers but not in themselves, school administrators expect improvement in their teachers but ignore their own need for change. This mental state erects a high wall between administrators and teachers and blocks communication between them. When this state of affairs exists, it not only bars important interaction between them but creates an emotional condition of distrust and re-

[4] K. D. Benne and B. Muntyan (eds.), *Human relations in curriculum change* (New York: The Dryden Press, Inc., 1951), p. 14.

sentment. The superintendent, for example, will often ignore the wishes of the teachers, and the teachers may frequently recoil in anger. Should they articulate their resentments, the superintendent will construe these as unreasonable complaints. He diagnoses the difficulties in his school, not as a human relations problem involving the personalities and prejudices of superintendent and teachers alike, but as expressions of antipathies between principals and supervisors, indifference on the part of teachers, and an unwillingness by all of them to cooperate in a common enterprise. If the superintendent should suggest or initiate changes in the school program, the teachers may conceive them as a waste of time or as the administration's way of "pushing them around." If a solution of their shared difficulty is to be effected, however, appeal must be directed not to teachers, supervisors, or administrators as separate individuals, but to their need to see it as an organizational problem of a functional group. A channel of communication must be established to enable each to see the other as a functioning member of a problem-solving group; for observation and study show that when they perceive it as a group problem they usually facilitate rather than resist change.

Perceptual change. The establishment of communication among the various classes of people involved in the task of education does not take place automatically when they are brought into contact with one another. Communication is aided or hindered by the perception which teachers, administrators, and supervisors have of one another and of their common problems. Since the administrator has the power of initiation invested in him by the nature of his office, much depends upon his willingness to entertain new ideas and experiment with new practices. It is not easy for him to accept new ideas, because, like most people, he is handicapped by deeply entrenched educational folkways and by an initial distrust of the unfamiliar. These attitudes present a strong barrier to perceiving educational problems in the light of research discoveries. This has been particularly true regarding the administrator's perception of the role of the group process in educational decision-making. He is often unready to see the value of group-dynamic research, especially since by virtue of his training and experience he tends to regard himself as eminently fit for his occupation. In this attitude he is, of course, partly right, but only as it applies to the role of individual knowledge and skill. This same knowledge and skill may either not function in a democratically oriented educational system or act as a serious barrier to the attainment of its stated objectives. There probably are few school administrators who do not consider themselves as experts in human relations, and who do not, therefore, resent the suggestion that familiarity with and practice of the techniques of group deliberation might solve many of their educational problems. They either do not know or avail themselves of the skills which theory and action research in group procedures have made available to anyone who takes the trouble to familiarize himself with them. Instead of participating in the group process, they too frequently act only as its judges and critics.

There are a number of effective ways in which group participation can effect results which will be of benefit to all who are concerned with the education of the child. Free and permissive discussion in which evaluation and censure play no part are more effective than is commonly realized. A group-centered discussion is not a "bull session" from which everyone emerges with his prejudices either intact or more strongly confirmed. On the contrary, in a democratic group bent on reaching decisions that will benefit all, everyone has too much at stake to permit himself the luxury of a rambling "talk." If he should use the group as a means of venting his own spleen thoughtlessly, he will be challenged by others who perceive the purely individual role he is enacting. A discussion group motivated by the feeling of partnership in a vital enterprise is guided in its deliberations by the task before it and by the strongly felt need to regulate its behavior in the interest of the group as a whole. A group discussion is, as Jenkins has pointed out, "an ongoing process."[5] Such a discussion, he tells us in the same article, has three characteristics—namely, a direction toward a goal, a rate of progress, and a position on the path toward its goal. A group that is aware of these qualities can intelligently guide itself in its deliberations and prevent them from becoming an aimless process or the occasion for aggressive or disgruntled people using the time for merely expressing their individual "gripes." The more "democratic" the group is, that is, the more freely everyone contributes to the group's discussion, the more every member will feel a responsibility to contribute to it.

Several of the studies that we have described in connection with other problems support the foregoing analysis. We would remind the reader of Hare's study of participatory and supervisory leadership in small discussion groups, which we described in our chapter on group leadership. The study demonstrated that groups in which leaders were members or participants produced a significantly greater amount of agreement than groups in which they were supervisory or dominating.

The sense of the foregoing analysis should be obvious. If the administrator is going to be more than a judge and a critic, his perception of his role in the educational process must change, He must become involved as an active participant in the group process. He must come to see himself, not as the center from whom decrees emanate, but as an individual who shares with others such recommendations, suggestions, and actions as will most effectively help all to learn from the collective effort. He will know what his own experience, if evaluated impartially, may have taught him: that unless the teachers believe in his ideas, on the one hand, they will not carry them out effectively, and that they will not believe them, on the other hand, unless they have had an active voice in formulating them. As one group of teachers put it, "We don't care to waste time in discussion and

[5] D. H. Jenkins, Feedback and self-evaluation, *J. soc. Issues, 4* (1948), 50-60.

exploration unless we can also recommend and move toward action."[6]

The limits of group decision. Democratic decision-making in the educational process, we have seen, is at once desirable and possible. There is no place in group-centered education for privileged persons or sovereign ideas. Every important problem is subject to group evaluation. The pages of this book are replete with theoretical and practical evidence confirming the foregoing assertions. However, some students of group-centered education tend to carry their enthusiasm too far. Benne, writing on the ethics of "social engineering," holds that "a democratic methodology [of social change] must be *anti-individualistic.*"[7] He adds, of course, that this view does not preclude the development of individual creativeness. He finds the rationale for his view in an imputed confusion of the ethics of liberal individualism with that of democracy, a confusion which is, in turn, based on "a false psychology and anthropology." This, however, may be only a contemporary trend, and the psychology and anthropology on which he implicitly bases his own view of individuality may itself one day be out of fashion. Benne sees only two alternatives in directed social change—collective planning or reliance upon "providential" effort, the latter of which, of course, he rejects. He asserts that individualism tends to "threaten rather than promote the values of individuality." Moreover, he seems to ignore the disclosures of the sociology of knowledge and does not explicitly recognize that his own position is partly a cultural product. A "true" psychology and anthropology is fully aware of the *Wertbeziehung* character of scientific ideas. Benne's defense of anti-individualism is, accordingly, a *tour de force.* The researches of group dynamics show that the group is no more indispensable than are the individuals who

[6] Quoted in A. Meier, A. Davis, and F. Cleary, The new look in school administration, *Educ. Leadership,* *6* (1949), 302–9.

[7] K. D. Benne, Democratic ethics in social engineering, *Progres. Educ.,* *26* (1949), 204–7. Italics ours.

compose it. A truly democratic group is highly sensitive to the wishes of the individual. Both the group and the individual lack any privileged position in the framework of the democratic ethic. Unless this is so, the group, like the king of old, becomes a tyranny in which submission, under the guise of consensus, becomes the criterion of social responsibility. *Democratic education is not anti-individualistic.* However one may rationalize or gloss over the fact, the argument for anti-individualism makes the individual and the group *antithetical* rather than inseparable. To argue on the basis of a "sound" anthropology and psychology that social planning must be a collective effort is to raise to an intellectual level what is known by common sense, namely, that the group is omnipresent and structures the individual's life everywhere.

The exponents of anti-individualism ignore the fact that their "philosophy" creates the very conditions which they deplore. Some creative individuals either flee from the collective strait-jacket or dilute their potential social contribution by timid compromises. Whyte, basing his analysis of this situation on extensive and documented evidence, makes a telling commentary on the anti-individualists when he writes:

> A committee member might be inclined to support an idea, but he is also not inclined to put up the fight for it that will be needed. He is constrained by good will. He feels an obligation to his fellow committeemen, who are, after all, only trying to do a good job, like himself. So he compromises, not from mere timidity but from a real desire to show respect for the opinion of others. Even if he has trouble mustering up the respect in some cases, his good will may make him feign it.[8]

The experiment by Maier and Solem, the reader will recall, demonstrated that a group's thinking can be up-graded by permitting an individual with a minority opinion to pre-

[8] W. H. Whyte, Jr., *The organization man* (New York: Simon & Schuster, Inc., 1956), p. 223.

sent his ideas without fear of rejection.[9] The results certainly do not justify the extreme view held by Benne and some other exponents of a closed system group which in effect argues the individual out of existence.[10]

Curriculum Change. We do not entertain the delusion that we can say anything about the need for change in the school curriculum that has not been said better and in more detail by others. Since, however, one cannot write on group dynamics in education without giving some attention to the curriculum, we shall examine the problem briefly.

A long-standing complaint of critics of the school curriculum, but one which seldom does much to improve the conditions which are deplored, is that it is not geared to the children for whose educational welfare it was designed. The traditional view conceives the curriculum narrowly as consisting of subject matter and the method of teaching it. While it is designed to produce a "thinking" individual, in practice the emphasis is on conformity to an authority, usually the teacher. The method of teaching is usually rigid and authoritarian, with little opportunity for the inquiring mind to follow its own interests. That the teaching procedures frequently go counter to what modern psychology has discovered to be the developmental pattern of children and youths seems hardly to disturb its practitioners.

From the group-dynamic view the curriculum is more than subject matter and a method of imparting it to more or less willing recipients. It also involves people in interaction with one another. Changing the curriculum to fit the needs of children and adults in living communities involves not only the deliberations of those who are officially designated to perform the task but of the entire educational community. The curriculum, as Alice Miel has emphatically shown, is "*everything that happens to young people in con-*

[9] N. R. F. Maier and A. R. Solem, The contribution of a discussion leader to the quality of group thinking: the effective use of minority opinions, *Hum. Relat.*, 5 (1952), 277–88.

[10] For reports on recent studies pertaining to school administration, see *J. soc. Issues, 10,* No. 2 (1954).

nection with their school life," and it will not be improved *"unless there is improvement in the aspirations, insights, and skills of the adults responsible for the pupils in the school."*[11]

Under ideal conditions the ideas of every interested citizen of a community can help in improving the curriculum. Practically speaking, the contemporary trend in curriculum-building is to enlist staff members and consultants who work cooperatively. The ways through which change is effected are numerous, but the most common and helpful are workshops, committees composed of teachers, students, and parents, designed experiments, research, and systematic and critical evaluation of both methods and results.[12]

The significant fact regarding cooperative efforts in changing and building school programs is that every interested person takes part in the process. In traditional education the teacher, for example, was not consulted on matters of importance. Like the pupils, she was a recipient, almost never a participant. Today even the pupil's opinions are sought, if not in committee conference then at least by means of soliciting his opinions in class discussions or by questionnaires.[13]

The Philadelphia project. In a report of the process of educational change Trager and Radke describe the difficulties and achievements in resistance to new ideas. While their study was made of more inclusive changes in school programs, it throws important light on the difficulties encountered in curriculum reform.[14] The authors describe a three-year project in the Philadelphia public schools. The resistance to change on the part of teachers was substantially reduced by giving them an opportunity to participate in a cooperative group process. The project was based on

[11] A. Miel, Let's work together on the curriculum, *Educ. Leadership*, 5 (1948), 295. Italics in original.

[12] See H. Alberty, *Reorganizing the high-school curriculum* (New York: The Macmillan Co., 1947).

[13] See U. H. Fleege, *Self-revelation of the adolescent boy* (Milwaukee, Wis.: The Bruce Publishing Co., 1945).

[14] H. G. Trager and M. Radke, Will your new program work? in Benne and Muntyan (eds.), *Human relations in curriculum change*, pp. 287–92.

assumptions which by now should be familiar to the reader.

The first assumption was that the teachers themselves must desire change before change could be effected. This desire was brought about by enabling the teachers to study the problems, by encouraging them to choose leaders from their own ranks, and by making it possible for the public to recognize their contribution to the ongoing research. These things were important to the teachers because they informed them of their own competence, instilled professional pride in them, and raised their status in the community.

The second assumption was that teachers, by virtue of their special talents and insights, are able to make a substantial contribution to the formulation of a school program. Teachers are in the strategic position of sensing and evaluating the reactions of all those who are involved in recommending changes—pupils, parents, administrators, and colleagues.

The third assumption was that changes are effected by the teachers, not by the program itself. This involved a synchronization of the teacher's values with the values of the entire program. Unless there is a felt compatibility between the two sets of values, the teacher's participation is lackluster, and she experiences no genuine change in herself. Her effect on her pupils is nonexistent or trifling.

The fourth assumption was that teachers, given the opportunity, are goal-directed and ego-involved in their work. This purpose and involvement resulted in the acceptance of themselves, others, and the task to be performed. Personal involvement, encouraged by a free and accepting social atmosphere, led to group involvement and task orientation.

The authors significantly add that "the project effected change in both program and in teachers by recognizing that what appears to be teacher resistance to change is really resistance to methods ordinarily used to introduce change, and by substituting methods that do not in and of themselves induce resistance. . . ."[15]

[15] *Ibid.*, p. 292.

The Teaching Process. Teaching in the United States has undergone significant changes during the past century. It began as a *teacher-oriented* practice. Where this orientation prevails, the pupil is almost wholly dependent upon the teacher and is expected to think and act in ways which are acceptable to her. The teacher's function is to maintain "discipline," direct the child's thinking and behavior into conformist patterns, and to concentrate almost exclusively on subject matter. In this process the guidance of the child toward becoming an independent but socially responsible citizen is adventitious rather than central. After the turn of the century teaching gradually developed, thanks to John Dewey and the philosophy of "progressive" education, into a *child-oriented* practice. While Dewey himself never subscribed to the excesses practiced in his name, many well-meaning imitators have helped to give "progressive" education a negative reputation which it ill-deserves.

Child-centered teaching recognizes the importance of the group. The teacher's function is to give every child an opportunity to become acquainted with members of the group but not to insist that he become a participating member if he does not wish to do so. Although the teacher acts as a guide, she fulfills this function only at the child's request, or voluntarily in situations where he might harm others or himself. Display of authority is minimized, and the greatest stress is placed on the attainment of independence.

A third approach to teaching is *group-oriented*. According to its advocates this is democratic education at its best. *Interdependence* is the watchword of group-oriented education, not only because democratically it is desirable, but because in practice interdependence is inescapable. The function of the teacher is not to compel or persuade the child to be a member of the group, but to help him to find his functional place in it, that is, to facilitate his active participation in the affairs of group living. In this form of education the child, through the very act of participation, develops an increasing measure of responsibility for self-direction and decision-making. It is Dewey's idea carried to its logical conclusion: the idea that genuine democracy can be established only when our schools encourage individuals to develop a free and critical intelligence. Democratic or group-oriented teaching, then, is a way of life, a means of rendering life more free.

There is no better source of information regarding the results of group-oriented education than the report of the Progressive Education Association on the experiment of thirty secondary schools under its sponsorship.[16] Although the chief goal of this study was curriculum reorganization, the improvement of teaching was an important objective. More than half of the schools reported that pupil-teacher planning was responsible for many favorable outcomes. Group activity was found to be an important cause of increased motivation, resourcefulness, social responsibility, and a sensitive regard for and acceptance of others.

EDUCATIONAL LEADERSHIP

Even this brief discussion of the problems of group dynamics in education highlights the importance of leadership not only in administrative and curricular changes but in teaching methods as well. While most people who observe and reflect upon the problems of education can see the need for reinterpreting and modifying administrative practices and overhauling outmoded curricula, they tend to forget the teaching function in the total educational reconstruction. The teacher is still too commonly conceived as an "underling" who must take orders from the top. While she has steadily gained in dignity and status, she has not been generally conceived as an educational leader. Group-centered education, however, has been correcting this defect, and the teacher's role as a classroom leader is rapidly being recognized.

Early Studies. We have already noted the role of the leader in the formation of "social climates." The study by

[16] Progressive Education Association, *Thirty schools tell their story* (New York: Harper & Bros., 1942).

Lewin, Lippitt, and White is by now a "classic." [17] By means of controlled experimental methods the investigators established three different patterns of leadership, observed the group atmospheres which the leaders created, and studied the effects of the induced atmospheres on the behavior of children in groups. Although the methodology of the investigators is open to criticisms and its weaknesses have been duly exposed, the experiments have increased our understanding of groups and leadership.

In the *democratic* atmosphere the leader's evaluation of the boys' work and his attitudes toward them was "fact-minded" and objective. He was a participant, not a commander, and shared with the boys whatever ideas and skills they found helpful in pursuing their work of mask-making. He permitted the boys to solve their own problems but was always ready to help in matters that were beyond the skill or competence of the individuals.

The *laissez faire* atmosphere, which by virtue of a long politico-economic history we associate and even identify with the democratic attitude, encouraged haphazard and wasteful activities. The leader, while occasionally consulted by the boys, was not a participant and took little or no part in their discussions and decisions.

In the *authoritarian* atmosphere procedures and decisions were determined by the leader with no consultation with the boys. His attitude toward the boys was personal, critical, and aloof. The whole atmosphere, in fact, was marked by hostility, discontent, and relative unproductiveness.

These social climates have also characterized teacher-pupil relationships in our schools. They correspond rather well with the orientations in our educational system. In the teacher-centered educational practice, the teacher is authoritarian, where "discipline" and punishment play the dominant role. In the child-centered system we find a loud echo of the *laissez faire* technique, where the teacher is not

[17] K. Lewin, R. Lippitt, and R. K. White, Patterns of aggressive behavior in experimentally created "social climates," *J. soc. Psychol., 10* (1939), 271–99.

truly a participant and where, if carried to its logical conclusion, she becomes almost superfluous. In the group-centered classroom at its best the education enterprise is a cooperative endeavor, in which everyone involved is a participating member. Self-discipline, rather than free-wheeling or punitive measures, is its motivating spirit.

Anderson and Brewer, in their comparative study of teacher-dominated and democratic atmospheres in the classroom, found important differences in behavioral outcomes. In the classroom where the teacher was basically a dominant, ordering-and-forbidding individual, the students displayed self-centeredness, frustration, hostility, and socially negative behavior. In the democratic, freer atmosphere in which the teacher was relaxed and normally permissive, the students were friendly, cooperative, and socially constructive in their relations with one another.[18]

In an attempt to test Cantor's theory of "non-directive group instruction," that is, instruction not by means of lectures but through class discussion, Gross found further confirmation of the "superiority" of the group-centered to the teacher-dominated classroom atmosphere. Gross compared the degree of "self-insight" achieved by Cantor's well-known method of teaching and that of a group designated as "Doe's group." Although the number of cases studied by Gross in the two groups was too small and the standard deviation of the sample was too large for any meaningful application of rigorous statistical formulas, his investigation lends "weight to the interpretation that Cantor's method does encourage the development of self-insight on the part of a majority of the students, though it may fail to reach a certain minority of every class."[19]

In a study dealing more directly with the effect of the social and emotional climate of the classroom upon the learning process, Withall adds more confirming evidence to the

[18] H. H. Anderson and J. Brewer, Studies of teachers' classroom personalities: I., *Appl. Psychol. Monogr.*, No. 6 (1945).

[19] L. Gross, An experimental study of the validity of the non-directive method of teaching, *J. Psychol., 26* (1948), 246.

importance of the teacher and the atmosphere which he creates in the behavior of the student. A dominating, hostile, and repressive teacher has a dispiriting effect upon the student and noticeably interferes with the effectiveness of his learning.[20] This is consistent with a well-established finding in individual psychology, namely, that emotional disturbances and excessive anxiety tend to disorganize learning and thinking.

Recent Studies. Many studies of the effect of leadership in the classroom have appeared since 1950. Lack of space precludes a detailed description and critical evaluation of these investigations. We shall briefly examine a few of them, as well as one study which contradicts, or at least seriously questions, the results of the others.

In a special issue on "Classroom Dynamics," published in the *Journal of Educational Research*, several good studies take up the issue of classroom leadership.[21] Flanders, in an investigation of the role of personal-social anxiety in the learning process found that self-centered and dominating teachers generated anxiety, hostility, and aggressivness in children, whereas accepting and supporting teachers elicited very little anxiety and induced individually and socially constructive behavior. Furthermore, in the learner-centered teacher behavior the student's ability to recall and elaborate the materials which they were asked to learn were both greater than in the teacher-centered situation. In some cases "emotional disintegration" was elicited in the demanding and teacher supporting atmosphere, whereas in the acceptant and problem-oriented classroom emotional readjustment frequently took place.[22]

Further support for the superiority of group-centered teaching is found in a study by Rehage, especially in an

[20] J. Withall, *The development of a technique for the measurement of social-emotional climate in classrooms*, Ph.D. dissertation, University of Chicago, 1948.

[21] Vol. 45, No. 2 (1951).

[22] N. A. Flanders, Personal-social anxiety as a factor in experimental learning situations, *J. educ. Res.*, *45*, No. 2 (1951), 100–110.

atmosphere of student-teacher planning. Cooperative pupil-teacher planning is "a method by which a problem-oriented, experimental-minded group can determine its goals and direct its efforts toward the achievement of those goals."[23] The study covered a period of thirty weeks in two eighth-grade social studies classes at the University of Chicago Laboratory School. In the experimental group the teacher and pupils cooperatively worked out the specific objectives of the classes and decided on the means by which the ends were to be attained.

The results were analyzed by means of a regression equation based on scores for the control group for predicting the final scores for subjects in the experimental group. The "t" test of significance was applied to the differences between means of the obtained and predicted scores. The differences overwhelmingly favored the experimental group, and showed that the latter was "markedly superior to the control group in their ability to discriminate between reasons which supported their choices of action and those which did not." The study shows, in short, that better working relationships may be effected more quickly in the pupil-teacher planning group than in the traditional teacher-oriented classroom.[24]

An interesting study along similar lines was made by M. J. Asch of nondirective teaching in psychology.[25] His aim in this study was "to evaluate the over-all effectiveness of nondirective teaching of an undergraduate course in psychology as compared to the traditional lecture-discussion method."

The subjects of the experiment were 124 students in the second semester of a year course in general psychology. They were divided into three control groups and one experimental group, and all were taught by the investigator. The experimental class was "nondirective," in which the subjects

[23] K. J. Rehage, A comparison of pupil-teacher planning and teacher-directed procedures in eighth grade social studies classes, *J. educ. Res.*, *45*, No. 2 (1951), 111.

[24] *Ibid.* See further H. V. Perkins, Climate influences group learning, *J. educ. Res.*, *45*, No. 2 (1951), 115–19.

[25] M. J. Asch, Non-directive teaching in psychology: an experimental study, *Psychol. Monogr.*, *65*, No. 4 (1951).

were permitted to choose their own goals, select most of the reading materials, and to write a weekly report describing their reactions to any experience in the course. They were, further, responsible for class discussions and for grading themselves at the end of the term. The instructor's main task was to help the group "to create the atmosphere for self-directive learning." The control classes, however, were conducted in the conventional lecture-discussion manner.

Omitting further description of the experiment itself, we shall briefly state the results. The students in the nondirective class were more satisfied with the group experience and with the results of their own participation. There was a noticeable improvement of the students' adjustments, as measured by the Minnesota Multiphasic Personality Inventory, in the experimental group. Particularly interesting and important is the fact that, although the students in the nondirective class performed significantly poorer on a factual final examination, they believed, what has not been verified, that their experience helped them to learn general psychology better than did the subjects in the control, or traditional, group. Asch's statistical analysis shows that in three of the four questions on a Course Evaluation Form "the results are statistically significant in favor of nondirective teaching."

More recently a rigorous investigation of democratic leadership in the classroom was made by Johnson and Smith which deserves careful study. The investigators' purpose was to test experimentally the effectiveness of democratic leadership in the classroom.[26] The experiment was designed to compare two classes taught by democratic methods and two taught by the widely used lecture-discussion methods. Variations between students were balanced by matching the two types of classes, and variations between instructors were controlled by requiring each of the experimenters to teach a lecture and a democratic group. A Class Evaluation Scale, A Democratic Attitude Scale, a 150-item achievement test with five subscores, and a test of "sensitivity to psychological

[26] D. M. Johnson and H. C. Smith, Democratic leadership in the college classroom, *Psychol. Monogr.*, 67, No. 11 (1953).

problems" were used for both groups at the end of the course.

The hypotheses to be tested by the experiment have been the subject matter of group dynamics for a long time, and have been on the whole confirmed by a variety of studies of group behavior. They may be stated briefly as follows: (1) students favor democratic classes; (2) they accept their own decisions more readily than those made by the instructor; (3) democratic classes are more effective than lecture classes in generating democratic attitudes; and (4) students learn more in democratic than in lecture classes.

The hypotheses were confirmed, but in varying degrees. Particularly important are the results regarding democratic attitudes. There were only "small, inconsistent changes in attitude in both the democratic and lecture groups." Neither the lecture method nor the democratic approach had any consistent effect. Attitude change consisted not primarily in their democratization but in their tendency to *conform to the norms* of the group—a finding confirmed by numerous studies of the group process. Again, while the democratic classes gained more knowledge than the lecture classes, the difference was not significant. The experiment strongly suggests that the democratic classes were group-oriented, whereas the lecture classes were grade-oriented. A warning is suggested by the results to the extremists and indoctrinators in group dynamics in the fact that the "isolated individualist made the greatest academic improvement."[27]

Johnson and Smith suggest three hypotheses based on their interpretation of the results of their experiment, which practitioners in group dynamics in the classroom might find useful. They assert that the most effective class is one in which (1) the subject matter facilitates teamwork; (2) the grading system provides a group reward; and (3) the instructor is accepting and delegates a considerable amount of authority to the class.

As so often happens in research, especially in the behavioral sciences, what is established by some good investiga-

[27] *Ibid.*, p. 17.

tions is challenged or contradicted by still others. Learning, it seems certain, differs with both individuals and groups, and good teaching is good, whatever technique of instruction is used.

An experiment by Wispe challenges some widely accepted conclusions of group-centered teaching.[28] The author was interested in finding answers to three questions: (1) What are the effects of "directive" and "permissive" teaching? (2) How do different kinds of students react to the two kinds of teaching methods? (3) What are the variables for analyzing results on the final examinations, and how well do they predict? "Directive" teaching was defined operationally as subject-centered, formal, and highly structured. "Permissive" teaching was student-centered, informal, and unstructured. The experiment was performed on eight sections of an elementary course in Social Relations at Harvard which were matched on the following items: an objective pretest on the contents of the course, Scholastic Aptitude Test scores, secondary school background, the year in college, and the size of each class. Four of the classes were taught by the "directive" method and four by the "permissive." At the final meeting of each class the students were given a TAT-type test and a sentence-completion test in order to elicit the more basic attitudes toward the classes and the instructors.

The details of the study and the experimental manipulation of the data are too intricate to expound within the limits of this chapter. Of crucial interest to the group-dynamic approach to education is the results. The findings may be briefly summarized.

The permissive groups were characterized by student participation, student-instructor interaction, keen interest, humor, and mutual acceptance. The directive groups were more course-relevant, and displayed the other characteristics to a lesser degree. Although the permissive sections were enjoyed more, the directive sections were preferred by most

[28] L. G. Wispe, Evaluating section teaching methods in the introductory course, *J. educ. Res.*, *45* (1951), 161–86.

of the students because, as Wispe points out, they were clearly defined and because of their "presumed value in preparing for examinations." The two groups, furthermore, showed no significant differences on the final examination when taken as a whole, but when the two teaching methods were examined for their effects on the students, it was found that the directive groups helped the poorer students more than did the permissive sections.

Even more important, perhaps, than the results of the experiment is its implication for teaching. It challenges the rather indiscriminate praise and use of the permissive method by showing that personality variables are important. It strongly argues for an intelligent consideration of the student's emotional and intellectual needs in deciding what kind of instruction will benefit him most. Teaching and learning must be viewed exclusively neither in terms of personality variables nor group dynamics, but in terms of the interaction of both.

THE CLASSROOM AS A "LABORATORY." The reader must have been struck by the fact that most of the studies on social climate were performed on contrived and "artificial" groups. This fact is a methodological limitation which has given us partial and one-sided presentations of the teaching-learning process. Studies like those which we have briefly described in the preceding pages have a significant advantage, the most important of which is, in our judgment, that the groups which were subjected to controlled experimental testing were observed under natural or normal conditions. In contrast to the early experimental groups of Lewin, Lippit, and White, and others, which were highly fluid and impermanent, the classroom is, as Johnson and Smith have pointed out, "a regular part of the student's routine for one term."[29] What goes on in the classroom is not incidental but constitutes a set of significant events in the life of both the teacher and the student. The events which take place can be controlled and manipulated by the experimenter, especially if

[29] Johnson and Smith, Democratic leadership, p. 1.

the latter is also the teacher. He can control the size of the class and its membership, influence the direction of the activities that take place in it, and observe what is going on.[30] To a great extent the teacher is responsible for the social climate of the class, and it is he who largely controls the effects of the classroom upon the intellectual and emotional development of the child. This puts the teacher not only in a strategic place for studying the group process but for putting into practice the principles of democratic teaching. It is the teacher who, by his arbitary authority, instills fear and resentment in the growing child, or who, by permitting pupils to disagree and to challenge, encourages personal independence and group responsibility. By not deliberately trying to structure the child's personality, the group-centered teacher, by a deft combination of firmness and respect for the dignity of the individual, can aid in the process of development. We agree with Cantor that "the *individual* is sovereign, *up to a point.*"[31] It is the class atmosphere created by the teacher, however, which has an important bearing on the degree of freedom of the student and his integration with the group. The classroom thus becomes an important testing ground for the principles of democratic, group-centered teaching. Every experienced teacher who creates a warm and accepting atmosphere in his class knows—what he may first discover with surprise—that both the inhibited and insecure student and the forward and aggressive one learn to understand themselves and each other better. No less important and surprising is the teacher's discovery that, in proportion to his own recognition of his attitudes toward students, he learns to understand himself better. We are thus brought around once more to the realization that in teaching, as in other areas of life, the individual and the group are inseparable and reciprocally influencing. Democratic education is reality-centered: it stresses the principle that education is not exclusively con-

[30] *Ibid.*

[31] N. Cantor, *The teaching-learning process* (New York: The Dryden Press, Inc., 1953), p. 33.

cerned with the individual nor the group, but with both in their effect upon each other.

CONCLUSION

We have described and analyzed but a small segment of the enormous research, theoretical and operational, which has been published on the group-dynamic approach to education. In a general way, and if we are not too critical in our evaluation of it, group-centered education has left a positive mark on educational theory and practice. It is not always clear whether the ethical premises of the democratic way of life obtrude themselves upon educational research and influence the interpretation we place upon the results. The belief that education is a problem in human relations, that it involves people and not primarily subject matter, would *a priori* tend to color our evaluation of what we observe. While this may not be wholly in the interests of truth, it is reinforced by a powerful moral disposition. Although it contributes to the humanization of education, it becomes dangerous when we become prejudiced adherents to its dubious claims.

The research data on group-centered education do not support some of its allegations. The instances in which a "directive" educational leader can effect planned but desirable results are too numerous to be ignored. Group-centered education is a royal road neither to education nor to democracy. The dangers of oversimplification are numerous, and they must be vigilantly guarded against.

The results obtained by Asch, Wispe, and Johnson and Smith, for example, leave us very much in doubt regarding the effectiveness of group-centered or nondirective teaching. Should we be influenced in our judgment by the students' own preferences, the structured or directive teaching fares much better than the democratic. Significant, too, is the fact that in Wispe's study there was no sharply distinguishable superiority in learning in either type of classroom instruction. Personality variables also, and not only group forces, are important in the teaching-learning process. Evidence from other studies support the conclusion that group-centered students acquire less knowledge and relevant information than those who participate in directed groups. In seems that almost the only thing which group-centered students derive from their experience which is not shared by those in the conventional classroom is a significantly greater amount of social and emotional satisfaction. This observation, too, cannot go unchallenged. Some evidence leads one to believe that group orientation takes on a kind of over-centralization of the interaction pattern of a classroom. As the group becomes centralized and dominant in its influence, some individuals become increasingly dissatisfied. Nor is the effectiveness of group learning always aided by group centralization. Effectiveness is in large part a function of the interaction pattern of the group, particularly its channels of communication. As the size of the group increases, the interaction pattern varies, and the effectiveness of the group diminishes. In a period of swollen school and college enrollments this factor takes on a special significance.

Adherents to the group-dynamic approach to education, finally, have paid insufficient attention to the time factor. There are no satisfactory studies or measures of the relative efficiency of the directive and nondirective methods of teaching and administrative work. While much of the strength of the democratic approach to education lies in its refusal to be hurried and precipitated into hasty and unwise decisions, hesitation can be fatal. As Barnard has discerningly pointed out, effectiveness and efficiency are not positively related, so that a procedural technique may be effective without being efficient.[32]

On the basis of published research on the subject we can conclude then, with the usual caution, that nondirective education, embodying the democratic principle of free discussion and mutual respect of teachers, pupils, administrators, and parents, can effect valuable educational experiences to all concerned. The truly great appeal of group-centered

[32] C. I. Barnard, *The functions of the executive* (Cambridge, Mass.: Harvard University Press, 1938).

education, however, apart from what scientific investigation has discovered regarding its technical superiority, is that it humanizes education by making *people* the focus of its deliberations. When our schools, their curricula, and the methods of teaching become truly group-centered, they will reflect or embody the revolutionary changes of life that have been going on apace in our society during the last quarter-century. Only then will our educational programs become revivified and equal to the task which they must face.

CHAPTER 9

Human Relations in Industry

Thirty years ago the psychological study of industry was almost nonexistent. It was the pioneer ideas of Elton Mayo that inspired his associates and students to first apply social-psychological principles to the industrial setting in the late 1920's. Since that time, however, a prodigious amount of theoretical and especially empirical research has been focused on various types of industrial organizations.

The first large-scale investigation of industrial relations was made at the Hawthorne Plant of the Western Electric Company. This study was initiated by the driving force of Mayo's ideas and was carried through to completion and publication by the now well-known collaboration of Roethlisberger and Dickson.[1]

A decade later Lewin, having escaped the oppressive atmosphere of German authoritarianism, and inspired with a deeply felt enthusiasm for American democracy, initiated a series of studies on group behavior and social climate. These studies were to have had profound implications for

[1] F. Roethlisberger and W. J. Dickson, *Management and the worker* (Cambridge, Mass.: Harvard University Press, 1939). For the social and psychological ideas which gave rise to the current interest in industrial problems, see E. Mayo, *Human problems of industrial civilization* (Cambridge, Mass.: Harvard University Press, 1933).

industrial psychology and our understanding of the whole range of human problems in business and industry.

Another impetus to the development of industrial psychology was the stupendous demands of the war effort in the early 1940's which impelled many industrialists to turn to scientific methodology and research, both here and abroad, for the solution of many perplexing problems of motivation, attitudes, morale, productivity, and the like. This application of science created a pattern of approach to problems of labor, management, and the unions which is stamped upon most current research in industrial relations.

Despite its brief history, industrial psychology has successfully raised our knowledge of human relations in large organizations beyond subjective and preconceived ideas. Programs of research during the past fifteen years have given us a more complete picture of the problems of industry and better techniques for solving them. To this extent the contributions of psychologists, sociologists, and anthropologists have appreciably added to our scientific knowledge of industrial behavior. Furthermore, the theoretical and operational research performed has attested to the scientists' skill in human relations and the workers' and industrialists' capacity for cooperative effort. Without these attributes much of the fine work in the area could not have been accomplished.

A CONCEPTUAL FRAMEWORK

A striking feature of the bulk of the early research in industrial psychology is the fact that it was initiated without the benefit of a theoretical model. There was no discernible order in the progress from subjective and unvalidated descriptions to scientific formulation. Almost from the beginning, empirical studies, many of them avowedly exploratory, were given attention and status. Concepts borrowed directly from psychology, especially from social psychology, were early applied to industrial problems, and with good effect.

This unsystematic procedure, while objectionable to the purist, was perhaps both inescapable and salutary. It was inescapable because there were few if any precedents, and because most of the current variables were either ill-defined or originated in the field of individual psychology. In either case the variables were carried over into the area of industrial relations without much concern for their real applicability to the study of complex human organization. It was salutary because the older conceptual frameworks were too rigid to permit an adequate description of a complex industrial organization. As a result, the early attempts to formulate the significant variables of industrial behavior were not saddled with the burden of an inflexible theory. As an example of the harm which a rigid model can impose upon research, we cite the study of the worker's incentive when it is conceived wholly in terms of individual motivation as described by conventional psychology, or in terms of wages, hours, and benefits as described by traditional explanations of what makes workers work.

It is not our purpose to propose a theoretical model for the dynamic study of industrial relations. Rather, ours is the more modest task of describing a few concepts which must go into any general discussion of the social and psychological factors which determine the behavior of men in industrial situations. Some of these concepts are already familiar to the reader of this book.

SOCIAL SYSTEM. All dynamic groups of the type we have been describing comprise a social structure or system. This structure, we have seen, is a complex pattern of relationships involving persons and their roles. Any alteration in the relationship of persons and their roles results in a change in the structure of the group, and any alteration in the structure of the group affects the behavior of the individuals. Accordingly, the behavior of workers and managers in an industrial plant is a function of the social system called the factory. The factory may effect desirable behavior either through the power devices inherent in its hierarchical organization, as has traditionally been the case, or through overlapping, integrated, or "democratic" participation, as is increasingly the practice. The factory as a social system is not a mere collection of individuals, but a social unity. Accordingly, neither the workers nor the management, neither the individual nor the social system, operates in isolation. The social structure influences the individual and the individual, to the extent that he can exercise a choice, affects the social structure. The structure is organized in proportion to the opportunity it gives to every unit to perform specific tasks.

The quality of the human relations in an industrial organization depends a great deal, nevertheless, on the ability of those in the upper-status hierarchy to perceive the extent to which their own actions are molding the fate of the group as a whole. This is true because the administrators, by virtue of their hierarchical position, constitute a center of high potential or influence in the total structure. To understand that they are molding the workers' actions requires no omniscience on the part of the management; but it does require a good deal of social insight for members of management to understand that they are themselves products of the social forces which they are trying to control in the interest of all. T. N. Whitehead well expressed the reciprocal relations of workers and managers when he said, "What is required is that the social sentiments and activities of groups be regarded, not as hurdles to surmount, but as an integral part of the objective for which the organizer is working."[2]

Turning to the specific aspects of the social structure of an industrial organization several things stand out. A factory, for instance, is a group of people and a pattern of activities whose chief goal is the production of commodities. To this end the people and their activities must be coordinated to achieve the goal. To the extent that every person who is involved in the process plays his role successfully, the organization will realize its cardinal objective. Accordingly, every member of the whole must understand his position in it and constantly adjust his behavior in the interests of the group goal. In this process he will be aided by the

[2] T. N. Whitehead, *Leadership in a free society* (Cambridge, Mass.: Harvard University Press, 1936), p. 85.

achievements of modern technology—machines, formal techniques, and inculcated skills.

Furthermore, the system is constructed on a pyramidal hierarchy. At the top is the director or manager, more formally designated as the president. At the bottom are the workers, whose chief function is to perform those activities which are necessary to make a finished product. Situated between these two and linking them by varying positions and communication systems are the "operational" members—the plant superintendent, department heads, line foremen, etc.

From the standpoint of group dynamics the most important variable in the pyramidal structure is the *human factor*. This human factor is comprised by the people who engage in the productive activities, their relationship to one another and to the management, their work motivations, the personalities of the members, the character of the leadership, and so forth. While the technical equipment of an industrial organization may be superb to the last detail, whether it be the latest machine of a factory or the most intricate electronic "brain," the thing that counts in the long run is the character of the human beings who control it. Gardner and Moore describe it well when they write:

> Behind the formal, paper façade is another organization, consisting of a group of people from various walks of life—people having varying interests, needs, and ambitions, and all of whom are making adjustments to the formal tasks which they are called upon to perform, adapting their own interests to the demands of the people with whom they are thrown into daily contact, making friends, and acquiring enemies. This is the realm of feelings and emotions, scuttlebutt and rumors, cliques and washroom repartee. This is the human side of doing business. Observing it, we get the "low-down," so to speak, on how organizations with all their "paper" dignity actually work.[3]

Many studies, some of which are described in the preceding chapters, attest to the importance of the human factor, especially in its group manifestations. Whether we study

[3] B. Gardner and D. G. Moore, *Human relations in industry* (Homewood, Ill.: Richard D. Irwin, Inc., 1950), p. 7.

group learning, collective problem-solving, group-centered education, human relations in industry, or group psychotherapy, the social-psychological characteristics of group relations are important. People on the job do not want bread alone; they also need the sense of well-being which comes from being with, and being like, other people.

The foregoing statements may be summed up by saying that the social structure of a factory or a business organization is an interlocking pattern of techniques, status hierarchies, and psychological relations among people. A neglect of any one of them not only leads to distortion but is, in a sense, a neglect of all.

Authority. Decision-making in industrial situations has traditionally been the exclusive function of management. The power structure of business and industry has been based on the concept of superordination-subordination and has been the matrix in terms of which organizational leadership was understood and practiced. Nevertheless, whatever one's philosophical preferences might be regarding the use of authority, it is but realistic to acknowledge the fact that authority and power are essential in any type of social organization, the democratic not excepted. There is no known social order that is not in part sustained by authority vested in some person or institution. No society, not even the most primitive, is exclusively regulated by informal custom. The controlling force of authority should be despised and combated only when it becomes tyrannical and contemptuous of the freedom that challenges it.

Our consideration in this section is not, however, with the formal properties of power and authority, but with the behavior patterns which it generates. Authority is a form of behavior exercised by people with reference to one another, and as such it is a problem in human behavior, particularly group behavior. In an autocratic group, authority is exercised by an individual in the form of commands, while others simply obey. In a democratic group, especially in the kind we have been describing, authority is usually diffused. Those who act in accordance with the expectations of the authority do so, not out of abject fear, but out of an awareness that in subordinating their own temporary interests to those of the group everyone will be better off. Democratic authority may thus be more adequately described as a form of persuasion in which no one completely abdicates his freedom of choice.

We have said that in a democratic group people subordinate themselves to an authority because they anticipate the welfare of all in their actions. However, this is a simple overstatement and an idealization. The process is more complex and involves several factors, which we shall describe briefly.

People obey laws, or subordinate themselves to authority, because they fear or dislike social disapproval. It is safe to say that social approbation, engendering a feeling of group acceptance and group belongingness, is the basic explanatory principle of man's subordination to a democratic authority. Indeed, there is much evidence in support of the view that acceptance by one's fellows is essential to normal living. The force of obedience to one's own group is startlingly brought out by Rebecca West in her description of the traitor, the individual who has renounced obedience to his country. She calls attention to the misery of the traitors standing in the prisoners' dock awaiting trial. They were miserable not only because they were going to be punished—the conventional social sanction—but because *"They had forsaken the familiar medium."*[4]

Next in importance in the acceptance of authority is an awareness of the advantages beyond that of social approbation, as such, that accrue to the individual who accepts authority. In the industrial situation this factor often stands out sharply. The worker knows that by obeying the boss his own position may be enhanced. It may secure his position, increase the possibility of a promotion, or an increase in wages, or initiate other benefits. The worker is thus ready

[4] The meaning of treason, *Harper's Magazine* (October, 1947).

to subordinate his own individuality and freedom, including even the freedom to protest, in order to realize the benefits which this subordination tends to beget. Furthermore, a large segment of any population obeys authority because it is easier than exerting one's own effort. While historical reasons explain in part this reluctance to assume responsibility—witness the case of Germany before World War II, when its people abdicated their desire to make governmental decisions—it is also true that many people are psychologically unwilling or incompetent to take the risks involved. They find it less painful and often positively more reassuring to accept the opinions and follow the suggestions of others.

In a democratic organization, finally, people subordinate themselves to authority because they are aware that only through concerted effort can certain desirable objectives be attained. This is not "obedience" in the usual sense, but is a positive effort to reach a group consensus. The subordination involved is a form of relationship in which the individual may find satisfaction of several important interests and needs, such as recognition, independence, a fair evaluation of his own behavior, and group belongingness.

Although authority is becoming increasingly shared by more and more individuals in a modern industrial organization, this is not, however, the pervasive pattern. Distribution of authority usually takes place vertically, so that managerial subordinates, for example, share in it much more than line foremen. Nevertheless, significant consequences affecting the entire industrial enterprise stem from a greater distribution of power. Production increases quantitatively and qualitatively, worker satisfaction increases, absenteeism and turnover are reduced, and the quality of managerial decision is improved. Delegation of authority and allocation of decision-making to those capable of assuming these responsibilities is an aspect of the "fine art of executive decision" which generates competence in others, heightens morale, and aids in the establishment of responsibility.[5] As the sharing

[5] See C. I. Barnard, *The functions of the executive* (Cambridge, Mass.: Harvard University Press, 1938), p. 191.

of authority is widened to include an ever larger population in an industrial organization, these positive consequences will be multiplied and strengthened; for what workers find intolerable in any working situation is their dependent and often degrading position in it.

COMMUNICATION CHANNELS. In earlier chapters we stressed the importance of effective communication for adequate group functioning. Communication can either facilitate or hinder participation in human activities. The example of "pluralistic ignorance," cited earlier, illustrates this fact. In working relations effective communication is absolutely essential, for it may affect production in measurable ways. Since an industrial plant is a social system in which hierarchical positions play very important roles, the linking together of the entire chain of command from top to bottom is a process of signal importance. This process, and particularly that of the distortions in communication, was illustrated in the brief description of the Bank Wiring Room in Chapter 3.

Communication is important for several reasons. When the manager or the boss is psychologically removed from those over whom he has authority, he cannot know everything that is going on in the plant. His knowledge is usually rather general and lacking in specific information. On the other hand, while he may transmit detailed instruction to his subordinates, the flow of messages from the bottom to the top is controlled and sifted.

The effectiveness of the whole working unit can be seriously impaired by defective lines of communication. An ineffective flow of messages, especially from the bottom to the top, may not only impair the productive effort directly but may generate misunderstanding and anxiety as well. This is particularly true of the boss who must link the worker below him and the manager above him into a communication arc. Although the workers are fearful of displeasing the foreman, the latter in turn may be even more concerned with anticipating the manager's wishes and with the possibility of making the wrong impression on him. Some of the ill-feeling and antagonism of the foreman may be an unconscious expression of his fear of displeasing the manager. This "neurotic" sensitivity of each person toward the expectations of the one immediately above may not be the result of the working situation as such but of the distortions and misunderstandings arising from impaired communication between them. In describing this type of situation in the Bank Wiring Room, we stressed the importance of communication and showed that there is a constant temptation by the worker to withhold adverse information from the foreman, while the foreman in turn sometimes conceals facts from the management. In this situation every communicant places himself in a defensive position, thus depriving the whole department —or even the whole plant—of the information that it must have for efficient production and effective management.

It would be a mistake for the reader to infer from the foregoing analysis that failure in communication arises only out of personal sensitivity or fear of the reactions and attitudes of the various members of the communicative process. For communication is also a problem in semantics. Worker and manager often live in different universes of discourse. The meanings of words often vary with the social context; and the social context in an industrial plant is largely determined by the role and status of the individuals who are involved in the productive effort. Manager and worker also fail to understand each other, therefore, because each occupies a different status in the social system of the factory. Roethlisberger pointed out that "a good portion of the executive's environment is verbal."[6] He deals with words and abstractions, for the most part, whereas the worker manipulates objects and commodities, the symbolization of which seldom reaches the same level of refinement. Even though both use the same words in trying to communicate with one another, both tend to use them as absolutes and react to them as if they were things. They unconsciously assume, as Hayakawa

[6] F. J. Roethlisberger, *Management and morale* (Cambridge, Mass.: Harvard University Press, 1941), p. 88.

has shown, that "the symbol *must necessarily* call to mind the thing symbolized."[7]

While misunderstandings will probably never be eliminated from human relations, they can be very substantially reduced. To date, the most effective technique in reducing misunderstanding in industry has been the creation of a worker-manager environment conducive to free exchange of ideas, feelings, and grievances. In this way cooperation—or at least coordination of effort—toward a common objective has been achieved in some industrial plants. But it should also be pointed out that in a complex organization like an industrial plant, as in a small informal group, every individual must participate, at least minimally, in shared knowledge and cooperative behavior. Only then can communication truly exist, and only under those circumstances can misunderstanding and ill-will be substantially reduced. Our description and analysis of group structure, group process, the technique of democratic discussion, the conference method of reaching consensus, and the like substantiate the foregoing conclusion.

Personality Variables. Perhaps in no other form of dynamic group behavior are the personalities of individual members so evident as in worker-manager relationships. Although personality plays a role in all groups, in the long run individual personality factors are oriented toward group norms or are submerged in the act of reaching group consensus.

Individual maladjustments are obviously one of the most serious barriers. The chronic troublemaker may have no just grievances, for his behavior may stem from individual frustrations or neurosis. Fortunate is the department which does not harbor at least one such individual in its midst and suffer negative consequences from his presence. Moreover, many workers, as was pointed out in an earlier chapter, are too unadaptive in their attitudes to enable them to fit into

[7] S. I. Hayakawa, *Language in action* (New York: Harcourt, Brace & Co., Inc., 1941), p. 31.

a changing work situation. Such misfits obviously gain little or no insight and improvement from a democratic participation in the deliberations of their shop.

The effect of personality variables are not, of course, limited to maladjustive or neurotic behavior. The "normal" person brings to his job whatever he is as a person, including his past conditioning and a whole complex of customs and beliefs, as well as his technical experience and skill. A young man just out of college who believes that he should become a junior executive in a few years will approach his job in a different manner from one who believes that his motives will be judged by the results which he produces. These distinctions will make for differences in the expectation which each has concerning his job, for they are based on a different conception which each has of himself as a person.

The perception which an individual has of himself is, of course, only one aspect of the problem of the relationship between personality and industrial organization. His image of others, especially of those who are in authority, is also very important. The docile individual will welcome direction and control, for these give him the security without which he cannot function. Such a person seldom assumes initiative and self-direction, regardless of how willing the manager and the group as a whole might be to give him greater autonomy and freedom of choice. The aggressive individual, on the other hand, especially if he is also rebellious against authority, presents a different situation. His image of others is of people who are critical and hostile, instead of encouraging and helpful. No matter how much the group may beat him down verbally, he persists in his attitude and dissipates his energy in chronic opposition.

There are people, furthermore, who have difficulty in relating themselves comfortably to others, no matter how accepting of them others may be. They are not to be classified with the rebels, neurotics, and malcontents whom we have mentioned, for they are not hostile and antipathetic. They deal most comfortably and successfully with ideas or objects. Consequently, they make poor managers or supervisors, for these positions involve important human and psychological problems.

INDUSTRIAL LEADERSHIP. From the role of personality to the role of leadership in industrial relations is not a giant step, for all complex industrial organization involves leadership authority. That is, no matter how much the decision-making act is shared by various individuals, decisions do not take place without the exercise of someone's authority.

Modern industrial decisions are made, on the whole, by bureaucratic minorities. (The nature of bureaucratic authority was described in Chapter 6, and we shall not repeat our discussion here.) But unlike the decision-sharing process of small groups, organizational leadership employs a certain degree of institutionalized power. Does this institutional power pose a dilemma, and, if so, can the dilemma be resolved? The problem, then, lies in the fact that bureaucratic leadership, no matter how fair and just it may be, seems to challenge the democratic norms upon which the bulk of the discussion in this book has been predicated. In seeking an answer, it is well to note that on several occasions we have been critical of the argument that leadership in a democracy must be completely shared. As we indicated before, some individuals have neither the ability nor the incentive to initiate group behavior. Since leadership and democratic action are not incompatible, our job is to understand how democratic leadership functions in an industrial situation, and what its strengths and limitations are. It is utterly unrealistic for us to expect a giant factory to direct itself after the manner of a free discussion group or a nondirective college classroom. Efforts in directing an industrial plant on the basis of "diffused responsibility" pose a difficulty no less baffling than that presented by institutionalized leadership in a democratic framework. The power inherent in leadership is bad only when it is used to exploit the followers. The complications of leadership in a democratic industrial society recede in importance provided, as

Bernard thoughtfully observed, leaders can be obtained in quantity and quality to survive the short periods when strong and directive leadership is indispensable.[8]

An experiment in group-centered administration. The extent to which group-centered leadership in a factory can be applied with success is described in an experiment by James Richard.[9]

The experiment was performed in a metalworking plant employing 325 men and women. There were three levels of management in the plant. The top management consisted of the chairman of the Board and the president. Executive department heads were the sales manager, controller and treasurer, the chief engineer, the director of purchases, the vice-president, and the plant superintendent. The supervisory group included ten foremen, the production control manager, the personnel director, and the production engineer. James Richard, the director of the experiment, was the plant superintendent.

The objective of the experiment was to operate the factory "through a leadership method that supported men in the use of their own capacities, rather than by controlling, guiding, and manipulating them."[10] Most of the work of the superintendent was problem-centered, and face-to-face discussion was the most frequent procedure. His desire was to generate an atmosphere of cohesiveness and to induce increasing self-reliance in each member. In this atmosphere decisions were made, policies were established, and the task of running the factory was accomplished. Every situation required the superintendent to play a different role—sometimes as a counselor, at other times as an authority channel for communicating sanctions, and at still other times as an accumulator of facts, as a reminder to others of the limits of freedom, or as a group therapist. The collaborative

[8] C. I. Bernard, *Organization and management* (Cambridge, Mass.: Harvard University, 1948), p. 40.

[9] In T. Gordon, *Group-centered leadership* (Boston: Houghton Mifflin Co., 1955), chap. xii.

[10] *Ibid.*, p. 315.

effort is best described in the superintendent's own words: "My intention was to act in such a way that the supervisors, foremen, and staff men could learn that their departments were, in fact, their own to run and that decision-making was a process which did not exclude me, but which included them in an important way as individuals and as an interdependent group."[11]

Inasmuch as it would require too much space to describe the operating methods used in the experiment, the reaction of the executive group, the daily events and experiences of the participants, the nature of the leader-initiated conferences, and similar matters, we shall have to content ourselves with a brief statement of the results.

One of the most important outcomes was the psychological growth of the individuals. An example of this growth was that of the stubborn, defiant, and inarticulate foreman who became a sound-thinking, stable, and articulate administrator. A second outcome was the development of strong group cohesiveness, which paved the way for the group's dependence on its own resources. The superintendent found a "measure" of this group dependence in the large number of instances where he found himself not needed. Another consequence was an improved morale. Concretely, this meant that the individuals assumed greater responsibility. The superintendent's problem was no longer one of maintaining discipline and motivating others, but of keeping up with the group's performance. As he expressed it, "I had to scoot to keep up." Important, too, was the reduction of unproductive tensions—the kind of tensions which, because of the fear, anxiety, and conflict which characterizes them, were psychologically crippling. (The investigator discriminatingly contrasts these tensions with the more "normal" kinds which motivate people to higher levels of aspiration.) Finally, and significantly, the increased productivity which took place had a special character which the superintendent described as "a quality of creativity."

[11] *Ibid.*, p. 319.

The men put themselves zestfully into their work and dis played thoughtfulness at the same time. To quote Gordo again, the people "argued and worked and sweated—bu with respect for themselves, respect for each other, respec for their men, and respect for the company."[12]

Scientific caution does not permit us to generalize from single instance. Many more experiments of the type con ducted by Richard are needed before we can speak of th efficacy of group-centered industrial organization with con fidence. Richard himself is fully aware that his experimen is only a beginning. Nevertheless, as he points out, "it *ca* be done." We would do well to consider this group-cen tered organization, as Richard does, as "a process and a attitude, more than a system"; for when the organizatio becomes a rigid system, power controls, bureaucratic ma nipulations, and institutionalized thought-patterns tend t strangle it. Meanwhile, however, we have to come to term with reality and accept the fact that in a complicated indus trial system the pyramid of power, while not democrati in the very best sense of complete group self-direction, ca be as efficient, just, and humane as the most advance knowledge and skill will permit. Power is wicked and im moral only when it is abused—when it exploits, divides, an disorganizes.[13]

PROBLEM OF MOTIVATION

Why do workers work? To answer this question, w must turn to the problem of incentives, a crucial area in th understanding of the psychology of work. The truth is tha every problem in production is a problem in human motiva tion. A deeply entrenched attitude (although, happily, declining one) is that man is inherently lazy and will wor only because he has been unable to invent a better way o

[12] *Ibid.*, p. 337.

[13] For other confirmations of the use of democratic techniques, especiall as it applies to supervision, see N. R. F. Maier, *Principles of human rela tions* (New York: John Wiley & Sons, Inc., 1952), especially chaps. vi and ix.

surviving. According to this view, the worker must be driven to produce, watched over by a foreman, and carefully paced if he is to produce the quota for which he is being paid.

Veblen long ago exposed the fallacy, if not the absurdity, of this view of the nature of man. While he wrongly ascribed an "instinct of workmanship" to man, Veblen was nevertheless right in his argument that work gives man a high degree of personal-emotional satisfaction.[14] If a man does not show the interest in his work that management expects, and if the wages he receives seem to him to be more important than the work itself, this condition is partly explained by the fact that the deadening routine of the machine process induces such an attitude. Thus the worker seldom experiences the sense of being a vital part of the productive process. "The conveyor belt," as we have said elsewhere, "is a living symbol of the repetitive routine of work, and frustration and taut nerves are its psychological symptoms."[15] Under more humane circumstances, especially those in which group self-direction plays a functional part, man can find joy in his work.[16]

There exists also a traditional and deeply entrenched belief that man works only for money. But reliable scientific data refute this notion. The reader will recall our brief reference in Chapter 2 to the experience of the girls in the Western Electric Company. These employees were given the opportunity of increasing their earnings substantially by working singly on the bonus plan, but they refused it, preferring instead to work for less in order to stay together. Group belongingness successfully competed with pecuniary gain. They chose the hourly rate over the bonus plan, not because they were insufficiently motivated, but because their

[14] T. Veblen, *The theory of business enterprise* (New York: Charles Scribner's Sons, 1904).

[15] H. Bonner, *Social psychology: an interdisciplinary approach* (New York: American Book Co., 1953), p. 294.

[16] For an eloquent and scholarly discussion of the satisfying nature of productive work, see H. DeMan, *Joy in work* (London: George Allen & Unwin, Ltd., 1929). Trans. from the German by E. Paul and C. Paul.

incentives were *different.* Motivation underlies both courses of action, but it takes a different direction in each. Man's attitude toward money is bound up with his attitude toward others. He no more reacts to money as an isolated commodity than he reacts to others as if they were completely self-contained individuals. Money, motives, and human relations are intertwined.

MOTIVATION AND ORGANIZATIONAL CONTEXT. There is a long tradition in American psychology of dealing with human motivation as if it were largely an individual phenomenon. This is due in part to the influence of biological accounts of the behavior of lower animals. While we no longer subscribe to the instinct doctrine in psychology, the theory of drives which has replaced it still conceives motives too rigidly in the framework of individual tension reduction.

Contemporary social psychology, on the other hand, defines motives as socially conditioned needs. Motives are derived from the social group in different learning situations; therefore, they vary not only with individuals but with groups. Men strive for such values as group belongingness, self-esteem, security, and similar goals, not because they are biological animals, but because they are social beings who respond to the attitudes of others.

Researches during the past quarter-century have abundantly shown that human desires are not satisfied in the same way in different social environments. The structure of the group has a noticeable effect on both desires and their satisfaction. Accordingly, the organizational structure of an industrial plant, which concerns us here, will define the nature and the means of satisfying the interests of its members. Thus, although the hunger drive is found in both the manager and the worker because they are both biological animals, the manner in which each satisfies his need is strongly conditioned by the status which each holds in the social system of the factory.

Incentives for production. The study of human motives in an industrial setting is important to the student of group dynamics in industry because of the strong bearing of motives on the problem of production. Every manager wants the workers to produce to the limit of their capacity, but the crucial question is how to motivate them to do so.

It is not necessary to stress again the fact that men prefer to do those things regarding which their own decisions played a substantial part. They produce more, reach their production goals more effectively, and experience greater satisfaction from their work through group decision than they do when they resentfully obey an order from above.[17]

The use of democratic means for inducing production increase contrasts sharply with the traditional conception of what makes a worker work. The "stick and the carrot" conception was the frame of reference in which industry operated.[18] In this framework, the worker was callously exploited for the benefit of the owners and managers of production. The humanizing quality which we stressed earlier was largely absent. Only those in the upper level of the industrial organization pyramid had any clear idea of the goal of their own endeavors. In this situation the worker could not be expected to develop pride in his occupation or show loyalty to the system which had degraded him. In this process, as Blum points out, industry singlemindedly undermined its own productive efficiency.[19]

Recent experiments using democratic techniques have demonstrated that the workers' incentives for increasing production are strengthened when the workers participate in setting up their own quotas. Employes do not accept production quotas merely because they are submitted to them from above. The production goal, as Whyte has pointed out, should not be established by the management alone. Workers "are moved much more strongly toward the

[17] We use the term "productivity" in both a quantitative and qualitative sense. A group is productive when it meets the required quota, when its work is accepted as fulfilling the qualitative standards of the shop, and when it is efficient in reaching its goal, etc.

[18] See F. H. Blum, *Toward a democratic work process* (New York: Harper & Bros., 1953), pp. 163–64.

[19] *Ibid.*, p. 163.

goals they themselves had a part in setting."[20] Even when the goals are entirely set up by the management the achievement of them is more likely assured when the group is given the initiative that it rightfully deserves. Workers and leaders of workers' groups take justifiable pride in setting their own sights and aiming for them unhindered by a crippling fear concerning the management's evaluation. The evaluation which they respect and which serves as an incentive to continue in their task is one that is reasonable and free of the personal bias of the manager. While all workers want a good pay rate—for who does not?—they want even more to be respected and appreciated by those with whom they spend their working hours. It is a psychological commonplace that all normal people want to be liked and to feel that what they are doing is important. In a recent survey of 2,500 skilled workers by Ian C. Ross and Alvin Zander, as reported in *The New York Times,* it was found that the need for recognition was a very significant factor in motivating the workers on the job. Indeed, the greatest difference between those who quit and those who remained on the job was degree of satisfaction in the area of recognition.[21]

Management has been traditionally blind to the role of the social system of the factory in the lives of its workers. This social system is generally not an abstract pattern of worker-management relations but a living reality. A third of every workingman's day is spent in close contact and interaction with others. "He may want money," as Whyte observes, "but he also wants to be liked and respected by the people he works with. An extra dollar a day and a pat on the back from the foreman are nice things in themselves, but they can hardly compensate (in most cases) for eight hours a day of ostracism from the work group."

For good results in production there must be a better feeling between worker and management than now exists in many industrial plants. Management has now at its dis-

[20] W. F. Whyte, *Patterns for industrial peace* (New York: Harper & Bros., 1951), p. 191.
[21] *The New York Times,* March 24, 1957.

posal a great amount of tested evidence from group dynamics and the psychology of industrial relations upon which to base a changed and improved policy. Neither management nor labor is so obtuse as not to recognize that each is constantly helping the other to reach its goal. Both are rewarded by increased productivity. If the worker does not want to help management attain its production quota, and thereby help management increase its own earnings, the reason often lies in his distrust of management. But antipathy and distrust must give way to esteem and confidence. "Only under those circumstances," says Whyte, "can it become a good thing for workers to take actions that help management, while they help themselves." Only when this happens are the workers no longer pulled in opposite directions. They can make money," Whyte continues, "and still be accepted by the work group." Their respect for one another is enhanced, so that instead of dissipating their energies by pulling in different directions they will aim for a common goal.

Whyte cites a striking example of this conflict and conciliation between management and the workers. The workers, at great financial loss to themselves, curtailed production in a factory throughout a protracted period of conflict between themselves and the management. However, when distrust of the management was eliminated, the pattern of interaction markedly improved, and with the improvement in the objective conditions the attitudes that the people had toward one another also changed. Describing the situation Whyte writes as follows:

> For the first time, stepping up production became a good thing to do—from any point of view. So the workers went out and stepped it up. They went after the money—to be sure—but only when it fitted into the proper social setting. Money had only limited drawing power in a social system shot through with conflict and distrust.[22]

The foregoing description and analysis make clear that motivation in an industrial organization is as complex as in

[22] W. F. Whyte, *Patterns for industrial peace* (New York: Harper & Bros., 1951), p. 194.

any other social system. Man responds to the total industrial set-up, not only to a single function. Thus, while money is important because it gives some guaranty of individual survival and safeguards the welfare of the worker's family, it is only one factor, albeit an important one, in his motivational complex. When money becomes excessively important, or perhaps all-consuming, the fault lies somewhere in the objective relations of the worker and manager, and it is a symptom of industrial pathology. In extreme cases the incentive to make money overshadows the worker's ethical judgment, and he will try to get as much as he can for as little work as possible.

There is no single formula for improving worker-manager relationship, and no simple psychology for directing human incentives into productive effort. We are not blind to the fact that the preservation of nondemocratic management serves needs and motives that are more impelling than even increased productivity. Nevertheless, the problem can be boiled down to the need for *democratic management*. It is not only anachronistic but also dangerous for industry to function autocratically in a democratic society. The numerous studies of the effects of group participation, group cooperation, democratic leadership, and the like bear an obvious lesson to modern industry. Only through management-worker cooperation, in which the individual is treated with dignity and respect, and where his needs of recognition, autonomy, and a just appraisal of his work by the managers are concrete practices, can modern industry get in tune with the basic values of democracy. Democratic management is an empty phrase unless it is implemented by a leadership practice that permits the worker to use his full productive and creative capacities. As we said before, production is partly a function of the organizational context, and not wholly of the amount of time and energy expended by the worker. In a study of supervisory practices in high-production and low-production groups in an insurance company, Katz and his collaborators found distinct differences in efficiency. Supervision in the high-production group was characterized by less supervisory direction, greater worker-participation, and more consideration of the motives and incentives of the workers. The study, like many others dealing with the same problem, confirms the importance of worker-participation in increased production.[23]

Further encouraging support for the importance of group decision-making in increasing group productivity is found indirectly in a study of the decision-making conference by Marquis, Guetzkow, and Heyns, which we have already cited.[24] These investigators were fully aware of the fact that the research findings regarding group productivity may vary with the type of group under investigation. For instance, a small discussion group and a labor-management conference would not necessarily yield the same results. There is no a priori reason, however, to doubt that each can throw valuable light on the nature of group productivity.

Omitting the findings on member satisfaction, participation, cohesiveness, and so forth, in this study, we may turn to the results regarding group productivity as measured by whether an agenda item was completed, not completed, or postponed to a later meeting.

One measure which was significantly related to productivity was the extent of self-oriented (as contrasted with group-oriented) need behavior. The relationship was found to be negative; that is, the more self-oriented the need behavior, the less productive the group. The implication of this for worker-managament relations should be obvious.

The second factor which was significantly related to productivity was directly motivational in character. It related to "the urgency of the problem." Problem urgency was found to "correlate significantly with productivity"; that is, the more urgent the problem, the more productive the group.

[23] See D. Katz, N. Maccoby, and N. C. Morse, *Productivity, supervision and morale in an office situation, Part I* (Survey Research Center, University of Michigan, 1950).

[24] D. G. Marquis, H. Guetzkow, and R. W. Heyns, A social psychological study of the decision-making conference, in H. Guetzkow (ed.), *Groups, leadership and men* (Pittsburgh: Carnegie Press, 1951), pp. 55-67.

The third measure of relationship was found in the area of "power" relationships. The possession of "power" by the group to proceed on its own authority "correlated significantly with productivity"; that is, the more adequate the group's power, the more productive it turned out to be.

Peripheral to our claim of the importance of the worker's participation, but supporting it nonetheless, was the investigators' discovery that "shared leader functions and informal group procedures, patterns of functioning which are often resisted by groups because they are regarded by members as inefficient, did not reduce productivity."[25]

The study by Berkowitz, which we described in our discussion of collective problem-solving, disclosed roughly the same results.[26] Particularly important, he found, was problem-urgency and the permissiveness of the leader. Problem-urgency was significantly related to group motivation, and leader-permissiveness was positively associated with "the percentage of all solution proposing done by the members when the group's problems are relatively urgent."[27]

The importance of self-esteem was until recently almost unrecognized in the incentive for production. Self-esteem is derived from different sources, but most frequently from social status. Although not identical with security, social status is closely linked with it. An industry that guarantees its workers security of employment and wages commensurate with the needs of the time can measurably increase the psychological well-being of its employees. This point is clearly confirmed in the well-known experiment in the democretic work process of the Hormel Company, a packing house in Austin, Minnesota, where wages and worker-satisfaction both increased. The average Hormel worker earned $4,590 in 1951, while the average worker in the American packing industry in that same year earned only $3,460.[28]

[25] *Ibid.*, p. 64.

[26] L. Berkowitz, Sharing leadership in small, decision-making groups, *J. abnorm. soc. Psychol.*, *48* (1953), 231–38.

[27] *Ibid.*, p. 237.

[28] Cited in Blum, *Toward a democratic work process,* p. 157.

But equally significant are comparative production figures. Blum shows that at Hormel production over and above the standard work requirement averaged 60 per cent in 1950, and in some departments it averaged over 100 per cent. Hormel workers have the same base pay, "yet they produced and hence earned, well over 30 per cent more while they put in almost 20 per cent less time than other workers in the packing industry: the average Hormelite worked 34.4 hours in 1951, the average packinghouse worker 41.5 hours!"[29]

The needs for security and self-esteem played a signal role in the productive process at Hormel, and the experience of the latter strikingly points up its possibilities in any industrial organization. The Hormel plant experiment eliminated the fear of losing one's job and the fear of a speedup. The guaranty of security is, as Blum, indicates, "an essential aspect of a democratization of the work process." "Fear of losing one's job," he adds, "is incompatible with a creative self-expression, and fear of speed-up is a sign of an undemocratic organization of work—it results from a lack of self-determination of the work performance." Guaranteed wages are in effect "a promise of security and a stimulus to freedom."[30] In the Hormel plant the worker has achieved a high degree of self-esteem because he is recognized, to quote Blum once more, "as a human being rather than as a cog in a wheel."[31]

Concluding Remarks. Our brief analysis of the role of motivation in productivity reiterates and confirms what the greater bulk of research on motivation in industry has borne out: Motivation is not wholly—nor even primarily—an individual variable. Certainly its force and direction are functions of the social situation in which it arises and is exercised. People work not because they are ambitious—although this factor must be recognized—but because their egos are in-

[29] *Ibid.*, p. 158.

[30] *Ibid.*, p. 161. The last statement is quoted by Blum from O. Tead, *New adventures in democracy* (New York: McGraw-Hill Book Co., Inc., 1939), p. 177.

[31] Blum, *Toward a democratic work process*, p. 162.

volved in the task which they perform. Whenever a person has a part in creating something, he wants to succeed in creating it; for success in a chosen task is a source of his self-esteem. A trait which distinguishes those who persevere in a task and those who give it up is a strong need for recognition, for an image of ones' self that is approved and appreciated by others.

Numerous researches in the area of group behavior in the past two decades show conclusively that when members of a group are involved in making their own decisions they will change in desirable directions. Democracy as a form of self-direction is not an empty folk-word nor a becoming sentimentality, but a creative force. The experience of sharing in the decision-making process effectuates changes which under imposed conditions would be either reluctantly accepted or outrightly rejected.

Since motivational energies are influenced by the organizational context in which an individual pursues his vocation, the management, whether in the person of the president, superintendent, or supervisor, also behaves according to the roles which it is expected to play. The constraints of this role expectation have changed enormously during the past fifty years. The executive, whether at the top or the bottom of the power pyramid, can no longer operate in an untrammeled way. He finds it both necessary and profitable to heed the needs and motives of the working group, which is constantly growing more articulate. While the maximization of profit is still a driving force in managerial behavior, it is increasingly circumscribed and constrained by the group-imposed democratic values. Like every normal human being, the manager is responsive to the values of society as they are filtered through to him by the status and role which are assigned to him, even though he may at times let other satisfactions take precedence. A complete theory of motivation, if such be possible, must accordingly be applicable to the behavior of both worker and manager in a context of mutually shared values.

Finally, if the democratic method in industry works—and research has established the fact that it works more effectively than was initially expected——it is not because the democratic process per se is superior to all other value systems, but because it is generally founded on a sounder theory of individual and group behavior. This theory is characterized by principles which in one way or another we have utilized in this book. These principles are briefly the following: (1) social pressure is a powerful motive to act in the interests of the group; (2) group belongingness is present in all normal persons and helps to destroy the barrier between the manager and the worker; (3) forcing another individual to submit arbitrarily to one's will is degrading to him, causing him to rebel against the other instead of cooperating with him; (4) recognition is important to every individual, and if this is denied him by excluding him from participation in the group's deliberations his hostility is aroused, and this makes cooperation difficult if not impossible; (5) ego-involvement in the group task is indispensable and desirable, for it increases an individual's desire to pursue the group's goal or solve its problem; (6) people are not exclusively motivated by the need for stability and safety, but strive for change and new experience, as well.

The foregoing principles are motivational categories. If they are sound—and research has supported them extensively—then the democratic behavior which they describe should be sufficient to serve as a basis for humane and meaningful controls in industry. They refute the notion, held paradoxically even by Kurt Lewin, that authoritarian means may have to be employed to achieve democratic ends.[32] They make it difficult for those managers and executives who not only want to retain their power but are searching for scientific rationalizations of their positions. This rationalization group dynamics not only cannot supply but has been effectively helping to destroy.

[32] See K. Lewin, *Resolving social conflicts* (New York: Harper & Bros., 1948), p. 50: "Sometimes people must rather forcefully be made to see what democratic responsibility toward the group as a whole means."

TRAINING FOR INDUSTRIAL PERFORMANCE

It is easy to see that if mutual trust and cooperation between workers and managers are to be increased, something positive has to be done to achieve them. Clearly, the techniques of group dynamics, founded on the premise that industrial relations constitute a problem in the management of people and not only of machines, are an educational device for bringing this condition about. This educational tool includes the more individual approach of the clinical psychologist, for it is cognizant of the fact, as we have shown, that some industrial problems are consequences of personal maladjustments. While we shall discuss this "clinical" approach only briefly in connection with counseling, it is effective in changing those defensive and destructive personality characteristics that interefere with the productive effort.

Training for improved industrial performance does not concentrate on the few with special talents, exceptional skills, or managerial potential. The democratic ethic, supported by group dynamic researches, conceives training or education not only for the upper ten per cent, but for the broad base of factory workers. Moreover, the tenor of the discussion permeating this book is that most, if not all, workers are educable, and that very many of them possess an ability that is seldom tapped. Besides, industrial education is not only concerned with developing aptitudes and skills, but even more with the vital process of attitudinal change.

The foregoing remarks take on an increased importance when we recognize the fact that the traditional concern of industry with the production potential of its workers has been, if not cynical, then unduly pessimistic. Until the advent of scientific training programs, especially those based on democratic values and group-dynamic principles, an unusually large percentage of industrial workers was considered to be incapable of appreciable improvement.[33] The

[33] See F. Cushman, The foreman's place in the training program, in W. J. Donald, *Handbook of business administration* (New York: McGraw-Hill Book Co., Inc. 1931).

evidence furnished by group dynamics and industrial psychology in recent years points to a reversal of this view and justifies an optimistic attitude. In every industrial plant there are only a few workers who are wholly unteachable or without a promotion potentiality. Among them are persons of congenitally low energy potential, deficient drive, and inferior mental capacity.

It is, of course, impossible to give a detailed description and analysis of the variety of training techniques used in modern industry. But since our task is not to describe specific programs, such as apprenticeship, training schools, staff officers' instruction, on-the-job training, and the like, we shall briefly indicate the role of group dynamics in the broader aspects of the training of industrial personnel.

THE CONFERENCE METHOD. Having discussed the conference or group-discussion method on several occasions, the main characteristics should by now be familiar. In many ways it is the democratic method *par excellence.* It consists in a free and critical expression in a highly permissive social atmosphere of ideas, opinions, and attitudes. There may or may not be a designated leader; in many instances the leader emerges from the interaction process by the stimulating value of his ideas or by the sheer "force" of his personality. If, however, the group should be more formal, it will have a prepared agenda and an established leader in the person of a chairman.

If the discussion does not degenerate into an interminable wrangle, the members find it not only productive but highly satisfying—even those who do not participate overtly. Consequently it generates good morale and "we-feeling," and results in cooperation and identification with the problem under consideration. In an industrial plant it is especially well suited to straighten out misunderstandings in departmental matters and resolve interindividual tensions and conflicts.

As a study in human relations the conference method is a good illustration of the pull and counterpull of psychological factors, and one which makes most members more aware and appreciative of the role of compromise and the productive nature of group consensus. While this process is slow and, in terms of time-consumption, expensive, the results it produces, both in the solution of problems and the improvement of group morale, fully justify its extensive use.

ROLE-PLAYING. Like the conference or group-discussion technique role-playing is a form of spontaneous communication among members of a group, and the results are similarly affected by the manner in which the members interact with one another. The fundamental difference between the two is that, unlike group discussion, which is confined to verbal behavior, role-playing consists fundamentally of acting out the problem which has been presented for solution. While discussion helps people to appreciate other points of view, role-playing sensitizes them to the effect which they have on others. Role-playing also generates a wholesome self-awareness. In the employment situation role-playing helps the worker and the boss to understand each other better, for each has an opportunity to put himself in the other person's place and to "see" the situation through that person's eyes. The boss, for example, by playing the role of the worker, will quickly discover how the latter feels when he gives him orders, or treats him in a peremptory manner. This awareness of the effect of one's own actions upon others is particularly sharpened when the interchange of roles takes place immediately and without the intervention of other roles.[34]

It is a serious mistake to conceive of role-playing as wholly or largely an intellectual process. It brings understanding not only by sensitizing people to one another but even more truly—judging by the writer's own observation

[34] For a good introduction to the use of role-playing in supervisory training, consult the following: L. P. Bradford, Supervisory training as a diagnostic instrument, *Person. Admin.*, 8 (1945), 3–7; L. P. Bradford and R. Lippitt, Role-playing in supervisory training, *Personnel*, 22 (1946), 358–69; A. Bavelas, Role-playing and management training, *Sociatry*, 1 (1947), 183–91. The social-psychological nature of role behavior is fully discussed in Chapter 12, below.

and experience—by presenting them with an opportunity to experience a problem on an emotional level. It has cathartic value because irritations and aggressions can be freely expressed without the penalty of someone's disapproval. By resolving his conflicts in role-playing an individual is free to face a problem situation constructively instead of defensively. As he learns to accept himself in the role-playing process, he also comes to accept others understandingly instead of critically.

Finally, role-playing is valuable and effective because, in addition to changing people's emotions and attitudes toward others and the work situation, it results in changed behavior, as Maier has pointed out. "Role playing," Maier says, "carries the training into action, even if the action is only at the level of play. Once an action has been expressed the resistance to a repetition of the action is reduced. . . . Role playing becomes the laboratory part of human relations training."[35]

THE SYSTEMATIC INTERVIEW. The interview technique is a group method in that it involves two or more people in interaction. The systematic interview is at once a technique for determining a worker's fitness for a job and a device for developing good public relations. When conducted by a skillful interviewer, this method can not only elicit valuable information but also stimulate free discussion. This is partly inherent in the systematic interview itself for—unlike the case of the conventional interview—in the systematic interview the questions grow out of the interview situation. Well-conducted systematic interviews can yield ratings that are diagnostic of a worker's future success on his job.[36] Moreover, the reliability of a systematic interview is increased when more than one interviewer makes an assessment of the applicant or the worker.[37]

[35] Maier, *Principles of human relations*, pp. 98–99; for cases, pp. 110–38.

[36] See H. C. Hovland and T. J. Wonderlic, Prediction of industrial success from a standardized interview, *J. appl. Psychol.*, 23 (1939), 537–46.

[37] We omit discussion of the nondirective interview, which is similar to the above, because it is so much like nondirective counseling that for practical purposes it is a kind of informal psychotherapy.

Although systematic interviewing is associated mostly with personnel selection and merit ratings, its greatest value lies in its disclosure of individual attitudes. A skilled interviewer can elicit attitudes without pressures, thus assuring that they are a true expression of the interviewee's real feelings and values. The latter are important, for as we said in the opening paragraphs of this chapter, the worker brings to his job not only his knowledge and skills, but a whole pattern of attitudes, sentiments, values, and other culturally conditioned dispositions.

The interview is valuable, finally, for the increased understandings that accrue from it to both the interviewer and his subject. An interview may clear up misunderstandings that originate in emotional situations, where neither the worker nor the boss was very rational. The interview session establishes a delay period during which the disturbed individual may find his bearings and clarify his thinking. The delay period is, in effect, as it is in individual behavior, a thought process during which hasty conclusions are checked and precipitate action is blocked.

Personnel Counseling. We approach this technique with considerable trepidation. The well-informed reader, we know, will be critical of a brief description of a very complex problem; and the elementary student may not get much meaningful knowledge from it.[38] We shall limit our discussion to nondirective, or client-centered counseling, terms introduced into the literature of psychotherapy by Carl Rogers.[39]

Nondirective counseling in an industrial organization is not intended for severely disturbed cases. These require the help of a psychiatrist or of a professionally trained psychotherapist. It can be used effectively with mildly disturbed,

38 For a concise but lucid discussion of nondirective counseling, with application to the work situation, see Maier, *Principles of human relations*, chap. xiii.

39 See C. Rogers, *Counseling and psychotherapy* (Boston: Houghton Mifflin Co., 1942), and *Client-centered therapy* (Boston: Houghton Mifflin Co., 1951).

frustrated, anxious, and hostile individuals. While such individuals may be recognized by the average foreman, they are usually misunderstood, avoided, or clumsily handled by him. Too often these persons are relegated to the category of "troublemakers," or they are discharged from their jobs. This practice is generally more wasteful than is commonly recognized, for with proper counseling they can be helped to change and to grow into efficient personnel. Even a patient foreman, eager to help and to preserve the worth of his men, can utilize the technique in mild cases. At any rate, he might help, and his help can do no damage for, as Maier points out, it "can have no harmful effects if improperly used."[40]

Superficially, client-centered counseling appears simple, for it seeks to do only two things for the maladjusted person, namely, to release his emotions and to reflect back to the individual his own tensions and anxiety. Actually it requires unusual empathy, intuition, skill, and forbearance. The most reassuring aspect of nondirective counseling to the maladjusted person is the permissive social atmosphere in which he is neither praised nor condemned but only encouraged to talk about his feelings more and more. This very *giving of himself*, the value of which is not always fully appreciated by the practitioners of the method themselves, has the effect of reducing anxiety and of accepting the giving of themselves by others. The result is mutual acceptance and mutual trust, which are essential qualities of democratic group relations.

Risk Technique. This technique, named and used by Maier, is very effective for reducing fear.[41] It integrates some features of the free discussion technique and nondirective counseling. It differs from both, however, in that it *directs the discussion into an expression of fears.* It is based on the principle that every person who has fears can help every other person with fears by communicating them to

[40] Maier, *Principles of human relations,* p. 414.
[41] *Ibid.*, pp. 62-73.

him. "The group's expression thus serves to clarify fears and at the same time creates a situation where such expression is acceptable. When all members express some fears, further expression of fears is facilitated so that even the lesser fears can become expressed."[42] The fear of a union shop, for example, as Maier points out, does not necessarily imply a desire for an open shop. But the rejection of one alternative places the individual in the open-shop camp. Suspicion thus falls upon him, even though his preference is clear. Fears of this type are based on "the imagined goals of the opposition," although "neither side has the goals attributed to it."[43]

This situation seems to be a special case of "pluralistic ignorance," and since imputed motives are the source of the fear it might be called *pluralistic fantasy*. The cure for this pluralistic fantasy, with its elements of risk and danger, is for the members concerned to discuss the risks involved and to disregard any discussion of possible gains; for when the fears have been expressed, they can be of further value because they can be re-examined and periodically evaluated.[44]

CONCLUSION

The subject of human relations is vast and complicated, and this chapter has presented only the large features of the problem. Much had to be omitted, and much has been treated only briefly. We have not even touched on the vital and social-psychologically intricate problem of the role of labor unions in modern industry. We must omit a discussion of the fact that the organization of labor into unions has given the worker not only a more advantageous bargaining power with industry, thereby increasing his share in policy- and decision-making, but it has won for him that dignity and self-respect which raises his work a level above sheer drudgery.[45]

42 *Ibid.*, p. 62.
43 *Ibid.*, p. 63
44 *Ibid.*, p. 63.
45 For a brief but enlightened discussion of the role of labor unions in modern industrial society, see Blum's *Toward a democratic work process*, chaps. i–iii.

The studies cited or described in this chapter, as well as many others which we have omitted, call attention to the important group factors and other social-psychological variables that affect worker-management relations. They show that an industry is fundamentally a social system, and as a social system it has a set of expectations regarding personnel. They demonstrate that the worker does not want money only, although it is the source of security for himself and those for whose welfare he feels responsible, but also such important psychological values as dignity and self-respect. He wants his employees and his fellow-workers to appreciate and understand him. He wants an opportunity to enjoy meaningful human association on the job. "When industrial leaders recognize these needs and act to fulfill them, they add decisively to industrial morale and the reduction of avoidable friction."[46]

Our discussion of training in human relations did not go to the roots of the problem of productiveness and the humanization of work. It was too brief to accomplish so difficult a task. In any case, the point to be noted is that the importance of techniques lies not in themselves but in how well they change people's attitudes and behavior and in what direction.

Finally, there is much more than understanding organizational structure and using the latest technical skills involved in the improvement of industrial relations. More than anything else, what is requisite is the determination by all concerned to subordinate technical proficiency and the alleged but spurious scientific objectivity to moral considerations. There may be scientists who are deluded enough to believe that their investigations transcend human values, but they must be a very small minority. Researches in the last fifty years have created a growing realization that the line separating scientific objectivity from value-relatedness is practically nonexistent. Where such alleged "objectivity" exists

[46] Bonner, *Social psychology,* p. 375. For the most up-to-date research on the more inclusive area of large organizations, see *J. soc. Issues, 12,* No. 2 (1956), 69 pp.

it is always an artifact of historical conditions and a narrow or distorted conception of the nature of science—especially as it relates to human actions and preferences. It is for these reasons that the ethics of democracy have persistently obtruded themselves on the pages of this book. Where this "ethical conception of human relationships" is absent, a contempt for human beings, however rationalized and concealed it may be by those who practice it, is found to be the basic philosophy. In such cases, no matter how pretentious the apparatus for solving human relations problems may be, "it does not come to grips," as Blum makes clear, "with the problem of the ethical nature of man." Consequently, he continues,

> . . . man is cut off from the life-spring of his being and scientific thought becomes shallow. It becomes often an instrument to implement existing power positions and to manipulate people to make them satisfied with a basically undemocratic industrial organization. This is the ultimate result of spurious "objectivity"—the worst idol worship of the *status quo* a scientist could be guilty of.[47]

[47] F. H. Blum, *Toward a democratic work process*, p. 176.

CHAPTER 10

Group Dynamics in Community Relations

There is a prodigious sociological literature on the structure, organization, and change of the human community. Anthropologists have added to this literature a number of excellent comparative community studies, especially from the cross-cultural point of view. The earlier studies were motivated largely by humanitarian interest, particularly by the urgency of ameliorating pathological conditions in our cities. While this interest should not be condemned, it did not lead to any theoretical and scientific understanding of community dynamics. This early period was followed by an interest in detailed ethnographic description, exemplified by the pioneering work of the Lynds in the 1920's.[1] Today, owing in part to the group-dynamics movement in social science, there is a growing interest in community dynamics—in action programs, intergroup tensions and conflicts, cohesiveness, community leadership, and similar problems. This interest is best described as *interactional* in contrast to

[1] See R. S. Lynd and H. M. Lynd, *Middletown* (New York: Harcourt, Brace & Co., Inc., 1929).

demographic, ethnographic, and purely ecological descriptions.

The group-dynamics approach calls for a more restricted definition of the human community. While there have been many definitions of the term, the most common or traditional view defined the community largely, but not exclusively, in terms of the local area—in terms, that is, of neighborhoods, towns, cities, and regions.[2] Group dynamics, on the other hand, calls, as we have said, for a more restricted meaning. From our point of view a community is not primarily a spatial, demographic, or ecological area—although it is these things, too, of course—but a social group in which interaction is the fundamental process.[3] Our conception recognizes the spatial or localized nature of the community, but the distinguishing mark of the latter, from our point of view, is its group-interactional character.[4] In studying the community, therefore, we are not deserting our main preoccupation, which is the study of dynamic groups, but extending our concepts beyond the small informal group to the viable human community.

THE COMMUNITY AS A DYNAMIC GROUP

Even a primitive community, which is conventionally described as stable and enduring, is subject to change when seen in the perspective of time. However, in this chapter we shall dwell on the modern community, which is subject to constant, and often rapid, change. Its members are present, not voluntarily, as in many of the contrived groups that

[2] See A. B. Hollingshead, Community research: development and present condition, *Amer. sociol. Rev.*, *13* (1948), 136–46.

[3] While R. E. Park described the community, particularly the city, in interactional terms as early as 1915, his conception was not fundamentally a group-structural and -dynamic definition. See R. E. Park and E. W. Burgess, *The city* (Chicago: The University of Chicago Press, 1925). His paper, "The City," was originally published in 1915.

[4] For an earlier formulation of a similar view, see E. T. Hiller, The community as a social group, *Amer. sociol. Rev.*, *6* (1941), 189–202. See also J. Bernard, Some social-psychological aspects of community study: some areas comparatively neglected by American sociologists, *Brit. J. Sociol.*, 2 (1951), 12–30.

we have described, but involuntarily, because there is no other way for them to survive as individuals. Involuntary membership at once suggests the question of why people work together in groups for the attainment of common goals. While the answer is complex, it can be simplified without distortion by reiterating a former assertion, namely, that group belongingness as such is a fundamental source of security and satisfaction. This has been a theme running through writings from Plato's *Republic* to Tönnies' *Gemeinschaft und Gesellschaft* to the most recent researches of group dynamics. The genuine community, characterized by common sentiments and understandings, is attractive and holds people together in the pursuit of a common objective. Consensus, agreement, concord—these have always been fundamental in community life.[5]

Modern social-psychological and anthropological researches, furthermore, have convincingly demonstrated that since we ourselves are products of group membership the feeling of community, of belongingness, is essential to normal living. It may very well be a truth which history might some day demonstrate, that the peace and freedom about which men dream will be realized when they universally share goals and obligations with one another.

THE PSYCHOLOGY OF NOT BELONGING. In his brief but psychologically sensitive analysis of group belongingness, A. J. Marrow presents a very perceptive description of the feeling of not belonging, especially as it pertains to those members of the community who are rejected because of racial, national, and religious differences. The unequal

[5] Students of group dynamics seem to forget or ignore the sensitive and discerning observations that Tönnies made regarding the elemental nature of belongingness and consensus. *Eintracht* (concord), he pointed out, is the community in its most elementary form. See F. Tönnies, *Gemeinschaft und Gesellschaft* (Leipzig: Fues Verlag, 1887). Community *(Gemeinschaft)* is characterized by "organic" as contrasted with "mechanical" connectedness and solidarity. No student of contemporary group dynamics has shown more consistently than Tönnies the *interdependence* of individuals and subgroups that constitute a community in the true, holistic sense. His frequent use of biological analogies was probably meant to underscore this quality of interdependence.

treatment accorded them results in two different forms of responses: it may increase *group solidarity* among some who are rejected by the dominant element of the community, or it may generate *self-hatred.*[6]

The development of group solidarity is a positive and constructive reaction to inequality of treatment. The rejected minority develops into an in-group of its own. This in-group formation involves, as in all in-group relations, a strong identification with the new group. Pride in the new group replaces the former self-consciousness and shame. Individuals experience confidence in themselves, and their self-esteem is heightened. When these experiences are integrated, they strengthen morale and help to make the group more cohesive. At the same time the solidarity of the new group is strengthened by its concerted protest against the unfairness of the larger community and so "provides a new strength for group survival."[7] What happens, in effect, is that a new community is established. The new community is obviously not an ecological entity, not an administrative unit, but rather a new framework of values and social norms, a social bond of common sympathies.

Self-hatred, on the other hand, is quite obviously a negative and psychologically destructive reaction because of its effect upon both the individual and the minority group. It does not lead to a new community of self-confident equals, for the aim of the individual who hates himself for his minority status is to escape identification with the subordinate group. The self-hating individual, obsessed with the need to deny his despised status, is found in most minority groups. Although it may at first blush appear puzzling, the self-hater despises his own people in a manner similar to the hatred shown by the prejudiced majority to minority groups. In its milder forms this self-hatred may consist of no more than a Negro trying to "pass," or in an immigrant changing his name. In its more virulent and cynical expression it reflects all the stereotypes and the derogatory characteristics

[6] A. J. Marrow, *Living without hate* (New York: Harper & Bros., 1951).
[7] *Ibid.*, p. 88.

which are imputed to the minority by the dominant community. The self-hater "seeks to leave the group because he hates to be a member. He may rationalize his rejection on the ground that it is the best solution to the minority problem. The self-hate overflows. Personal deficiencies are projected on the group, its culture, its traditions, its goals."[8]

There is, further, a complicating factor in self-hatred that too often goes unnoticed and which contributes to the self-hater's psychological dilemma. While he has rejected his own community, he remains bound to it, as Marrow notes discerningly, in preserving a defensive sensitivity to the behavior of the group from which he is desperately trying to escape. While he loathes to admit his kinship with it, he cannot fail to recognize that his destiny is nevertheless tied up with it.[9]

Kurt Lewin describes a telling example of this hypersensitivity. While dining in a fashionable restaurant with a non-Jewish friend, a Jewish woman was annoyed by two other guests who talked loudly and were intoxicated. For some reason she felt that these guests might be Jewish. A remark made by her non-Jewish friend, however, set her at ease, for it apparently convinced her that they were not Jewish. From that moment on, Lewin informs us, she "was amused rather than annoyed by their boisterousness."[10]

The chief value of the foregoing description of unbelongingness is the light it sheds upon the *psychological* nature of the community, which is our exclusive interest in this chapter. To repeat a former observation, while we fully realize that the human community is a unity of ecological and psychological elements, as students of group dynamics our interest is focused upon the psychological process of consensus and attitudinal change. Although this approach inevitably yields only a partial account of the total community, the picture which it presents is of the community in its most vital

[8] *Ibid.*, p. 91.

[9] *Ibid.*, p. 92.

[10] K. Lewin, *Resolving social conflicts* (New York: Harper & Bros., 1948), p. 190.

aspects, namely, as a group in which tensions, conflicts, social solidarity, and collective harmony are the dominant characteristics. The unity of the modern community—its social cohesiveness—lies less in the likeness of its individuals or its populational units and more in the kind of interdependence and acceptance of differences which we have described in this book.

GOAL-DIRECTED ACTION. In earlier chapters we introduced the terms *act* and *interact*. If we are going to go beyond the structural analysis of the community, which has been the dominant approach to its study, we must examine it within the framework of *action*. If we wish to go farther than a spatial analysis, we must study the community as a form of goal-directed behavior. *Action toward a goal* is a characteristic of the community as it is of the individual. *Participation* in the solution of community problems is the most important goal of all individuals who are concerned with the community's welfare. Action research has convincingly demonstrated that the surest way of involving citizens in the affairs of their community is, first, to ascertain their own wishes and needs and, second, to encourage them to take active and responsible roles in improving its conditions. This is another way of saying what we have repeatedly stressed, that, given the opportunity, people in interaction will develop into self-directing groups. This is saying, too, that community change and improvement are forms of group decision-making, and that they involve most of the features of collective problem-solving which we have examined—communication, leadership, consensus, and the like. There is no democratic community in the absence of collective participation in the thinking, planning, and acting of the entire group.

It is beyond the limits of this chapter to consider in any detail the objectives of community action. They may be subsumed under the general category of community planning. Since this has become a technical subject in itself, only the barest outline is stated here.

Every community must first satisfy the physical and economic needs of its members. This obviously entails such specific items as employment, the accessibility of consumer's goods, and a sound fiscal economy. It also includes a community organization that makes provision for sanitation, recreation, and livable housing conditions.

The community must also provide its citizens with opportunities for full social and psychological development. This refers to such important matters as adequate educational facilities, cultural opportunities exemplified by art, music, and other aesthetic enjoyments, and similar pursuits. In this connection the role of adult education must play an ever-increasing and important role.

Finally, a genuinely democratic community must instill in its people something that usually is not consciously planned, namely, *a sense of awareness of itself as a community,* as a civilizing agency of the highest order. This awareness is more than civic pride, important as the latter is; rather it is in the deepest sense *a loyalty to itself as a free and democratic society.* Research evidence supports the belief that this view of the community is not an idle fancy. Many of the dynamic groups which we have described exemplify this condition, and students of community life attest to its existence. Arthur E. Morgan, an authority on community life, assures us that "it is approximately the actual condition in numberless small villages and neighborhoods."[11]

Like the dynamic groups which we have studied, the organic community recognizes the rights of dissenters, minority peoples, and the economically underprivileged to play a functional part in its deliberations. In many communities, even those organized on democratic principles, these people are too often ignored and left out of the group's affairs.

Furthermore, there is a tendency of a few people, by reason of their status, prestige, educational qualifications, or economic position, to be overchosen for the management of community leadership and civic affairs. This is a sure

[11] A. E. Morgan, *The small community* (New York: Harper & Bros., 1942), p. 132.

inducement to passivity on the part of many citizens and to their eventual indifference to community well-being. When this happens, it is a sign that the community is not living up to its full responsibilities as an integrating agency in the lives of its people.

The negative effect of excluding any segment from participating in community action is explained by a principle of group dynamics already stated in Chapter 8 and which has been rigorously analyzed by Thelen.[12] It operates in all problem-solving situations, and not only in the classroom. The principle asserts that the solution of a problem must include all levels in the group structure, including all individuals whose actions might create barriers to the solution of the problems. If dissident elements, for example, are ignored, or if their objections are not considered along with the suggestions of others, the freedom of action of the whole group is endangered. Even if their cooperation is not given, or is deemed to be unnecessary by the majority, it should not be overlooked; for the possibility of its being present has an influence on the group.

THE INDIVIDUAL'S PERCEPTION OF THE COMMUNITY. In several places in this book we called attention to the importance of the group's perception of itself and the attitude of its members toward the group. Group self-perception ranks among the most significant features in the life of a community and plays a vital role in the quality of its morale. A sense of awareness of itself as a community, we pointed out, is an integral part of its nature. Whether or not joint action by its members toward a goal will be consummated will be determined in the end by their attitudes toward the group as a whole. People who feel that they "belong" and that the community is their home will approach its problems in a significantly different way from those who do not share this identification. This was made clear in our discussion of the psychology of not belonging.

[12] H. A. Thelen, Engineering research in curriculum building, *J. educ. Res., 41* (1948), 579–96.

An important index of the sense of community belongingness is the sensitivity of individuals to the urgent problems of the group. When group belongingness is strong and community morale is high, people are almost invariably more conscious of the community's needs. What little research exists on this subject, together with our own observation of communities in action, unequivocally points to the fact that persons with positive community self-perceptions are usually the one's who identify with and call attention to the community's needs. This may run the gamut from improving the local schools to the technical problem of water flouridation.

Community self-perception not only generates sensitivity to people's needs but also arouses in them the need for action. This feature is another index of the sense of community belongingness. It is not enough merely to recognize problems; something must be done to solve them. Research in group dynamics has demonstrated that problem-solving is most successful when groups are cohesive and members are task-centered. Likewise, community problems are more likely to be solved when citizens identify themselves with the group and "lose" themselves in the needs of its members. We have made much of the fact that when a group strives for goals that it has itself set up, or when members participate in solving problems themselves, they are much more likely to act upon their solutions than when the latter are externally imposed upon them. People will follow a desirable course of action only when they have themselves had the opportunity to discover and acknowledge its desirability. Community problem-solving is an additional confirmation of this well-established principle.[13]

Bound up with one's perception of the community, and especially with acting on one's perception, is the factor of motivation. It is self-evident that goals exist only because human beings have needs which they strive to satisfy. We

[13] For an illustration of the impairment of collective action when people perceive themselves as dependent and incapable of directing their own affairs, see R. Munoz, B. M. Serra, and A. S. de Roca, Research and evaluation in a program of community education, *J. soc. Issues,* 9 (1953), 43–52.

have seen that a cohesive group is characterized by a strong motivation to engage in mutual activities and by a powerful need to solve the group's problems collectively. Obviously, the goal of community well-being will mean nothing to a group insensitive to the need for collective problem-solving. The more vague and ill-defined people's goals are, the less they will be motivated to strive for their achievement. Social-psychologically, group motivation means community involvement. The more community-involved a person is, other things being equal, the stronger will be his motive to contribute to the community's welfare; and, conversely, the more socially motivated he is, the more community-involved he becomes. This is not a circular argument, for social facts impose their own stamp upon human behavior, especially dynamic and developmental, behavior.

The emphasis on mutual participation and social action does not minimize a principle which we have stressed on many occasions, namely, the place of the individual in the community self-perception. Democracy, we have said, must leave room for the individual. It is a way of life, not a set of rules imposed upon the individual by external pressures. When a community is so overorganized that it coerces its members, even if only by indirect and subtle pressures, into unwilling participation, it is to that extent tyrannical. It must tolerate the unsocial dreamer, for in so doing it may be encouraging the pioneer. It owes him "the freedom to be unsocial if he chooses."[14]

There is no evidence from the comparative study of societies that this form of individualism is harmful either to the person or to the group. On the contrary, even a nodding acquaintance with the history of ideas will show that in the long run society stands to gain from it. Morgan, writing on the place of democratic leadership in a free community, shows a sensitive regard for it. He writes,

> Society has a right to insist that the contacts a man has with society shall be helpful and not harmful, but the number and intensity of such contacts should be for each man to decide for himself. . . .

[14] Morgan, *The small community,* p. 282.

> Relatively solitary persons like Spinoza or Henry Thoreau by their very separateness may get new viewpoints of great value to society. And who knows what degree of intensity of social contacts will give life its greatest value? A man may prefer to have as his intimate associates the great minds of all times in books, or the quiet beauty of nature, rather than his neighbors. He will find some common ground of interest, and will discover ways in which to bring to them some of the values he has found. Otherwise he may be a parasite, taking his living from society, and giving nothing in return. His community may tolerate him, but will not love him.[15]

The pronouncements of some students of group dynamics have been based, not on what man actually is but on what their abstractions have made him out to be. There runs through their thinking the implicit premise that the more men interact with one another, the more they will like one another, and the happier everyone will be. But this view overlooks the well-attested fact that, while men tend to be unhappy in isolation, they are also miserable when they are deprived of the restorative power of isolation and privacy. Human beings are social—even gregarious—animals, no doubt about it; but they also want and need apartness and individuality. When togetherness becomes engulfing and inescapable, men erect emotional barriers between themselves. When this happens, the limits of participation and community have been dangerously overextended.

COMMUNITY ORGANIZATION

Although certain forms of community organization are consequences of rational planning and design, an informal structure is implied in the very concept of community. A community is a form of social organization. From the standpoint of group dynamics, community organization is not necessarily effected by a committee of experts, nor is it merely the group's stamp of approval of the decision of another. In a democratic social group the citizenry makes the decisions and puts them into action. Participation is the basic process, and collective responsibility is the driving

[15] A. E. Morgan, *The small community* (New York: Harper & Bros., 1942), p. 281.

force. The wisdom of its decisions and actions is rendered dependable by the strong identification which the group makes with the community's well-being, and by its readiness to heed the advice of anyone who is deeply involved in its problems. As before, the stress here is not on the ecological, demographic, or geographic arrangement of the human community, but upon the needs and desires of interacting men. Community organization in a democratic society is not primarily a consequence of economic competition, population distribution, and ethnic identity, as some sociologists believe, but comes into being even more in response to purposeful discussion and collective action.

Again, the organized community, despite its name, is not a rigid blueprint or a set of rules. These are necessary, for one cannot learn to know one's community all at once; and in the absence of guides that have grown out of group living they have their uses, especially in the immaturity of growing up. A participating member of a democratic group acts, rather, upon ethical motives, is guided by trust in others, and grows in confidence by being a fellow-member.

Techniques of Community Organization. Since our approach to the problem of the community is that of group dynamics rather than of sociology and of community planning, we shall omit a discussion of such technical matters as community size, zoning, sewage disposal, the location of parks, and the like. Ours is the more difficult task of indicating how men in groups act together to achieve common ends. Some of the means which men in groups use for this purpose, we shall now examine briefly.

The discussion method. We already described this method on several occasions. The chief aim of any discussion is to reach consensus by encouraging the free expression and exchange of ideas, facts, and opinions. In the preceding chapter we described it as the democratic method par excellence. For a substantive illustration of this method, but more particularly to show its effectiveness in maximizing people's participation in policy decision-making, we shall briefly describe Wilson's study of policy formulation in a college community.[16]

Wilson based his investigation on the belief that a pattern of government could be developed "in which the electorate is constantly aware of crucial issues and is active in their solution." He believed, further, that a community discussion program, which we shall describe presently, would enable people to examine differing points of view and would serve them as a means for developing the ability to withhold judgment while the alternative arguments were being reviewed. He assumed, finally, that "the sense of community could be enhanced while, at the same time, attitudes of critical analysis and constructive change were encouraged."[17]

Wilson's study is based on a community discussion program which was initiated at Antioch College in the fall of 1948. The program involved a discussion of college policies by all members of the college community: administrators, students, teachers, clerical workers, and others. Wilson describes the program as "a decentralized town meeting." The membership was assigned to small groups of no more than 25 persons. Minorities like the faculty members were spread randomly throughout thirty discussion groups, which totaled about 750 persons. Attendance was voluntary, ranging from 43 per cent to 69 per cent during the 1949–50 school year. The discussion leaders took care to create a social atmosphere in which the free expression of different points of view would take place.

The discussion topic, which is reported at length by the author, dealt with educational objectives. The range of issues involved in the consideration of this topic was extensive. It included, to mention only several, the desirable size of the college population, pooling of job experiences, self-help on needed construction projects, clarification of the powers and relationship between the community government and the

16 See E. K. Wilson, Determinants of participation in policy formation in a college community, *Hum. Relat.*, 7 (1954), 287–312.

17 *Ibid.*, p. 288.

college administration, intensifying efforts in placing minority-group students on jobs, and so forth.

Wilson's study presents a detailed and interesting description of the factors making for participation in community affairs. Here, however, we shall examine only three factors which were related to participation in the discussion program, namely, the subjects' conception of the democratic process, critical thinking, and identification with the community.[18]

The democratic process was conceived, not as consisting of "internalized social intercourse," that is, not as an imaginary give and take, but as participation in the presence of other individuals. When an individual engages only in internalized social intercourse, he has no opportunity to demonstrate his capacity to others nor to contribute actively to the task of the group. His relationships with others consist mostly of imaginary constructs. His behavior is characterized largely by "self-concern or status anxiety." On the other hand, when he *actively participates* in the presence of others, his interest becomes problem-oriented. He is induced by the "coercive" effect of "public opinion" to do a job or to find a solution to a problem. Since failure to carry a commitment through is observed and evaluated by others, the individual increases his effort to complete the job. There is an unwillingness—perhaps a fear?—to be judged as irresolute by others. "There is," as Wilson asserts, "self-coercion in commitment to a group or to its decisions." This is, of course, in line with the point we have frequently asserted—and which Lewin was one of the first to emphasize—that people are more ready to act upon a decision which they have themselves agreed upon.

Democratic participation, furthermore, affects thinking in ways which we described in detail in Chapters 4 and 7. Active participation in group deliberation exposes people to differing opinions, checks faulty judgment, and eliminates more errors than individual thinking. The total impact of

[18] *Ibid.*, p. 301.

the group's deliberation is to challenge self-oriented and idiosyncratic views by confronting them with authentic contrary views. In this way, Wilson believes, "we come closer to the scientific objective of controlled observation."[19]

The foregoing study of people's identification with the community is in agreement with what we have related in numerous places in this book. We have shown that active participation in community affairs is related to people's interest in community well-being. Their concern with the community's welfare is reflected in "other-directed" attitudes and a problem-centered approach to the community's important issues. People who are ego-involved in the affairs of the group, who identify themselves with the needs of the community, are, on the whole, much more sensitive not only to group pressures but to the well-being of others. They rely less, finally, on established leadership and more on the decisions of the group.

The community council. Typically, a community council is composed of representatives from various public-interest bodies, such as the Chamber of Commerce, service clubs, the League of Women Voters, the Parent Teachers Association, and the like. These groups generally are public-spirited, and their concern is with community well-being. Since it cuts across racial, political, and religious lines, the community council is usually invulnerable to the manipulations of special-interest groups. Its over-all aim is to coordinate the work of the various agencies or institutions of the community whose purpose is to improve the life of the people within it.

When the council is sufficiently large and its welfare interests are considerably varied, the practice has been to divide it into functioning committees. Each committee then concentrates on some special problem, such as juvenile delinquency or the economic improvement of the community. In pursuing these interests, however, the committee does

[19] *Ibid.*, p. 308. We wish to remind the reader that, while there is much truth in the above statement, there is danger that social pressure may destroy originality and suppress the expression of ideas that may appear bizarre only in the cultural context in which they are expressed.

not forget its place in the larger context of organization, but aims to coordinate its activities with other bodies—the committee on economic improvement, for example, will form a liaison with the community's budget office, and the committee on juvenile delinquency will work closely with the law-enforcement body.

Unfortunately, it has been the fate of small communities that they have been unable to bear the financial burdens involved in the performance of certain services. For this reason the community council has been not only a spiritual help but an economic asset as well. Workers in community councils have been volunteers, freely giving their service without financial remuneration, out of loyalty to their community and to their fellow-men. They have been democratic citizens determined to preserve the values of a free society.

An example of a functioning community council may be described briefly. We are referring to the "Citizens' Advisory Committee" in a small Midwestern community. This is a nonpartisan local study and action group which is attempting to find solutions to its school problems through the broad base of participation by its citizens. Its membership is representative of the whole community: there are teachers, farmers, business and professional men, office workers, and other "ordinary citizens." Some are taxpayers and some are not; some have children in school and some do not. They are not experts, they have no axes to grind, no sectarian or political doctrines to disseminate. They have only one purpose: to improve the community by bettering its schools. The meetings are informal, although called to order by an elected chairman. His main function is to see that the agenda items, when there are any, are carefully considered by the group. Deliberations are carried on by means of free discussions in a permissive social atmosphere. Discussions range from the need for curricular changes to the design and location of a new high school building. The members disseminate information concerning school problems and try to enlist public interest in and support of a new school levy to finance a badly needed high school building. The sole remuneration which these devoted citizens hope to get is the satisfaction they anticipate in heightening their community's well-being.

Adult education. When a social system, be it a nation or a small community, begins to become rigid or formalized, the easiest way for it to maintain itself is to remain static and perpetuate ignorance. Thus knowledge has always been an enemy of social complacency and cultural lag.

The implication of the foregoing remarks is clear. In order to maintain a community's health, to promote its growth into a democratic group interested in the well-being of its citizens, education cannot stop at the end of a growing period, or at the terminus of a formal program. Democratic education is continuous. Adult education is continuous education. It is an effort by people in concert to instruct one another in a self-active improvement in the quality of group living. It does not rest on coercion or even on subtle persuasion, but upon an intelligent awareness that education is the surest guaranty of the continuance of each man's choices within the framework of a democratic community. Keeping citizens of a community ignorant is a sure way of perpetuating injustice and cruelty; working together to help one another understand the sources of injustice and cruelty is a positive means of raising the level of life for the whole community.

Furthermore, adult education is based on a principle that differs from the philosophy underlying many other forms of education. Higher education today in particular is founded on the principle that there are wide intellectual differences among men. Its philosophy is that education can benefit only a small segment of the community's population. It would take us beyond the limits of our discussion to examine this philosophy critically. We pause only to point out that it has serious limitations and defects, and that it has been vigorously challenged by responsible thinkers. Adult education, on the other hand, proceeds on the premise that people can govern themselves only when their deliberations are infused with dependable knowledge and with a system of values in which justice and fair play are its highest virtues. This democratic education is designed not only for the individual but for the community in which he will inescapably live. It affirms that in the absence of an informed social intelligence the democratic community will wither and die. It holds that the fruit of adult education is a better civilization for all.

Adult education, however, is not successfully effected by traditional methods of teaching. Lectures and recitations, which are so important in conventional classroom teaching, seldom achieve the same results in adult education. Similarly, course credits and grades seem to afford insufficient motivation for learning among adults. Although adult education has not altogether freed itself from the traditional pattern, it is at least experimenting with new ones. Among these, group discussion is rapidly displacing lectures and recitations. In this pattern the teacher is not the "leader" but a learner like others in the group. In a democratic classroom, as in a democratic community, leadership is shared as fully as the learning situation permits.

We must not, however, deceive ourselves. Desirable and effective as the new pattern of adult education may be, it has not attained its full power. Tradition dies hard, and at the moment adult education has not fully emancipated itself from ancient practices. It is, accordingly, a not-too-happy amalgamation of traditional and group-dynamic methods.

Community self-surveys. Earlier in this chapter we asserted that a democratic community gives to its people a sense of awareness of itself as a community. Its perception of itself, if we may for the moment use a rhetorical figure, is an important element in its being, just as an individual's image of himself sheds light on his psychological nature. The community self-survey can furnish a community with such a perception, with such a portrait of itself. It is a technique for effecting community action on the basis of facts regarding vexing community problems. While to date most of the published surveys deal with the problem of ethnic or racial discrimination, the self-survey technique is in principle applicable to any problems dealing with human relations in the community.[20]

The community self-survey technique which we have in mind was devised by the Commission on Community Interrelations (C.C.I.) and includes a "Discrimination Index," which, as its name indicates, measures the bias or prejudice which people have toward minorities.

Several surveys of American communities have been made by this technique, and the results were published in the *Journal of Social Issues.*[21] The self-surveys were made of Minneapolis, Montclair, New Jersey, and "Northtown," an anonymous community of 40,000 people near New York City. We shall present only the "Northtown" survey.

The survey of Northtown was initiated in 1947. The overall procedure consists of four steps, namely, bringing the people together, stimulating their participation in establishing policies and procedures, gathering facts, and initiating action.

Margot Wormser, of the C.C.I. staff, who headed the study, got a picture of the city by talking with businessmen, teachers, ministers, Negro leaders, a YWCA officer, and others. She next secured sponsorship of the survey by such organizations as the Council of Social Agencies, the Council of Jewish Organizations, the League of Women Voters, the Ministers' Association, the National Association for the Advancement of Colored People, and others—thirteen in all, to be exact. In informing the delegates from the sponsoring organization at the first meeting, Mrs. Wormser clearly indicated that the survey was not of people's attitudes but of discriminatory practices in vital areas of community life.

The general nature of the findings should not surprise us. They revealed widespread discrimination against Ne-

[20] For an early discussion of the "self-survey," see J. Harding, Some basic principles of self-surveys, *J. soc. Issues,* 5 (1949), 21–30. Harding concentrated on civil rights.

[21] C. Selltiz and M. H. Wormser (issue eds.), Community self-surveys: an approach to social change, *J. soc. Issues* 5, No. 2 (1949).

groes and Jews, and the emotional disposition behind the discrimination was shown to be acute. Discrimination and antipathy were especially strong toward Negroes. The discrimination and hostility were classified according to their manifestation among four important community functions, namely, employment, housing, public facilities, and education.

In the area of employment the discrimination was glaring, especially as regards the disadvantaged position of the Negroes. A large percentage of the Negroes was employed in "menial" occupations, such as janitorial and other unskilled work. Over twice as many Negroes as Christian whites were engaged in unskilled or semiskilled work. The difference was most pronounced at the higher levels of employment: 34 per cent of the white Christians and only 7 per cent of the Negroes were managers or professional workers.

The treatment of Jews was much better in this respect. There were many more Jews than white Christians in managerial and professional positions—52 per cent and 12 per cent, respectively. Prejudice toward Jews did, however, exist, as is shown by the fact that some employers did not hire Jews, and many more did not reply to queries regarding the Jews' qualifications and the employers' satisfaction with the work of Jews.

The worst discrimination existed in the area of housing, especially as it pertained to Negroes. While there was prejudice against Jews, as indicated by the refusal of real estate dealers to sell or rent to them, they fared much better than the Negroes. Real estate men gave the usual rationalization of their attitude, namely, that the Gentile residents objected to their presence in their neighborhoods. Negroes made up approximately 12 per cent of the population, but they were restricted to about 5 per cent of the residential area. Most of the existing housing for Negroes was substandard.

Discrimination against Negroes also existed in restaurants, hotels, and health services. Jews did not experience discrimination in those facilities. Negroes were either directly barred from most of the restaurants or were discouraged from going into them. None of the hotels accommodated them. Private physicians had a better record. Only one doctor refused Negroes, and one accepted them on a segregated basis.

While the schools did not discriminate directly, the poorest school buildings were located in the Negro areas. Indirect discrimination was subtly and insidiously practiced in the fact that in the only school that had Negro teachers, 92 per cent of the pupils were Negroes.

Now, the importance to the community of a self-survey is the changes it can effect. Since our present concern is with community organization, the value of the survey data lies in the action it stimulates and the evils it eradicates. From this standpoint, the self-survey of Northtown is its own best vindication: it changed the social and human relations of most of its people by the democratic process. It impelled its citizens to become ego-involved, participating people who discovered their own faults as a community and collectively set out to correct them. Through the help of the Northtown Committee on Human Relations, which the sponsors had themselves voluntarily set up, the community reduced the inequalities which we have briefly described. Social policies were changed, public practices were modified, a new social atmosphere was created, and a better understanding by various groups of the *human* factor, as contrasted with the racial, ethnic, or other minority factor, in community relationships was effected.[22]

It would be interesting to discuss the important implications of the method of community self-survey and some of the questions which it poses. This would involve a detailed and critical examination of the precise relation between the

[22] For a description of four other communities, studied along similar lines but in less detail, see H. Y. McClusky, Comments on four case studies of community organization, *J. educ. Sociol.*, 23 (1949), 183–88. See further, M. W. Perry, Community action to eliminate racial discrimination, *J. educ. Sociol.*, 23 (1949), 168–75.

self-survey and the changes in discriminatory practices. But it is reasonable to suppose that, with the knowledge and insight which the self-survey made possible, Northtown was able to reorganize its collective life on a new level of integration.

COMMUNITY LEADERSHIP

The beginning student of group dynamics might well be occasionally puzzled by the stress on leadership—a word which connotes the direction of one person by another—in a field of study that espouses a democratic philosophy as its foundation. However, our detailed discussion of leadership in Chapter 6, as well as our frequent reference to it in practical group situations, should have reassured him. It is by means of democratic leadership that dogmatic and capricious regimentation can be averted. Democratic leadership, we saw, is based not on authority but on group consensus. It is leadership that is participatory; it is a teamwork in which, in a real sense, everyone is a leader. This is what we mean by "shared leadership." In the long run this kind of leadership will, paradoxically, make leadership unnecessary. The function of a leader is to facilitate, not to control, cooperative behavior; and a successful leader, as we have said, is one who, by playing his own role well, enables others to play their own roles productively. In this situation the work of the community is effected without anyone feeling that he is being coerced or dominated. The leader does not lead or command in the popular sense; instead, he behaves in a manner that will bring about the most effective group relationships.

As before, however, we must call attention to the limits of this kind of leadership. There are times in community deliberation when the chosen leader, by virtue of his competence or skill, must inject direction into the area of group participation. Participation that does not get the job done is not efficient, for it is wasteful of time, money, personnel, and individual creativeness. So, while the democratic leader will aim to make himself dispensable, he will not surrender his obligation to that fatal vacillation which often destroys effective community action.

The Leader's Place in the Community. The human community, unlike the small face-to-face groups organized for specific purposes which we have described in previous chapters, is not an artificial group designed to test scientific hypotheses. Rather, it is a viable group with a history and a tradition. Its citizens cannot be manipulated in the same easy way as the subjects of a contrived experiment. Many persons are restrained by tradition and paralyzed by inertia. Contemplated changes arouse suspicion and induce a sense of insecurity in many people. In this state of mind they tend to be uncooperative, if not indeed hostile. Hence, when change is badly needed, it will not usually take place spontaneously. It waits for the initiative of those who have imagination, who are basically group-centered, and who have the self-confident courage to assume responsibility.

Since community change, especially in its beginning phase, depends so strongly upon the initiative of others, the presence of citizens who are sensitive to the needs of the community as a whole, and not those of any special interests, is a matter of great importance. What the community needs more than executive and administrative ability is the capacity of some of its citizens to sense the needs of the entire community, to reflect them back to men in the group, and to enlist their aid in carrying out a proposed action.

The leader's place in the community, furthermore, is not that of a dispenser of good will. Good will is, of course, good, for it is motivated by humanitarian impulses; but it is not good enough. We can never have too many good impulses, but they do not solve our problems, even though they make living a little kinder. While hortatory attitudes, too, have their value in adding encouragement and enthusiasm to the life of the group, they leave basic issues mostly untouched and almost never remedied. In fine, the democratic leader must have above all else dependable knowledge of men and communities and the skill to put his discoveries into action. The first is essentially an individual achievement, the second is a problem in effective teamwork.

Finally, a democratic community leader is not only an originator of action but a producer of followers. In this dual condition the act of role-playing, which is an important factor in our conception of leadership, is especially noticeable. A community leader, no matter how potentially skillful he may be, is helpless without an intelligent and well-intentioned group of followers. If he fails to stimulate effective role-playing in others, he will be unable to play his own role successfully.

Democratic followers, for their part, display only one unfailing characteristic: they do not obey blindly; they do not confuse obedience with loyalty. It is open-minded loyalty which enables a follower to choose between good suggestions and bad ones, between a sincere leader and a charlatan, between important issues and trivial ones. Confronted by such followers, the democratic leader will perforce grow; for they are bound to challenge him and impel him to widen his own horizon. Morgan put it astutely when he wrote, "Great followership requires interest and preparation as much as does great leadership."[23] On no other basis, it seems reasonable to suppose, can cooperation between leaders and followers be effectively established; for as we pointed out in Chapter 6 when citing experimental data in evidence, the leader cannot successfully perform his function if he is too advanced for his followers. In a democratic society the only way for leaders and followers to come closer together is to raise the level of followership. With the widespread dissemination of knowledge and the extensive increase in adult education this goal can be transformed into a reality.[24]

[23] *Morgan, The small community,* p. 177.

[24] Group dynamics has largely ignored the personal satisfaction and the sense of community usefulness which dedicated followers experience in their work on community problems. Research in this area should throw valuable light on both the leader and the led. A brief consideration of this problem is found in Leadership, by C. A. Gibb, being chap. xxiv in G. Lindzey (ed.), *Handbook of social psychology,* Vol. II (Reading, Mass.: Addison-Wesley Publishing Co., Inc., 1954).

PLANNING AND LEADERSHIP. At the beginning of this chapter we indicated that the community has been chiefly the concern of sociologists, and that their study of it has been extensively as an ecological unit. This has also been true of the problem of community planning. Ecologists have concentrated on the problem of design: the best distribution of peoples and residences, the layout of streets and the regulation of traffic, the location of parks, trading areas, and sewage disposal plants, and the like. These matters are, of course, of the utmost importance. From the standpoint of group dynamics, however, community planning aims at the understanding of people in groups and the means by which they can improve their relations with one another. When we speak of community planning, therefore, we are thinking of the ways in which the human relations factor can add to the quality of community living. Planning consists not of rules to be followed, but of goals to be achieved. One pursues it not as one does when one builds a house, but as an individual interested in the welfare of the group. Community planning is an *attitude*, a way of conceiving human relationships in a group.

Since community planning as we conceive it is not an engineering skill but an understanding of people living together, it calls for a "planner" or leader who, while he may be deficient in designing a strategy or preparing a program, is unusually skillful in tapping the creative energies of men. *He plans in community with others.* Since community planning is an attitude, changes in community life can be effected only by changes in attitudes. The example of Northtown confirms this view. A technical knowledge of community planning, while very helpful, is not a substitute for skill in effecting constructive relations with others. The democratic planner does not exploit people; on the contrary, as Gordon well put it, he "tries to prepare himself *to guard against* the tendency to manipulate the group."[25] If he may be said to have one over-all plan, it is, to borrow Lilienthal's power-

[25] T. Gordon, *Group-centered leadership* (Boston: Houghton Mifflin Co., 1955), p. 155. Italics in the original.

ful phrase, to awaken in the whole people a common moral purpose—the material and spiritual well-being of all men.[26]

The TVA is an excellent example of community planning with few regulatory measures and a minimum of leadership pressure. While voluntary methods, such as those employed in democratic groups, may result in many mistakes, the good they produce far outweighs the dangers of coercion. Lilienthal makes the point eloquently when he writes,

> . . . I feel strongly that the admitted limitations of voluntary methods, distressing and tragic as their consequences sometimes are, do not invalidate the wisdom of a *minimum of coercion* in carrying out plans for resource development. For coercion is insatiable. In whatever guise, once coercion becomes the accepted reliance for making planning effective, more and more coercion is needed. I am deeply persuaded that high as the price of voluntary methods may be, in delays and errors, in the end the price of arbitrary enforcement of planning is nothing less than our freedom.[27]

TRAINING FOR COMMUNITY LEADERSHIP. Training for leadership in the community does not differ, in principle, from training for leadership in any other democratic group. The common denominator of all democratic leadership training is the conception of the leader as a *change agent.* The continued need for change in the democratic community is not confined to the followers, but holds with the same force for the leader himself. The effective leader aids in changing the attitudes of others, but in the process of changing others he undergoes change himself. This is usually the more difficult aspect of the change process. Change in the leader's attitude seems to be unrelated to his knowledge, showing that "getting the facts," as we are often admonished, is of itself insufficient to effect the needed change. People who possess more knowledge about a problem than others do not necessarily change their attitudes more easily. As a matter of fact some authoritarian leaders possessing very limited knowledge of the subject involved have been found to

[26] D. E. Lilienthal, *TVA: democracy on the march* (New York: Harper & Bros., 1944), p. 198.

[27] *Ibid.*, p. 202. Italics in the original.

change their attitudes with greater ease than some better-informed democratic individuals.

At the present time a large number of organizations, ranging from schools and factories to military services and local communities, have established leadership training programs. The chief stimulus to leadership training came from the psychological theories and investigations of Kurt Lewin, although the progressive education movement some years before was deeply concerned with the training of leaders for a democratic society. The views of Lewin, especially as they were being tested then (1946) at The Massachusetts Institute of Technology, and the philosophy espoused by the National Education Association were joined into a program in the First National Training Laboratory on Group Development, in 1947. In June of the same year the Laboratory established the first Workshop for training in various phases of group life, and particularly leadership, at Bethel, Maine. From its very inception, the Laboratory has demonstrated that *practice* in human relations techniques is the most satisfactory means of establishing and maintaining a democratic community of men.[28]

Before the Bethel program was established, however, an initial test of the use of group dynamics in community relations was established at New Britain Teachers College, in Connecticut, under the auspices of the Connecticut State Interracial Commission.

At the first Workshop, in New Britain, which lasted two weeks, 41 persons were enrolled. Over half of the members were Negroes and Jews. There was a sprinkling of business and labor leaders. The religious affiliations were representative of the three important denominations in our society, namely, Protestant, Roman Catholic, and Jewish. The whole effort of the group was to secure the collaboration of social scientists, educators, and professional leaders toward the

28 For some earlier discussions of training techniques, see R. Lippitt, The psychodrama in leadership training, *Sociometry*, 6 (1943), 286–92; J. R. P. French, Jr., Retraining an autocratic leader, *J. abnorm. soc. Psychol.*, 39 (1944), 224–37.

integration of research, training, and social action, with a view to the application of the knowledge and skills derived from it to harmonious living in the modern community.[29]

Role-playing was used extensively as a method of training. Role-playing, we pointed out in the preceding chapter, goes beyond discussion or verbal behavior and stimulates the individual to act out verbal decisions and sensitizes him to the effect which he has on others. It thus serves—and in the Workshop this was vividly brought out—as the connecting link between a conceptual understanding of what must be done and concrete performance in a task situation.

The results of the training in the Workshop were positive. They confirmed the main principles of group behavior as they apply to community relations. Stating only the major finding, we can say that, while both individuals and groups benefited from their Workshop experience, the groups had far exceeded the individuals in the quantity and quality of progress and performance in establishing better community relations. The largest gains were made by those groups that had the strongest community feelings, that is, belongingness, cohesiveness, and high morale.[30]

It is to be noted and repeatedly stressed that the technique of the Workshop—and by implication the goal of all methods of training for community leadership—is not to train leaders as such but, through developing group understandings and skills, to enable them to aid their communities to help themselves. It is to be noted, furthermore, that training in group leadership is directed toward developing a strategy of community action. To the extent that this kind of training is achieved and its principles understood, it will do what Lippitt perceptively saw in the action research of

[29] See R. Lippitt, *Training in community relations* (New York: Harper & Bros., 1949).

[30] For a comprehensive and detailed report on the methods and findings by one who played a key role in the Connecticut Workshop, namely, Ronald Lippitt, see *ibid.*, *passim*, but particularly chaps. vii–ix, xi–xii. For an evaluation of Lippitt's book, see *Hum. Relat.*, 3 (1950), 201–14.

Lewin, namely, help "to engineer between a science of human relations and a sounder practice of human affairs."[31]

Inasmuch as the chief function of a democratic leader is to stimulate his community to help itself, the process of mutual help is by definition collaborative. But how may collaboration be achieved? The community self-survey and the afore-mentioned Workshop give us the answer. We shall sum up the answer briefly.

In all collaborative efforts, particularly those involving the community's needs, both the leaders and followers and the researchers and men of affairs must have a common perception of their relations to one another. If the lines of communication are open, if each is able to see himself through the eyes of the others, and if each feels secure enough in his relation to others to permit him to bear both a permissive and critical atmosphere without feeling personally threatened, the collaboration can become a reality.

Close on the heels of collaboration is the capacity, which comes through practice, of integrating the insights of others into a consistent plan of action. Even more, it means the integration of ideas and actions, which is difficult even at best. The technique of role-playing has been used successfully to achieve this difficult integration. While the community leader may at times be a specialist, most of his tasks are to integrate a number of skills.

In community relations the practice of shared leadership is probably more essential than in any other form of human relationship. In a democratic community, as we have pointed out, everyone is a leader, and the leadership that is practiced will itself make leadership progressively less essential. This is further supported by the principle, as we have shown, of leader-follower interdependence. As problems and functions change, leadership must be transmitted to that person or group which is best qualified to effect desired results. Trainer and trainee, leader and follower, must inter-

[31] Lippitt, *Training in community relations,* p. vii.

change roles whenever the community situation demands it. Academic scholars can testify to the salutary nature of this rotation. The theorist can gain insight from the applied scientist, and the two, in turn, can benefit from the practical knowledge of the man of affairs. When the three get their heads together, the emergent ideas are neither coordinations nor compromises merely, but new creations, novel decisions, and more effective understandings. Research in community relations has demonstrated again and again that fruitful investigation requires the integrated approach of several disciplines, if not by collaboration then through the increasingly more difficult route of the single individual. The study of the community is no longer the exclusive interest of the sociologist investigating crime, delinquency, poverty, and other crucial problems, but the student of community dynamics focusing on the productive and harmonious relations of people in groups.

Whether community life will be satisfying and productive of genuine human relationships will depend finally—irrespective of dynamic leadership and intelligent effort—upon the character of the larger membership. People who live in a community against their will, like people in any group who have nothing to say concerning their fate, will have little or no interest in its welfare. This is sharply revealed by the case of Regent Hill, a community investigated by Festinger and Kelley.[32]

Regent Hill was a government housing project established during World War II. A project of about one hundred housing units, it was located in the center of a residential area of a medium-sized town. Most of the residents lived there either because wartime work in the shipyards brought them there, or because a serious housing shortage made it impossible for them to find houses elsewhere. Finding themselves in this unwanted and undesirable situation, they had no interest in their community and its people. Indeed, because the community at large considered their neighbors

[32] See L. Festinger and H. H. Kelley, *Changing attitudes through social contact* (Ann Arbor, Mich.: Research Center for Group Dynamics, 1951).

as undesirable people, they disassociated themselves from others and lived largely in isolation. An association that normally gives satisfaction was feared and rejected because people perceived it as a relationship which they did not want. To this was added a spirit of hostility. Pluralistic ignorance led them to believe that people outside their own neighborhood had the same attitudes, and thus they deprived themselves of social relations with outside areas likewise. Their perception of their community was, consequently, largely negative. Since emotions and attitudes have a tendency to spill over and attach themselves to many areas of daily life, the residents of Regent Hill not only disliked their homes but the community and its people as well.

After diagnosing the community and its ills, Festinger and Kelley tried to change the pattern of isolation and hostility. However, they found it exceedingly difficult because the first step, that of enlisting their cooperation, was almost impossible to effect. This fact, together with the hostility and resentment that prevailed, made their progress on the whole discouraging. One important implication of this study is very clear, however: unless membership in such projects is voluntary and need-gratifying, it will maim or destroy an identification with others which, under more favorable social conditions, would produce wholesome community feelings and relationships.

CONCLUSION

In this chapter we have attempted to take a fresh view of an old problem. The study of the community as a spatial and demographic unit is far from new, and interest in its social and cultural life has been a concern of the cultural anthropologist since the beginning of his science. The contributions of the sociologist and the anthropologist to our knowledge of these aspects of community life have been, on the whole, important, and all social scientists are grateful for their contribution to our better understanding of these matters.

Our objective in this chapter, however, has been different. We have been investigating the nature of community dynamics. A crucial element in this community dynamics has been the perceptions, both veridical and distorted, which people in dynamic groups have of each other, and the harmony and conflict which each respectively generates. We have described some of the tensions and conflicts which upset the community equilibrium, generate social disharmony, and impair normal human relations. We have described some of the means by which harmony is revived, hatreds are diminished, and a sense of community is restored.

The investigations into community dynamics have left a dual impact upon the student of group life. First, they reveal rather sharply that a community's perception of itself is a vital factor in its well-being. The people of Regent Hill were lonely, hostile, and frustrated because they could not identify themselves with one another. Their emotional investments were largely negative and self-destroying. They had no interest in their housing project because they had no sense of community. Their behavior can be partially explained by the psychology of not belonging: they rejected and were rejected because of a strong element of self-hatred. No community can endure on a base of disloyalty to itself. Second, while there are many ways for a community to become aware of itself as coacting and cooperative individuals, an effective technique is the community self-survey. It would be a wholesome experience if every community made periodic self-surveys in order to diagnose both its ills and its potentials for healthy growth.

Group leadership, like leadership in other areas of human activity, is essential to community organization. In a democratic society it is based on the principle of rotation. It operates only to the extent that in its absence the community might suffer; for as we said before, one of its characteristics is to enable people to rely less upon it and more upon the will of all—or at least the will of the majority.

Like all skills, community leadership can be cultivated. There are tested methods for developing leadership skills. Some of these we have briefly described in this chapter.

Viewing the contents of this chapter as a whole, the facts show that we can perceive the human community not only as a fit place to satisfy needs, but as a laboratory for the experimental investigation of democratic living. This experimental investigation will be challenged by vested interests, for nothing frightens self-centered people more than confrontation by their own selfishness. Their hostility will not be feared by the courageous scientist, for he knows that seldom does anything fine come into existence without someone enduring the wrath of the uninformed and the bigoted.

CHAPTER 11

Group Relations in Political Behavior

Political behavior is as old as organized social life. However, until recently the study of politics has been largely concerned with political structure and organization—with political institutions rather than political behavior. To say this is not to be unmindful of the fact that historians and political scientists have generally been aware of the behavior of statesmen and politicians and have pondered over the intricate and devious ways of the latter's minds in reaching important decisions. Moreover, we are aware that the study of political behavior and political decision-making have been the special concern of some outstanding contemporary political scientists, notably Arthur Bentley, Charles Merriam, and Harold Lasswell, to mention only those which come to mind immediately. Students of decision-making in politics owe these scholars a signal debt; for they have not only given us important leads but, what is more important, they have emancipated the study of politics from preoccupation with political institutional structures. We may be mistaken in judging present trends, but the signs seem to point toward an increasing development of political science into a behavioral discipline.

From our point of view, then, the study of politics is a behavioral science. Like the other problems concerning group conflict and adjustment, which we have discussed in Part III, political behavior is a process of group tension-reduction, group problem-solving, and collective decision-making. In these problems lies the chief relevance of political behavior to the science of group dynamics.

The concepts of conflict, adjustment, resolution of tensions, and the like which describe group processes have their counterparts in political theory. It is interesting to see present-day political scientists wrestling with some of the same fundamental problems as social psychology and group dynamics. The concept of equilibrium—of consensus, concord, harmony, agreement—has been made into an important theoretical issue by at least one contemporary political scientist. David Easton, while wisely rejecting a particularistic conception of equilibrium, finds it useful in his discussion of political dynamics.[1] He notes the fact that social equilibrium, in contrast to thermodynamic states, always involves human beings in constant activity. Like the dynamic groups which are the subject matter of this book, other social groups, including political systems, are ceaselessly changing. A political group, like other dynamic groups, while reaching for equilibrium in deliberation and decision-making, never achieves a state of complete rest; its condition must be described as a *dynamic* equilibrium; it is always a *process*. The basic concepts of political dynamics are then substantially the same as those of group dynamics, for both assume change, action, interaction, goal-direction, and the like to be fundamental to political and other forms of social behavior.

[1] See D. Easton, *The political system: an inquiry into the state of political science* (New York: Alfred A. Knopf, Inc., 1953), chap. xi, and Limits of the equilibrium model in social research, a paper read by him at the American Psychological Association, Cleveland, Ohio, Sept. 8, 1953, and published as a part of a symposium in the Chicago Behavioral Sciences Publications, No. 1.

THE POLITICAL SYSTEM AS A GROUP

A besetting weakness of much historical and political thinking has been particularism. The latter has accounted for political institutions in terms of a particular causal nexus. For example, some writers traced these institutions to the ambition of a strong leader; others, to the force of majority opinion; others, to an unexplained "will" of the people; and others still, to the cementing and expanding power of military aggression; and so on. From the standpoint of group dynamics the foregoing factors are effects, not causes. The behavior of the leader, the role of majority opinion, the consent of the governed, the overwhelming force of war are consequences of human interaction. They do not make the human group; they are products of human association. Popular or democratic government, we shall see, is group organization in action.[2]

The Source of Political Authority. Few topics in political science reveal its tradition-mindedness more than the concept of political sovereignty. While no scientific student of political institutions and behavior today traces sovereignty—or political authority, as we prefer to call it—to a divine power, or to the will of the monarch, the word retains much of the original flavor of power or dominion vested in a person or in an abstraction called the State. But in a *democratic group,* which is the essential meaning of the State as we conceive it, authority or control is derived from the group itself. Since contemporary society is a complex

[2] It is an astounding fact that political scientists are just now coming to realize that as early as 1908 Arthur F. Bentley had formulated an interactional view of political life. As a matter of fact his analysis of political behavior was in essence a theory of *intergroup* relations, for he perceived the group not as acting in isolation but in specific relations to other groups. That he argued individual psychological variables out of existence is important in assessing his complete theory, but this fact in no way detracts from the group-centered nature of the political process as he defined it. The subtitle, A study of social pressures, of his well-known treatise on government, is itself indicative of the modernity of his ideas. See A. F. Bentley, *The process of government* (Chicago: The University of Chicago Press, 1908), especially chap. vii.

of many and often conflicting groups, authority is shared by many of them. Since at the same time groups are perpetually striving to reduce tensions and conflicts among themselves, agreement, while hard to achieve, becomes the most significant goal of every democratic community. The integrating function of the community we have already described at length, and it is sufficient to point out here that the performance of this function is best achieved in the ways which we described in the last chapter.

Failure to acknowledge a world community is probably at the basis of much of the conflict of sovereign rights. While international law has effectively prevented the rise of permanent predatory states and has strengthened security and heightened morale within nations, it is not the final answer to the attainment of collective well-being.

Political authority, moreover, is vested in the democratic group and is conceived as a process of group self-discovery. This authority is not a majority opinion, nor a compromise, nor a consensus arrived at through timidity in facing criticism. Rather, it lies in the group in which everyone contributes according to his capacity and experience. "Sovereignty" then lies in the people who, by their own productive efforts, have reached a decision or embarked on a course of action. Authority springs from the collective deliberations of people. This is so because, as our analysis of group structure and process has shown, group behavior is characterized by the fact that no single individual, no matter how skillful he may be, determines collective action. As the group structure changes, the deliberations within it change also. Who has not observed that no individual will act as he would if the other members were different or absent from the group?

Democratic authority—or the sovereign power of the state, if one prefers—resides, then, in a community of free men. It is never the prerogative of an individual, nor is it power inherent in the abstractions called the State or the Government—both of which are in truth convenient fictions. It lies, rather, in the system of values which holds a democratic people together. The essential feature of democratic authority based upon common values is not the fact of *sharing* it, but of having *produced it together*. The so-called "collective will" is neither existent nor collective: it is a condition of working and thinking together in order to reach decisions that will result in the well-being of all. The energizing impulse which lies behind it is not some mysterious patriotism, of which our professional politicians speak so rapturously, but the sense of community solidarity which impels us to act together toward a common objective.

Law as a Group Imperative. From the standpoint of group dynamics, the law is not only a contract that binds people together to observe an agreement made in common. It is not merely a permanent code of principles, not merely a set of rules, but legal principles which change in accordance with the needs of the growing community. In other words, in a dynamic group, legal principles are dynamic, too, changing as the living community changes. The history of tyranny has demonstrated beyond doubt that when laws become fixed and unchangeable, when their permanence has become encrusted in tortuous legalistic interpretations, they favor vested interests and perpetuate the evils of special privilege.

It has been widely believed, the reader will recall, that men are inherently lazy and will work only because they cannot survive without the economic benefits which their labor bestows upon them. An analogous belief exists regarding the "lawlessness" of man. According to this conception of man, law is a necessary restraining measure to curb his dishonest and antisocial tendencies. Law so conceived is fundamentally coercive.

No rational person would deny that some individuals—perhaps many—have to be "forced" by legal codes to act on grounds other than complete self-interest. But modern social psychology gives credence to the view that men obey laws not out of fear of sanctions or of punishment only, but for various other reasons. The motivation behind obedience is the same in kind as the impulse of people in groups to reach consensus because of the positive consequences which flow from it. While we lack for the legal-political area the kind of experimental evidence which we found useful for demonstrating the valuable consequences of consensus, of group participation in problem-solving, decision-making, and learning, in education, industry, and so forth, there are neither a priori nor empirical reasons that cast doubt on the validity of extending these principles to politics. Men obey laws for the same reasons that they conform to other social pressures. Group conformity, attitudinal uniformity, the feeling of group belongingness, and similar factors condition men's ethical behavior. People identify themselves with the State as they do with their reference group or their community. "Law-abidingness," MacIver said, "is the pragmatic condition of and response to the whole firmament of social order."[3]

If this is not fully convincing, let us reconsider still another fact of group life, already reviewed on more than one occasion in this book. Men work in and for their groups because only through safeguarding the rights of others are their own rights preserved. The greatest individual freedom, we saw, cannot be attained in isolation, but is achieved in interaction with others. Man gets his freedom by living with other free men. This freedom through collective sanction reinforces the other obligations to group adherence. In this condition "the various groups that constitute the community, no matter how divided by separatist interests or conflicting doctrines, can alike identify themselves with the broad purpose of the state. They may or may not agree with the policies of a particular government but since it leaves their faiths alone and since it does not suppress their opinions they can still be in accord with 'the spirit of the laws.' "[4]

[3] R. M. MacIver, *The web of government* (New York: The Macmillan Co., 1947), p. 77.

[4] *Ibid.*, p. 79.

The law so conceived is a living thing, not a court document or the arguments of a governing body. The latter are merely external means of identifying it, of giving it "a local habitation and a name." The integrating force of the law lies not in what the judge and the criminal do with it, but how the group of people called an organized community uses it to foster its own development. When the group uses the law to improve itself, it is not merely obeying the legal statutes. Obedience is passive, if not negative, behavior. The group that uses the law to enhance its well-being is *creating* law, for in so doing it is diffusing justice throughout the community. People now act lawfully, not out of a sense of fear or duty, but because they have a new conception of the all-embracing community—a community built by people for themselves and for one another.

A popular way of conceptualizing the growth of democracy by political scientists and jurists has been to describe it as a growth from status to contract. In an aristocratic or authoritarian state justice was meted out in accordance with a man's social position. Often, the elite of the community was above the law. With the growth of democratic institutions and the liberalization of jurisprudence the notion of contractual regulation developed. In this atmosphere all men were considered "equal under the law," and each case was adjudicated accordingly.

Contemporary society is still largely controlled by the contractual conception of human relations. There are signs, however, that juridical actions are becoming group-centered. As democracy becomes more group-oriented, contract will give way to community. As Mary Follett explained it forty years ago: "We see contract diminishing because we believe in a different kind of association: as fast as association becomes a 'community' relation, as fast as individuals are recognized as community-units, just so fast does contract fade away."[5] The growth of the law now going on is from con-

[5] M. P. Follett, *The new state* (New York: Longmans, Green & Co., Inc., 1918), p. 125. This book is a pioneer attempt to think of politics as a dynamic group process.

tract to community. When the community does in fact become the foundation of law, we shall have democracy in its best sense: a community of interdependent individuals acting freely in the interest of the whole group.[6]

The implications of the foregoing discussion for a group-centered view of law are worth noting. It implies, first, that relation is taking the place of contract, and that the relation is not personal. We now ask not for "the strict terms of the contract, but what the relation demands."

Second, personal relation is being displaced by the concept of dynamic relation—a "*relation in relation*" in which the judge considers "not landlord and tenant as landlord and tenant, not master and servant as master and servant, but of that relation in relation to other relations, or, we might say, to society."[7]

The third implication serves as a bridge between political authority and the law as a group imperative. It argues for the pluralistic nature of authority—or political power, if one prefers. It should be clear, in view of what we have said, that, from the standpoint of political science and group dynamics, power or authority is only one element of the political structure; it is, indeed, diminishing in importance. "Political life," observes Easton in a cautious understatement, "does not consist exclusively of a struggle for control; this struggle stems from and relates to conflict over the direction of social life, over public policy, as we say today in a somewhat legal formulation."[8] The goal of power, in other words,

[6] Examples of community-based laws are the regulation of hours and conditions of labor, workmen's compensation and employers' liability, limitations on the part of creditor or injured party to exact satisfaction, water rights, social security, etc. See *ibid.*, pp. 126–27. This theory of law was anticipated by Duguit and Jellinek, and more recently developed by such eminent jurists as Holmes, Brandeis, Pound, Cardozo, and Frankfurter.

[7] *Ibid.*, pp. 128–29. Italics in original.

[8] D. Easton, *The political system*, p. 117. For a systematic formulation of the dynamics of power in non-face-to-face groups the reader should consult the rigorous theories of Goldhammer and Shils and Talcott Parsons, which are grounded on Max Weber's well-known views on the subject. See H. Goldhammer and E. Shils, Types of power and status, *Amer. J. Sociol.*, *45* (1939), 171–82 and T. Parsons, *The social system* (Glencoe, Ill.: The Free Press, 1951). For a theory of power in small groups, see L. Festinger,

becomes less important as the relation in relation to other relations—that is, the well-being of the community—becomes central in political as in other group decisions.

POLITICS AS A GROUP PROCESS. One of the delightful elements in interdisciplinary research is the discovery of the influence of one discipline upon another. For at least half a century sociologists have been describing society as a process, and students of group dynamics have been led to follow suit. Since political scientists have been interested in political change, it was but natural and logical that they, too, came to perceive political activities as processes.[9] The result has been that the concept of political institution has been receding into the background, and group process and interaction are rapidly taking its place.

The concept of political process is particularly relevant to group dynamics because it is the framework in which many political decisions take place. Social or public policy is not a static thing; it emerges from a process of interaction between people and groups, usually called pressure groups, lobbies, class-centered interest group, and the like. Policies and other political decisions are thus viewed within a flowing matrix of deliberating groups. Group dynamics and political science are accordingly linked together by the concepts of social interaction and social change. Policy-making, in turn, is rescued from the sterility of institutional description by placing it squarely in the interactive process. It is thus perceived to be, not a static product, but a mode of action toward a goal, a dynamic consequence of interacting individuals.

S. Schachter, and K. Back, *Social pressures in informal groups* (New York: Harper & Bros., 1950). The latter study owes much to Lewin's definition in terms of "influence." See K. Lewin, *Field theory in social science* (New York: Harper & Bros., 1951). For a very perceptive and rigorous conceptualization of power theories, see F. L. Neumann, Approaches to the study of political power, *Pol. Sci. Quart.*, 55 (1950), 161–80.

[9] See O. Garceau, Research in political process, *Amer. pol. Sci. Rev.*, 45 (1951), 69–85. European sociologists and political historians used the concept at the end of the nineteenth century. See also Bentley, *The process of government.*

The upshot of the foregoing analysis is that politics is not a formal structure, but an ongoing activity, a group process. The process view of political behavior, whether in the form of a conflict over policy-making or in the form of a struggle between a multiplicity of interest groups, is fundamentally conceived as group behavior. One astute observer of political behavior shows the relationship clearly. He writes,

> . . . The process conception views social elements as in constant tension or power struggle over policy, and the task of the political scientist is to extricate the various elements for independent study in order to determine the exact role of each. But for most political scientists, the political process is not only a complex network of human interaction; it is also specifically the interaction of groups. Political life is primarily to be viewed as group life."[10]

In an interesting article on the group character of international relations by Landecker, we find further support for our main thesis.[11] Political states, as we have said, are groups. Since international relations are, as he points out, relations between groups, they may be appropriately described as "intergroup relations." Dividing intergroup relations on the basis of whether they are *direct* or *transmitted*, Landecker attempts to show that the relations between states in a federal union are direct, whereas those between national states are transmitted. The relations between federal states are direct in that the contact between the participating members is immediate without the aid of intervening media. Thus the relations between an inhabitant of Ohio and one of New York are affected very little, even politically, by the fact of geographic separation. The loyalty of members of each state to the nation is not appreciably affected by the fact that each state has also a relatively independent existence.

The interaction between two sovereign nations, on the other hand, is a transmitted intergroup relation. The process

[10] D. Easton, *The political system: an inquiry into the state of political science* (New York: Alfred A. Knopf, Inc., 1953), p. 175.

[11] W. S. Landecker, International relations as inter-group relations, *Amer. Sociol. Rev.*, 5 (1940), 335–39.

of interaction between people in sovereign states is effecte through each state. The function of the states in the international community is thus different from that of the state in a federation. Hence, although the constituents of a federal state are individuals, the function of the constituent of the international community is determined by their participation in the life of the nation.

There is no inherent reason why the foregoing conditio must be permanent. As long as nations function as "transmitting agents in international relations," this conditio will prevail. When international associations at some futur time, however, become intergroup relations, they will be a direct as those of federal states. They will then be subjec to the same dynamic principles that govern small groups More specifically, international relations require the sam sort of voluntary subordination to the whole that characterizes a small cohesive group at its best. "The internationa community," Landecker observes, "is not an aggregate o 'I's but 'We's." As structural units, he points out, they ar not subjects of this aggregate. Nevertheless, as structura units some of their functions in the international communit are like those of individuals in other aggregates. "Therefore," he continues, "since the international community i an aggregate composed of a small number of structure units its characteristics are in various respects the same as those o numerically small groups."[12]

The emphasis on the group-bound nature of politica decisions and actions does not blind us to other features o political behavior. Even an amateur in the study of politica science soon discovers the force of institutional factors i political decisions, especially governmental bureaus an legal agencies, whose relations to people are not psychologically but formally defined. We have stressed the grou factor for two reasons: first, the law or some other forma agency is not the exclusive means by which rights and privileges are allocated; and, second, political science itself i

[12] *Ibid.*, p. 337.

now fostering the notion that it must be interested in every technique by means of which policies are established and exercised. This is admittedly a broad view of the nature of political decisions, and consequently many political scientists will prefer to cling to the narrower and more manageable phases of their discipline. It suggests, what every political scientist knows and admits, namely, that political science is not only related to other social sciences, but that it should form productive liaisons with them. As a behavioral science, the study of politics is, as we have said, interdisciplinary.

The role of psychological variables. As an illustration of only one phase of the interdisciplinary approach and at the same time as a means of adding to the group-process analysis, we mention the psychological nature of political decisions. The recognition of psychological variables is perhaps as old as political theory itself. Plato recognized their importance, and Hobbes and Bentham made them important factors in political analysis. Their views of man as a political animal, however, were too narrow: they stressed individual psychology and largely neglected the role of psychological groups. Most psychological approaches to political behavior conceive it in individual terms. The stress on individual motivation is perhaps strongest in the political conceptions of Harold Lasswell.[13]

Our stress is of course on group-psychological variables. We are interested in politics as a *group process.* This fact must be emphasized because, in their enthusiasm over their rediscovery that politics is a behavioral as well as an "institutional" discipline, some political scientists tend to ignore politics as a group-dynamic process. A more complete science of politics conceives group behavior as a vital aspect

[13] See especially his earlier works with their psychoanalytic orientation: *Psychopathology and politics* (Chicago: The University of Chicago Press, 1930); *World politics and personal insecurity* (New York: McGraw-Hill Book Co., Inc., 1935). This is partly rectified in his analysis of groups, without, however, specifying its relation to politics, in H. D. Lasswell and A. Kaplan, *Power and society* (New Haven: Yale University Press, 1950).

of behavioral science.[14] It analyzes political behavior in terms of *human relations;* that is, on the basis of group organization and group process.

Political organization and political behavior can be fruitfully studied as problems in group dynamics. It is interesting to see how some students of politics, while avowedly analyzing political organization by means of the variables of individual psychology—specifically *personality*—are, in fact, dealing with it in the conceptual language of group psychology. Thus Simon, Smithburg, and Thompson, in their highly commendable book on public administration, while stressing the role of personality in political organization, are describing mostly the powerful effect of the group on administrative functioning. Administrative organization, their chief concern, is, they point out, the organization of a *group of people.*[15] The motivations which they describe are not primarily individual but are largely the products of individuals in interaction. Individuals in administrative groups do not usually act on the basis of individual motivation alone. Their private feelings and motives merge with those of others to become a product different from the emotions and aspirations of any one of them separately. The group structure of the administrative unit of which the individual is a part strongly determines his own decisions and actions. Indeed, these actions and decisions are not his own; they are the resultant of the actions and decisions of all other members considered as a totality or whole.

A natural retort to the foregoing statement may well be: Who has denied it? There is a deceptive familiarity in what we have said, and the cynical reader might describe it as *mere* common sense. The literature on political behavior, however, shows that the critic's observations are in reality afterthoughts. The political scientist has paid lip-service to

[14] There is much confusion in recent political writings between the role of individual motivation in political behavior and the effect of situational, particularly group-centered, action.

[15] H. Simon, D. Smithburg, and V. Thompson, *Public administration* (New York: Alfred A. Knopf, Inc., 1950), especially chap. iii. See also H. Simon, *Administrative behavior* (New York: The Macmillan Co., 1947).

the concepts of interaction and interdependence, but not until recently has he conceived them as fundamental to a theory of political process and political behavior. A vice of much critical scholarship is the belief that nobody says anything new; hence, it is easy to conclude that if certain contemporary concepts were used in the past they were used with their current meaning. For instance, the vitalistic and mystical accounts of group behavior, as we indicated in Chapter 1, have been thoroughly discredited. The group mind of Le Bon and McDougall has been superseded by the functional-dynamic view of contemporary social psychology and group dynamics.

We have been careful to present a balanced view of the comparative importance of individual and collective factors in group behavior. The reader will recall numerous places in the pages of this book where, despite our emphasis on the group factor, we did not overlook the individual. The psychological variables of human behavior are both individual and collective. We must, therefore, take another look at the role of the person, this time regarding his place in the political process.

We shall begin with the interesting, perhaps novel, observations of Winnicott.[16] An essential part of the democratic process, according to him, is that "it is a *person* who is elected." He differentiates between the vote for a party, a principle, and a person. An individual may, of course, vote for both a party and a principle, but what marks him as psychologically and politically mature is the fact that he votes for a person. Voting for a person implies that the electorate believe in themselves as persons, and therefore they believe in the person whom they nominate and elect.

The importance of this philosophical view of the role of the person in political life, however, does not lie, in our judgment, in the fact that the individual who is elected is a person, but in Winnicott's assertion that the person who is

[16] D. W. Winnicott, Some thoughts on the meaning of the word democracy, *Hum. Relat.*, 3 (1950), 175–86.

elected "has the opportunity to *act* as a person."[17] The President of the United States, for example, pressed though he is on all sides by the nature of his office, by the legal structure of the Constitution, and by a host of special interest groups shapes the presidency considerably by the stamp of his personality. He acts not only as an elected officer but as a person. The most dynamic of our presidents have left their mark indissolubly on the presidential office. The Cabinet of the same members presided over by Dwight Eisenhower and by Richard Nixon, on different occasions, would have different properties as groups. Each brings to the situation his personality and other individual and social variables which change the character of the whole.

There is yet another reason, a logical as well as psychological one, for recognizing the place of the person in political dynamics. We believe in part with Lasswell and Kaplan when they describe political science as dealing with "persons and their acts, not 'governments' and 'states.'" The latter terms, which have been central in the language of political science, are, as these writers say, "of ambiguous reference until it is clear how they are to be used in describing what people say and do." Quoting Catlin, who early recognized the behavioral character of the political process, they add: "'The subject matter of politics is the acts of individuals, not of states; the individual will is the political unit.'"[18]

In the face of our definition of group structure, group process, and group behavior, the point made by Lasswell and Kaplan, although partly true, is not as basic as they seem to believe. Their assumption of the priority—not the psychological importance, as we would say—of the person is based on a conception of the group which research in group dynamics explicity denies. While recognizing the importance of group behavior, these writers define it as "a pattern of individual acts." This definition gives no hint—indeed,

[17] *Ibid.*, p. 180. Italics ours.

[18] Lasswell and Kaplan, *Power and society*, p. 3. Their quotation of Catlin's view was taken from G. E. G. Catlin, *Scinece and method of politics* (New York: Alfred A. Knopf, Inc., 1927), pp. 141–42.

t seems to deny—that the behavior of the parts of a whole, or of members of a group, is modified by the relationships involved in membership.

The important thing in the present context, however, is that Lasswell and Kaplan, as well as a growing number of younger political scientists, recognize the importance of psychological variables, including the individual personality, in determining political behavior. Important in other words, is the fact that they deny the centrality of political entities, like states and governments, and emphasize psychological groups and individuals, in the study of politics.

Further confirmation of the human, as contrasted with the merely formal, element of political behavior is found in a recent investigation of the dynamics of voting.[19] This study challenges the widely held opinion that voting behavior is largely influenced by the techniques of mass media, such as newspapers, magazines, radio, and television. Certainly in the case of the undecided and uncommitted voters, personal contacts and group discussions were extremely effective in molding their final opinions. Political discussions, particularly, were influential in producing changes in attitudes. "On any average day," the investigators write, "at least 10% more people participated in discussions about the election—either actively or passively—than listened to a major speech or read about campaign items in a newspaper."[20]

People who deferred their choice of candidates to a later period in the campaign more often attributed their final decisions to "personal influences." "Three-fourths of the respondents who at one time had not expected to vote but were then finally 'dragged in' mentioned personal influence."[21]

Furthermore, the study reveals an interesting point regarding the "opinion leader" in the network of personal relationships in which political opinions are determined and modified. Unlike the undecided voters whom he influences,

[19] P. F. Lazarsfeld, B. Berelson, and H. Gaudet, *The people's choice* (2d ed; New York: Columbia University Press, 1948).
[20] *Ibid.*, pp. 150–51.
[21] *Ibid.*, p. 151.

the opinion leader, while engaging much more in political discussions than the others, reported that the formal media of communication influenced him more effectively than personal interactions. "This suggests," the investigators point out, "that ideas often flow *from* radio and print *to* the opinion leaders and *from* them *to* less active sections of the population."[22]

The foregoing facts add confirmation to a repeated assertion in these pages. Under normal circumstances—we exclude rebelliousness and nonconformism—the pressure of the ideas and attitudes of others influences one's own behavior. The impersonal and remote nature of the newspaper and the radio lacks the constraining psychological effect of the presence of real people. The compelling influence of group attitudes should by now be well understood. Group sanctions, such as approval, criticism, and personal rejection, are too powerful for most people to challenge or ignore.

A word should be added, finally, to explain, as Lazarsfeld and his associates have done, that the personal contacts which we have described are not those furnished by the "*professional* political machine" which operates so energetically during election campaigns. Rather, they are contacts with relatives, members of one's family, friends, congenial neighbors, and other face-to-face associations.

POLITICAL DECISION-MAKING

We must remind the reader once more that decision-making in the political process is a search for a dynamic equilibrium, for the resolving of group and intergroup tensions. It is a phase also, as we have shown in Chapter 7, of collective problem-solving. It should be clear, furthermore, that our interest was, as it is now, in decision-making within an organizational or group context.

We have touched on this problem in our brief consideration of policy-making in the political sphere. We described it as the process of producing and sharing preferred values.

[22] *Ibid.*, p. 151.

We affirmed that it emerges from the interaction of people in the process of deliberation.

If the process of decision-making strikes one as a mystery still, it may be because students of policy-making conceive the process in too narrowly individualistic terms.[23] An increasing number of political thinkers are grappling with it and making sense out of it.[24] Thus far, group dynamics suggests the most plausible explanation. While group dynamics seeks scientific explanations, it cannot close its eyes to the value preferences and choices of the democratic frame of reference which we have already briefly described.

THE MATRIX OF CHOICE. Our conceptual scheme invariably leaves room for the acts of an individual. Decision-making acts in the political arena have been overwhelmingly personal. Politics, like the rest of life, is a system of preferences. We daily choose between two or more alternatives. The maker of decisions, the forger of public policy, is perpetually faced by options. The choices he makes are usually his own. In a highly formalized situation, such as a governmental bureaucracy, the task is made easier by established rules. The psychological value of the set of rules is like that of an escape clause. As we said in our discussion of bureaucratic leadership (see Chapter 6), if a poor choice is made, one can always blame the "system"—that is, the rigidly established rules. However, the important thing to note is that, traditionally, governmental personnel were responsible for many decisions that pertained to the welfare of all.

Political science as we have said, has come a long way in the past quarter-century in emancipating itself from the shackles of institutional formalism. At the same time, the imputation of conspicuous decision-making to individuals,

[23] It is still a mystery to some. See E. P. Ulrich *et al., Executive action* (Cambridge, Mass.: Harvard University, Division of Research, 1952).

[24] See H. A. Simon, *Administrative behavior*, and D. Black, On the rationale of group decision-making, *J. pol. Econ.*, *56* (1948), 23–34. See also H. Guetzkow, An exploratory empirical study of the role of conflict in decision-making conferences, *Internat. Soc. Sci. Bull.*, 5 (1953), 286-300.

which has characterized much political thought, has been due to a subtle confusion. It has confused decision-making with the translation of policy into action. Today, we know that policies are made more and more by groups—though, unfortunately, they often are special-interest groups—even though their execution may be the task of individuals.

The gist of what we are trying to say then is this: Although the choice of options in decision-making is often an individual one, it is not always wholly so. In a democratic society choices are increasingly made by people in concert within a collective value system. Any theory of choice which minimizes the organizational system and the pattern of values upon which it is based, is inexcusably narrow and one-sided. Even when the choices are not determined by the give and take of group discussion and negotiation, they are partly group-derived in the sense that they are the resultant of the directional forces of organizational rules and precedents, not of the putative actions of a single individual. Finally, if one is determined to be hypermeticulous, it can be shown that the individual decision-maker is markedly influenced in his range of choices by such group-bound factors as education and class membership.

It was pointed out before in this chapter that some of the conditions which we have been describing are more in the nature of ideals than concrete realities, and that contemporary society is successively approximating the values which it is setting up. In the realm of choice approximation is elementary. With the increasing complexity of contemporary society the range of purely individual choices is narrowing. While it is true that in this impersonal and complex society governmental agencies are assuming an increasing share of decision-making, this need not be so. Running through the subliminal minds of some political theorist is the implicit assumption that for policies to be formulated and executed a central agency is absolutely essential. The successful functioning of primitive societies and of international organizations in the absence of a central government challenges the validity of the assumption. As Easton has astutely remarked, "authoritative allocation of values," that is, the establishment and execution of policy, does not necessarily presuppose the need of "a well-defined organization called government."[25]

THE ROLE OF LOCAL ADVISORY GROUPS. Group participation, we have shown, is a fundamental concept in the discussion of group behavior. The psychology of choice and consent in group affairs presupposes participation by the group's members. But the larger and more complex our society becomes the more difficult, *yet necessary,* is the need for our citizens' participation in the direction of their own affairs. This fact was strongly emphasized in our discussion of group dynamics in community relations, where we showed the valuable work performed by advisory committees.

Democracy in the "best" sense is always a community, rather than a formal government, important as the latter is for the performance of certain functions allocated to it by the community. In a democracy the community controls the government, as MacIver has cogently argued. "In the community," he writes, "develops the law behind law, the multi-sanctioned law that existed before governments began and that the law of government can never supersede."[26]

In the community, if any place, decentralization of functions will become a reality. Decentralization is necessary if democracy is to escape formalization and the freezing of authority in persons and rigid governmental bureaus. One of the admirable things about the democratic state, when compared with other kinds, is the diffusion of power—of policy creation and decision-making. But the diffusion of power is seriously hindered by the overcentralization which accompanies expansion and increasing complexity. To permit increasing participation in governmental activities, therefore, the state must once more return to the status of a community group. If people carry out decisions more willingly and are more satisfied with them when they have had a

[25] Easton, *The political system,* p. 137.
[26] MacIver, *The web of government,* p. 193.

voice in making them, the safety of democracy lies in the continuing participation of people in directing their own affairs. The findings of group dynamics forcefully attest to the belief that the larger the participatory base of "ordinary" citizens is, the more dispensable are the minority of directors at the top.

An effective technique for increasing the participation of ordinary community members and combating the evils of overcentralization is through the type of advisory groups to which we have already referred. These advisory groups will concern themselves not only with local but with national problems as well. In a complex society like our own there is no other means by which the mass of citizens can take part in determining their own destiny. Nor is there a better way in which the citizens can learn to understand the intricacies of government and to become other-minded and competent citizens. In these advisory groups discussion and self-education would be effective means of planning and executing programs for the benefit of the whole community. Our detailed discussion of group learning and collective problem-solving, of democratic education and group relations in industry, brought into sharp focus the generally ignored fact that group participation wakens interest and releases unsuspected creative energies in the solution of a complex problem.

An important characteristic of advisory groups is that they are voluntary organizations. They are not confined by formal rules. They perform their function within the pattern of needs and the system of expectations of the people who breathe life into them. They are as varied and numerous as the problems which people find pressing for solution. While their chief interest is the advancement of democratic life and government, they are nonpartisan and nonsectarian. This enables them to conserve their energy and to apply it to what is urgent. From the standpoint of human relationship the greatest merit of advisory groups lies in the fact that they permit —or better, encourage—direct participation by people in the affairs of the government conceived as a democratic community. In this way these advisory groups might well dispel the indifference and apathy with which complainants of the political scene are chronically saddling it.

Since advisory groups are not yet widely used for making important political decisions, their efficacy cannot at the present time be evaluated. They are primarily a promise rather than a fulfillment. Their use contributes little to the science of government, but they indicate what is possible in practical politics. We can say of them, as MacIver said of the mythology of scientific governing, that they show not how men *are* governed, nor even how they *should* be governed, but how they *can* be governed.[27] If the analysis and recommendation of advisory groups add anything to a better understanding of the political process, it lies in the fact that they underscore once more the important shift from the institutional to the behavioral approach in the study of democratic politics. The accumulation of factual data regarding the efficacy of advisory groups must wait for future research.

SOME LIMITATIONS ON THE DECISION-MAKING PROCESS. In Chapter 7 we described very briefly the main decision-making procedures—the techniques of voting, consensus, postponing decisions, and delegation of decision-making authority. While even in small face-to-face groups these procedures are more complex than our brief description of them would lead one to believe, they are even more involved in the area of political policy-making. Since political groupings tend to be more formal and impersonal than the face-to-face groups which we had in mind in Chapter 7, they are more subject to institutional restraints. We shall examine these limitations in the present section by following the fruitful lead by Snyder, Bruck, and Sapin.[28]

27 See *ibid.*, p. 8. For a detailed discussion of decision-making in the community, see F. Hunter, *Community power structure: a study of decision makers* (Chapel Hill: University of North Carolina Press, 1953).

28 R. C. Snyder, H. W. Bruck, and B. Sapin, *Decision-making as an approach to the study of international politics,* Foreign Policy Analysis Project, Foreign Policy Analysis Series No. 3, Organizational Behavior Section (Princeton: Princeton University, 1954), pp. 64–66.

The authors divide the limitations on decision-making into three categories, namely, those that are external to the system, those that are internal to it, and those which are a combination of the two.

1. External limitations. The authors are far from clear in their identification and description of these limitations. Interestingly enough, while these limitations have an independent existence, "their significance depends on the judgments of the decision-makers, who may be operating under internal limitations as well." The extent to which they limit the decisions of an actor will partly depend on the degree to which he perceives them as subject to his control. More concretely an external limitation is one that is not conducive to the achievement of stated objectives. Thus, to supply an example, while a candidate may succeed in convincing voters of the soundness of his platform, his ideas may be nullified if they fail to go to the polls. A state or a government bureau cannot achieve its objectives unless it has techniques for making them materialize. These limitations are external, in other words, because the judgments and perceptions of the actors are determined by their participation in a decision-making process, or because the decision-making situation is external to them.

2. Internal limitations. These are limitations imposed upon the decision-makers by the decision-making system itself. Thus if the bureaucratic committee which makes the decision is afflicted with untoward or pathological conditions, such as suspicion and distrust among its members, or if its thinking is warped and deflected by crippling rules and precedents, the resulting judgment will be different from one originating in a context where these conditions do not prevail. The most common internal limitations, however, are a lack of, an insufficiency or inaccuracy of information, failure in the communication of messages, unyielding precedents, the character of the decision-making setting, and the paucity of such resources as time, skill, and money.

3. *Combined limitations.* As should be clear, and as Snyder, Bruck, and Sapin remind us, the limitations internal and external to the decision-making system are related; and so may not only be combined, but may be either mutually diminishing or reinforcing. The external limitations, while having an independent existence, may be interpreted and manipulated by the judgments of the decision-makers, which are fundamentally internal. For sound decision-making it is, therefore, very important that both kinds of limitations and their combinations be discovered, intelligently interpreted, and effectively guarded against.[29]

POLITICAL LEADERSHIP

From decision-making to the decision-makers may be but a small step, but the understanding and description of the latter are not easy. Here we are entering once more the area of group leadership which we have found to be one of the really significant problems of group dynamics. Our task in the present context is made more difficult by the fact that most political scientists have traditionally described leadership in the context of power, a concept which group dynamics has consistently challenged.

Let us make ourselves clear on this matter at once. It is historically obtuse not to recognize the validity, within certain periods of time, of the political scientist's conception. It is blind to the realities of political life to write as if the conception of leadership formulated and espoused by students of group dynamics is unassailable. In every political system in secular society leaders have exercised power. With the growth of democracy, leadership has, to be sure, changed from the absolute authority of an individual or of an elite, to an increasing participation by many in the deliberations of the political community. In any event, in a democratic political system the group as a whole is taking a larger share in the selection of leaders, if not in leadership itself. In a democracy where formal leadership has not been fully banished—and this would include all democratic states

[29] See *ibid.*

—the effect of power investment is partly mitigated by the followers' identification with the leader. Leadership is thus more readily endorsed because the followers accept the leader instead of opposing him. This relationship between leaders and followers is variously defined in terms of respect, status, deference, prestige, and the like, which the leader bears in relation to other citizens.

In a democratic state, then, power is defined *not by how equally it is distributed but by the access which people have to it.*[30] Even in the most democratic state power is not distributed among all its members; it is democratic in the sense that everyone has an equal opportunity to acquire it. It varies from state to state, as Lasswell and Kaplan point out, by the principles according to which the leaders are recruited. "The principles of elite recruitment," they write, "may be such as to provide equal opportunity for acquisition of power, or they may severely restrict its acquisition in various ways. The rule is equalitarian in the degree to which the elite is recruited in the one way rather than the other."[31]

LEADERS AND BOSSES. Lasswell and Kaplan distinguish between leaders and bosses. Leaders are decision-makers because, as the authors inform us, they are wielders of power or because they are invested with *effective* and *formal* authority. Bosses, on the other hand, are not invested with formal power or authority. "A *boss,*" they say, "is an informal holder of effective power."[32] His power, they explain, is not authoritative; it is not legitimized and justified by the larger society. More than that: his power is often covert and indirect; and when it is overt, Lasswell and Kaplan describe it as "naked power," that is, power assumed without the consent of a constituency. When the boss's power is informed by

[30] This is essentially Lasswell's and Kaplan's distinction. See Lasswell and Kaplan, *Power and society,* pp. 226 f.

[31] *Ibid.,* p. 227. We state emphatically, however, that Lasswell's conception is too broad, for it also includes recruitment which restricts the acquisition of power, and because it exaggerates the function of power in political relations.

[32] *Ibid.,* p. 159.

enlightened values, he often exercises considerable influence. His power lies in his close advisory relation to the legitimized leader. A group of such advisers, as the authors point out, has been used extensively in policy decision-making, and has been given the half-contemptuous appellation of "brain trust."

Unfortunately, the political boss has had a powerful position and influence in American political behavior. In many instances he has established an almost impregnable machinery for the exercise of his power. The political machine, as every schoolboy knows, often forces men upon us who are not leaders but party bosses. Too frequently these men are chosen by the political machine, not on the basis of merit or skill or a sense of their responsibility, but by their popularity and by their readiness to dispense patronage. Much of the corruption in our political life, as is well known, is a product of boss rule and machine politics.[33]

Boss influence is not, according to our definition, a form of leadership. Even when it is not based on unquestioned loyalty to the boss, its power lies in arbitrary decisions and in iron discipline. The strict discipline helps to keep the boss in power; for when discipline weakens, the boss's power is easier to challenge. In this situation he is deprived of his power only when his party is defeated in an election, or when the corruption of which the boss is guilty is of such enormity that public clamor makes it imprudent to permit him to continue abusing his office.[34]

The view of leadership which we expounded in Chapter 6, and in scattered other places in this book, challenges the

[33] Our analysis is, and will continue to be, oversimplified, for we are omitting any consideration of the problem of party politics. In party politics one machine is always trying to keep another machine out of power. A discussion of this struggle lies outside the limits of this chapter.

[34] We wonder why situations of the foregoing kind, especially since they are not infrequent, did not a long time ago suggest to political scientists the ubiquity of the group. The dramatic nature of boss-behavior in such instances seems to have blinded them to the role of the group in the boss's downfall. Political dynamics as a group process could have been born before the advent of group dynamics.

somewhat Machiavellian view held by Lasswell and some others. Earlier in this chapter we voiced our objection to Lasswell's conception of leadership on the ground that it describes it in too narrow individualistic terms. "The distinguishing trait of the personality type, *common to all leaders,*" according to this view, "is an emphatic demand for *deference*—chiefly in the forms of power and respect. . . . *The leader, as a personality type, is preeminently a politician:* his conduct is directed by considerations of the acquisition and enjoyment of deference."[35]

The authors do not, however, follow the logical lead of their assertion: they should specify that deference is not located in the "heart" or in the "mind" of the leader; it implies others who will defer. Respect is a way in which others relate themselves to an individual. It is a group phenomenon as well as an individual motive. In saying this, we are not challenging the definition as applied to many cases of leadership, but its overextension. No one, we assume, doubts that some individuals are motivated largely by the desire for power. Self-centered behavior is too common to be denied.

There are people, including political leaders, however, whose behavior in groups, including political associations, is not motivated by the desire for personal power, or the type of respect from others which is based on deference to the leader. While we know substantially less about the political leader's dedication to the group than we know concerning his lust for power, we have already given a partial explanation. What we cannot demonstrate by empirical data, we can support by means of inferences from them.

Group-Centered Political Leadership. From the standpoint of group dynamics, leadership, we saw, is viewed not in terms of individual psychological traits, although these are elements in the total scheme, but in terms of group actions. The leader, we said, is a person who plays his roles in such a way as to aid others in playing theirs; and in this relationship he facilitates group action toward a goal. We

[35] Lasswell and Kaplan, *Power and society,* p. 153. Italics are ours.

established this view by describing numerous investigations and researches published during the last two decades.

Can this view of leadership be applied to political behavior? We believe that it not only can, but that it is supported by what is known of the political process as a group phenomenon.

To begin with, we must take note of the fact which is usually ignored or forgotten, that a political group by its very nature performs a leadership function. A political group —say a party, a legislature, or an administrative body—is identified and defined by the fact that it acts at the behest of a chairman, a functionary, or a mediator. Each group, however, acts not in response to the leader only, but in answer to the expectations of other members. In political science these expectations are called public opinion. The political leader, therefore, like any group leader, is responsive to the wishes of the group of which he is a member. He leads while he follows.

The foregoing illustrates, if it does not confirm, the concept of relation in relation to other relations. In political behavior, as in other forms of group behavior, "groupness" facilitates action in the interest of the group. There is nothing in the psychology of human nature—not even excepting Freud's pessimistic view—to support the belief that man in all his self-centeredness is completely selfish. The need to belong, whether its source be biological or acquired, tends to vouchsafe the group's existence and perpetuation. Men incontestably "come to will the will of others," as Catlin phrased it, "and make conformity to an intelligent social authority their own interested choice."[36]

If in this tendency to will the will of others some achieve a superordinate status, they do so not because of the desire for power inherent in their leadership position necessarily, but because the group itself bestows it upon them. If they exercise "control" over others, it is in part because others would have it so. In a study of interaction in a government

[36] Catlin, *Science and methods of politics*, p. 221.

agency, Blau found that the esteem for a government agent shown by his colleagues usually induced them to follow his recommendations. The members who were originally the chosen agent's peers showed regard and deference for him, and bestowed superior status upon him. He not only initiated more acts in the work of his department, but his initiation of acts was increased by the security which the bestowed prestige created in him. "The frequency of the contacts an agent received . . . not only expressed but also helped to determine his status in the group."[37]

In an experiment reported by Pepitone, similar results were found. These results confirm once more the belief that not all leaders are motivated by individual craving for power and deference but are moved instead by a feeling of responsibility to and acceptance by the group.[38] In this experiment some members of the group were told that their task was more important to the group than were the tasks of other members. However, in reality, the tasks of all the members were identical, although the members were unaware of this fact. The experiment demonstrated that those who perceived their task as being more important developed a stronger sense of responsibility to the group and were more willing to give time and energy to it. As Cartwright and Zander point out in commenting on Pepitone's findings, it seems that "a feeling of worth and acceptance by the group stimulates a readiness to perform functions needed by the group."[39]

The place of loyalty in group-centered leadership. The sense of responsibility to the group which we have just described has its equivalent in the political sphere in the attitude of *loyalty*—the feeling of support for and the desire

[37] P. M. Blau, Patterns of interaction among a group of officials in a government agency, *Hum. Relat.*, 7 (1954), 348.

[38] E. A. Pepitone, *Responsibility to the group and its effects on the performance of members* (unpublished Ph.D. dissertation, University of Michigan, 1952), reported in D. Cartwright and A. Zander, *Group dynamics: research and theory* (Evanston, Ill.: Row, Peterson & Co., 1953), pp. 546–47.

[39] Cartwright and Zander, *Group dynamics: research and theory,* p. 547.

for the continued existence of the group, either as a nation or as an international community.[40]

In times like the present, when our nation is concerned with its security and the loyalty of its leaders, the problem of multiple loyalty is thrust into the foreground of attention. In his discerning analysis of the problem, as it applies to both the general citizen and the political leader, Guetzkow's observations deserve our careful attention. In answering his own question of how leaders are influenced in their loyalties, Guetzkow shows that, contrasted with other citizens, the leaders "serve as chairmen of the Chamber of Commerce's international trade committee . . . work on UNESCO's commissions . . . are elected to the foreign policy posts of American Legion chapters, and so forth."[41]

Let us consider a concrete example described by Guetzkow. What, we ask, is the nature of the loyalty of an international secretariat which is composed of individuals from a variety of national states? Citing the views of people experienced in the affairs of international bodies, Guetzkow quotes them as saying that international loyalty is "'not the denationalized loyalty of the man without a country, but . . . is the conviction that the highest interests of one's own country are served best by the promotion of security and welfare everywhere.'"[42]

[40] Although "patriotism" has been used extensively as a synonym for loyalty, the latter is more inclusive. Patriotism has traditionally been reserved for one's country—*patria*—and is too narrowly associated with nationalism and chauvinism, to be descriptive of the group-centeredness which we are talking about in this book. Since the group loyalty which we envisage must ultimately include all groups, including a world community, the concept of patriotism is less satisfactory because of its exclusiveness. Despite the "multiple loyalties," as Guetzkow calls them, which exist in the world, it is still possible to develop a sense of world community. Loyalties can be, as he points out, complementary. "National and supranational loyalty may exist side by side." H. Guetzkow, *Multiple loyalties: theoretical approach to a problem of international organization* (Princeton: Center for Research on World Political Institutions, Princeton University, 1955), p. 57.

[41] Guetzkow, *Multiple loyalties*, p. 52.

[42] *Ibid.*, p. 52, quoted from Royal Institute of International Affairs, *The international secretariat of the future: lessons from experience by a group of former officials of the League of Nations* (London: Oxford University Press, 1944), p. 18.

Viewed on the background of the principles of group dynamics, the foregoing conclusion is not surprising. Just as the well-being of the individual depends a great deal on the group of which he is a member, so a nation's security and welfare depend, in the final analysis, upon the health of the world community of which it is a part. Patriotism and loyalty are neither incompatible nor mutually exclusive; they complement each other to form a higher integration, a more inclusive faith in the interbelongingness of men.

The sketchy knowledge which we possess, furthermore, suggests that while the world community is not a small face-to-face group writ large, the solutions of its problems still lie in the area of interaction and communication. Obligation to peoples remote from one's self can be exercised through the mechanisms of mass media. There is no evidence for believing that in the practice of loyalty the face-to-face group is superior to the group that is limited to indirect and remote contacts.[43] The significant fact regarding both levels of decision-making is that the leaders and general citizens alike make loyalty to a world community an integral part of their social ethics.[44]

There are cases where world bodies have persisted in the face of divided and opposed public opinion. While the preservation of the leaders' jobs no doubt played a part in the durability of these international groups, they have persisted largely because of the strong allegiance of its leaders and followers to the ideal of international cooperation. The successes of international organizations resemble those of individuals: they are cumulative and this cumulative effect has the force of perpetuating the groups' existence. In these bodies, as in smaller face-to-face groups, consensus and agreement "give participating national delegates feelings of

[43] See Guetzkow, *Multiple loyalties,* p. 55.

[44] We are fully cognizant of the many powerful barriers which stand in the way of leadership toward international cooperation and a world community. To discuss them would require many more pages. For a good initial coverage of these barriers, see G. Myrdal, Psychological impediments to effective international cooperation, *J. soc. Issues,* Suppl. Series, No. 6 (1952), 31 pp.

belonging and of satisfaction in serving the larger community. . . ."[45]

The idea of a progressively more inclusive political community is not a wild dream. When one considers, for example, the bitter hatreds and distrusts which have so long existed between France and Germany, it is hard to believe that these countries should be able to progress as far along the road to unity as they have in recent years. For they have now joined with other West European powers in a six-nation economic union and a six-nation agency for the development of atomic power. Together with Italy and the Benelux countries, they thus envisage a customs union, economic bloc, and atomic power pool embracing 170 million people.

It is important to note several factors in this striving for unity. The plan will pool the economies of 170 million people. Its control will be vested in a nonnationalistic parliament responsible to the six nations. France and Germany have made two significant concessions, namely, the yielding of her political control of the Saar by France and the reduction of tariff walls by Germany.

These are the facts. Can one safely make a prediction regarding the future? Astute political observers see in this accomplishment and in the new atmosphere of cooperation believable signs of eventual *political* union. Europe seems to be moving toward an eventual union of cooperating peoples.

The place of the individual in group-centered leadership. Some critics of group dynamics, including the present writer, are occasionally disturbed by its tendency to neglect the individual in the group process. We have made this plain enough by always attempting to keep him in the proper perspective with reference to the group. We have also stressed over and over that the leader is not independent, since in the light of our field-theoretical framework there is no local determination of events. Even at the risk of wearying the reader, we must say once more that individual and

[45] Myrdal, Psychological impediments, p. 30. Examples of such persisting groups are the Bank of International Settlements, its offspring, the European Payment Union, and the International Labour Organization.

group are not antithetical but together form a more or less integrated whole. The dynamic relation of man, we said, is a relation in relation to other relations.

The political leader must have most what traditionally he has had least, namely, the capacity to create an integrated community with the help of others. It is to be noted that we use the phrase, *with the help of others.* While he is of course an individual, the leader is also a part of the group. He leads not from the outside but from within the group. A weakness, if not a cancerous condition, of American political life is that the leader, especially the machine politician and political boss, has too often established either personal allegiance or party patronage as the test of his performance. In this there is no expression of the community's will, no recognition of law as a group imperative, no awareness of the principle that the leader does not control through power, "naked" or otherwise. The democratic leader is his own best vindication, for in his devoted behavior he is expressing the political community, not his individual will.

This leadership is no wishful chimera; it is functioning efficiently in American government. We mention only two outstanding examples, namely, civil service administrators and executive leaders. The achievements of the first, not only in the United States but in other countries, notably England and Sweden, are well known. The executive leader, who is most prominent in the government of the United States, has proved to be exceptionally capable of effecting united action. Charles E. Merriam, a learned and astute political scientist, has described executive leadership as "one of the great contributions of modern democracy to government." It nicely blends "the elements of effective popular responsibility with those of unification of action." It rests on "a genuine system of institutionalized responsibility," and "is a factor of vast strength in the future development of government." Two examples illustrating this form, according to Merriam, are Woodrow Wilson and Franklin D. Roosevelt.[46]

[46] C. E. Merriam, *The new democracy and the new despotism* (New York: Whittlesey House, McGraw-Hill Book Co., Inc., 1939), p. 256.

It is an interesting fact that our democratic philosophy has often looked with disfavor on the idea of leadership. This is in part due to the fact that the conception of leadership most prevalent in the minds of men has been that of an external control. Domination rather than leadership, to use again Pigors' distinction, has characterized this concept in both theory and practice.

In our view of leadership, the leader and followers, while integrated in a community of wills, are yet semiautonomous persons. Their individual freedom has not been abrogated. In merging their personalities with those of others in the political community, they have not lost their freedom. Individuality is free to develop to its full and creative capacity. Only those individual differences, whether of leader or followers, which cannot be integrated with the group without injuring or destroying it, must be curbed. The abuses of machine politicians and the eccentricities and pathologies of potential dictators are inimical to political integration and must be excluded from the body politic.

The greatest potentiality for the individual leader to become even more creative lies in the area of racial discrimination. A fact of the greatest significance in contemporary American life is that the problem of racial discrimination has made a full circle. The problem began as a political issue in the middle of the last century, developed into an anemic social problem at the hands of humanitarians, sentimentalists, and do-gooders after the Civil War, and today has attained again (but in an intelligent and enlightened form, thanks to social scientists and wise jurists) the status of a constitutional decision. It was no ordinary group of governmental leaders, but men with the ideal of an integrated community, who made this come to pass. While narrow and selfish men will continue to claim "the magic of unearned merit" for themselves, their claim will daily sound hollower and less convincing even to themselves.[47]

The full impact of the Supreme Court Justices' decisions has not yet been felt by the American people, and the great-

[47] The phrase in quotation marks is MacIver's. See R. M. MacIver, *The more perfect union* (New York: The Macmillan Co., 1948), p. 103.

ness of their leadership is not yet appreciated. They acted at once as individuals and as dedicated members of the American community. What could be more autonomous, what more lonely and solitary in fact, than for the great judges to pronounce against the most shameful social and psychological corruption in our social life?

At the same time, there is in this independence and solitariness the relatedness to others that is deeply social. The life of the group is expressed through each and yet each reflects the spirit and the collective purpose of the whole. While it may not please the taste of the *hyperfactualists* to describe it so, every creative act of the individual not only sets him apart but establishes him more firmly in the pattern of the whole.[48] The political leader is a leader precisely because of this relatedness of self to other selves. He helps to sustain society while society even more truly sustains him. Political leadership, in sum, like any group-democratic leadership, is a strong sense of personal responsibility for the well-being not only of one's nation but for one's nation's contribution to the well-being of the world community.

CONCLUSION

While group dynamics is a young and immature science, it is regrettable, nonetheless, that so few workers in the field have seen fit to use their imagination and skill in the study of political problems. We do not wish to detract from the importance of the issues which they have investigated, often rigorously and creatively. Yet they have largely neglected the art and science of government, perhaps the noblest and most civilizing activity of all. Had their energies been directed as vigorously to the political process as they have been consumed with the problems of education and industry, for example, we might have to rely less on rational analysis.

There is a mitigating factor, however, in this evaluation. The theory and principles of group dynamics, supported in

48 Easton describes the political scientists' preoccupation with fact-gathering by the term "hyperfactualism." See Easton, *The political system*, p. 66.

part by the researches which we have reported, and in part suggesting the researches themselves, have given us some leads. We have proceeded in this chapter on the premise that the dynamic principles which govern group learning, collective problem-solving, and human relations in education and in industry are also valid when they are applied to political problems. While we have adduced some facts and observations from political science to confirm our conclusions regarding political behavior, we have also relied heavily on inferences and theoretical constructions. Where we have been unable to say what *can* be done in political situations, we have had what we hope is an informed courage to suggest what *ought* to be done. The extrapolations from group dynamics to political dynamics, even when on rare occasions they appear to be scarcely more than poetic flights, are no less logical and realistic than extrapolations from the behavior of lower animals to the complex acts of human beings in an organized community.

May we, finally, be granted the luxury accorded to investigators in other areas, of saying, what is wearisomely repeated by some of them, that the answers to the questions which we have raised must await more and intensive research? Future research in and applications of the principles of group dynamics to the political process will extend consent-democracy to a point where, through group participation, a much larger segment of the human community will share in the decision-making of national and international governments.[49]

[49] For an excellent comprehensive review of international tensions, with valuable references, see O. Klineberg, *Tensions affecting international understanding*, Social Science Research Council, Bull. No. 62 (New York, 1952).

We should add here that since this chapter was written further evidence supporting the view of political behavior herein discussed, especially as it relates to the view that persons and groups are able to make wise political decision, has been adduced by the "Special Studies Project" of the Rockefeller Brothers Fund, Inc., and published in the daily press on January 6, 1958. The study shows that in a crisis American citizens no longer rely on politicians, but on the investigations of the best and most experienced minds of our country. Unlike the planning staffs of government departments, these able individuals have no policies to defend, no axes to grind, and no political motives to protect.

Part IV

THE PERSON IN THE GROUP: GROUP DYNAMICS AND INDIVIDUAL BEHAVIOR

CHAPTER 12

Role Dynamics

Perhaps nowhere else in the area of group behavior is there as clear a synthesis of individual and group variables as in the concept of role. The functioning of any group, from the most informal face-to-face association to large social groupings such as communities and nations, takes place through a set of interrelated roles. A role, however, we shall see, is always an individual action. It is enacted by an individual but *in a group setting.*

It is unfortunate that failure to note this obvious fact has led to a mischievous confusion. Because roles are psychologically individual variables, some devotees of group dynamics have mistakenly described individual roles as inimical to group-functioning. Some of them have gone so far as to brand individual roles with such opprobrious names as "blocker," "aggressor," "dominator," and the like. We agree that these roles impair purposive group action, but it is because they are played not *in* a group setting but *against* it. The "idea man," the "social oiler," the "compromiser," and the like are also playing their roles as individual selves; but these roles are relevant to the group's task, and aid the group in maintaining itself or in solving its common problems. What we are saying is that both group-task roles and group-building-and-maintenance-roles, as Benne and Sheats call them, are performed by individuals. A role is detrimental or nonproductive, not when it is played by an individual—for every role is so played—but when it is "individual-centered," or when it is "nonoriented or negatively oriented to group building and maintenance." In this situation an individual-centered role is undesirable because it in effect works against the group's welfare.[1] In this connection it is worth noting that we do not speak of the group's role, but only of the individual's role in the group. Also, we usually describe a role as something that a person *occupies* in a group. In either case it is the individual who "has," "plays," or "occupies" a role.

Perhaps we have said enough to show that the word role has no simple and clear meaning in social psychology and group dynamics. While the concept is used extensively, both in theoretical and empirical investigations, there is no consensus, regarding its definition, among psychologists, sociologists, and anthropologists, all of whom use the term freely and loosely. In the face of its unstable meaning it is necessary to discuss the concept with the view of arriving at a workable definition.

ROLE: ITS NATURE AND FUNCTIONS

Common sense and anecdotal conceptions of role abound both in daily thinking and in the literature of social science. Wordsworth, describing the recollections of his early childhood in his *Ode on the Intimations of Immortality,* writes perceptively that "the little Actor cons another part." The delightful line is, in turn, an echo of the same idea in Shakespeare's description of the "seven states of man."

One of the first rigorous applications of the concept of role to the study of human behavior, although a philosophical rather than an empirical one, is that of G. H. Mead, whose view of the self is intimately tied up with the process

[1] For a well-known discussion of the three main kinds of roles and their specific expressions, see K. D. Benne and P. Sheats, Functional roles of group members, *J. soc. Issues, 4* (1948), 41–49.

of role-taking. In his concepts of psychodrama and sociodrama Moreno has added to our understanding of role and its place in individual and group behavior. "*Man*," as the present writer remarked elsewhere, "*is a role-taking animal*."[2] For a more complete understanding of man's individual and group behavior, therefore, a knowledge of the nature and function of role and role behavior is essential.

Definitions and Distinctions. Role per se cannot be defined, for as such it has no existence. It derives its meaning from the *status* of the person who "occupies" a role. Status (also called position) and role are inseparable. It is a set of rights and duties, as Linton pointed out.[3] These rights and duties determine the individual's "place" or position in the group or community. In view of this position or status the individual can expect, through a long process of socialization, certain forms of response and behavior from others, and others, in turn, can anticipate definite reactions from him, for these responses or reactions are determined by the set of rights and duties embedded in the culture.

A role, on the other hand, refers to the *action* performed by an individual who holds a certain status, in anticipation of others' expectations. When he acts in response to the rights and duties embedded in his culture, he is said to be playing the role that is expected of him. It is wholly impossible to participate in any group or in any social relationship except by means of the status-role, which every adult individual develops through the course of learning his culture. This is obvious in the case of the infant who has not yet acquired any of the customs of his group. He cannot actively participate in the life of the group because he has not yet acquired or been assigned any clear-cut role. He can play roles only symbolically through the expectations of others. He is a "baby," and as a "baby" he has

[2] H. Bonner, *Social psychology: an interdisciplinary approach* (New York: American Book Co., 1953), p. 44. Italics in the original.

[3] R. Linton, *The study of man* (New York: Appleton-Century-Crofts, Inc., 1936), p. 113.

status in the eyes of others; but the status, and hence any symbolic roles attached to it, are nonfunctional. His role, in other words, is performed not by himself but by others, which is to say he has no role. Lest this sound improbable, we might put it in another way. An infant's position in society is that of an "infant," and the role he will "play" in his family will be that of an infant. This may be no more than eating, sleeping, and crying.

As the infant develops, especially as he begins to acquire a language, his statuses in the group become more clearly defined, and the roles which he plays increase in number and complexity. The human self develops in the process by which the individual becomes an object to himself, or in the process of taking the role of another person, by means of which he learns to understand the point of view of the other. A child becomes a functional member of a group when he can take other people's roles. This is distinctly seen in the child's participation in games, as Mead and Piaget convincingly describe it. In a game, Mead points out, a child learns to organize his roles. If he did not, he could not play the game. "The game," he writes, "represents the passage in the life of the child from taking the role of others in play to the organized part that is essential to self-consciousness in the full sense of the term."[4]

Clearly then, role is intimately associated with the growth of the self as well as with the development of group behavior. When an individual plays a role, he acts in accordance with the cultural norms of his group, usually a reference group within the larger social organization. By knowing the status and roles of an individual, we can predict with some feeling of certainty how he will behave. This initial analysis of role-status may be summarized as follows:

Personality is a way of behaving which we attribute to others because we perceive it in ourselves, because we can imagine ourselves feeling, thinking, and doing what others are feeling, thinking, and doing.

[4] G. H. Mead, *Mind, self and society* (Chicago: The University of Chicago Press, 1934), p. 152.

Behavior is thus interpreted in terms of social interaction, role-perception, or the kinds of experiences which an individual has by virtue of participating in close personal relationships with other members of his group. It is this assumption of another's role in oneself that gives meaning to one's own behavior.[5]

Roles and attitudes. Reciprocal and cooperative behavior are direct functions of role-playing. In cooperative activities the growing child learns to take the attitude of another person and respond to it in more or less expected or prescribed ways. He is learning to act in terms of the values and standards of the group—his family, his playmates, and eventually the larger community. Particularly important is the fact that the rules of his group, which originally seemed to be absolute impositions upon him by others, are becoming self-imposed. To the extent that he has internalized the norms and standards of his group, they become his own, and are no longer completely felt as external impositions. The group's "will" has become his own, and he appraises his behavior in the light of the group's wishes and expectations. The attitudes of others in the group have become his attitudes, and without the attitudes of others he would have no attitudes of his own. Outside a group his dispositions would not develop into attitudes, and acts based upon them would be meaningless: they could not be anchored, for there would be no standards by which the individual could judge their relevance to his own and others' behavior.

If Mead's elusive term, "the generalized other," is conceived as the integrated norms of the group, it is a useful and penetrating idea. It is through "the generalized other" that the acts of an individual become meaningful to himself and to others. Through it the norms or attitudes of the group become *his* norms or attitudes, and by means of it he finds his own locus in the inclusive pattern of human rela-

[5] H. Bonner, *Social psychology: an interdisciplinary approach* (New York: American Book Co., 1953), pp. 44–45. For a good experimental study of role behavior, see T. R. Sarbin and D. S. Jones, An experimental analysis of role behavior, *J. abnorm. soc. Psychol., 51* (1955), 236–41.

tionships. Carrying the analysis a step further, the "normal" or "well-adjusted" person is one whose attitudes are generally like those of the group of which he is a member, and who generally behaves in accordance with its definitions. The deviant or "abnormal" person, accordingly, is anyone who rejects the group-expected roles and enacts roles which have no acceptable place in his group. Many group tensions and conflicts, no less than individual ones, result from a deep and sometimes unbridgeable disparity between an individual's self-image and the role and status that his group has assigned to him.[6]

The upshot of the foregoing theoretical and abstract discussion is that an individual's attitudes are markedly influenced by his role in the group structure. This has been suspected for a long time, and a theoretical formulation has been given to it by numerous writers on the relation of roles and attitudes, notably by Parsons and Newcomb. There is, however, an embarrassing paucity of empirical evidence to support the theoretical discussion. It will be helpful, therefore, to describe Lieberman's recent investigation of this problem, which lends empirical support to the formulation.[7]

Lieberman's study was part of a larger investigation of a medium-sized plant engaged in the manufacture of household appliances. The study reported in this section investigated the effect of roles on attitudes. The experimental variables were changes in roles, and the experimental period was the length of exposure to changes in roles. The experimental groups were all the employees who experienced

[6] The foregoing condition should not be confused with the "undifferentiated absolute," or the state of "autism," which Piaget ascribed to the infant before he acquires roles, during which he is largely absorbed in pleasure-giving fantasy. See J. Piaget, *Judgment and reasoning in the child* (New York: Harcourt, Brace & Co., 1928), p. 244, and *The child's conception of physical causality* (New York: Harcourt, Brace & Co., 1930), p. 128.

[7] S. Lieberman, The effects of changes in roles on the attitudes of role occupants, *Hum. Relat.*, 9 (1956), 385–402. For a general discussion of the problem, see T. Parsons, *The social system* (Glencoe, Ill.: The Free Press, 1951) and T. M. Newcomb, *Social psychology* (New York: The Dryden Press, Inc., 1950). Parson's book is difficult but very much worth the effort of a careful reading.

changes in roles during the period; and the control groups were all the employees who did not change their roles during the experimental period. The design of the experiment permitted a three-step process of measurement, which Lieberman designated as "before measurement," "experimental period," and "after measurement."

The *before measurement* step was the administration of an attitude questionnaire to practically all personnel in the plant, a total of 2,354 workers, 145 stewards, and 151 foremen. The questionnaire was designed to elicit the employees' attitudes toward the company, the union, and their jobs.

The *experimental period* covered the time between October, 1951, and July, 1952, during which 23 workers became foremen and 35 workers became stewards.

The *after measurement* was the period in December, 1952, when the forms that had been filled out by the rank-and-file workers in 1951 were administered to the following:

> 23 workers who became foremen during the experimental period; 46 workers in a control group who did not become foremen during the same period; 35 workers who became stewards during the experimental period; and 35 workers in a control group who did not become stewards during the same period.

The control groups were matched with their parallel experimental groups on demographic, motivational, and attitudinal variables. Consequently, as Lieberman says, "any changes in attitudes that occurred in the experimental groups but did not occur in the control groups could not be attributed to initial differences between them."[8]

The hypothesis tested in this experiment was that people who occupy a certain role will acquire the set of attitudes which are consistent with the expectations of that role. Thus, since the role of foreman implies that the latter is a representative of management, workmen who become foremen would tend to show sympathy or attitudes of partiality toward management. Since the role of steward is one that

[8] Lieberman, The effects of changes, p. 387.

implies that he is a representative of the union, the expectation is that the workers who become stewards will become more favorable toward the union. Finally, to the degree that the values of the union and of the management are either incompatible or in conflict with each other, we should expect that workers who become foremen will be less favorably disposed toward the union, and the workers who become stewards will be less favorably inclined toward management. "In general," says Lieberman, "the attitudes of workers who become foremen tend to gravitate in a pro-management direction and the attitudes of workers who become stewards tend to move in a pro-union direction."[9]

Statistical significance of the results were determined by the chi square method. Most of the differences were found to be significant, but a number of them were not. The differences that were statistically significant were all in the expected direction, and most of those that were not significant were also in the expected directions.

Lieberman raised a natural question concerning the changes in attitudes. Are the shifts in attitudes and allegiances that accompanied people's changed roles stable or temporary phenomena?

It was possible to answer this question by virtue of a set of circumstances in the plant. Shortly after the 1952 resurvey the nation experienced an economic recession, and the factory found it necessary to reduce its work force. This resulted in the laying off of many rank-and-file workers and the return of a number of foremen to nonsupervisory jobs. By June, 1954, 8 of the 23 workers who had become foremen were returned to the status of worker, 12 were still foremen, and 3 had voluntarily left the plant. In the same period, 14 stewards were returned to the worker role, leaving only 6. Fifteen, or almost half, had voluntarily left the factory.

[9] *Ibid.*, p. 393. It should be noted that in the control group either no attitude changes took place, or they were less marked, from the "before" situation to the "after" situation.

The research team now readministered the questionnaires that the personnel had filled out in 1951 and 1952. While the number of cases was now small, they suggest a reasonable answer. In general, "most of the 'gains' that were observed when workers became foremen were 'lost' when they became workers again."[10] In most cases the foremen who retain their positions either retain their positive attitudes toward management or become even more favorable toward them, while the foremen who become workers again "show fairly consistent drops in the direction of re-adopting the attitudes they held when they had been in the worker role. On the whole, the attitudes held by demoted foremen in 1954, after they had left the foreman role, fall roughly to the same levels as they had been in 1951, before they had ever moved into the foreman role."[11]

In summary, the data in Lieberman's experiment support the hypothesis that an individual's attitudes are influenced by the role he occupies in his group.

Role behavior. Newcomb has made a useful distinction between role and role behavior which is germane to our discussion of the nature and functions of roles.[12] Role, says Newcomb, is a sociological concept. It refers to a pattern of action which is expected of all members of a group who occupy a specified position, regardless of who they are. There are many daily acts which are not forms of role behavior, for they are not in most cases determined by any status or position which the actor occupies in his group, and they do not involve any assumption on his part as to how his position is perceived by others. Examples of such acts, given by Newcomb, are brushing one's teeth, going to the movies, and buying bubble gum. People engage in these acts simply because they are motivated to do so. There is nothing gained, Newcomb adds, by calling them role behaviors.[13]

10 *Ibid.*, p. 395.
11 *Ibid.*, p. 395.
12 See Newcomb, *Social psychology*, pp. 328–34.
13 *Ibid.*, p. 331.

"Prescribed roles" fall into the same category. A prescribed role consists of acts "required of the occupant of any position." They are based on the *ascribed* status of the actor; that is, the position given to an individual on the basis of an identifying characteristic, such as age, sex, or vocation. The ascribed status of a teacher, for example, is based upon his profession and of a grandfather upon his seniority. The difference, then, between role and role behavior is the difference in the function and the act performed by the individual: it is the *function* performed which identifies a role and the *specific act* which distinguishes role behavior. Bill Jones, for example, describes the Battle of Waterloo to his students, and Ed Smith teaches his grandson to shoot an arrow. Each is assuming a role, but the motive patterns involved in the act of each is not a role but a role behavior. "A role behavior," Newcomb asserts, is "a *motive pattern on the part of a specific individual as he takes a role*."[14]

A role behavior, as we see it is a person's internalization of his social roles, as he perceives them, in such a way that his individual behavior is synchronized with the expectancies of other members of his group or community. The synchronization of individual behavior and others' expectancies is determined by how accurately the person perceives his role in the group and by how strongly he is motivated to play it. The clearer and more accurate his role perception, and the stronger his motive to enact his role, the more his behavior will agree with the expectations of others.

A role behavior differs from an attitude in that the former is always the *behavior* or *action* of a person who occupies a defined or recognized status. An attitude is not fundamentally described by an action; it is a *tendency* or disposition to act. It can be, and often is, as we remarked, concealed from the inspection of others. Being a tendency, it can only be inferred from the concrete responses of a person occupying a specific role position.

[14] *Ibid.*, p. 330. Italics in the original.

Role and role behavior are related by the fact that both are objective and observable forms of human action. Unlike motives and attitudes which can be concealed and falsified, role and role behavior are open to public inspection. The roles which we play in relation to others are observed and reacted to by others. They form an interactive pattern of behavior which we call the group. The group is a dynamic configuration of roles and role behaviors. Lewin's assertion that a "group atmosphere can be conceived as a pattern of role playing" expresses our point exactly.[15]

Probably every social psychologist is dissatisfied with the terminology of role theory. In an unpublished analysis of role theory, Martin Martel has recently injected a considerable amount of clarity into this vague subject. As reported to the present writer in a private correspondence by J. McV. Hunt, Martel holds that there are three basic constructs in role theory. These constructs are the following: (1) the status defined in terms of criteria which are often formal and named, such as in the case of the President of the United States; (2) the norms or expectations on the part of people concerning what an individual in a given status or position should do; and (3) the actual behavior or action of an individual in a status.

Individual Role Behavior. This and the next two chapters, the reader will observe, examine the person in the group. They investigate the relation between group dynamics and individual behavior. Group dynamics has understandably neglected the place of the individual, but in so doing it has narrowed its scope and impaired its fuller understanding of group behavior. We are, therefore, extending the conception of group dynamics to include personality, especially in the next chapter. In so doing we hope to widen the horizon of the study of group behavior, in consonance with recent developments, thus deepening

[15] See K. Lewin, *Resolving social conflicts* (New York: Harper & Bros., 1948), p. 50. There are other terms which describe this, most of which we have used in different parts of this book. The most common are shared norms, interlocking roles, and role system.

our potential insight into the nature of both individual and group dynamics.[16]

Every normal individual is in some ways "unique"—or at any rate different from others—and in some ways like others of his group. This difference and likeness is characteristic of his role behaviors also, but it is due to different factors. Self-perception is one of them. Self-perception is a pattern of role perceptions—an experience which results from an individual's personal relationships with other members of his group. It involves the ability to anticipate another person's behavior. Of course, there are significant individual differences in this ability. The person in whom this skill is well developed easily and correctly perceives another's point of view. The individual whose perspective is poor or undeveloped shifts with difficulty from one role to another. By playing the role of another, a person reproduces the other's actions, incorporates them into his own behavior pattern, and acts in ways similar to the other person. Yet in the whole process he is expressing his own role, because his role behavior is bound up with his perception of himself as an individual. The timid person, for example, relates himself to others or plays his role with reference to them in a hesitant and dependent manner. He acts within a frame of reference which, although it is public, it is also deeply private. This situation confirms our earlier statement that nowhere else perhaps in the whole area of group phenomena is there as clear a synthesis of individual and group variables as in the concepts of role and role behavior.

The distinct character of individual roles is normally obscured by their strong tendency to form networks of interrelated roles. They act in sets or patterns. The network conceals their strongly individual nature. The sets

[16] As is always the case, one is not alone in such matters. A few others have been similarly concerned. See, for example, H. H. Jennings, Sociometric structure in personality and group formation, being chap. xiv in M. Sherif and M. O. Wilson, *Group relations at the crossroads* (New York: Harper & Bros., 1953).

r patterns themselves, furthermore, tend toward individ-
ality; they are characteristic of the person. We thus come
o identify a person, not by any single or isolated role, but
y the pattern in which the roles are integrated. The set
f interrelated roles *is* the person. Accordingly, we recog-
ize a person not only by his physical features and the
ituational conditions in which the roles arise and function,
ut by the set of attitudinal and normative acts which con-
titute his individual roles. In knowing the roles he plays
nd the manner in which he enacts them, we know *him.*

Social-psychological research and evidence from psycho-
herapy attest to this observation. Every mature individual
levelops directionality in the socialization process, no mat-
er how hemmed in he may be, or feel himself to be, by the
onstrictive effect of the group norms. Every healthy adult
ehaves in accordance with goals which he has himself
stablished, no matter how much they may have been
acilitated in their development by the values of the group.
harlotte Bühler, who made an intensive study of this
'thrust into the future" that characterizes every normal
erson, found that each person was impelled in his own
pecial way to achieve a desired objective.[17]

Interpreted in the light of the concept of role perception,
his anticipation of future acts and their consequences is the
apacity of an individual to play the role of another. One
erson understands the psychological state of another be-
ause he has learned through his own perception to see that
ther as being a person like himself. In this condition he
an anticipate the acts of another and relate himself con-
tructively to him. Anticipation thus makes role behavior
ossible and human actions within limits predictable.

There is no intention in the foregoing analysis to suggest
hat there is always consistency and harmony in the direc-
ionality of individual roles, or in the anticipation and pre-
liction of individual acts. On the contrary, most individual
ole behavior is marked by some inconsistency. There is no

17 C. Bühler, *Der Menschliche Lebenslauf als Psychologisches Problem*
(Leipzig: S. Hirzel, 1933).

complete integration of roles. A man who is a gentle father at home may be an autocrat in his office or factory. Another one may be a self-assured chess player but show no confidence in a business transaction. Life is full of such examples, and it is improfitable to belabor the point. The crux of the issue is that the inconsistencies are individual, not group, incompatibilities. Each role behavior is a means by which the individual tries to meet the demands made upon him by the groups to which he belongs. The whole process of socialization, of growing to be an acceptable member of a group, lies behind his role-playing. The child learns to perform one role rather than another, to behave this way rather than that way, because through the guiding restraint of his parents and others, he is striving to fashion his own life. To the extent that he has succeeded in emerging from the process as an individuated person, he has played his roles adequately.

Place of Motivation in Role Behavior. In calling attention to the directional nature of the self, to its impulsion toward a desired objective, we implicitly suggested the place of motivation in role behavior. The brief description of role behavior in terms of expectancy or anticipation also suggested the relationship. Not all role behaviors, however, are performed in response to the expectancies of others or to the demands of group norms. Since individual role behaviors, however shaped they may be by social influences, are also private and personal, they may also be described as based on individual motives. When he enacts a role, a person is not only responding to the expectations of others; his behavior is also guided by his private wishes. He may perform a role for no other reason than that he finds the act pleasurable and satisfying. The wish for group belongingness may be satisfied by playing expected roles, for playing the expected roles is accompanied by the reward of acceptance by others. The reward of acceptance strongly reinforces the motivation to play one's roles expertly. Every normal individual wants social acceptance, and he will strive to please others—that is, play the role of a friendly and accepting individual—because of the anticipated belongingness that will accrue from it.

The foregoing description but emphasizes once more the combined individual and social nature of role behavior. Clearly, playing one's roles accomplishes both personal and social functions. The individual satisfies his personal needs, especially that of acceptance by others, and the group's security and continuity is assured by the individual's performance of whatever acts the group's value system may expect of him. Yet, while the individual enacts most of his roles in response to the expectations of his group, he has a wide latitude for their performance. Although each role is played in conformity with society's rules, each is, nevertheless, distinct and individual, because the act which the individual performs has its own specific place in the network of role behaviors. No two roles can be played identically, and no two persons enact their roles similarly, in every detail. Roles are shared, but they are not shared exactly alike.

The clearest example of this fact is found in the role of the leader. Our detailed analysis and description of leadership should make this clear. Role-playing in a group reaches its maximum degree of individuality and personal motivation in the leader. As we saw, he is a center of high potential. He is more "free" in the sense that he initiates more role behaviors than others. Insofar as he is motivated —as indeed he is—not only by the desire to facilitate role-playing in others, but by a strong personal motivation to *initiate* role behavior in others, his actions are individualistic. Obviously, we have in mind the democratic leader. The authoritarian or autocratic leader is motivated by different role behaviors. His primary wish is not to facilitate and initiate the role behavior of others but to create a state of dependency in his followers. To be sure, when they depend upon him they are also playing roles, but their roles are those of passive submission, lacking in individual motivation and initiative. While there is no empirical support for the distinction, we venture to say that there is a degree of sameness in autocratic leadership-followership roles that is seldom duplicated in the democratic situation.

Summing up the foregoing discussion, we can say that in informal groups of the type we have been describing, role behavior is characterized by individual—some would say unique—qualities of motivation and action.

Role Behavior and Group Membership. Although the subject matter of this chapter is roles and individual role behavior, our discussion of it is intended primarily to shed further light on the nature of group structure and group behavior. Since a group is a pattern of functional roles or an integration of status-acts into a unified whole, a knowledge of the part played by the membership is very important. We must understand the role of group members in the maintenance and growth of groups.

Benne and Sheats a decade ago called attention to the fact that students of group dynamics, especially in their practical concern with leadership training, have traditionally relegated membership roles to a position of secondary importance. Even worse, most investigators have tacitly identified membership with followership. This identification, however, seems to be inconsistent with their avowed interest in effective group functioning. For if members are only followers who must be guided by skillful leaders, the concepts of group responsibility and group productiveness which loom large in the researches of group dynamics have a dubious status. For this reason the argument for greater stress on membership roles in group psychology, particularly in group training, is sound and timely.[18]

Benne and Sheats proceeded on the premise that moving toward a group goal is a group responsibility, not the work of a few dominant individuals or of a formal leader. The latter, as we pointed out in Chapter 6, is himself a member who, together with other members, shares in the responsibility of working toward a collective goal. The organiza-

[18] See Benne and Sheats, Functional roles of group members.

tion, maintenance, and productivity of a group are the task of its member roles. This has been our meaning of group-centered behavior. This view of membership roles excludes from group functioning those self-centered roles whereby individuals use groups to satisfy wholly personal, and therefore "group-irrelevant," needs.

With this distinction in mind, Benne and Sheats, whose chief concern was the training of members to perform group-centered roles, classified member roles into three main categories, namely, group-task roles, group-building-and-maintenance roles, and individual roles. Before describing the first two, we must comment on the third, or individual roles.

First, we have no objection to this category itself; for individual roles, as defined by the authors, no doubt exist and function as they describe them. These individual roles are "irrelevant to the group task," no doubt about it, and are either "non-oriented or negatively oriented to group building and maintenance."

However, we believe that individual roles should be differently conceptualized. Enactors of individual roles, while physically present in the group, are not participants in it. They are potential "out-groups" whose main interest, as with all out-groups, is to act against the in-group. In terms of our conceptual scheme these individuals are subgroups, and are more appropriately treated as elements in intergroup behavior, as in Chapter 5. These roles should be called *egocentric* roles.

Benne and Sheats themselves provide us with specific descriptive examples which, we believe, give credence to our view. Here is a summary of their typology. They describe the *aggressor* as one who is engaged in "deflating the status of others . . . attacking the group or problem it is working on," and so forth. The *blocker*, they say, "tends to be negativistic and stubbornly resistant, disagreeing and opposing without or beyond 'reason.'" The *playboy*, to choose just one more example, "makes a display of his *lack of involvement* in the group's process. This may take the from of cynicism, nonchalance, horseplay, and other more or less studies forms of '*out of field*' behavior."[19]

The main points of the foregoing observation are first, that these individual roles must not be confused with the individualized character of role enactment as we described it in the preceding two sections; and second, that they are in actuality simple forms of intergroup conflict.

We turn now to those classes of roles, as outlined by Benne and Sheats, which truly involve individuals in group functioning.

1. *Group-task roles.* As the term implies, these roles are task-centered. Its enactors, both leaders and nonleaders, work together to solve a common problem. Since no specific role is formally assigned to any member, each individual may successively participate in as many role behaviors as the occasion permits or demands. The main thing is that every member participates, or has the freedom of choice to participate, in the facilitation and coordination of group effort toward solving the group's problem.

Since roles are played by individuals, not by groups as such, group-task roles express themselves in specific forms. They are briefly described below, in the order in which they appear in Benne's and Sheats' report.

The *initiator-contributor* suggests new ideas or different ways of regarding a group problem. This may take the form of proposal of a new goal, a new definition of the problem, a suggested solution, or a new way of mobilizing the group's efforts and skills in problem solving.

The *information-seeker* asks for elucidation of proposals and for factual or authoritative information pertaining to the problem.

On the other hand, the *opinion-seeker* is looking not for facts but for a clarification of the value premises which are related to the problem.

[19] *Ibid.*, p. 45. Italicizations of descriptive phrases are not in the original.

Compared with the information-seeker, the *information-giver* presents facts, brings his own experience to bear on the problem, or formulates reasonable generalizations.

Unlike the opinion-seeker, the *opinion-giver* expresses whatever beliefs he thinks might be relevant to the task, particularly his opinion of what the group's values ought to be.

The *elaborator* concretely spells out or illustrates ideas, presents reasons for suggestions made by the group members, and tries to predict how a suggestion or a proposed solution would work out.

A *coordinator* clarifies relationships among ideas, tries to pull the ideas together, or attempts to coordinate separate activities into an effective group effort.

An *orienter* summarizes the discussions and activities of the members in order to enable them to see their position with respect to the group goal, or raises questions concerning the direction which the group discussion is taking.

The *evaluator-critic* attempts to evaluate the group's achievement in terms of the group task. He may do this by evaluating the logic or feasibility of proposals made by the members.

Since groups do not always perform at a high peak, an *energizer* is a useful member. His function is to stimulate the group not only to perform, but to perform at a higher qualitative level.

There are many groups whose actions are aided or impeded by the performance or neglect of various "mechanical" procedures. The *procedural technician* fulfills this function. He expedites the group's work by performing such routine tasks as distributing materials, rearranging the seating, and so forth.

The *recorder* plays the role of "group memory." He keeps an account of suggestions, decisions, the results of group discussion, etc.

2. *Group-building-and maintenance roles.* The roles in this category are concerned with the functioning of the

group as a group. More specifically the function of these roles is to foster and maintain group-centered attitudes and behaviors for the purpose of maintaining, strengthening, and perpetuating the group as a group. Like the group-task roles, these are performed by individuals and, therefore, are manifested in specific and identifiable forms. In presenting them below, we again follow the classification and description given by Benne and Sheats.

The *encourager* accepts the contributions of the members with warmth and approval. He radiates a spirit of acceptance and understanding of others' ideas and suggestions by means of praise and encouragement.

Since all active and productive groups are marked by dissension and disagreements, a *harmonizer* plays an effective part in creating and maintaining group cohesion. He is a mediator in disputes and disagreements and a facilitator of tension release in the members. Because of this skill in conciliation, he has been called a "social-oiler."

The *compromiser* facilitates the group's progress toward a goal by yielding his own position in a dispute. He may do this by admitting his own mistake, by modifying his own ideas for the sake of group productiveness, by self-control in the interest of group harmony, and the like.

The importance of effective communication in group behavior has been frequently emphasized. The *gatekeeper and expediter* fulfills the function of keeping the channels of communication open. He does this in various ways, depending, of course, on his imagination and skill. The most common way is by encouraging and helping others to participate in the group's deliberations. Concretely, he may do this by asking for member A's ideas or by suggesting that individual contributions be limited in length, in order to permit as many persons as possible to make suggestions.

The *standard-setter* sets up a goal for the group to strive for and establishes a criterion for evaluating the quality of its achievements.

The *group-observer* keeps a record of different aspects of the group's activity and reflects his observations and interpretations back to the group's evaluation of its own processes.

The *follower* serves primarily, and perhaps exclusively, as an audience in group decision-making. He goes along with the group's procedures and passively accepts the ideas and suggestions of others.[20]

ROLE ALTERATION AND BEHAVIORAL CHANGE

We distinguished between role and status on the ground that the former indicates action, behavior, or change whereas the latter suggests occupancy, position, or condition. While it is not strictly accurate, we can designate the two by the overworked terms *dynamic* and *static*.

Sociologists are constantly calling attention to the mobile and changing character of modern society, and the changes of roles and status that are bound up with the dynamic social process. Social psychologists have for a long time been investigating personality and attitudinal changes. Group dynamicists have been deeply concerned not only with the larger and more unmanageable problem of group change but also and particularly with the specific and urgent problem of attitudinal change as a method of reducing or resolving intergroup conflicts.

Since role behavior and attitudes are, as we have seen, intimately related, this relationship can throw light upon the question of behavioral change, which is an important practical problem in group dynamics. The problem may be phrased as follows: What group factors cause a change in role to be followed by a change in behavior? We phrase the question in this manner because, as was shown in preceding pages, a change in role tends to lead to a change in attitude. Since attitudes are not actions but tendencies to action, we want to know the mechanism which would explain the origin of a person's act from a change in his role.

[20] The foregoing roles are described in Benne and Sheats, Functional roles of group members, pp. 43–45.

SHARED FRAMES OF REFERENCE. The term "frame of reference" is widely used in contemporary social psychology. It refers to the context which determines our perceptions of objects, persons, and events; or "the system of functional relations consisting of influences operative at a given time."[21] A frame of reference not only determines our attitudes but our perceptions of our roles. Roles derive their meanings from the frame of reference, from the pattern of functionally related perceptions by means of which we unconsciously or habitually evaluate our experience. The frame of reference is a "scale" by means of which we judge the social environment and our position in it. An object, an event, or an experience is structured or organized into a meaningful whole by the frame of reference, or the scale of values, which as we shall see, we acquire, largely from the group in which the object, event, or experience is embedded. Accordingly, while we act in a limited way on the basis of individual frames of reference—our behavior, as we have said, is always to some extent individualized or "unique"—our actions are for the most part "anchored" in a frame established by the groups with which we identify ourselves.[22]

Group frames of reference. While attitudes have an individual locus and mode of expression, they are for the most part group-determined. We acquire them from others, and they express themselves largely within the group's boundaries. If people perceive objects, persons, or events similarly, it is because they share the same frames of reference. If they reject Negroes or Jews, it is because the groups with which they identify themselves avoid or condemn these minorities. The frames of reference are not only internalized by every individual but are communicated to and shared with other persons. All social attitudes

[21] M. Sherif and C. W. Sherif, *An outline of social psychology* (rev. ed.; New York: Harper & Bros., 1956), p. 41.

[22] A review of this subject, including numerous empirical studies, is found in M. Sherif and H. Cantril, *The psychology of ego-involvements* (New York: John Wiley & Sons, Inc., 1947).

are acquired within a public frame of reference. This is largely what makes them rigid and enduring. When they change, it is not generally because a person "sees the light" or perceives the error of his ways, but because the frame of reference which he has shared with others has been modified by all of them. A change in social attitudes, then, is a group phenomenon, not solely an individual change of mind.

Our chief concern in this section, however, is not with change of attitudes but with behavioral change. The frames of reference are group-shared perceptions; they function mostly in groups. Change in behavior, as contrasted with change in attitudes, has its origin in the reference frames of informal and established groups. In order to answer our question regarding what group factors cause a change in roles to be followed not only by changes of attitudes but even more importantly by changes in action, we must examine the nature and functions of certain groups in which frames of reference operate.

1. Reference groups.[23] The concept of reference group has been used extensively in the last decade to indicate the source of attitudes and their modification. A reference group is one with which an individual closely identifies himself. The internalization of values of which we have spoken on several occasions, which impels a person to perceive the group's values as his own and to feel that he is acting not under compulsion but on the basis of the group values which he has appropriated, takes place in a reference group.

Reference groups differ from other kinds of groups in the readiness of persons to establish a close identification with them. An individual normally belongs to various groups, to some of which he is only externally or passively related, or to some in which his membership confers practical ad-

[23] The term "reference group" was first used by Hyman in his investigation of frames of reference. See H. Hyman, The psychology of status, *Arch. Psychol.*, No. 269 (1942). For a comprehensive discussion of reference groups, see Sherif and Wilson, *Group relations at the crossroads*, chap. ix.

vantages, or to others largely against his own wishes. A reference group is an association of persons to which he *wants* to belong and in which he finds satisfactions which other groups do not generally afford him. This group he feels is *his* group, and the functions which it performs are activities with which he wishes to identify himself. A reference group not only expects devotion from him but it gives him devotion in return. This mutual satisfaction helps to breed the sense of solidarity of which we spoke at length in Chapter 3.

From the paucity of empirical evidence at hand one may tentatively assert that changes in role are associated with changes of status in the group or with shifting one's allegiance to another reference group. The first perceptible changes in these situations are in the attitudes of individuals. These changes are consequent upon a change in frames of reference followed by changes in self-perceptions which lead to changes in attitudes.

Now, since a change in reference group inevitably involves a change from one group to another, or a modification of functions within the original group, the individual's behavior changes to meet his new status in the group. He acquires a new role, or set of roles. These roles call for new forms of behavior; for unless his behavior changes to fulfill the new functions, he cannot serve as an effective member. We saw this situation illustrated in the examples of changing from worker to foreman or to steward. In changing his status from one to the other, the individual changed his roles to meet the demands of the new position. This involved a reorientation of attitudes. Attitudes could not remain locked up inside the self of the individual; they led to the performance of new functions. His actions now differed in definable ways from those which characterized him before he changed his roles. The foreman, for example, now had to assume a position of superordination, or perhaps even of dominance. The manner of relating himself to his former fellow-workers underwent a change. Many of his functions obviously had to change, and these changes of function were, in effect, forms of changed behavior; for unless he changed his behavior to meet the demands of the new role, the functions themselves could not be performed. When the promoted foremen reverted to a worker status, their behavior once more underwent change, especially in those instances where the reversion to a former role was a painful psychological experience. While the number of cases was statistically too small to permit generalization, there was a tendency among some of them to engage in behavior quite different from that before the reversion of roles took place. Some, according to Lieberman, blamed "uncontrollable situational determinants" and consequently were not too much bothered by their demotion. Others blamed management; others, still, blamed themselves, and were emotionally disturbed by their demotion. In any case, the overt behavior of some of them was modified by the change of role and shift of reference group relationships.[24]

The reference group principle which operates when a change in roles involving a change in reference groups ends in changed behavior is summed up by Lieberman as follows: "A change in roles involves a change in reference groups . . . which leads to change in attitudes . . . which leads to change in actions."[25]

2. *Membership groups.* Reference groups and membership groups may serve the same functions and yet be different. A reference group, we have said, is one to which a person wishes to relate himself and with which he strongly identifies himself. In a simple and stable society practically every group with which a person associates himself is a reference group. The more integrated the society, the more likely will this be true.

In a rapidly changing society, however, where there is much differentiation of status and where there is a multiplicity of groups, an individual does not relate himself to all of them in the same way. There are groups in which a per-

24 Lieberman, The effects of changes, p. 396, n 4.
25 *Ibid.*, p. 400.

son's feelings are characterized by a weak or nonexistent sense of loyalty and relatedness. This is true of many secondary groups in which an individual's contacts are formal and less ego-involved, and whose norms he has not clearly internalized. His relation to them is largely marginal. These membership groups may run the entire gamut of affiliations from the family to the clique, the church, and the political party. While each one of these is usually also a reference group if the individual closely identifies himself with it, it is a membership group in that the individual exercised little or no choice in becoming a member.

When it differs from a reference group, a membership group is thus one to which a person either *actually belongs* or "in which," as Newcomb points out, "a person is recognized by others as belonging," whatever his membership aspirations may be.[26] In the membership group, as in the reference group, an individual is influenced in his attitudes and behavior because of his membership in it. We are, of course, also influenced by groups with which we are *not* identified, as well as by the attitudes and actions of members of groups to which we belong. For this reason the function of the two kinds of groups is frequently the same: both affect attitudes and behavior.

Good examples of membership groups—which may, however, also have characteristics of reference groups—are those loose associations which, having no formally defined anchorages or frames of reference, impel individuals spontaneously to form groups in order to achieve some stability in their interrelations. Cliques and gangs illustrate this type of group formation. Each gives to its members a frame of reference,

[26] Newcomb's definition is found in his *Social psychology*, p. 225. See further M. Sherif and C. W. Sherif, *Groups in harmony and tension* (New York: Harper & Bros., 1953); R. K. Merton and A. S. Kitt, Contributions to the theory of reference group behavior, in R. K. Merton and P. F. Lazarsfeld (eds.), *Studies in the scope and method of "the American soldier"* (Glencoe, Ill.: The Free Press, 1950), pp. 40–105; and H. H. Kelley, Two functions of reference groups, in G. E. Swanson, T. H. Newcomb, and E. L. Hartley (eds.), *Readings in social psychology* (rev. ed.; New York: Henry Holt & Co., Inc., 1952), pp. 410–14.

or a system of anchorage points, by means of which they locate or place themselves in a web of social relationships.

The interrelation of reference and membership groups. The relationship between reference groups and membership groups is anything but simple. Our description of the two has shown that, while abstractly they are separable, in concrete practice they tend to merge or interpenetrate. Common sense as well as empirical research shows that attitudes and actions are influenced by the values of the groups in which one has membership. At the same time the researches of Hyman, Sherif, Newcomb, and others which we have cited demonstrate the strong need to orient one's attitudes and behavior in the direction of selected groups, that is, reference groups.

The close relationship between the two is sharply brought out in the study by Merton and Kitt, which we have cited.[27] In this study membership groups are one kind of reference group. This is illustrated in soldiers' evaluations of promotion opportunities in the armed forces.[28] A paradoxical finding was that the *less* the opportunity for promotion the *more favorable* the attitude toward promotion opportunity. Thus, for example, while the Air Corps had a very high promotion rate, Air Corps men were much more critical of promotion opportunities than, say, the Military Police, in which promotion opportunities were probably the worst in the whole Army. The same critical attitude characterized the better educated soldier, even though his chances of promotion were much higher than those of the poorly educated ones.

The explanation of the paradox lay partly in the frame of reference of group rates of promotion. Since a high rate of mobility affords frequency of social contacts and change of jobs, it stimulates strong hopes of promotion. Since, however, the supply of desirable jobs is limited, many men are

27 Merton and Kitt, in Merton and Lazarsfeld (eds.), Contributions to the theory of reference groups.

28 As reported in detail in S. A. Stouffer *et al.*, *The American soldier*, Vols. I and II of *Studies in social psychology in World War II* (Princeton: Princeton University Press, 1949).

frustrated in their wishes and become discouraged by the poor prospects for promotion. This represents a disharmony between their hopes and achievements relative to others in their group. It means that their membership groups are not their reference groups. If we then think of the soldier's rank as the group—say of corporals—to which he belongs (membership group) and his aspired rank—say of sergeants—as the group to which he wants to relate himself (reference groups), his attitudes and actions toward the Army are the resultant of the combined influence of the two groups.

Newcomb's well-known Bennington study (1935–39) also shows that, although membership groups and reference groups are distinct, they interchange frequently. Individuals in the Bennington community acquired widely approved attitudes to the extent that the membership group served as a *positive point of reference.*

The Bennington membership group was composed of about 250 women students, "relatively homogeneous in respect to home background . . . from urban, economically privileged families whose social attitudes were conservative."[29]

Most individuals in this membership group of 250 women went through marked changes in attitudes toward important public issues. In most cases, as we shall see, the membership group also served as the reference group in which their attitudes changed.

Information concerning the membership group was obtained by means of a Likert-type scale of Political and Economic Progressivism which dealt with such contemporary public issues as unemployment, public relief, and the rights of organized labor—all vital questions in the 1930's.

Individual prestige at Bennington was associated with nonconservatism, the study revealed. The measure of prestige was the frequency of choice as one of five students

[29] T. M. Newcomb, Attitude development as a function of reference groups: the Bennington study, in G. E. Swanson, T. H. Newcomb, and E. L. Hartley (eds.), *Readings in social psychology* (rev. ed.; New York: Henry Holt & Co., Inc., 1952), p. 421.

"most worthy to represent the College" at an intercollegiate gathering. Nominations were submitted by 99 per cent of the students in two successive years, "with almost identical results." "The nonconservatism of those with high prestige," Newcomb writes, "is not merely the result of the fact that juniors and seniors are characterized by both high prestige and nonconservatism; in each class those who have most prestige are least conservative."[30]

The attitudes of the membership group was not, however, uniform. Some individuals were unusually nonconservative and others revealed this trait not at all. The variance was a function of the reference groups with which they identified themselves.

Information regarding the reference groups was obtained directly from the students themselves, or indirectly from other students and from instructors. One of the indirect methods used was to obtain indexes of "community citizenship" by a guess-who technique. Each of 24 students, representing every grouping of importance, was asked to name three individuals from each of three classes "who were reputedly most extreme in each of twenty-eight characteristics related to community citizenship." A "reputation index" was constructed "on the basis of the frequency with which individuals were named in five items dealing with identification with the community, minus the number of times they were named in five other items dealing with negative community attitudes."

Most students were aware of the pronounced trend away from freshman conservatism to senior nonconservatism, but a few, especially among the conservatives, were scarcely aware of it. This means, of course, that those who were unaware of it had not been using the community as a reference group for their attitudes. Since, however, it was inappropriate to assume that those who were aware of the trend had necessarily been using the community as a reference group, a measure of awareness had to be constructed. This was done by asking students to answer in two ways a

[30] *Ibid.*, p. 422.

number of statements taken from the Political and Economic Progressivism Scale. The two ways were as follows: (1) to express agreement or disagreement with such statements as "The budget should be balanced before the government spends any money on social security," and (2) to estimate the percentage of freshmen, juniors, seniors, and faculty members who would agree with the statement. From their responses an index of divergence of own attitudes from the estimated majority of juniors and seniors was computed. In his analysis of this index Newcomb writes that,

> . . . a positive index on the part of a senior indicates the degree to which her own responses are more conservative than those of her classmates, and a negative index the degree to which they are less conservative. Those seniors whose divergence index more or less faithfully reflects the true difference between own and class attitude may (or may not) be using the class as an attitude reference group; those whose divergence indexes represent an exaggerated or minimized version of the true relationship between own and class attitude are clearly not using the class as an attitude reference group, or if so, only in a fictitious sense.[31]

The results of the investigation support the view of the distinctness and relatedness of membership groups and reference groups. In the Bennington community, as in most others, membership is not necessarily a reference point for acquiring attitudes; yet at the same time, the acquisition of attitudes depends on the process of relating oneself to a group. These findings support the thesis, in other words, that a person's attitude development "is a function of the way in which he relates himself both to the total membership group and to one or more reference groups."[32]

What is the relevance of this type of knowledge to the understanding of roles and role behavior? The answer is quite clear, and can be stated briefly. The character of a community, which is to say a group, is reflected in the roles

[31] T. M. Newcomb, Attitude development as a function of reference groups: the Bennington study, in G. E. Swanson, T. H. Newcomb, and E. L. Hartley (eds.), *Readings in social psychology* (rev. ed.; New York: Henry Holt & Co., Inc., 1952), p. 423.

[32] *Ibid.*, p. 430.

which it accepts and rejects. In Bennington the approved role was nonconservatism. A person's role behavior expressed itself in attitudes and actions which were community-oriented; that is, it reflected absorption in community affairs, interest in student activities, acceptance of campus standards and codes of behavior, and the like. The unapproved role was conservatism, or a lack of interest in community problems and affairs and a resistance to its codes of behavior. Every individual, whether conservative or nonconservative, adjusted herself to the total community through the specific roles which she played in the membership group to which she belonged or the reference group to which she aspired.

Leader Roles. In our discussion of role behavior and group membership we argued that aiming toward a group goal is the responsibility not only of a formal leader but of the entire group. The leader, we said, is himself a member who shares responsibilities with other members. As we have said repeatedly, his chief role is to facilitate role behavior in others, even though he plays other roles besides. This is obviously a broad and general statement; the fact of course is that, beyond this general role of inducing others to play their roles effectively, the leader, like everyone else in a group, plays many roles and in various ways. The variety of roles which the leader plays is a function of his personality, the structure of the group situation, the nature of the group task, the roles of other members, and so on. Also, we must remind the reader, we do not refer here to all types of leadership, but only to the democratic leader in a group among other members. In Chapter 6 we excluded domination as a trait of leadership. In so doing we did not deny the existence of a type of directive behavior characterized by the need to dominate others and to have others depend upon the designated leader. Neither domination nor dependence by others marks the genuinely democratic leader.[33]

In addition to the general or basic role the leader also performs whatever specific roles the expectations of his

[33] We return to this in a more detailed discussion in Chapter 15.

group require. A number of these we described briefly in our discussion of group-task roles and group-maintenance roles. An important fact about these roles, which was not stressed in the former discussion, is that these specific leader roles are also shared by other members. The sharing of leader roles stimulates the group awareness and mutual participation which we have just mentioned. More yet, it tends to increase group productivity. Sarbin, describing the results of an unpublished study by Sarah Mazelis, shows that the sharing or diffusion of leader roles maximizes both the quantity and quality of a group's performance. The leader roles of each individual in four independent work groups were counted and recorded. Mazelis' hypothesis, as stated by Sarbin, was as follows: "productivity will be greater among groups where the various leader roles are enacted by most of the group members; productivity will be less where the leader roles are enacted by a small proportion of the group members."[34] This agrees with Hare's findings in his study of participatory and supervisory leadership in small discussion groups, which we described in Chapter 6.

Mazelis' hypothesis was confirmed. In a group task requiring planning, for instance, it was found that "the quality of the product, as rated by the judges, was directly related to the diffusion of the various leader roles among the group members. Spearman rank difference correlation between index of role diffusion and production rating was .75."[35]

While it would be grossly unwarranted to generalize too much from so little evidence, the results strengthen the view that leadership is not only a uniquely individual role but also a group-membership role. The effective group leader seeks neither to dominate others nor to place them in a position of dependence on himself. His role is to guide rather than direct. At any rate, democratic leader roles can function effectively in the absence of the conventionally ascribed

[34] T. R. Sarbin, Role theory, being chap. vi in G. Lindzey (ed.), *Handbook of social psychology* (Reading, Mass.: Addison-Wesley Publishing Co., Inc., 1954), Vol. I, p. 233. The original study, The relation of role-diffusion to work productivity, is an unpublished manuscript (1953).

[35] Sarbin, Role theory, p. 233.

attributes of dominance, aggressiveness, or even assertiveness. In a case history of a leader role published a decade ago, it was found that the most effective and productive leader role was expressed in "unassertive, socially sensitive and supportive behavior."[36]

The lack of dominance and assertiveness in the leader described by Deutsch and his associates, may well be embedded, as they suggest, in his personality–specifically in underlying "dependency and affiliation" needs. As the authors point out, by assuming the role of equality with other group members–by being a *member*, in other words–he can escape the rather lonely responsibility that is required of the directive leader. "His noticeable avoidance of aggression and his tactfulness, to a certain extent represent the cautiousness of a person who is affiliatively dependent and who is sensitive to the possibility of being rejected."[37] At any rate, the effective role-functioning of this type of leader challenges the notion of leadership in which the desire for dependence upon himself by others is considered to be the common trait-role of all leaders.[38]

The leader role, while a member role similar to those of others, is differentiated from them by a stronger motivation by the leader to stimulate others to perform their roles in a united effort to achieve a shared goal. He stimulates others to play their roles because, like they, he is enmeshed in a value system which conditions his motives and actions. This fact is further confirmation, if more is needed, of the widely accepted view that the leader is not a free agent. If he does not successfully anticipate the expectations of others, which is to say if he does not enact the role demanded of him, he will have little or no success in aiding others to play their roles successfully. A man is "chosen" for the leader role, not

[36] M. Deutsch, A. Pepitone, and A. Zander, Leadership in the small group, *J. soc. Issues, 4* (1948), 34.

[37] *Ibid.*, p. 39.

[38] See, for example, Newcomb's analysis which holds to the desire for dependence by others as the common trait of leaders. Newcomb, *Social psychology*, pp. 651–60.

primarily for his abilities and ideas, but by how purposefully he participates in the group's discussion and deliberation.[39]

In this view personality variables and role behavior are integrated to account for the place of the leader in a system of interlocking roles.

CONCLUSION

We opened this chapter with the assertion that the concepts of role and role behavior mark the beginning of a synthesis of individual and group variables in the study of group behavior. Role theory is the meeting ground also of psychological and sociological conceptualizations of individual and social behavior. If the synthesis is not as much an actuality as it might be, the difficulty lies in the paucity of experimental data and the inherent difficulty of the subject matter itself. While astute social-psychological thinkers like Cooley and G. H. Mead have given us flashes of insight into the extraordinary importance of roles in human behavior, they did not base their formulations on experimental data. It has remained for more rigorous investigations like those of Sherif, Newcomb, Parsons, and the researches published in the *American Soldier,* which deals with a variety of attitudes among servicemen in World War II, to raise the subject to a more dependable form of conceptualization.

This research has given us a better understanding of the nature of roles and role behavior. We can now define roles as a set of expectations by others regarding a person occupying a determinate status. Role behavior, then, is a system of actions in response to the set of expectations established by the group in which we have membership. Group life itself may thus be conceived as a dynamic process of role assumption and role behavior.

The reader may have bogged down in trying to understand the precise difference between membership groups and reference groups. He is not alone in this, for neither

[39] See P. E. Slater, Role differentiation in small groups, *Amer. sociol. Rev., 20* (1955), 300–310. See further, G. B. Bell and R. L. French, Jr., Consistency of individual leadership position in small groups of varying membership, *J. abnorm. soc. Psychol., 45* (1950), 764–67.

the present writer nor others who have made the distinction have been altogether clear. This imprecision is due in part to the fact that it is very difficult to ascertain whether a person *assumes* that he shares certain values with other individuals. If we know that he assumes shared values, we can be sure that the group with which he shares them is a reference group. Unless we know that he shares a frame of reference, we cannot know the group in which he acts.

Again, we must note that, while membership groups may also function as reference groups, not all reference groups, as Newcomb has pointed out, are membership groups, for "most of us are also influenced by the norms of some groups in which we are not recognized by others as belonging." Thus any group to which a person aspires, even one to which he hopes to belong in the future, for example, a college fraternity or sorority which a high school student hopes one day to join, can affect his attitudes and behavior by what he interprets to be its system of norms.[40]

Finally, the relation of roles to personality which we have only sketchily treated, complicates the problem of role behavior. While other problems in group dynamics may be difficult and vague, there probably is none that is more complex. Indeed, when we attempt to give a theoretical account of human behavior in terms of roles and role enactment, we are moving on a highly abstract and complex level of explanation.

All in all, despite the halts, false starts, and relative neglect of role behavior, our knowledge of it has clearly and unquestionably moved from philosophical analysis to empirical research. Given the time, the energy, and the ingenuity of an increasing number of investigators, role psychology is destined to make an important contribution to the understanding of both individual and group behavior.

[40] See Newcomb, *Social psychology,* p. 226. See further the Sherifs' statement: "When the group with which the individual is actually associating is also the group with which he identifies himself, interiorizing its values and norms as his own attitudes, then his membership and reference groups are one and the same," Sherif and Sherif, *An outline of social psychology,* p. 631.

CHAPTER 13

Group Dynamics and Personality Dynamics

On several occasions we stressed the idea—and the evidence we have adduced tends to support it—that one cannot say much concerning the behavior of a group by knowing only the personality variables of its members. Yet, the situation is not so simple, and in this chapter we shall present a detailed and more balanced discussion of this subject.

Modern social psychologists agree that personality is effectively molded by the group in which the child is socialized. Modern group dynamicists are of one mind in believing that the attitudes and behavior of persons are modified, as was shown in the preceding chapter, by their membership and reference groups. Together, the two disciplines—social psychology and group dynamics—have solidly established the conclusion that personality organization and group organization are intimately related. They have shown that every person reflects in his own personality the structure of his group; and that all groups are to some extent affected by the personalities of their members. Group dynamics and personality dynamics, like other individual and social phenomena, are inseparable.

We have seen that different kinds of groups have different effects on the individual members. This was particularly evident in our comparison of the effects of organized and unorganized group structures upon the individual members. Organized groups, we have also seen, stimulate a greater equality of member participation than unorganized ones, induce a greater sharing of responsibilities, show more "we-feeling" and a stronger individual motivation to complete assigned tasks, and experience more frustration when the tasks are not completed.[1]

On the other hand, the individual also affects, but in a more limited degree, the structure and functioning of the group. Aggressive, dominant, and independent persons produce different group effects than submissive, dependent, and unassertive individuals. The individual roles, better called egocentric roles, to which we briefly referred in the last chapter, have different consequences from those of the group-task roles and group-building-and-maintenance roles. The "aggressor," it was shown, attacks the group or the problem on which it is engaged; the "blocker" is negativistic and resistant, opposing the group unreasonably; and the "playboy" indulges in horseplay and other "out of field" behavior. Each in his own way affects the group and its activities. However, those who are deeply involved in the group's tasks and in building and maintaining it, affect it quite differently.

The effect of the individual leader on the group process should by now be very clear. Although the democratic leader works in the interests of the group and is affected by his membership in it, he also influences it in a variety of ways. This was shown in our discussion of leadership in Chapter 6, in several other places where leadership was described, and again in our description of the leader role in the preceding chapter.

We have, in short, presented enough evidence to suggest the hypothesis that group structure and personality organi-

[1] See the description of French's experiment on the disruption and cohesion of groups in Chapter 3.

zation reciprocally influence each other. In this chapter we shall examine this relationship in detail, placing greatest emphasis on the effect of personality variables on group functioning.

GROUP FACTORS IN PERSONALITY DYNAMICS

A full discussion of the effect of the group on the individual would require a complete review of what we have expounded in this book up to now. This is neither necessary nor feasible. Besides, the unraveling of society's effect on the individual, its formation of the self, and its integration of the personality are the proper domain of general social psychology. Accordingly, we must concentrate on the concrete group factors which impel a person to behave in certain, and within narrow limits predictable, ways. We begin with the personality that is already formed; we do not describe the process of its formation. We seek out the group factors which, despite definable personality variables, cause a person to work with a group, change his attitudes toward it, engage in the solution of its problems, and the like.

Students of collective behavior have long known what they have yet not adequately explained, namely, that an individual will perform acts in a group that he would not commit as a solitary individual. The psychology of crowd behavior, for example, has stressed the state of heightened suggestibility as being largely responsible for its irrational and often violent form of expression. There is in this form of behavior a reduction, or even the complete obliteration, of self-consciousness. Under these conditions people easily relax, and even discard, their normal and conventional restraints.

We are not interested in this book, however, in the nature and forms of collective behavior, but with the effect of the small group upon the attitudes and behavior of people.

THE PRESSURE TOWARD CONFORMITY. While it is usually impossible and therefore unwise to fit complex processes into simple statements, we shall assert that, when all is said and done, the effect of the group upon the person is a *pressure toward conformity.* This pressure, which we also called the pressure toward uniformity (see Chapter 3), is a marked characteristic of all groups, from families and other informal groups to communities and nations. We have repeatedly shown, by means of theoretical and empirical research, that uniformity or conformity of behavior in groups is due to the directive force of group norms and standards. Our description of the interracial housing projects in Chapter 5 demonstrates the validity of the assertion. Group norms affect people and create uniformity through the group's attractiveness to its members and by the ease of communication among them. Whenever a group norm operates to influence people's behavior, the degree of conformity (or uniformity) is related to the cohesiveness of the group. The more cohesive the group, the more it tends to influence its members to conform to its standards; whereas the less cohesive it is, the more it induces deviant behavior.[2]

Group pressure and attitudinal change. We have shown that attitudes seldom change much in response to verbal persuasion, propaganda, appeals to good will, and similar influences. Lewin's experiment in changing food habits, and other studies which we have reviewed, show that attitudes change most readily when an entire group makes its own decisions regarding important problems.

There are several good investigations (some of which we have already described) which show that, as the pressure for conformity increases, the magnitude of change in opinions and attitudes also increases. In a study by Festinger and Thibaut, it was shown that the *degree* of pressure toward uniformity makes a measurable difference. Dividing the pressure groups into high, medium, and low, these authors found that changes in the subjects' responses correspond to these three degrees of pressure, the low-pressure

[2] The reader would do well to review Chapter 5, above, and L. Festinger, S. Schachter, and K. Back, *Social pressures in informal groups* (New York: Harper & Bros., 1950), chaps. v and vi.

group changing least and the high-pressure group changing most in the amount of uniformity.[3]

The tendency to change one's attitudes or to be resistant to changing them is related to the degree to which one relates himself psychologically to other groups. Influence coming from some other group than the one in which a person has membership, or one in which he has no strong reference orientation, tends to be resisted by him. This confirms what sociologists have been saying for many decades, namely, that the pressure by the primary or face-to-face group is powerful; and once an individual has committed himself to its standards, he persists in his attitudes and behaviors in the face of powerful influences exerted upon him by other groups. The researches of group dynamicists have rendered the sociologists' observation more certain. The investigations of reference groups add further support to the importance of group pressures in creating social uniformity. The more a person perceives others as a reference group for himself, the more he tends to conform to their norms.[4] There are no experiments, however, that test the frequently observed phenomenon that uniformity often leads to complacency.

Group pressure and performance. A recent experiment by Brehm and Festinger gives further support to the importance of group pressure toward uniformity.[5] In this experiment sixty groups, thirty in each of two conditions designated as "High-Importance Condition" and "Low-Importance Condition," participated in group-training sessions concerned with "teaching people how to make accurate judgments about others." Each group was composed of five college students who had volunteered to take part in the training sessions. The groups were divided equally by sex, the subjects were

[3] L. Festinger and J. Thibaut, Interpersonal communication in small groups, *J. abnorm. soc. Psychol.*, *46* (1951), 92–99.

[4] See, for example, L. Festinger, Informal social communication, *Psychol. Rev.*, *57* (1950), 271–82, and Festinger *et al.*, *Social pressures*, chaps. v and vi.

[5] J. Brehm and L. Festinger, Pressure toward uniformity of performance in groups, *Hum. Relat.*, *10* (1957), 85–91.

chosen randomly, and friends were not assigned to the same group. The subjects in half of the groups, in the High-Importance Condition, and before the training began, were told that the Dean had asked the experimenter to announce that several students in the University were to be chosen for a paid tour through England that summer. The purpose of this tour, they were told, was to spread good will, so that those who were to be chosen would be selected on the basis of their sensitivity to others. They were then given the time and place for an interview if they were interested in the trip. In this High-Importance Condition, in other words, "the ability in question was made particularly and immediately important for them."

However, in the Low-Importance Condition the foregoing instructions were not given. For half of the groups, consequently, "whatever importance the ability in question had for the subjects was left unchanged."

The experimenter next described the way in which the training session was to be conducted. The subjects were asked to get acquainted, form judgments of how each individual might behave in certain hypothetical situations, and discuss their judgments. Each judgment was written on a separate sheet of paper, the sheets were collected, and each person received the sheets containing the judgment made of him by others. Each person was next asked to score from 0 to 100, that is, from completely wrong to completely accurate, each judgment made of him by the others. The scoring was done in such a way that each would know the score assigned him by each person making the judgment but not his identity.

Three successive judgments were made in the above manner. When all the judgments had been made and scored, the experimenter put *prearranged* scores on the blackboard. In these scores one person always scored high and another one always low, while the other three clustered together between the two.

After the third set of scores had been posted, the experimenter announced that for the remainder of the session each letter by which judgments and scores were marked would be identified. For this identification each person's name was written alongside the letter which had up to then identified him. The subjects were then asked to complete a questionnaire, which was ostensibly intended to aid the experimenter in preparing for the second session, but whose real purpose was to measure attraction to the group, evaluate their capacity of judging others, determine their confidence in the evaluation of their own ability, and so on. When the last questionnaire had been submitted, the real purpose of the experiment was explained.

The results may be stated briefly in the investigators' own words:

> Each subject could try to affect the scores of other persons in the group by giving them high or low ratings on the judgments that the others made about him. If pressure toward uniformity exists we should expect that the high scorers would rate other people higher and low scorers would rate other people lower in an attempt to bring others close to their own level. It would also be expected that the stronger the pressure toward uniformity the more marked this effect would be, and that the pressure toward uniformity would be stronger in the high-importance condition. . . . The second ratings were given, of course, after the subjects knew the scores people had made the first time. The third ratings were made after everyone knew the scores each had made the first two times . . . In both high- and low-importance conditions, on both the second and third ratings, the high scorers give the highest ratings and the low scorers give the lowest ratings. The differences, however, are more marked in the high-importance condition, where we should expect the pressure toward uniformity to be greater. For the second rating the difference between the average ratings given by high and low scorers is significant at the 2 per cent level in the high-importance condition but is not significant at all in the low-importance condition ($t = 1.08$). On the third rating the difference between the high and low scorers is significantly beyond the 1 per cent level for the high-importance condition but only at the 5 per cent level for the low-importance condition. However, the difference between these differences in the high- and low-importance conditions does not reach significance either for the second or for the third ratings.[6]

[6] J. Brehm and L. Festinger, Pressure toward uniformity of performance in groups, *Hum. Relat., 10* (1957), 88–89.

Summarized, the experiment shows that the pressure to conform is effective in the situations described, and it furthermore suggests, as the investigators point out, that the degree of the pressure increases as the importance of the ability to the person increases.

The results of the foregoing experiment add objective confirmation to the well-known fact that group pressures—whether in the form of rewards or punishments, whether through customs, institutions, or primary groups—produce similarities in attitudes and behavior. To understand this phenomenon, together with the more complex pattern of the personality, we must know a great deal concerning the structure and functions of the group.

A recapitulation. The foregoing investigations confirm what has been amply established by a large amount of research in the social sciences. We have demonstrated in this book that the group in whatever form—whether large or small, informal or institutionalized—molds an individual's attitudes, behavior, personality, or any psychological variable. We have described the effects of adolescent cliques and gangs; of the Corner Boys; of Middletown and Elmtown; of the Bank Wiring Room in the Western Electric plant; of the autokinetic phenomenon; of social climates, leadership, and membership; of learning groups, problem-solving groups, and decision-making groups; and of membership groups and reference groups. All these and others too numerous to mention give us solid knowledge of the nature of the structure and behavior of groups and their effect upon the behavior of the individual. The "driving force" behind these groups, we find, is self-maintenance and the achievement of common goals.

In order to maintain itself and achieve its goals, every group exerts pressure upon its members to conform; for in conformity lies a partial guaranty of its self-maintenance and perpetuation. No group can achieve its goals in the face of perilous divergences and divisive disputes. While it may, as in the case of democratic or self-directing groups, encourage differences, it does so with its eyes focused on the larger consensus that promises to follow when all persons and ideas have had an audience. While members of democratic groups desire choice in their contribution to group maintenance and goal-achievement, they know from experience that a sure way of accomplishing the group's purpose as well as their own is through uniform or conforming behavior. To this extent conformity is practiced, not with a sense of oppression or rebellion, but with the sure knowledge of its advantages. The types of data which we have submitted challenge the traditional notion that the individual opposes the group and hates the conforming behavior which it induces in him. The data show that every normal individual is conscious of the presence of others and adjusts his behavior to their expectations. Even the act of challenging or opposing the group is a sure sign of the individual's awareness of its pressure or its inducement to conform. Even the rebel has to compromise and adjust his behavior to group opinions and expectations.

The group pressures to conform are not necessarily consciously imposed upon members by initiating leaders; customs and traditions alone are often sufficient to effect uniformity. The process of institutionalization to which we have called attention, that is, the cultural process of standardizing people's behavior, is often more powerful than the influence of any individual or group of individuals. This is a sociological commonplace which was systematically formulated in a study by Merei.[7] Institutionalization, perhaps more than anything else, makes group norms rigid, uniform, and difficult to change.

The preceding analysis calls attention to the need for interdisciplinary investigation in group dynamics. The groups that we have described and analyzed are typical of Western society, and the researchers who have studied them are almost entirely products of its culture. They see groups through Western eyes, and their methodology is embedded in the conceptual framework of Western social science. We

[7] F. Merei, Group leadership and institutionalization, *Hum. Relat.*, 2 (1941), 23–39.

do not know if the group-dynamic principles which account for the behavior of the groups that we have studied also operate in groups in other cultures. This problem belongs in the category of "future research."

THE PERSONALITY DIMENSION IN GROUP BEHAVIOR

We ask the reader to recall the many instances when, while stressing the ubiquitous influence of the group and the almost universal tendency of people to participate in its affairs, we called attention to the function of individual psychological variables, particularly the personalities of its members, in group formation and change. We return to this subject now and shall consider it in something of the detail that it rightly deserves.

It is interesting and instructive to note the fact that most early studies of the structure and functions of the group were also (though unintentionally) contributions to the understanding of the role of the individual. There is no *explicit* recognition of this fact in the literature of group dynamics. Consider, for example, the pioneer study of Lewin and his associates on social climates. These climates were not the "givens" of the investigation. Strictly speaking, they were not even entirely artifacts of the methodology employed. They were to a large extent functions of the individual attitudes and acts of the leaders who tried to influence the group members. The authoritarian atmosphere was created by an autocratic person; the democratic, by a permissive and task-oriented member; and the laissez faire, by an indifferent and group-uninvolved individual. Each in his own way made the group what it was.

In the remainder of this chapter we are going to give serious attention to the personality variables in group behavior, a problem which, to repeat, has received less attention that it deserves.

SELF-ENHANCING FACTORS. In Chapter 2, where we gave some consideration to the role of the individual in the group, we called attention to the fact that group-dependency needs are powerful motivating factors in group formation and group functioning. We also pointed out, however, that, while group dependency plays a major role in group life, the cooperation and agreement which they exact from the individual may also be deterrents to independence and individual creativeness. This theme has been repeated in various places in the pages of this book. Again, everyone who has had experiences with groups will have discovered that the goal of consensus may result in a conformity which leaves problems unsolved and disruptive tensions unresolved. Instead of reducing our conflicts in groups, we thus sometimes tend to conceal them. We are then in a state of pluralistic ignorance where an objective solution of our problems cannot be easily found.

Again, in our analysis of the psychological structure of the group we described some of the most important motivating forces in group belongingness. We wish to examine this topic again, but more systematically, in order to bring into sharper focus the importance of the individual psychological variable in group behavior.

A glance at the Freudian view. If one is not troubled by a paucity of empirical and experimental data in his theory of group development, one cannot find a more individualistic explanation than Freud's. According to Freud, group belongingness is based on the repression of libidinal and aggressive instincts or impulses. This repression is normally initiated in the family in the early years of a child's life. Group belongingness, the wish to associate with others, the desire to love and be loved by them, and so on are transformations in group life of the early emotional dependence of the child upon his parents. Roughly speaking, then, dependence on the family is the prototype of all social groups and group processes.

The resolving of group tensions and conflicts according to this view, can be achieved only when the individuals who make up our society succeed in establishing libidinal, or individual-affective, ties with one another. This would hold true of both small face-to-face groups and a suprasocial world community.[8]

There are, of course, characteristics of group life which lend themselves to this type of explanation, but only on theoretical grounds. The chief limitation of Freud's explanation is that it is essentially untestable. Its main value is that it forcefully calls attention to the role of individual psychological variables in group behavior.

Self-actualization. In Chapter 2 we asserted, following Gordon, that groups satisfy the desire for self-actualization. Every healthy personality has a tendency to grow, to fulfill, and to enhance itself. A person wants to belong to groups because they afford him opportunities to gain recognition and acceptance. Self-actualization, we said earlier, is a way of realizing individual goals objectively, in the presence of others. Thus, such associations of persons as discussion groups, problem-solving committes, and "action" groups provide some individuals with a high degree of self-actualization, with the realization of their potentialities. In this connection Helen Jennings has made a sound and useful distinction which is relevant to our discussion. Sociometric findings, she asserts, indicate that people tend to form two kinds of groups, each satisfying different needs. There are groups in which "the individual as a person receives sustenance, recognition, approval, and appreciation for just being '*himself*.'" There are also groups in which "the individual's efforts and ideals are focused towards objectives which are not his alone but represent the fulfilling of goals which a number of individuals agree to seek."[9] The latter kind of

[8] Besides Freud's own formulation of group relations in his *Group psychology and analysis of the ego* (London: International Psychoanalytical Library, 1922) and *Civilization and its discontents* (London: International Psychoanalytical Library, 1930), we highly recommend the following: S. Scheidlinger, *Psychoanalysis and group behavior* (New York: W. W. Norton & Co., Inc., 1952), especially chap. vi.

[9] H. H. Jennings, Sociometric structure in personality and group formation, being chap. xiv in M. Sherif and M. O. Wilson (eds.), *Group relations at the crossroads* (New York: Harper & Bros., 1953), p. 332. Italics in the original.

group has been the chief concern of the preceding twelve chapters. The former is our present interest.

Self-actualization in group relations is dependent on the individual's capacity to relate himself to others "without preoccupation with 'what is the other thinking of me?' " as Jennings puts it. It is enhanced, further, by the person's ability to enhance this feeling in others. Self-actualization is a condition in which the person is not helplessly dependent upon the group, is relatively autonomous, and independent of it; yet not wholly detached from it. Indeed, the self-actualizing person easily identifies himself with others. He has, as Maslow has shown, a deep capacity for identifying, even fusing, himself with others without losing his individuality.[10] This is, despite its surface paradox, in line with our whole analysis of group structure and group behavior, namely, that the individual, no matter how autonomous he may be, is always in a relational complex with other people; and that the group, no matter how extensively it may engulf the individual, is always dependent upon him.

The foregoing characteristics are not found in all group-related people. There is no rigidly established evidence to account for their presence or absence. Maslow's data suggest that persons possessing such characteristics are relatively small in number, and even common-sense observation reveals that there are few people who can accept themselves only as pursuers of highly individual goals. It is not improbable that most healthy persons have potentialities for self-actualization in groups, but these are thwarted by an essentially inhibiting socialization. Sociodramatic data add credence to this hypothesis, showing that the capacity to exercise *choice-daring* and *choice-initiative* in establishing positive human relationships develops early and may be permanently damaged in childhood and adolescence.[11]

[10] See A. H. Maslow, Self-actualizing people: a study in psychological health, in W. Wolf (ed.), *Values in personality research* (New York: Grune & Stratton, Inc., 1950), Symposium No. 1, pp. 11–34.

[11] See H. H. Jennings, Sociometric structure, in M. Sherif and M. O. Wilson (eds.), *Group relations at the crossroads*, p. 360. The italicized terms are hers.

Social psychology and psychoanalysis have amassed an enormous quantity of evidence in support of the view that every normal individual seeks response from others and values their positive attitude toward himself as a person. When he has the esteem of others, his regard both for himself and for members of his group increases. When regard by others is deficient, his relatedness to them is damaged, and group life becomes unproductive and chronically unfulfilling. The number of persons whose esteem he desires may be quite few. Indeed, they are those usually with whom he can associate in a "person-to-person way," to borrow Jenning's phrase. He seeks these persons because they are less hedged in by custom and rigid expectations, and because they most nearly resemble himself. These choices comprise what Jennings calls his *psychegroup*, that is, the "personal-reference-group" in which the more or less formalized restrictions which characterize other groups are absent.

Self-actualizing behavior is also characterized by a high degree of spontaneity. Spontaneity carries with it a strong flavor of unconventionality. This unconventionality is not, however, like that of some Bohemians, a rebellion against demands for conformity, but is based on the need to expand one's behavioral choices. Jennings describes this condition clearly, and we can do no better than to quote her directly. She writes:

> Sociodramatic exploration supports a theory that choice behavior intrinsically involves and is undergirt with a spontaneity component —the individual chooses others to *facilitate* his expression, aiding him by *stimulating* his spontaneity, and this process shows itself in his greater creativity and productivity and ease of approach to attacking more confidently and effectively problems with which he is confronted when in interaction with those he chooses than when not so situated. . . .[12]

Self-consistency. Self-enhancement can be achieved not only through actualizations of the self, or through "choice-daring," but through the maintenance of self-integrity or self-consistency. The healthy or "strong" personality finds

[12] *Ibid.*, p. 362.

satisfaction and self-esteem in attitudes and actions that are internally consistent. He can participate and discharge his obligations in a group most effectively and gratifyingly if he can be true to himself. A group that brings pressure to bear upon an individual to conform must take due cognizance of his tendency to resist it if the demand for agreement is inconsistent with his image of himself. It is a prejudice to label the resistance "negativism" and to describe a person behaving in this manner as "maladjusted." It ignores the group-dynamic principle that a person will change his behavior—barring force or coercion, of course—only when he knows that he has done so on his own initiative. The principle of self-consistency points to the urgent need for researchers in group dynamics to investigate the role of the self in group behavior, a problem that has been almost completely neglected. In any case, we must recognize what common sense knows to be true, that every healthy personality will resist such encroachments as are inconsistent with his self-image. If agreement and consensus demand a surrender of his selfhood, an individual will either actively resist them, engage in group-irrelevant activities, or indulge in out-of-field behavior.

Research in mental health has documented the claim that neither extreme rebelliousness nor timid conformity are characteristic of a healthy personality. A psychologically healthy individual conforms to the expectations of others only if the conformity enhances his and others' well-being, but the choice to conform must be his own. The sense of independence and the choice-daring which is a part of it make for creativeness and leadership actions. The ability to work constructively with others is derived in part from the self-confidence which is generated by freedom of action. Confidence in one's self leads to confidence in others, which in turn leads to group-enhancing relationships.

There are situations, however, where the integrity of the self can be maintained only by complete involvement in and loyalty to the group, especially the group in which the individual has a deep anchorage. There are many cases of this in combat situations during a war. In battle an individual can often survive only through the concerted actions of his comrades. He accordingly develops an unshakable loyalty to them, for he knows that he owes the preservation of his self to them. Any other road leads to injury, death, or breakdown of the self. His self-consistency now lies in his image of himself as a loyal member of his combat union.

In his attempt to account for the fact that a change of roles not only leads to a change of attitude but also to a modification of actions, Lieberman, it will be recalled, ascribed the process partly to the influence of reference groups (see Chapter 12). He also tried to account for it by the *principle of self-consistency*. This principle affirms that people need to have their attitudes "internally consistent with their actions."[13] The principle of self-consistency enables an individual to orient his changed behavior to his changed role. Although Lieberman partly describes this consistency as a form of justification or of rationalization (which it no doubt is in many cases) he is more right, it seems to us, when he says that it enables the role occupant "*to make rational*" his changed role behavior—that is, to place his actions in a familiar frame of reference. In contrast to the reference-group principle, whereby a person's attitudes influence his actions, the consistency principle holds that a person's actions influence his attitudes.[14] In view of the reciprocity of individual-social actions this circular form of argument should no longer astonish anyone. As Lieberman remarks, although data are not available to settle the issue, both principles might plausibly account for the results.

Interpersonal compatibility. It is clear that no group can arise—certainly it cannot function and endure—unless its members bear toward one another at least a minimal acceptance. There must be a basic compatibility if the barest communication is to take place. When a constellation of compatible people exists, it forms the kind of group that

[13] S. Lieberman, The effects of changes in roles on the attitudes of role occupants, *Hum. Relat.*, 9 (1956), p. 399.

[14] *Ibid.*, p. 400.

comprises the subject matter of this book. There can be no consensus if people are basically incompatible as individuals. When competitiveness, rebelliousness, withdrawal, and the like exist, interpersonal sharing cannot take place, and the group must eventually disintegrate.

Nothing points up the importance of the personality in group behavior as much as this compatibility component, this capacity of the individual to relate himself with some degree of acceptance and intimacy to other people. Social psychology has amply demonstrated the existence of this personality component, although it cannot yet tell us for certain its source. It may very well originate in the early associations of the child with his parents and siblings. Whatever its source may be, people in interaction must possess it to form a functional group.

Like all other human traits, interpersonal compatibility varies with the person. In some individuals it is strongly developed, in others it is weak. Bennis and Shepard describe two extremes of this component, which they call "overpersonal" and "counterpersonal."[15] Each refers to the degree of intimacy that a person can establish and comfortably bear with another individual. The overpersonal member is one who is not satisfied until he has established a high degree of intimacy with other members. The counterpersonal individual feels uncomfortable in intimate relations with others and tends to avoid them.[16]

Besides being overpersonal and counterpersonal, individuals are also described by the degree of their dependence upon one another. "Dependent" persons are those who find comfort and stability in highly structured group situations, such as are characterized by agendas, rules of procedure, a leader, an expert, and the like. "Counterdependent" per-

[15] W. G. Bennis and H. A. Shepard, A theory of group development, *Hum. Relat.*, 9 (1956), 415–37.

[16] *Ibid.*, p. 418. Since the word "intimate" has connotations which have no place in this discussion, we simply remark that it refers to acceptance and liking of other persons in such a way that the relation between them is relaxed and comfortable instead of anxious and defensive.

sons are frustrated, perplexed, or confused by structured situations.

The importance of these degrees of interpersonal compatibility lies in the fact that they clearly affect the development and behavior of a group. They are responsible for the degree of conflict prevailing in a group. Thus a highly "conflicted" individual who is overdependent upon a strong leader or authority may create confusion by his contradictory behavior: he may distrust authority and at the same time be unable to rely upon himself.

The "unconflicted" person, on the other hand, relies more upon himself and forms a more objective judgment of the group situation. Being relaxed and trusting, he does not create the doubt and confusion so characteristic of the conflicted individual's effect upon the group. It is the "unconflicted" person who is usually responsible for producing effective communication and constructive group development.[17]

The operation of these phenomena, which we have integrated in the term "interpersonal compatibility," may be briefly summarized. People in a group must have some compatibility, as measured by their capacity for entering into friendly relationships with one another, before they can develop into more than an external association of persons. Both excessive and deficient intimacy create confusion and conflict. Optimal interpersonal compatibility is found in those groups where "unconflicted" persons have the maximum opportunity to establish communication among the members. Bennis and Shepard sum up this situation as follows:

> The core of the theory of group development is that the principal obstacles to the development of valid communication are to be found in the orientations toward authority and intimacy that members bring to the group. Rebelliousness, submissiveness, or withdrawal as the characteristic response to authority figures; destructive competitiveness, emotional exploitiveness, or withdrawal as the characteristic response to peers prevent consensual validation of experience. The

[17] *Ibid.*, pp. 417–18.

behaviors determined by these orientations are directed toward enslavement of the other in the service of the self, enslavement of the self in the service of the other, or disintegration of the situation. Hence, they prevent the setting, clarification of, and movement toward group-shared goals.[18]

In short, personality variables are an integral part of the study of group dynamics. They help in significant ways to make or dissolve a group, they help or hinder in effective ways its development, change, productiveness, and the like. The process of change from dependence to independence to interdependence represents not only "a change in emphasis from power to affection, but also from role to personality." It represents not only a change from such distinctions as "class, ethnic background, professional interests," and similar differentiations, but also "a deeper concern with personality modalities, such as reaction to failure, warmth, retaliation, anxiety, etc."[19]

The principle of interpersonal compatibility is further validated in an interesting and ingenious study by Schutz.[20] This investigation is, however, too intricate to lend itself to a clear summary. Accordingly we shall select those features which are directly relevant without destroying the essential unity of the investigation. However, while we shall not discuss all the factors in the experimental design, we believe it is necessary first to enumerate them in order to provide the context for those that are relevant to our immediate interest.

The study is divided into two main sections, namely, *a description of the method for constructing compatible groups,* and *a discussion of the sociometry of persons and groups.*

The method for constructing groups, in order to test their productivity, includes: (*a*) an exposition of the personality assumptions that account for the concept of compatibility, (*b*) definitions that supplement and specify the basic ideas,

[18] W. G. Bennis and H. A. Shepard, A theory of group development, *Hum. Relat.*, 9 (1956), 417.

[19] *Ibid.*, p. 436.

[20] W. C. Schutz, What makes groups productive? *Hum. Relat.*, 8 (1955), 429–65.

(*c*) a technique for constructing a personality test to measure an individual's interpersonal relation tendency, and (*d*) a method for constructing compatible and incompatible groups.

The sociometry of persons and of groups was investigated by means of a sociometric questionnaire administered at the end of the fifth meeting of the group, and again at the end of the tenth or final meeting. Here, however, we shall concentrate exclusively on the first, namely, the compatibility of groups and the role of personality in creating compatibility.

Compatibility, or agreement on making interpersonal decisions, is based on a "fundamental personality trait." There are two sources of this trait: (*a*) the "power relations" involved in interpersonal decisions, such as rules, laws, leaders, and so forth; and (*b*) the "love relations," such as closeness and liking, which exist between people when they make decisions.

If people agree on the relative importance of the power relations and the love relations, they generally work together effectively. If they markedly disagree on their importance, cooperative efforts are difficult to achieve. "This difficulty," Schutz writes, "will not be easily resolved since it is based on *deep and fundamental personality characteristics*."[21] These personality characteristics are either *compatible* or *incompatible* patterns. A *compatible* pattern is composed of acceptant, supportive, and socially secure ("unthreatened") individuals. These are personal and independent in their orientation. An incompatible pattern is comprised of persons resistant to close personal relations, dependent on others, especially leaders and power figures, and of low to medium assertiveness.[22]

Inasmuch as the chief problem of Schutz's investigation is to determine the effect of interpersonal compatibility on group productivity, we shall examine the problem briefly.

[21] *Ibid.*, p. 456. Italics are ours.

[22] Schutz characterizes the compatible pattern by the term "personalness" and the incompatible pattern by "dependence." *Ibid.*, p. 458.

By group productivity is meant the extent to which a group approximates "the optimal performance of a task."

Three group tasks or problems were given to 120 enlisted men from the Naval Training Station at Bainbridge, Maryland, between the ages of seventeen and twenty-one. All members of each group had been in the training unit for eleven weeks. They were divided into groups of five subjects each. Acquaintance among any five men in a group varied from close friendship to casual acquaintance. No five men had ever met as a group before. They varied in intelligence scores (I.Q.) from 76 to 132. The tasks were new to everyone and there was no reason to believe that any subject had a background that would give him an advantage over any others. A prize of five dollars was offered for the best individual performance among four groups. A prize of fifteen dollars was offered for the best performance in each section of four groups.

The three problems or tasks may be briefly described. The *intercept problem* required agreement among the group members for every decision made in an "alternate-move, enemy-versus-friendly" board game. Each move presented the same problem situation for each member. Judgment of what made a good decision or move could not be made immediately. The time allowed was gradually changed from unlimited time, to one minute, then to thirty seconds.

The *plotting problem* required cooperation and division of labor to perform many tasks at the same time, namely, to plot the course of many planes on a large vertical plotting-board. The task required speed. Time pressure was varied by increasing the rate of information transmission to the group.

The *coding and identification problem* required minimal cooperation. It consisted of two "highly intellectual" problems, namely, decoding messages and a "logical exercise phrased as a naval problem," to be completed in the shortest time and with the fewest errors.

Each group was given from two to five runs on each of the three tasks. It should be added that the tasks differed in complexity. The intercept problem required a great deal of cooperation for maximal performance. It was assumed that the more cooperative a group was, the more alternatives it could suggest rapidly and accurately. The plotting problem also required much cooperation, but of a different sort. Everyone had a different job to perform in contributing to the whole, so that the group product could be good only if each member performed his particular task well. The coding problem required individual concentration rather than cooperation. It was assumed that "one individual working alone could do at least as well as a group—no matter how cooperative the group."

The purpose of the experiment as described in the preceding five paragraphs was to test the following six hypotheses:

1. The compatible groups will score significantly higher on the intercept problems than the incompatible groups.
2. Compatible groups will win over incompatible ones on intercept problem contests significantly more often than they will lose.
3. The compatible groups will score significantly higher on the plotting problems than the incompatible groups.
4. There will be no significant difference in performance on the coding problems; but if there is a trend, it will favor the compatible groups.
5. Productivity differences between compatible and incompatible groups will increase with the increase in time pressure.
6. There will be greater superiority of compatible over incompatible groups on the intercept problems than on the plotting problems.

The six hypotheses were confirmed by the experiment. The conclusion to be drawn from the investigation is a twofold one. First, compatible groups are generally superior to incompatible groups in the performance of tasks, and, second, compatibility is a function of fundamental personality traits. The trait, finally, that is most conducive to cooperation and productiveness is that which we have designated by the term "interpersonal compatibility," or the ability to establish warm, affectionate, and acceptant relationships between one's self and other individuals.

Individual differences. Although we shall describe them more briefly than their significance deserves, individual differences are an important set of psychological factors in group behavior. They operate in most human relationships; but since we obviously cannot discuss these relations here, we shall instead select an area of human behavior, already discussed at length in this chapter, which has a direct bearing on the problem of personality structure in group relations —namely, individual differences in group conformity.

In the section on group pressure and attitudinal change we asserted that the tendency to change one's attitudes or to be resistant to change is related to the degree in which one relates himself psychologically to other persons. The concept of interpersonal compatibility has shown that, generally speaking, the overdependent or "conflicted" person responds differently to group pressures than the independent or "unconflicted" individual. The extent to which a person can free himself from the ubiquitous influence of the group is in large part a matter of individual differences, which are sometimes very extreme. The study by S. E. Asch, which we have already described, bears this point out very well.[23]

Asch's investigation showed, for example, that there were individuals subjected to identical group influence who remained independent in their judgment throughout the experiment, and that there were others who almost invariably agreed with the majority. One-fourth of the critical subjects, it should be noted, remained completely independent. A similar difference was found in the subjects' feeling of self-confidence in the face of the majority judgment. Some subjects remained completely confident throughout the experiment, whereas at the other extreme were persons who became doubt-ridden and even disoriented. Since the experi-

[23] S. E. Asch, Effects of group pressure upon the modification and distortion of judgments, in H. Guetzkow (ed.), *Groups, leadership, and men* (Pittsburgh: Carnegie Press, 1951).

mental situation, that is, the degree of group pressure, was the same for all the subjects, the differences must be ascribed to individual psychological characteristics.

The foregoing differential reactions to group pressure may thus be briefly summarized. The *independent* individual's independence was based on personal confidence in his perception and experience. Asch particularly stresses the independent person's vigorous tolerance of the group's opposition, even though he was sensitive to it, and his persistent reliance upon his own perception.

The independent but *withdrawn* retained his own judgment not spontaneously but "on the basis of explicit principles concerning the necessity of being an individual."

The independent but *doubt-ridden* person adhered to his judgment "on the basis of a felt necessity to deal adequately with the task."

Among the subjects who yielded to group pressure the following individual differences were found: (1) Those *whose perceptions were distorted,* of whom there were few, but who were not aware that the distortion was due to the majority influence. (2) Those—and there were many—*whose judgments were distorted.* They experienced doubt and lacked confidence in their own judgment, and were accordingly impelled to agree with the majority. (3) Those who experienced distortion of action, but who, strictly speaking, neither yielded nor admitted that they were wrong. They had an overpowering need to appear to be different and could not tolerate the idea that they were inferior in the eyes of others. They suppressed their perceptions and sided with the majority, fully aware of what they were doing.

Asch makes the following final observation: "The results are sufficient to establish that independence and yielding are not psychologically homogeneous, that submission to group pressure (and freedom from pressure) can be the result of different psychological conditions."[24]

[24] *Ibid.,* p. 184. For an earlier, sociometric, study of individual differences in interpersonal relations, see H. H. Jennings, Individual differences in the social atom, *Sociometry, 4* (1941), 269–77.

Further testimony to the role of personality differences in group behavior is to be found in Gorden's study of the relationship between an individual's private opinion and definition of the situation and his expression of public opinion in a group.[25] Gorden's investigation was a participant observation of 24 members of a cooperative living project. Approximately half of the members were students; the rest were engaged in a variety of professions, semiprofessions, and occupations ranging from college instructor in one case to a waitress in another. All but one member had a college education. They ranged in ages from twenty-one to thirty-five years. They were equally divided by sex. They shared the household tasks and ate the evening meal together in the common dining room. Politically, there were fifteen Democrats, fourteen ex-Progressives, four Socialists, one Communist, and one Republican. All the seven Negroes were Democrats, but were noticeably more conservative than the white members.[26]

For the experimental situation opinion on Russia was selected because of its emotional content, the wide range of feelings toward the Soviet Union, and the narrowing range of expression of public opinion regarding it.

Three types of data were collected. The *private opinion* of each person regarding Russia was obtained by a Likert-type attitude scale. The *public opinion* of the subjects was elicited by the expression of their views in the presence of their fellow members. The *estimate of group opinion* as a measure of each person's definition of the situation was made on the same items.

The 24 members were divided into two subgroups matched according to race, occupation, sex, and rank order of the total score on their *private opinion.* The two groups were simultaneously interviewed but in different rooms. Two interviewers worked with each group. In one group both

[25] R. L. Gorden, Interaction between attitude and the definition of the situation in the expression of opinion, *Amer. sociol. Rev., 17* (1952), 50–58.

[26] The discrepancy between the political totals and the total number of subjects is due to the fact that the group was originally composed of more members.

were co-op members; in the other, one was a member and the other was a disinterested person representing a nationally known opinion research organization.[27]

The results of the study show considerable individual variation. There was a marked tendency for the individual to estimate correctly the trend of the median opinion of the group. Those whose private opinions were more pro-Russian tended to estimate correctly the group opinion as being more anti-Russian than their own. Twenty of the 24 people were correct in this respect. However, the pro-Russians on the private opinion scale tended to estimate group opinion as more pro-Russian than it actually was, and vice versa. This shows that, "although the estimate of the direction of the group mean from the individual's private opinion is correct, the conception of the absolute position of the group appears to be influenced by the individual's own feeling as well as the actual group opinion."[28]

It is important to note, furthermore, that in general there were no persons who changed from the pro-Russian category in their *private* opinion to the anti-Russian category in their *public* opinion, and vice versa.

Although private opinions in this study, as in others, tended to approach the opinion of the group, or what the individual thought was its opinion, the opinions of some persons remained strongly individual. The attitudes of eight individuals were counter to their group's attitudes, three were in no way influenced by the group, and thirteen conformed to opinions of the group.[29]

SELF-CONSTRICTIVE FACTORS. In contrast to the self-enhancing factors the self-constricting traits markedly narrow the individual's range of interactions and damage himself and the group of which he is a part. These factors must not be confused with the independence and nonconformity which we have described, for the latter characteristics are fundamentally constructive *on an individual plane*. The in-

[27] See Gorden, Interaction between attitude and the definition, pp. 50–51.
[28] *Ibid.*, pp. 52–53.
[29] *Ibid.*, pp. 53–54.

dependent person does not withdraw from the social field; he contributes to it in his own way and usually experiences a feeling of exultation in being a part of the group, yet not being engulfed by its pressures and demands. Just as the healthy personality maintains his independence without deserting his social world, so the self-enhacing personality is group-related, yet relatively autonomous.

Furthermore, the self-enhancing person, especially the one who is characterized by interpersonal compatibility, enriches the group's activities and, as we saw, increases its productivity. It would be appropriate to describe his role as creative; for he not only enhances his own personality, but also increases the well-being of the group. He assimilates other people's anxieties, thereby enhancing the "emotional tone" of the entire group. This quality we said seems to be manifested early. In describing a twelve-year-old pupil to the writer, a school principal remarked that the boy enthusiastically took on other children's problems—for other pupils were constantly seeking him out—without bothering them with his own. The presence of such an individual, whether he be a child or an adult, effectively changes the atmosphere of his group.

The self-constrictive factors, no less than the self-enhancing traits, are deeply embedded in the personality or character structure of the individual. While we know no more about their source than of those of the self-enhancing individual, the self-constrictive factors are generally believed to be rigid and relatively enduring.

For reasons that would vastly overextend our definition of personality variables, we shall exclude from our discussion of self-constrictive factors obvious pathological conditions. While pathological individuals do participate in functioning groups, and while their effect on these groups may be damaging, they generally do not long remain as effective participants before they are rejected by others. First let us consider the most important factor: self-isolation.

Self-isolation. This is obviously a relative term, ranging all the way from occasional contacts to complete withdrawal.

Since the completely withdrawn person is probably psychotic, we shall exclude him from consideration. We shall consider only the type of individual whom Helen Jennings describes as relatively *self-bound.*[30]

The isolate is characterized by a diminished sensitivity to the feelings and actions of another person. This insensitivity is distinguished from physical aloneness which does not necessarily constitute psychological isolation. An individual may be physically isolated and yet be keenly responsive to other people. He is an isolate when he is deficient in perceiving the effect of his behavior upon others. In comparing him with the more socialized person, the isolate is not as skillful in taking the role of another. The personality of the isolate is constricted because he cannot easily imagine how another person feels and thinks; for personality is a pattern of behavior which we attribute to others because we perceive it also in ourselves.

When an individual's insensitivity to a specific other individual is generalized, or transmitted to a whole group, it may have damaging consequences for both the person and the group. Certainly there can be no satisfactory group movement of any kind, either in the form of solving problems, learning, productivity, modification of goals and attitude, or whatever. The isolate's presence has adverse effects on the group even if it is minimal, for it dampens the group's *esprit de corps.* It is damaging to the isolate because responsiveness toward him is curtailed and choice of him as a social person is minimized or completely withheld. Acceptance of him depends markedly on how he relates himself to others, how well he internalizes in his own role-system the roles of other people.

An interesting and penetrating analysis of this isolation of the self was recently made by Goffman.[31] His study

[30] H. H. Jennings, Sociometric structure in personality and group formation, being chap. xiv in M. Sherif and M. O. Wilson (eds.), *Group relations at the crossroads,* p. 340. See also H. H. Jennings, *Leadership and isolation* (2d ed.; New York: Longmans, Green & Co., Inc., 1950).

[31] E. Goffman, Alienation from interaction, *Hum. Relat., 10* (1957), 47–60.

brings out sharply the nature of self-isolation, or alienation from interaction, and its effect on both the isolated individual and his audience.

Interaction, we have shown, is more than a contact between two individuals. It is a conjoint cognitive and affective involvement of two or more people in a common experience, in which each participant gives something of himself to the other, and in which the personality of each is modified by the encounter between them. Using a spontaneous conversation as his example of this relationship, Goffman describes it as "a little social system with its own boundary-maintaining tendencies; . . . a little patch of commitment and loyalty with its own heroes and its own villains."[32]

Conversation between two or more people exemplifies a fundamental characteristic of social control and is a vivid illustration of the role-playing process. In conversation the individual must not only be keenly involved himself, but play his role in such a manner as to impel others to maintain involvement. At the same time he must be able to rely upon the others to place their own sympathies at his command. Conversation is thus seen to be truly and deeply a group phenomenon.

Because of its fragility conversation readily permits alienation or "misinvolvement." It is, as Goffman points out, "a precarious unsteady state that is likely at any time to lead the individual into some form of alienation."[33] This alienation takes various forms, some of which are described in Goffman's article. We shall describe these forms of alienation in the following paragraphs.

1. External preoccupation. As the term implies, this form of behavior is not focused on the conversation. In this state an individual's concern may be unconnected either with the subject of conversation or with his fellow participants, or with either. His preoccupation may still be focused on something antedating the conversational encounter or on

[32] *Ibid.*, p. 47.
[33] *Ibid.*, p. 49.

something that may arise later in the course of interaction. It may also take the form of irrelevant activity, or of exclusive involvement with one or two of the total participants. These external preoccupations may be deliberate or involuntary, and the offensiveness of the person's alienation is judged by others accordingly.

2. *Self-consciousness.* This is not primarily a preoccupation with one's self, not a form of self-centeredness, as, for example, when a person makes himself an object of conversation; rather, it is the giving of his attention to himself "as an interactant at a time when he ought to be free to involve himself in the content of the conversation." This condition arises most typically in a situation where the person's image of himself is threatened. In order to defend himself against the threat he hurriedly withdraws from the conversational encounter and tries to repair whatever damage may have taken place. Who has not witnessed an embarrassed person engaging in behavior that externally is irrational and makes no sense, but which gives the self-conscious person a sufficient breathing spell to regain his psychological balance? Goffman analyzes the condition nicely when he says that if the embarrassed individual's correction of the situation raises his standing in the group, "his flight into self-consciousness may be a way of rejoicing"; whereas if the occasion discredits his self-image, then "flight into self-consciousness may be a way of protecting the self and licking its wounds."

3. *Interaction-consciousness.* While this is in some ways similar to self-consciousness, its essential characteristic is a conscious preoccupation with the interaction itself, instead of the topic of conversation. Hosts and hostesses at social gatherings often practice this form of preoccupation. A hostess, while being herself involved in the group's conversation, may become excessively preoccupied with the course of the conversation if it does not go well. Accordingly, she may become "so much concerned with the social machinery of the occasion and with how the evening is going as a whole

that she finds it impossible to give herself up to her own party."[34]

The dissipation of "small talk" is a further illustration of interaction-consciousness. The purpose of small talk is to provide a supply of conversation that will keep the process going. When the small talk is depleted, people find themselves in "a state of talk but with nothing to talk about." The usual interaction-consciousness in this condition is typically described as a "painful silence."

4. Other-consciousness. As in self-consciousness so in other-consciousness the individual is distracted from the focus of conversation. His attention is distracted by another participant who becomes an object of attention. There are many reasons for this preoccupation with others, but the most typical in conversational encounters are insincerity and affectation. People who display these traits break the emotional ties between people in conversation because they attract attention to themselves instead of the subject. Not infrequently they arouse hostility in others. "When the individual senses that others are insincere or affected," Goffman writes, "he tends to feel they have taken unfair advantage of their communication position to promote their own interests; he feels that they have broken the ground rules of interaction."[35]

As forms of self-isolation the foregoing types of alienation from interaction are important for their effect on the group. They are not only a source of offense or injury, but are causes of group disequilibrium and disruption. People's feelings are aroused by the impropriety or offensiveness of the alienated person's behavior. The alienated person suffers for his offense by becoming an object of resentment. Both are offenses against "involvement obligations," for both endanger or destroy the integrity of the group. As Goffman so nicely phrases it, "The mere witnessing of an involvement offense, let alone its punishment, can cause a crime against the interaction, the victim of the first crime himself being

[34] *Ibid.,* p. 51.
[35] *Ibid.,* p. 52.

made a criminal. Thus, during spoken interaction, when one individual is stricken with uneasiness, others often come down with the disease."[36]

THE LEADER AS A PERSON. We have given a great deal of attention to leadership in this book. Our discussions of the subject have been largely concerned with the leadership relation and the leadership acts initiated by central persons in a group. Except tangentially, we have said very little about the personality of the leader. This personality varies, of course, with the group and the task to be performed by it, as well as with the individual character structure of the leader. Thus, the democratic, authoritarian, or laissez faire leader functions best in groups which most strongly elicit the individual attitudes, values, and characteristic behaviors which make up his personality. These traits, however, are not easily changed by the group of which he is leader, for they lie deep in the personality structure of the individual as a consequence of his life experience.

Leadership, we have frequently said, is always a function of a central person in interaction with other persons, and always implies the existence of persons who act upon his suggestions or his initiating acts. However, whether the central person or leader will use others to satisfy private or social ends will be determined very largely by his personality.[37] Whether he will be skillful in relating himself productively to other people will depend largely on such psychological characteristics as skill in role-playing, perceptiveness of people's motives and the place of these motives in group relationships, skill in communicating with others, the capacity to engage in teamwork problem-solving, and others.

It is a mistake to think of all democratic leaders, to refer only to this kind, as being very much alike. Democratic leadership is initiated by different kinds of democratic personalities. While this cannot yet be empirically established,

[36] *Ibid.*, p. 54.

[37] We urge the reader to review in this connection the contributions of Adorno *et al.*, on the authoritarian and democratic personalities, and our discussion of E. Frenkel-Brunswik's description, in Chapter 6, above.

democratic leaders possess one sure trait in common: they will not indiscriminately play all kinds of roles, but only those which are compatible with their democratic value system. Thus, a democratic leader, regardless of the expectations of others, will not assume a dictatorial or autocratic position in relation to others; and in an authoritarian structure he will establish a set of roles that will change it to a more free and permissive one.

If this is true—and we believe it is—then the personality of the leader may very well be the one common denominator, despite individual variations, of all leaders.

The validity of the foregoing assertion will more likely be confirmed by intensive case studies, than by detailed experiments of the type we have described. This will involve intensive but largely unstructured interviews and clinical investigations. Such studies, of which there are too few, will probably show that leadership is a complex function which is determined as much by the personality of the leader as by the structure of the group.

As an example of a democratic leader whose behavior is described exclusively neither by the situation nor by such conventional leader traits as dominance, aggressiveness, self-confidence, and the like, we shall present a condensed account of the personality of "Ray Andrews," in a Basic Skill Training Group at the National Training Laboratory.[38] While the investigators' account is largely interpretive, it is based on data obtained by a variety of psychological techniques, including the Rorschach Test, the Thematic Apperception Test, the Sentence Completion Test, an Ideology Interview Questionnaire, and a self-administered Life History Interview.

Andrews was found to be a highly intelligent person with creative imagination. Although he was an academic man his thinking was practical rather than theoretical and abstract. The Sentence Completion Test revealed that this was probably due to strong doubts about his intellectual competence.

[38] M. Deutsch, A. Pepitone, and A. Zander, Leadership in the small group, *J. soc. Issues, 4* (1948), 31–40.

The test and interview situations showed Andrews to be good humored but reserved. Socially he was at ease, unassertive, and frank. Personally he was anxious, showed a tendency toward depression, fear of failure, and escapist in the face of difficulty. Nevertheless, his strong ego and social adaptiveness enabled him to adjust to difficulties without permitting them seriously to interfere in his relations with people. He tended toward introversion, despite his easy social responsiveness. This responsiveness, however, was controlled and curbed by a deep spontaneity of feeling. He did not usually, as the authors say, "let himself go" except in very unusual circumstances.

The clinical material reveals that Andrews has been deeply concerned with "the conflict between his passive dependency needs and his desire to assume the responsibilities of an adult." The authors suggest that this conflict may have been initiated in early experiences of rejection and lack of encouragement by his father. This has impelled him to identify himself with the underdog and to direct his energy toward social betterment. In his relations with others he is markedly equalitarian and is particularly resentful of discrimination toward minorities and underprivileged people. In referring to his conflictual state, the authors explain that, having assumed adult responsibility, "he feels burdened by the effort, feels himself to be under considerable pressure—an effort and pressure he is occasionally tempted to escape."

All in all Andrews is intellectually superior, "non-aggressive, non-dominating, equalitarian and affiliative with peers and subordinates. He is sensitive to the feelings and wishes of others and is also sensitive to criticism. He wishes to please, to be considered a 'regular guy,' yet it is evident that there exist fairly strong autonomy needs which would make him react to being 'pushed around' and which would make him wish to be free and independent of social approval and recognition."[39]

[39] The above description is found in *ibid.*, pp. 32–33. The reader should also review the role of personality variables in industrial relations in Chapter 9, above.

The picture of Andrews, the highly successful discussion leader, does not correspond to the conventional image of a highly ascendant, dominant type of individual who, by his "strong" personality, impels others to accede to his wishes. Rather, it confirms our repeated observations that leaders differ as do other people. So types of personality structure function effectively in some group situations and ineffectively in others. Leadership behavior, to repeat once more, is a function of personality variables and objective group situations.

CONCLUSION

After many repetitions of the theme it should now be crystal clear that the individual and his group are interdependent. A self-directing, democratic group is built by free and socially responsible individuals; and independent, group-centered individuals are molded by the collective atmosphere in which they have their being.

In this chapter we have purposely stressed the role of individual psychological variables, especially personality, in the life and action of a group. This was done to give a more balanced view of group phenomena than one can get by looking too closely and too long at the associative characteristic of social life.

Collaboration in collective efforts does not, obviously, take place automatically. It requires not only individuals who are interacting with one another, but such individual characteristics as good intelligence, communication skills, the ability to relate one's self productively rather than defensively to others, leadership capacity, especially the kind that is best described as syncretistic or collaborative, and other psychological traits.

In considering the force of personality in group relations we must carefully distinguish between those who are basically self-seeking and those who, through their self-actualization and independence, help the group to move toward its objectives. Independence and autonomy are wholesome goals only if they enhance the well-being of the group.

Otherwise, they end in self-isolation or alienation from interaction and other self-constrictive conditions which are harmful to the individual and the group alike. Unless we bear this distinction in mind, we become anti-individualistic in our attitudes and worshipers of a new deity: the group.

CHAPTER 14

Group Psychotherapy

It is not unreasonable to suppose that since nonorganic psychological disturbances are largely group induced they should be amenable to group treatment. Since frustrations, inhibitions, suppressions, repressions, and the like arise in response to group expectations and demands, the tensions and conflicts to which they often lead should be resolvable through constructive interaction with other people in a therapeutic situation. In a world where the individual is irrevocably joined with other individuals, where he begins *human* life in intimate association with other human beings, where he actualizes himself or becomes a person through participation, *restoration* of psychological health when it has been dissipated can be effectively achieved in therapeutic groups. The group process by means of which an individual's psychological health is restored is known as group psychotherapy.[1]

[1] This term creates various and mixed reactions. The historical and linguistic purist will object to it on the ground that, since a group does not have a sensorium or psyche, it cannot be treated by psychological techniques. This difficulty, if such it be, need not detain us; for we mean by it no more and no less than the psychological treatment of individuals in a group setting. This will be made clear in the pages to follow.

Psychotherapy in groups is a natural product of the history and development of social psychology and psychopathology. For this reason alone it is not a temporary phenomenon or fad. For at least forty years psychotherapy has recognized the fact that a maladjusted individual is a member of a social group, not a self-contained pathological unit. While Freud had no explicit conception of group therapy, he recognized the importance of an individual's relation to others. His *Group Psychology and Analysis of the Ego,* which we cited in the preceding chapter, stresses the interpersonal character of the human personality, and thus helped to pave the way to the contemporary view of human behavior.

An early formulation of group therapy was made by Moreno. His method of psychodrama is invariably described as therapy through the spontaneous acting out of internal tensions. While that is correct as far as it goes, the therapeutic group as he conceives it is *structured.* The conflict situation of a patient, for example, is acted out with the help of auxiliary egos who may be members of Moreno's staff. The activities are thus partly staged, and the process is partly contrived, not wholly spontaneous.[2]

At about the same time Trigant Burrow was developing the idea that a neurotic individual's distorted self-image could be corrected if he were put into a social situation where he might see himself as he really is and be accepted by others.[3]

The pioneer work of Schilder must not be overlooked either. He treated many individuals in the out-patient department of Bellevue Psychiatric Hospital. He was an uncompromising exponent of the view that since social factors are causative in the formation of mental disorder they must be fully utilized in its treatment. Through his own experi-

[2] See J. L. Moreno, *Who shall survive?* (2d ed.; Washington, D.C.: Nervous and Mental Disease Publishing Co., 1934), and *Psychodrama,* Vol. I (New York: Beacon House, 1946).

[3] See T. Burrow, The basis of group analysis, or the analysis of the reactions of normal and neurotic individuals, *Brit. J. med. Psychol.,* 8 (1928), 198–206, and *The biology of human conflict* (New York: The Macmillan Co., 1937).

ence he found that an effective way of correcting faulty personality development is through group therapy.[4]

The increasing popularity of group psychotherapy has been accompanied by errors which it is well to point up at the very beginning. First, it is not merely an application to several persons in a group of a method that is used in the treatment of an individual. It should be very clear by now that any psychological process in isolation—if that indeed be a reality—is changed when it is brought into relation with other psychological processes. The composition and size of a group, the character of the interaction between its members, and so forth make differences in the total process. In the second place, group psychotherapy is not a substitute for individual psychotherapy. It is, rather, the use of group relations for the improvement of the personalities of group members. As such it requires a knowledge of group dynamics and the skill to effect desirable changes in individuals in a group context. It differs from other forms of group direction, such as learning or problem-solving, by being employed exclusively for *therapeutic* purposes. This means that the therapist in a group situation must understand not only individual therapy, but must be able to utilize group forces for the achievement of individual mental health. A knowledge of individual therapy is not, however, a guaranty of success in group therapy.

Group psychotherapy is not, contrary to a popular belief, a therapeutic short cut. Important as are the economies of time and money, group therapy when properly used is as thorough and time-consuming as individual psychotherapy. Like good individual therapy, group therapy is fundamentally a process of re-education, and re-education takes time.

Again, unlike individual therapy, in which the development or restoration of role-playing is primarily verbal, group

[4] P. Schilder, Introductory remarks on groups, *J. soc. Psychol., 12* (1940), 83–100; Social organization and psychotherapy, *Amer. J. Orthopsychiat., 10* (1940), 911–26. For a more comprehensive review of the literature on group psychotherapy up to 1943 consult G. W. Thomas, Group Psychotherapy: a review of the recent literature, *Psychosom. Med.,* 5 (1943), 166–80.

therapy consists in the *enactment* of roles in the presence of others who are playing their roles. If there is any economy of time in group therapy, then it is due considerably to the fact that in group therapy one's roles are played directly in relation to other people's roles. It is easier to become aware of one's inadequate and defensive behavior, for example, when faced at once and in the same situation by the defensive and the self-satisfying behavior of other people in a permissive group atmosphere. It is usually easier to identify one's self and be accepted by others objectively in a group than in the socially restricted atmosphere of individual treatment.

This does not mean, furthermore, that group therapy is either superior or preferable to individual therapy. Only skilled diagnosis of individual cases, on the one hand, can determine which individual will gain more from one than from the other; and only an individual with full understanding of the nature, limitations, and possibilities of the group process, on the other, is qualified to make a final judgment.

It is important, finally, to note the fact that group therapy and "social group work" are not identical. While both are concerned with effecting changes in the individual, social group work aims, usually by informal discussion and recreational activities, to guide small-group members toward increased self-regulation and individual well-being.

THERAPY AS A GROUP PROCESS

In our discussion of human relations in industry in Chapter 9, we called attention to the fact that at the beginning of systematic research in that area there was no model to follow and no conceptual scheme to give it direction. In the industrial field this did not prove to be a disadvantage. In expounding the research contributions, however, we found that the construction of a conceptual framework was distinctly helpful.

In the field of group psychotherapy, on the other hand, a unifying framework is a necessary first step to a clear understanding of it as a group process and in order not to impose a preferred system of ideas upon it. In the absence of a framework therapists of various persuasions will unconsciously perceive the task before them through their professional orientation. Thus a psychiatrist, a social worker, and a group worker, each interested in therapy through the group process, might easily interpret its meaning differently.

THE THERAPEUTIC FRAMEWORK. A descriptive scheme in group therapy must place proper and balanced emphasis on the different factors involved. It must be able to account for the integration of the individual with the group from which he has become alienated, without reducing his status as an individuated person. On the contrary, successful group therapy enables an individual to accept himself while he is being accepted by others. Self-acceptance and acceptance by others go together. It is not necessary to establish the priority of one over the other. The process is continuous and cannot be sliced into parts. This is but a further confirmation of a basic group dynamics principle, namely, that the part and the whole, the individual and the group, are deeply intertwined. As in any other group, in a therapeutic group participation leads to a better understanding and acceptance of individual differences. The only groups in which there is a loss of self are those in which the individual's self-consciousness is obliterated, as in mobs and other crowd formations.[5] They do not concern us in this book.

Our descriptive framework is a simple one. It stresses three integrated factors in the therapeutic situation: (1) the *clientele* who are to be helped; (2) the *therapist* whose chief tasks are to clarify, reflect back to others their affective and other psychological tendencies, and serve as a catalyzer of group locomotion; and (3) the *interactive cognitive-affective process* taking place among all the "units" of the

[5] Students of collective behavior have long been aware of this loss of self in the crowd, and the beginnings of experimental research confirming it have been made by Festinger and others, who describe the process as *de-individuation*. See L. Festinger, A. Pepitone, and T. M. Newcomb, Some consequences of de-individuation in a group, *J. abnorm. soc. psychol.,* 47 (1952), 382–89.

herapeutic situation. These three factors in the therapeutic situation will be discussed in detail in the pages that follow.

1. The clientele. Since the individuals seeking or getting help in therapeutic groups are not "patients" in the conventional sense, we use the term "clientele" instead.

There is no strong agreement among group therapists concerning the selection of the clientele. Much reliance has to be placed, therefore, on the judgment and experience of those who have done extensive work in group therapy.

The judgments of Hinckley and Hermann illustrate the complexity of the problem.[6] Describing the work of the Mental Hygiene Clinic of the Students' Health Service at the University of Minnesota, which began in 1924, the authors point out that the first therapeutic group was formed in 1941. This group, composed of both men and women, was established to help patients in social adjustment. It remains to date the only group in the Clinic in which both men and women participate. Later other therapeutic groups were organized in which only persons with similar symptom complexes were admitted. One group was made up of individuals with skin afflictions. Another one was comprised of persons suffering from epileptiform seizures. Still another contained persons with primary high blood pressure.

Slavson, in his extensive experience in group therapy, especially with children, selects persons on the basis of two large classifications, namely, social maladjustment and typological criteria.[7] In Slavson's category of *social maladjustment* are all those persons—children in Slavson's groups—whose difficulties lie in the area of social relationships. Among the most common social maladjustment problems which are amenable to group psychotherapy are aggression, submissiveness, overdependence, withdrawal, and habit malformation.[8]

[6] R. G. Hinckley and L. Hermann, *Group treatment in psychotherapy* (Minneapolis, Minn.: University of Minnesota Press, 1951), pp. 3–5.

[7] S. R. Slavson, *An introduction to group therapy* (New York: International Universities Press, Inc., 1943), chap. iv.

[8] *Ibid.*, pp. 88–91.

Typological criteria, according to Slavson, are forms of behavior which are consequences of the "personality type" of the individual. Examples are the hyperkinetic or overactive individual, who disturbs others around him; the motor type, who finds satisfaction primarily in doing things and cannot adjust himself to a more inactive situation; the originative person, whose proclivities toward inventing and experimenting are not satisfied and who consequently becomes a "problem" for his group; the fantasy-laden child, who builds a fence around himself and keeps everyone outside it; the schizoid individual, who withdraws excessively; the "egoic" child, who responds too exclusively in terms of himself; and the emasculated boy, who is generally unable to fulfill his biological role and may eventually become hypochondriacal and homosexual.[9]

The clientele can also be selected from the more restricted population of mental hospitals. This permits the inclusion in group therapy of more severe cases of mental disorder, thus far difficult to treat by the group method. While the earliest work with this clientele was done in England, it is rapidly developing in the United States. Maxwell Jones, the British psychiatrist, describes this group-therapy population as the therapeutic community.[10]

The therapeutic community group differs from other therapy groups in two respects. First, it incorporates auxiliary figures as an integral part in the therapeutic situation in addition to clients and the therapists, namely, the nurses and job supervisors. The latter are important because they give the clients work experience in genuine jobs in place of "the mere time-killing characteristic of 'occupational therapy.' "[11] Second, it develops a culture of its own. The culture is largely maintained through the staff rather than through the patients, and consists of educational techniques, such as discussion groups, the provision of social and vocational roles, and the like.

[9] *Ibid.*, pp. 91–98.

[10] M. Jones, *The therapeutic community* (New York: Basic Books, Inc., 1953). Published in England under the title of *Social psychiatry.*

[11] *Ibid.*, G. Watson's Foreword, p. vii.

The clientele of group therapy, it is clear, represents a large segment of the universe of the mentally ill. They include children and adults, neurotics and some psychotics, psychosomatically disturbed, socially maladjusted, and personally unhappy and frustrated individuals. They are also, as Jones describes them, the " 'failures' in society"; many of them come from broken homes and many are unemployed; because of their failure, they have developed "antisocial attitudes in an attempt to defend themselves from what appears to them as a hostile environment." About half have broken marriages, and they make little effort to maintain the conventional standards of domestic behavior.[12]

A knowledge of the clientele of group therapy is necessary because, although the process of treatment lies in interaction, it is always directed toward the individual. The group is used, as Illing remarks, "to further individuation, to stimulate and to complete it."[13] Group therapy, unlike the forms of group behavior which we discussed in other chapters, is not directed toward a *group* goal. It consists, rather, in the use of group processes to make constructive psychological changes, such as reduction of anxiety, say, or an increase in self-confidence, in individuals in a group setting. In group therapy the clients "use" one another and the therapist—or better, they use the group process—to effect personal growth and social adjustment.

It should be added, parenthetically, that even some nontherapeutic groups, such as problem-solving groups, may have therapeutic consequences. By becoming task-centered, group-involved, and group-goal-oriented, a person finds emotional satisfaction and self-fulfillment. To this extent he experiences personal growth and individuation which are, as we noted, important objectives of group therapy.

There is, finally, a type of client who is unusually well suited for group therapy because he finds individual therapy too threatening and anxiety provoking. The transference

12 *Ibid.*, p. xvii.

13 H. A. Illing, C. G. Jung on the present trends in group psychotherapy, *Hum. Relat.*, *10* (1957), p. 82.

phenomenon that is aroused in individual psychotherapy creates some anxiety in all clients, but in some it is overwhelming to the point of producing panic. Although group therapy also arouses anxiety, it does not, as Slavson has shown, reach the intensity manifested in individual therapy. The presence of others in a group allays anxiety and "transference is diluted and modified by inter-member transference and mutual identification." It seems that awareness that others in the group have the same feelings and the security which comes from support by others in the same predicament dissipate anxiety.[14]

Clients in therapeutic groups enact different roles, as do members in other kinds of associations. Successful group therapy results in no small degree from the opportunity for clients to play roles and from the therapist's understanding of their place in the total group therapeutic process. That such roles recur—probably because most neurotic individuals are wrestling with similar psychological problems—has been noted by several investigators.[15] At the beginning of treatment, and for some time later, these roles serve as techniques of self-defense. When the roles give way to more constructive ones, the client may be said to have "recovered." It will perhaps increase the reader's understanding of the group therapeutic process if we identify and briefly describe some of these roles.

Although Redl designates the patterns of behavior which we are calling roles as "forms of group resistance," the difference is essentially terminological. The forms of resistance are ways of responding to the total therapeutic group; they involve images by the client of himself, of other members, of the therapist, and of the nature of what is going on in the therapeutic process. They are characteristic psychological stances, positions, or roles which the client is assuming through the course of treatment.

[14] S. R. Slavson, Differential dynamics of activity and interview group therapy, *Amer. J. Orthopsychiat.*, *71* (1947), 293–302.

[15] See, for example, F. Redl, Resistance in therapy groups, *Hum. Relat.*, *1* (1948), 307–13; T. Bry, Varieties of resistance in group psychotherapy, *Int. J. group Psychother.*, *1* (1951), 106–14.

Since the term "resistance" may not be clear to the reader, we shall explain it briefly. In psychotherapy it refers to the effort by which, according to most therapists, the client repels external influence. Its psychological function is to protect the ego by averting the client's attention from the weaknesses and shortcomings which he lacks the strength to face. In individual psychotherapy this resistance is directed against the therapist, since he is the person who "threatens" to expose the client's weakness. In group therapy it is directed at anyone in the group, since every member, and not only the therapist, is a potential agent of exposure.

Although Redl calls a form of resistance which is shared by several individuals in the same group toward the same therapist *group resistance*, it is plain to see that the resistance is displayed by individuals, however much they may be of one mind.[16] Again, it is important to note, as Redl warns us, that the forms of resistance—or the role enactments as we would say—which he is describing were those found in therapeutic groups of delinquent children, and that generalization from them may or may not be fruitful. The following, then, are the role enactments discerned by Redl.

Escape into love was one form of resistance, or one role enacted by the children. This is a role played in order to avoid the genuine change which all therapy requires of the individual. It consists in modifying one's behavior only enough to get love or friendship from the therapist. Thus, the boys in Redl's study, once they received signs of friendship from the therapist would refuse to change their attitude beyond being superficially "good." There was no genuine identification between the boys and the therapist, since the roles they enacted were functionally unconnected with genuine love.

The role of *protective provocation* is another assumed guise, and an insidious one, and may easily fool the unwary therapist. It consists of attempts to provoke the leader into acts that will justify the boys' distorted images of those adults whom they blame for all their troubles. As Redl puts

16 Redl, Resistance in therapy groups, p. 308.

it, the boys "literally 'ask' for punishment," in order to confirm their image of the punitive adult. They "ask" for the punishment not as a means of atonement but as a defense against "identification-surrender." To this end they use all sorts of irritants and exasperating acts to upset the therapist so that they can put him "into any one of the categories of their traumatic life history, so as to get rid of this dangerous enemy of their delinquent fun."[17]

Guilt escape through displaced conflict is a role often resorted to in which the individual begins to feel guilty but in which he will act contritely only toward his therapy group. This still leaves him a great deal of room for hating and combating the world outside. Thus, the boys may with no sense of guilt "offend an innocent bystander at the public bathing beach, and throw stones at motorists who pass them on a hike." In this role they resist "the total surrender of guilt-exempt delinquent fun." Having already made reluctant concessions to the therapist and the therapy group, "they try to rescue the rest of their life from being engulfed in the process of domestication."[18]

Role confusion consists of a state of bewilderment regarding the expectations of others, particularly those of the therapist. The boys in Redl's group quickly learned what they could and could not expect of the therapist. Thus they expected him to be a "good sport" and to overlook minor infractions or offenses, but they did not expect him to lie for them, to get them out of trouble, or to pretend that he approved every aspect of their misdeeds. This very differentiation, however, caused confusion; for they could not anticipate all his reactions. Thus, many boys accused the therapist of being an informer or "squealer" whenever he consulted with other staff members, even about matters that were unrelated to discipline. As Redl points out, by using words like "squealer," which are used to describe *group members*, and applying them to the group *therapist*, "they got away

[17] *Ibid.*, p. 310.
[18] *Ibid.*, p. 311.

with quite a lot of subversive antileader propaganda before the other kids even recognized it." In this way the other boys would become angry with and accusing of the therapist without bothering to check the veracity of the reports made by others.

Escape into virtue refers to the role of seeming recovery, especially if it begins soon after treatment. It is very common in individual therapy, where it is called "escape into health." It develops as soon as the client senses the oncome of identification, faces his defective state, and recognizes the need to change. It consists of concealing the symptoms or the offensive behavior that occasioned the need for therapy. The client, in short, improves noticeably and quickly in the unconscious hope that the treatment will be terminated. Redl, describing this situation regarding delinquent boys, tells us that he has had boys in his groups who, after an exceptionally short period of treatment, developed "a most laudable improvement in the management of their affairs, an astonishing accessibility to reasoning, and an astounding reduction in their open delinquent exploits. . . ."[19]

An interesting study of role behavior in group therapy is presented by Frank and his associates.[20] Although the investigators use the term "behavior pattern," what they are in fact describing is role behavior.[21] There are two client roles or behavior patterns described in this study which Frank and his associates term "help-rejecting complainer" and "doctor's assistant." These roles emerged early in group therapy and were therefore little if at all modified by it. They were, in other words, the habitual expectancies of the individuals, not a set of behavior prescribed by the therapeutic sessions. They were the roles which they brought with them to the therapeutic group, and the explanation in

[19] *Ibid.*, p. 312.

[20] J. D. Frank *et al.*, Two behavior patterns in therapeutic groups and their apparent motivation, *Hum. Relat.*, 5 (1952), 289–315.

[21] *Ibid.*, p. 290. Their definition of behavior pattern applies to role behavior: "Patients would be said to show the same behavior pattern if they appeared to be trying to handle the same conflict in the same way, that is, if their behavior had the same meaning or intent."

part of the persons' maladaptive behavior.[22] It was early found that some patients rejected the therapist's advice, antagonized other clients, and generally disrupted the group. Others offered advice, concealed their symptoms, and tried to keep the group process going. How reminiscent these are of the blocker, aggressor, dominator, opinion-giver, harmonizer, and encourager whom we discussed in Chapter 12!

The *help-rejecting complainers,* of which there were two women and one man in a group of seven, usually did not seek help directly but "complained in an aggrieved way" to the therapist or other clients in the group. Being strongly self-oriented they ignored the needs and attitudes of the others, except as potential rivals for the therapist's favors. Their self-centeredness blinded them to the ill-concealed ridicule which they frequently elicited from others. Characteristically they belittled other clients' complaints and tended to blame others for their difficulties.

Their behavior was typical of maladjusted and of certain paranoic patients who, as Cameron pointed out in applying the concept of role-playing to behavior disorders, were neither able to play their roles skillfully nor correctly to perceive the roles of others.[23] Frank and his associates sum the situation up clearly when they write: "While needing the help of others, they seemed to see them as unappreciative, indifferent, or unable to meet their needs, which made them angry. This led them to anticipate anger in return and strengthened their belief in the potential help-giver's ill will."[24]

The *doctor's assistant roles* were enacted by four clients. These individuals, even while addressing other clients, were overconcerned with the therapist's or doctor's reaction to

[22] *Ibid.,* p. 298. The therapeutic group roles were observed in treatment sessions and were corroborated by data from interviews and from the Rorschach and Thematic Apperception tests which were administered prior to the beginning of treatment. Care was taken to confirm or deny the hypothesis that "the behavior pattern in the group was the response generally made by the [client] to similar stimuli in outside life."

[23] See N. Cameron, *The psychology of behavior disorders* (Boston: Houghton Mifflin Co., 1947), chaps. iv and xiv.

[24] Frank *et al.,* Two behavior patterns, p. 300.

their behavior. Although their manner toward him was respectful, it was extremely deferential and placatory, especially if they anticipated his disapproval. In their relations to others they behaved in accordance with the stereotype of a physician. The authors point out that three of these four "doctor's assistants" were, in fact, initially suspected by other clients to have been real doctors who had been "planted" in the group.

As "doctor's assistants" they naturally assumed an air of superiority toward other clients. Their manner was usually "patronizing," "dogmatic," or "judicial." They belittled others' problems while concealing their own, "except as something in the past they had already overcome." They were very sensitive to criticism regarding their "solved" problems, a criticism "which they tried to dispel, usually by becoming placating or joking, occasionally by becoming more dogmatic."[25]

In support of an assertion in Chapter 12 that roles, although enacted in groups, are highly individual, and to add confirmation to the claim that personality disturbances can be partially explained as conflicts in roles, we cite the fact that the help-rejecting complainers' and the doctor's assistants' behavior was different in the therapeutic group from that in other situations. This difference is largely due of course, to the fact that the two experiences have different meanings for the client. The complainers showed more self-assertive behavior toward their bosses than toward the therapist. This may reflect the fact that the work situation called for the role of a competent individual rather than for a weak person. On-the-job behavior, on the other hand, did not arouse the "conflict between the need to appear superior and fear of exposing weakness" as much as it did in the therapeutic situation. Again, the persons playing the role of "doctor's assistants" reported in their interview that they were in open conflict with their bosses at work. This contrasted sharply, as the authors point out, with their need to avoid conflict in the therapeutic group. While there are

[25] *Ibid.*, p. 305.

other possible explanations for the difference in behavior, it was probably due to the fact that the work situation was different and therefore elicited different roles.

2. *The therapist.* The role of the therapist is to some extent similar to that of any central person in interindividual relationships, such as the group leader. Any central person is a focus of interest to other members, and an effective one creates a comfortable atmosphere for deliberation or action. Creating an atmosphere, however, for solving problems say, is not quite the same as creating the kind of permissive group effect which encourages individuals to lay bare before others their well-concealed hatreds and anxieties. While we do not wish to magnify the importance of trained skill, a group therapist must not only understand the group process, like other central persons, but he also needs a technical equipment which is usually not required in learning and problem-solving groups.

Lest the reader infer from the foregoing statement that the therapist interposes his own intellectual and technical scheme upon the therapeutic group, we hasten to point out that this is not true. After structuring the initial therapeutic pattern, which is necessary for stimulating at least a minimal participation, the therapist permits the group forces to generate freely. As in all productive group behavior, in therapeutic activities the central person—in this case the therapist—engages in a minimum amount of activity while keeping in close interpersonal contact with every member. As in other productive groups, where leaders become members, and leadership acts are diffused throughout the group, so in therapeutic group sessions the clients also become therapeutic change agents. It is no exaggeration to say that the group therapist's greatest skill lies in his sure judgment of when to refrain from interjecting his own ideas and attitudes. If, for example, a client reaches a place in the therapeutic process where facing an unconscious trend may stimulate an emotional crisis should the therapist probe him further, the consequence may be emotionally disastrous. To make clear our meaning, suppose the emotional crisis was motivated by an unconscious wish for death. Should the therapist, at this point, interpret the wish to the client as a suicidal tendency, he will have made an egregious error in timing. Hinckley and Hermann state the matter with admirable finality: "One never imposes a greater burden on that which is admittedly frail; one accepts, rather, that fragility as present reality and seeks to reinforce the enfeebled ego."[26] Slavson expresses the same idea when he describes the discriminate use of a rule in his own work: *"Don't do anything; don't say anything; when in doubt, don't!"*[27]

Like a successful group leader a good therapist plays different roles in the therapeutic group, depending on the needs of the clients and the requirements of the therapeutic situation from moment to moment. We saw the importance of role dynamics in Chapter 12, and we learned there something of the variety of roles which members enact in a group. Group therapists likewise are called upon to enact a variety of functional roles; and, generally, the more skillfully they perform them, the greater is the likelihood that the clients will be able to help one another to treat themselves.

The first role of the group therapist is that of a *catalyst* or change agent. He fulfills roughly the same function as the energizer in other groups. There is no group locomotion of any kind unless someone initiates it. In typical groups of the type we discussed in other chapters this function may be fulfilled by any member, although most commonly it is a central person, such as the leader. In a therapeutic group, movement is *initiated,* but seldom sustained, by the therapist. More specifically, the therapist must create a satisfying relationship between himself and the clients. This consists of establishing an atmosphere of security with a minimum of restraint upon the expression and behavior of the clients. As a catalyst or change agent the therapist, by infusing freedom and security into the group, encourages the release of repressed feelings and memories in the clients, thereby

[26] Hinckley and Hermann, *Group treatment in psychotherapy,* p. 25.

[27] Slavson, *An introduction to group therapy,* p. 157. Italics in the original.

ensuring the constant flow of material which is necessary for the continuance and therapeutic value of the group.

Experienced group therapists know that the creation of the initial atmosphere is difficult and delicate. There is a strong tendency to structure the group along certain lines; and the clients, by virtue of their initial dependence, tend to accommodate themselves to such structuring because they perceive their security to lie within it. The skillful therapist, however, like the effective group leader, encourages the members of the group to become their own change agents. He avoids, as we said before, interjecting his own frame of reference upon the group.

The establishment of a proper group setting is difficult, furthermore, because of diversity in the clientele. Some clients, for example, are much less self-reliant than others; some need direct guidance for longer periods than others, and cannot become active and productive members easily. Some persons talk easily and freely, whereas others are frozen into silence. The therapist knows how embarrassing the silences are to the clients, but he also knows that in time they will generate relaxation and ease. "The only ease allowed," however, "is that of maintaining silence."[28] But silence is productive only, Hinckley and Hermann tell us, when both the therapist and the clients can endure it comfortably. The therapist, accordingly, must quickly get to know his group well to be able to judge how much direction he should practice and how much can be handled by the group itself.

The therapist is, next, a *supporter*. In this he plays a role very similar to—or it may be the same as—the *encourager* whom we briefly described in Chapter 12. In this role the therapist reacts to the clients' contribution with warmth and approval. The clients thus see him as a sanctioner of whatever socially unacceptable tendencies they might show, rather than as a repressor or critic like others in the outside world who disapproved of them. While the therapist as a supporter is always potentially accessible, he plays this role

[28] Hinckley and Hermann, *Group treatment in psychotherapy*, p. 18.

actively only in periods or situations when the clients are helpless or dependent. During such periods the therapist's support and encouragement almost invariably reduces or alleviates the client's anxiety, if only temporarily. The support which he gives has, as Hinckley and Hermann point out, "the integrative function of keeping the patient's personality together, but makes no effort to change his basic patterns, for this may not be important or even endurable."[29]

Unlike the support given to the patient in individual therapy, however, its use in group therapy is much more restricted. This is in keeping with what we know regarding group productiveness. In active groups the leader holds his activities to a minimum, encouraging instead as full a participation by all as possible. In a therapy group the situation is the same. Since the aim of group therapy is for the clients to treat each other, the therapist does not interfere with the process by giving more support than he thinks the group needs. As Hinckley and Hermann inform us, in a therapeutic group "where the members themselves are expected to serve as practitioners, the therapist holds himself in abeyance until it is evident that he must supply what is not forthcoming from the group members."[30] In his capacity of a supporter he thus also takes the role of the catalyst, the initiator of action when the group process slows down or stops altogether. He helps to put the group back upon a self-starter basis.

The therapist's supportive role is often, however, perceived in different terms by the client. The latter sees the supportive role as that of either a *parent substitute* or *an ideal parent*, depending upon the client's own life experience with one or the other of his parents. When he is viewed as a parent substitute the client relates himself in a manner similar to his earlier relatedness to his real parent. Like his parent, who loved and accepted the client during his childhood dependence, the therapist accepts him as he is and gratifies some of his dependency needs. As the therapeutic process continues successfully, this parent-child relationship

[29] *Ibid.*, p. 37.
[30] *Ibid.*

aids the client in his reach for maturity, just as his parents helped him to grow from a dependent child to a self-directing adult. If, on the other hand, the client's experience with his parent was ungratifying because of real or fancied faults or weaknesses, there is a strong tendency for the client to ascribe the role of ideal parent to the therapist. The latter, seen now as an ideal parent, has all the virtues that the client's own parent lacked. His own parent may have been rejecting and punitive, whereas the therapist-ideal parent is acceptant and sanctioning. The latter accepts him unconditionally, without enmeshing strings attached to every favor.

Every successful group therapist plays the role of a *clarifier*. This is a locus in the group therapeutic process where he forsakes his dispensability and takes a more "active" part. While he does not engage in manipulation and control, he helps the therapeutic process along by identifying for the clients at the proper moment the disturbing emotions and their place in the psychic economy of the individual and the group. He interprets for the group the meanings of the tensions which disturb all of them, so that they will be able eventually to cope with them themselves. He supplies the clients with the emotional language of the tensions by means of which he can reflect back to them their own feelings. As they progress in group therapy, most clients come to observe their own feelings; but they cannot verbalize them or state them directly. Thus when one of them attempts to convey his feelings in a fearful, halting, and confused manner, the therapist restates the client's words in a manner that will make the feelings clearer to the latter. This function is called *reflection* in both individual and group therapy. When, for example, a client reacts to the taking of a personality test by saying, "Who wants to believe that he is a psychopathic deviate?" and the therapist reassuringly answers, "It is hard to accept something unpleasant," he is *reflecting* back to the client the latter's own unclaimed or rejected feeling regarding a suspected condition of his personality without passing judgment on him.[31]

[31] See *ibid.*, p. 45.

The group therapist is also an *information-giver,* although the function of this role in therapy is generally more restricted than that of the information-giver whom we described in Chapter 12. The purpose of information-giving is to reduce the trial-and-error by means of which clients acquire understanding of themselves and the therapeutic process. If clients in a group engage in long discussions in order to understand the nature of anxiety, the therapist can give practical help. If clients describe anxiety as not being able to eat or sleep as just "nerves," as "my stomach closes up," or as "tension—but what's tension anyway?" the therapist can give them authoritative information concerning its nature. Thus he may tell them that tension is "alertness for action," and anxiety, unlike fear, which is an avoidance of realistic situations, is a "sense of dread that comes from within you."[32]

We might say in summary that the functions of the therapist in group treatment are described by the roles he takes or has ascribed to him in his relationships with the clients. His skill in playing his roles determines the degree of success he will have in attaining the objectives for which the therapy group was established, namely, to enable each person *through group participation* to become emancipated from defensive modes of adjustment and to attain constructive, mature, and personally gratifying ways of behaving. Whether or not this purpose is achieved is determined much less by the therapist than by the clients themselves.[33]

3. *The interaction process.* This is the third and final interrelated element in our therapeutic framework. It is but another way of describing the group. It supports the premise that since persons become psychologically ill and unhappy in social groups they can re-establish their emotional equilib-

[32] *Ibid.,* p. 47.

[33] The "power" of the leader in a therapy group, however, should not be minimized. In contrast to the role of the leader in nontherapeutic groups, where initiative acts are performed by everyone, in a therapy group these are performed relatively more by the therapist. See H. E. Durkin, Group dynamics and group psychotherapy, *Int. J. group Psychother., 4* (1954), 56–64.

rium in productive human relationships through social interaction.

Social psychology and child psychology have pretty well established the fact that every normal child and adult wants to be accepted by others. This need of belongingness we pointed out in Chapter 2 impels individuals to join groups and to work with others for the attainment of common goals. This need is probably the strongest single incentive to personality change in group therapy. The desire to be accepted by others, Slavson says, "serves the same function [in group therapy] as does transference in individual treatment. Just as the patient in individual therapy improves in order to please the therapist, in Group Therapy the child alters his behavior and attitudes so that he may be accepted by the group."[34]

The interactive cognitive-affective process of the therapeutic situation is thus the major phase of group treatment; indeed, it *is* the therapeutic process.

In describing the interactive process, we shall answer the question, What goes on in the therapeutic process? We shall answer the question first in a general way by saying that, through the help of a therapist and of clients in the group, psychologically disturbed persons are relieved of their anxieties by learning to share them with one another and thus once again becoming independent and self-directing individuals.

Transference is a vital factor in both individual and group therapy. In either instance, however, it is a social, or interpersonal, not an individual process. It is a psychological condition *between* individuals. At the same time, the *capacity* to relate one's self to another person lies in the individual. When this relationship is directed toward the therapist, it is called *transference*. More rigidly defined, transference is the client's act of directing the emotions and attitudes which he has for his parents to the therapist. These psychological dispositions may be positive or negative or both. When the transference is positive, the client feels

[34] Slavson, *An introduction to group therapy*, p. 15.

warm and accepting of the therapist; when it is negative, the contrary condition prevails. Since, however—at least according to psychoanalytically oriented therapy—every person has feelings of both love and hate toward his parents, the client's relationship to the therapist is at least initially *ambivalent;* that is, a mixture of acceptance and rejection, of dependence and independence.

However, while the client's feelings for the therapist fluctuate between the two dispositions, he must eventually reach a point in the process where they are positive if the treatment is to be successful. Most therapists are agreed that any client who cannot establish a positive transference to the therapist cannot be successfully treated. "When the positive transference is established," says Slavson, "the client, having accepted the therapist as his parent, aims to please him as he aimed to please his real parents when he was a child."[35]

While the foregoing description is no doubt accurate in its essentials, it is more true of children (who are the subjects of Slavson's therapy groups) than of adults; and it is more true of individual than of group therapy. "Falling in love" with the therapist, as it has been described, is possible to a far greater degree in individual or "deep therapy" than in group therapy. The difference between the two is one of depth rather than kind.[36]

Perhaps it would be appropriate at this point to compare more fully transference in group therapy with the same process in individual treatment. To begin with, and as was just indicated, in group therapy transference seldom reaches the emotional heights and psychological dependence on the therapist that are characteristic of individual psychotherapy. The therapist aims to create positive feelings of acceptance in group therapy, to be sure; for without them the necessary re-education of the client could not take place; but he does so only to the degree necessary to keep the group process flowing. This has the important advantage of reproducing

[35] *Ibid.*, p. 137.

[36] Hinckley and Hermann, *Group treatment in psychotherapy*, p. 53.

real-life relations among all members of the group, and is more in keeping with the adult roles that the clients must maintain. Hinckley and Hermann state the matter lucidly when they say that "transference in the group is limited to a deepening of trust to the point where patients are enabled to accept support but not to the degree where prolonged regression is permitted to stages of earlier development," as is true in individual psychotherapy. "While being always parental," they explain, "the group therapist allows only a minimum of satisfaction to accrue to patients from the process of being dependent."[37]

In group therapy with children, however, the therapist is a stronger parental image; and the transference is strikingly similar to parent-child relationships. Slavson, who probably understands the group-therapy process with children better than most psychologists, has found this to be true. He reports that children tend to look upon the therapist as the acceptant or forbidding parent. This is vividly shown in the widespread tendency among children in therapy groups to address the therapist as "Pop," "Mom," and "Unk." Citing the case of a boy who addressed the male therapist as "Mom," Slavson points out that, since the child had an extremely dominating mother, only a woman could in his mind be in a position of authority.[38]

Unlike transference in individual therapy, in group therapy relations with the therapist have to be shared with other clients. This makes group therapy to that extent more realistic: clients have to realize that they are among others who have equal claims to the therapist's time and attention. The relationship of transference is social in the widest possible way that the size of the group will permit. The client relates himself not only to the therapist but to other clients. Transference is thus a group phenomenon in which the therapist plays the role of a catalyst on the one hand and an agent of cohesion on the other.

[37] *Ibid.*, pp. 53–54.

[38] Slavson, *An introduction to group therapy,* p. 138.

Using the analogy of the parental group or the family for what it is worth, the transference situation resembles the complicated relations of a family. This, again, is somewhat more true of children's therapy groups than those of adults. Slavson calls this relational complex a *family substitutive group*. He considers this as being more than a theoretical concept, for it is based on the actual day-by-day relations of members in his own therapy groups. In this relationship "the therapist is a parent-substitute, the members are sibling substitutes, and the total group pattern a substitute family to which the children look for their satisfactions."[39]

The "familial" quality of group-therapy relations has been noted by many practitioners and investigators of group psychotherapy with adults as well as with children. Hinckley and Hermann point to the difference in the relationships between clients and therapists and between clients themselves. The relationship with the therapist and the client, they note, is always a "loosely parental one." The interactions of clients with one another constitute a "sibling relationship," although not invariably so. While the therapist maintains a permissive attitude toward the clients, clients sometimes restrict one another severely; and while the therapist is always acceptant and supportive, clients alternately support and attack each other.[40]

In a preceding paragraph we remarked in passing that in the absence of positive transference re-education of the client cannot proceed. This implies that group therapy, like individual treatment, is an *educative* process—a process in which an important change in the client takes place. So conceived, group therapy can be related to an important psychological process—namely, the *learning* process. This in turn suggests a relationship to group learning which we discussed in detail in Chapter 4.

Practicing group therapists are not accustomed to interpreting the therapeutic process in terms of learning the-

[39] *Ibid.*, p. 39.
[40] See Hinckley and Hermann, *Group treatment in psychotherapy*, p. 49.

ory, but it is fundamentally a learning process. It is not enough to say that in therapy we aim to aid the individual in reacquainting him with the social world of other people and helping him to feel more relaxed with them. Changing one's relations to other people involves cognitive, affective, and motivational learning. Since maladjustive behavior is largely learned, it can also be unlearned.[41]

Learning to relate one's self positively to others involves, as Lewin pointed out, a change in the cognitive structure of the individual. This means that he must acquire knowledge that is realistic and veridical, to replace the distorted cognitive organization which is partly at the root of his trouble. He can acquire this in a therapy group through the opportunity of comparing his conception of himself and others in the give and take of group interaction. However, since behavior is never a purely cognitive process, he also acquires and modifies his likes and dislikes of people. Acquiring new attitudes toward people, in other words, is a change in motivation toward himself and others. A client must *want* to change, must *want* to get well, no matter how much he may resist the therapist's effort to change him.

Finally, therapy as a learning process involves a change in group belongingness, as Lewin also pointed out. The client must change his distorted interpretation of the cultural values of the group and learn a new set of standards. He is ill in proportion to his rejection of the group's values, or the degree of his sense of not-belonging, which, as we saw in Chapter 5, is the root of both his self-hatred and his hatred of others. If the client does not change, which is to say relearn, emotional valences, he cannot be "cured." But he cannot change his emotional attachments unless he also accepts belongingness to the new group.[42] Growing into the

[41] The view that neurotic behavior is learned is a basic hypothesis of Dollard and Miller. See J. Dollard and N. E. Miller, *Personality and psychotherapy* (New York: McGraw-Hill Book Co., Inc., 1950), especially chaps. ii and iii.

[42] See K. Lewin, *Resolving social conflicts,* pp. 56–68. For a detailed discussion of learning in the above sense, see K. Lewin, Field theory and learning, *41st yearbook of the National Society for the Study of Education* (Chicago: The University of Chicago Press, 1942).

culture of a group is a process of learning its values and forming positive and constructive relations with its members.

Although therapy is a learning process, the form it takes is not necessarily an act of conditioning in the conventional psychological sense. Nor does it take place automatically in the appropriate stimulating situation. For the client to learn, or to become aware of the meaning of what he has learned, or to get *insight* into his experience, he often needs someone to interpret the meaning for him. *Interpretation* is one of the therapist's important functions, and gaining insight is the client's most important learning achievement. The two form a unified process by means of which the client acquires a changed view of himself and of his relation to other people.

Interpretation is the act of explaining to the client the meaning of his behavior. In the state of anxiety and the eager seeking of escape from it, the client often gets confused and frightened. He cannot account for his irrational behavior, and his failure to understand it adds to his anxiety and confusion. The function of the therapist's interpretation is to help the client see the connection between his present behavior and the original experience in which the client learned it. When the client sees the connection, he is said to have insight into his behavior. As his insight increases, accompanied always by emotional release of hidden fears, the client steadily improves.

A note of caution must here be exercised. When we say that the therapist interprets the meaning of the client's behavior, we do *not* mean that he presents the latter with a ready answer to his problems, but only that he aids him to discover his own solutions. Nor is the interpretation purely intellectual. It is doubtful that any client is ever "cured," either in individual or group therapy, by only a cognitive grasp of his difficulty. The therapist's interpretation is such as to lead the client to changes of feelings and emotions, and not only to an understanding of the process through which he is going.

In a description of the interaction process of group therapy it is also necessary to pay attention to *group size,* for it is an important condition of successful treatment. We already gave some consideration to this problem when we discussed the optimal size of problem-solving groups in Chapter 7.

In his work with children Slavson, for example, found that the "ideal" group numbered five or six members. He added, however, that the number can be increased to eight at later stages of treatment. If the group exceeds this number, the atmosphere becomes surcharged with excessive activity, and too many conflicting currents arise. Moreover, the therapist cannot play the parental role if the number becomes too large. He cannot attend to the individual children and their activities. "We found," he says, "that a roll of eight members brings to the meetings approximately the desirable number. . . ."[43] Hinckley and Hermann have found the same group size to be most satisfactory in their work. Their groups are composed of from six to eight clients. They have experimented with larger and smaller groups, but did not find them satisfactory.

Most group therapists who have reported on group size are rather well agreed on the consequences of using groups that are either too large or too small. The reasons are about the same as those for the effect of group size on problem-solving; thus showing that all small dynamic groups, irrespective of their functions, operate on the same basic principles.

When a group is too small, it slows down from sheer lack of sufficient interaction and stimulus value to the members. A kind of indolence and complacency takes the place of the urgency and spontaneity which are characteristic of all psychologically productive groups. There may also be the "inertia of inhibition," as Hinckley and Hermann describe it, or of hostility and mutual disagreement, which do not tend to develop when larger numbers would furnish the "necessary catalyst members."[44]

[43] Slavson, *An introduction to group therapy,* p. 120.
[44] Hinckley and Hermann, *Group treatment in psychotherapy,* p. 95.

If, on the other hand, the group exceeds the optimal number, interaction and participation are diminished; for there is insufficient time for each client to take part in the therapeutic process. The therapist likewise cannot fulfill his function, for his attention almost inevitably becomes too diffuse. Equally damaging is the fact that in an oversized group many feelings and ideas, even if they are expressed, do not get the attention they deserve. These factors set up a condition in which the movement of the group is effectively diminished, and it is slowed up "to the point of separation or a loss of the sense of belonging."[45]

The *composition* of the therapy group also enters into its success or failure. We saw the importance of this factor when we described interpersonal attractiveness and the effect on the group of participatory and supervisory leadership in Chapter 3. The composition of the group is, however, less important of nontherapeutic than therapeutic groups. Perhaps this is only seemingly so, for we do not have sufficient data to establish it as a fact. In therapy groups, clients are deliberately and systematically selected, whereas for the most part this is true of other groups only when they are set up for experimental purposes.

Although groups composed of clients with divergent complaints create more group movement than "segregated" types, group therapists tend to exclude certain types of cases. In a college community, as a rule, psychotics, "psychopathic" personalities, and homosexuals are rejected.[46]

The composition of children's therapy groups is particularly important. Slavson found that the age span originally selected, that between fourteen and seventeen years, was unsatisfactory; hence this was later changed so that the majority were under fourteen. Chronological age grouping, however, must frequently give way to considerations of personality maturity. The child's *personality* is also a crucial factor. Slavson observes that groups consisting of withdrawn and self-effacing children are poor subjects for group

[45] *Ibid.*, p. 96.
[46] See *ibid.*, p. 98.

therapy. They do not stimulate that minimal interaction which is necessary for group movement. Each child is too preoccupied with his own interest, and he tends to isolate himself from others. In such cases active and aggressive children are added to the group to stimulate interpersonal behavior.

On the basis of his wide experience with children's groups, Slavson has, moreover, found it advisable to confine membership to one sex. Still, the separation, as he points out, is arbitrary rather than pragmatically based. Hinckley and Hermann, too, as we have indicated, set up their later groups on the basis of one sex, but give us no hint of the rationale behind it. No doubt the fact that the sexual content of therapeutic sessions is often frank and unabashed, even at times uninhibitedly "vulgar," is a practical consideration. Custom and cultural imperatives probably play a part too.

Both experience and theoretical considerations point to the conclusion that the most therapeutically productive groups are those in which interactional balance is achieved and maintained. The aim is to have a group containing both inhibited and spontaneous, dependent and independent, aggressive and submissive, clients. In a dynamic group, where opposing forces are always pressing for equilibrium and locomotion, one element in the totality is often able to change the structure of the whole. Thus, one hyperactive client can upset a group more than two passive and retiring ones, especially if the former is also aggressive and the latter are submissive. To gain the maximum therapeutic value for every client, in short, the group must afford each of them the greatest amount of intellectual and emotional extraversion and the "right" amount of clinical support.

Concluding Remarks. From the foregoing description of the group-therapy process it is clear that it is essentially no different from the dynamic group relations which we discussed in preceding chapters. It contravenes none of the principles of group dynamics. On the contrary it supports and exemplifies them in a special area of group behavior. The group-therapeutic process is a dynamic group experience in which persons with a variety of psychological deficits learn to identify themselves with the therapist and other clients. In the process of identification they learn to accept others because they are warmly accepted by others, particularly the therapist. The process of acceptance strengthens or restores their capacity of relating themselves to other people, thereby restoring their self-esteem and increasing their emotional adequacy and their confidence in human beings. For a disturbed person perhaps nothing is more important for giving him a sense of well-being than the recognition of the fact that, despite his current shortcomings, he is accepted by the group. This is made possible by the fact that after the group has developed some degree of togetherness it accepts and understands its members. Their difficulties are recognized as common human weaknesses which can and will be straightened out. The therapeutic group, in short, is a device for mobilizing all the individual's potential resources, especially his emotions and newly gained insight, for making him at one with himself and his fellow human beings.

There is much that a brief survey like the present one has had to omit. For example, to describe the specific techniques which the therapist employs in group treatment lies outside the scope of this chapter, which is concerned with group therapy as a problem in group dynamics. These techniques are the mechanics, so to speak, of treatment, or the procedural acts, the trained skills, and the set of attitudes by which the therapist performs his work. This is a technical subject, a knowledge of which is not essential to an elementary understanding of therapy as a group process.

Closely related to the techniques are the *forms* of group psychotherapy, a discussion of which we also omit. The forms of group therapy are the particular social configurations in which the treatment takes place. The best known of these are *activity group therapy, psychodrama,* and *therapeutic discussion groups.*[47]

Activity groups, which have been used by Slavson since 1943, are children's club-like associations, in which they play, engage in artistic and handicraft work, hold meetings, give parties, and the like. All the conditions which arise in the groups that we have discussed may develop, but the therapist does not, as in the other groups, identify and reflect the children's feelings nor engage in interpretations of their psychological trends. The therapeutic benefits are derived from *membership* in permissive groups in the presence of a gentle, sympathetic, but impartial, therapist.

Psychodrama, used by J. L. Moreno, is a social situation, or a staged play but without rehearsal, in which the clients spontaneously act out, before others, their inner tension, fears, and aggressions. Contrary to a popular belief people can be induced through participation to express freely their private and concealed emotional and ideational trends. Judging by Moreno's reports, there can be little doubt that in a psychodramatic relationship highly constricted and inhibited persons experience a liberation of feelings and develop a health-inducing spontaneity.

Therapeutic group discussion has no official proponents. It is a part of group dynamics which is well known but whose therapeutic value has not been the object of much study. It may take place in any dynamic group, especially problem-solving groups; and it will have therapeutic value if it enables the individual to discover his problems, air his feelings, and develop confidence in interpersonal relations. The role of the therapist, *as therapist,* is minimized to the point where he becomes a member among members more than in other therapeutic situations. When he occasionally interjects himself as a therapist into the group process, it is only to interpret to the group the source of its tensions.[48]

[47] While we are aware that these forms are usually referred to as *techniques* of group therapy, we believe that they are the social or group situations, or the contrived conditions, in which the techniques are exercised.

[48] See J. Kelnar, Treatment of inter-personal relations in groups, *J. soc. Issues,* 3 (1947), 29–34.

We must also forgo any discussion of the application of group psychotherapy to other than conventional personality and adjustment problems, such as overcoming racial and cultural tensions.[49] It is clear that race prejudice and cultural conflicts are no less forms of learning deficits than many other difficulties in human relations. Race prejudice and discrimination, as social psychologists have shown, are injurious to the mental health of both the discriminator and his victim. It is not, therefore, impractical to propose an extensive use of therapy groups to correct these dangerous and harmful distortions in human relations.

CONCLUSION

Our aim in this chapter has been to present a comprehensive rather than a detailed report on the nature of group psychotherapy. We have in no sense concerned ourselves with the *practice* of group psychotherapy, and no reader should delude himself into thinking that a knowledge of the content of this chapter will fit him for the role of a group psychotherapist. We have included it in a book on group dynamics out of the conviction that it exemplifies group-dynamics principles in clear and highly charged forms. It demonstrates the power of group influence, especially its capacity for inducing desirable psychological changes in human behavior. Just as the wavering individual finds confidence in his beliefs when they correspond with those of others, so the anxious and fearful client gains ego strength through the supportive attitudes of the therapist and other clients. Therapeutic groups differ from others in their *intent*, not in their dynamic processes, for these are essentially alike in all groups; and where they differ, they do so in degree not in kind. In illustration of the latter we cite the fact that, generally speaking, the *identification* of clients with the therapist and with one another—or the libidinal tie, to use a psychoanalytical term—is usually more intense than in non-therapeutic groups. Because they are fundamentally ego-

[49] See G. Konopka, Group therapy in overcoming racial and cultural tensions, *Amer. J. Orthopsychiat.*, 17 (1947), 693–99.

supportive, and not only pleasure-giving, problem-solving, or decision-making, they are truly *psychotherapeutic*.

While individual psychotherapy has worked for a long time on the premise that functional behavior disorders are essentially disturbances in human relationships, it has not proceeded on this assumption as consistently and indefatigably as has group therapy. As far as treatment is concerned, no other approach employs the concept of disturbed human relations as fully as group therapy, and no other technique can afford the same realistic setting. In group therapy the client not only verbalizes his disturbance; he actually experiences it in his relations with the members of the group. Although in individual therapy the patient can give free expression of his hatred for the parental figure and speak freely of the envy for his siblings, in group treatment he experiences these feelings in concrete interaction with others in the group. It is very difficult in individual therapy for the patient to show, except verbally, the attitudes that other people in his life had toward one another—of parents toward each other, of siblings among themselves. In group therapy the attitudes of clients toward one another and toward the therapist are there to see and experience. This enlarged group experience is mostly denied to the client in individual treatment, but it is an indisputable reality in group therapy. This enlarged group experience aids the client in forming a more realistic image of himself and of others, and to accept positively rather than rebelliously the demands of the living group.

Finally, the therapeutic group has a maturing effect upon the clients because it affords opportunity for close social relations with others. Many people are psychologically deficient, as we saw, because they cannot establish warm relationships with others. One of the greatest values—perhaps the greatest—of therapy groups is that they offer many individuals the humanizing influence which only intimate relations with others can fully generate.

Slavson states the foregoing well, and we can do no better than to quote him in full. He writes:

> The ability to relate oneself to other persons is the crux of human happiness. To many all relations have brought unpleasantness. The prime aim of psychotherapy is to help the patient establish constructive relations first with the therapist, later with other people, and finally with the larger world.[50]

[50] Slavson, *An introduction to group therapy*, p. 202. For the reader who wishes to learn the practical techniques of group psychotherapy, we suggest the following: G. R. Bach, *Intensive group psychotherapy* (New York: The Ronald Press Co., 1954); R. H. Corsini, *Methods of group psychotherapy* (New York: The Blakiston Division, McGraw-Hill Book Co., Inc., 1957). For a technical treatment of the subject, including the methodology of research and the therapy of psychotics, see F. B. Powdermaker and J. D. Frank, *Group psychotherapy* (Cambridge, Mass.: Harvard University Press, 1953).

Part V

CONCLUSION: GROUP DYNAMICS IN PERSPECTIVE

CHAPTER 15

A Critique of Group Dynamics

In the foregoing chapters we presented a detailed exposition and analysis of the most significant problems of group dynamics. We discussed the nature of dynamic groups, their formation and development, and those topics which have to date made up the crucial issues of our discipline: intergroup relations, leadership, collective learning and problem-solving, and role dynamics. We also devoted a chapter to a topic on which agreement is not easy to reach, but one which has obtruded itself into group-dynamics research and theory—the role of personality structure in group behavior. We brought together many facts and ideas, furthermore, which bear important relations to education, group therapy, and industry. Finally, we presented two topics which are not yet a part of the "tradition" of group dynamics, although, as we tried to show, they deserve the most careful attention of the group dynamicist, namely, a conception of the community as a dynamic group and the interpretation of political behavior as a group phenomenon.

In this review of the field of group dynamics we have made every effort to discuss principles and generalizations based on published empirical and experimental research.

This has inevitably posed the problem of selection, for the literature on most of the problems is enormous. In the process of selection many investigations had obviously to be omitted. Our criteria have been clear and simple. We selected those studies, first, which thus far have stood the test of time and have become standard references in our field. By this standard a number of references are, even in our new discipline, somewhat old! In the second place, we chose those studies, irrespective of their status in the stream of development, which are most germane to the structure and organization of the chapters as we have presented them.

In view of the foregoing considerations the reader should have a fairly clear and comprehensive knowledge of the subject matter of group dynamics; and he should now be ready to take an over-all look at the field, observing its possibilities, limitations, and some of its defects.

AN OVERVIEW OF GROUP DYNAMICS

When one carefully studies the prodigious literature on the relation of the individual and the group, both in psychology and sociology, one is struck by a marked characteristic. Not only in the past but to a lesser extent even today discussions are shot through with dichotomies and disjunctions, with "ands" and "ors." Thus the individual, if he is not pitted against the group is separated from it, even though he is always recognized to be a "part" of it. The leader is often conceived as a towering individual who by virtue of his "gifts" stands above the "crowd" and exhorts, compels, or persuades it to do his bidding. However, to those for whom this picture of the leader is offensive, there is another one: the leader is but one among others, prudent and self-effacing in the web of democratic interactions.

Again, we call attention to the fact that we have extended, and we hope thereby enriched, the meaning of group dynamics by relating it to the more inclusive societal organization. This should be salutary. In any event, we have expanded the horizon of group dynamics to include educational, industrial, community, and political organizations. We take group dynamics beyond the narrow confines of "small group" research by relating the group to larger functional units, such as organization groups, and the more inclusive social environment, at the same time, always keeping our attention on the main problem of *group behavior.* We have also given attention to group therapy and have related it, as such earlier workers as Bion and Redl have done, to the intensely emotional aspects of group relations. In so doing we are in line with recent developments in group dynamics.[1]

We hope that the preceding chapters have dispelled in the reader the narrow and faulty impressions of person-group relationships, widened his conception of the group, and helped him to understand better its holistic character.

Finally, while there is much disagreement among group dynamicists regarding numerous problems, while inconsistencies abound, and while there is no complete consensus regarding the subject matter of group dynamics, there are growing indications of what our discipline is about. The preceding chapters give the reader, we believe, an introductory glimpse of its subject matter today.

To help the reader form a coherent picture of group dynamics, let us present an over-all view of the field.

FACTORS IN GROUP MOVEMENT. The fundamental aim of group dynamics is to understand the factors that underlie group locomotion, especially those that initiate and sustain group productivity. This involves a search for the numerous and complex forces in groups that facilitate or inhibit group action. Among these forces are the character of the interaction process among individuals, such as the amount of participation; the degree of cohesiveness of the group; the value premises upon which the group's acts are per-

[1] See C. I. Barnard, *The functions of the executive* (Cambridge, Mass.: Harvard University Press, 1938); W. F. Whyte, *Patterns for industrial peace* (New York: Harper & Bros., 1951); H. A. Simon, *Administrative behavior* (New York: The Macmillan Co., 1947); G. C. Homans, *The human group* (New York: Harcourt, Brace & Co., Inc., 1950). See also F. Redl, Resistance in therapy groups, *Psychiatry, 5* (1942), 573–96. Also, W. F. Bion, Experience in groups, I-VI, *Hum. Relat., 1* (1948), 314–20, 487–96; *2* (1949), 13–22, 295–303; *3* (1950), 3–14, 395–402.

formed, such as democratic or autocratic standards of behavior; the kind and quality of leadership acts initiated by any of its members; the internal structure of the group, such as degrees of permissiveness, freedom, communication, and competitiveness; and the like. These forces have been described and their roles in group locomotion made clear.

Practically all serious discussions of changes in group relationships, even those that consciously question the importance of the leader as an initiator, recognize the function of a central person in group movement.[2] For this reason research on leadership has been very extensive.

Few, if any, topics in group dynamics bear out more clearly the difficulty in conceptualizing important factors than leadership. Our own struggle with the problem is evident. At the present writing it is impossible to determine the exact relation between the personality of a central person and the activities of a group. Some research has shown that not much can be inferred concerning group operation from a knowledge of the personalities of its members, the leader included. The study by Cattell and Stice, however, shows that personality is important, but not in the traditional sense of dominance. Sanford found that the needs of members influenced leadership in groups.[3] Even physical prowess seems to play a part, although its influence varies with class membership, it being important in disturbed lower-class, but unimportant in normal middle-class, boys. Factors like cautiousness and, to use Jennings' terms again, choice-daring and choice-initiative on the part of the leader, have been found to affect consensus.[4]

[2] The concept of a *central person*, which we used on several occasions, naturally presents itself to anyone contemplating on the changes in centers of potential that take place in a dynamic group. To our knowledge the term was introduced into the *literature* of group dynamics by F. Redl in the article in *Psychiatry* cited in footnote 1. The central person is also called the *focal person* by W. C. Schutz, in What makes groups productive?, *Hum. Relat.*, *8* (1955), 429–65.

[3] F. Sanford, *Authoritarianism and leadership* (Philadelphia: Institute for Research in Human Relations, 1950).

[4] See M. Horwitz, The recall of interrupted group tasks: an experimental study of individual motivation in relation to group goals, *Hum. Relat.*, *7* (1954), 3–38.

As we have often said, the dynamic group, like the individual, is always a part of a larger group, institution, or societal organization. Consequently, a great deal of recent research in group dynamics has focused on the effect of the more inclusive social relationships upon group behavior. The vast literature on human relations in industry, some of which we reviewed in Chapter 9, has attempted to deal with this problem. The discussion in Chapter 5 of intergroup relations, focusing on the fate of minority groups in the larger community, deals with the same problems. The cohesiveness of the minority or of the dominant group depends, of course, not inconsiderably on its status in the community. Lewin, in 1935, and Thibault, in 1950, found a definite relation between the cohesiveness of a group and its status among other groups.[5] Especially interesting is the almost wholly neglected study of the effect of cultural variation on group performance. In this connection Gyr's study of the effect of culture on committee behavior furnishes us with an interesting lead.[6]

The psychological structure of the group, which we discussed in Chapter 2, may be *conceptualized* on the basis of interindividual influence, sociometric choice, role dynamics, group norms, and attractiveness to members.

Interindividual influence refers to the ability of a leader or members to guide the behavior of others or of the whole group along desirable channels. In a recent study, to add to the list already cited, this influence, described as the "dynamics of power," is shown to be of two main kinds: *behavioral contagion* and *direct influence*. Behavioral contagion is "the spontaneous pickup or imitation by other children of a behavior initiated by one member of the group where the initiator did not display any intention of getting the others to do what he did." Direct influence is of a kind "in which the actor initiates behavior which has the mani-

[5] K. Lewin, Psycho-sociological problems of a minority group, *Charact. & Pers.*, 3 (1935), 175–87; J. W. Thibaut, An experimental study of the cohesiveness of underprivileged groups, *Hum. Relat.*, 3 (1950), 251–78.

[6] J. Gyr, Analysis of committee member behavior in four cultures, *Hum. Relat.*, 4 (1951), 193–202.

fest objective of affecting the behavior of another member of the group."[7]

Interindividual influences, or power relations, as they are typically described in political science, hold a significant place in political behavior, as we saw in Chapter 11. In the political sphere power or authority is often vested in a leader, who may be democratic or autocratic; or it may reside, as in a genuine democracy, in the collective deliberations of a people. As we have frequently noted, power in such a group is diffused or shared. It lies in the "wills" of people, in a community of free men, not in the "sovereign power" of a nation, or in an abstraction called the State.

Since complete diffusion of power, however, is only an ideal and not an actuality, some people are bound to be frustrated and dissatisfied in their desire to share authority. This has been found to be true even in small groups, especially as they increase in size. Thus in a small discussion group everyone has an "equal" opportunity to direct or influence others, whereas in a business organization the opportunity diminishes with its size and complexity.

Because influence or power is always subject to curtailment, especially as the size of the group increases, there is a tendency to develop splinter groups, or subgroups. In Chapter 5 we gave some attention to their formation. We can add to what we said there that, generally speaking, as the size of the group membership increases the formation of subgroups also increases. This was demonstrated in a recent investigation of consensus and disagreement by Paul Hare.[8]

Sociometric choice we have discussed only superficially. Briefly, the sociometric view holds that the structure or organization of a group may be determined by the valence of its members—by the positive and negative choices persons make of other individuals. Homans' study of the Bank Wiring Room disclosed that attraction among individuals was

[7] R. Lippitt, N. Polansky, F. Redl, and S. Rosen, The dynamics of power, *Hum. Relat.*, 5 (1952), p. 37.

[8] A. Paul Hare, Interaction and consensus in different sized groups, *Amer. sociol. Rev.*, 17 (1952), 261–67.

a function of interaction. The point that we are trying to make is that the structure of the group can be studied by investigating the attractions and repulsions of people toward one another.[9]

The structure of the group is affected, further, by the organization of the functional roles of its members. The very meaning of group organization implies a distribution of functions, or the enactment of functional roles. Even in a democratic group structure the leader's role does not remain his own throughout the life span of the group, but is distributed among the membership. So conceived, any person is a leader at any time when he enacts an expected functional role. Thus, although a considerable body of research on group structure has centered about the leadership role, it is important to note the fact that group structure is determined by the totality of the functional roles assumed or enacted by all its members, and not only by its leader.[10]

People in groups also behave in ways motivated not by their role position but by the set of values or norms of their groups. This was discussed at some length in Chapter 12, with particular emphasis on the importance of reference groups. The norms of one's reference groups have much to do with the structural formation of groups. We are referring to the pressures toward conformity which we examined in Chapter 13. Asch's study of group pressure in modifying judgments, Newcomb's study of the effect of norms in a college community, Whyte's description of the "corner boys," and others testify to the powerful influence of social norms upon the structure or organization of groups.

[9] See H. H. Jennings, *Leadership and isolation* (2d ed.; New York: Longmans, Green, & Co., Inc., 1950).

[10] This is one of the confused areas of group dynamics. The difficulty is in part semantic no doubt, but it is also due to the divergence in point of view and the inconsistencies of investigational results. For a variety of views, see R. Lippitt, *An experimental study of authoritarian and democratic group atmospheres*, Univ. Iowa Studies in Child Welfare, Vol. 16, No. 3 (Iowa City: University of Iowa Press, 1940); F. Redl, Group emotion and leadership, *Psychiatry*, 5 (1942), 573–96; R. B. Cattell, New concepts for measuring leadership in terms of group syntality, *Hum. Relat.*, *4* (1951), 161–84.

Finally, the structure of the group is conditioned by its attractiveness to its members. This factor was discussed in detail in Chapter 3 in the analysis of the nature of group cohesiveness. Cohesiveness exists in proportion to the need of belongingness by the group's members and to the opportunities which the group affords in satisfying the need. Thus here once more we see the inseparability of the individual and the group. Inasmuch as group attractiveness and cohesion are discussed in detail in Chapter 3, no more need be said here.

Action Research. We have not discussed "action research" as such, although its methods and results have appeared in various places in this book. We did in effect deal with it in our brief reference to changing people's food habits, in our account of research in certain industrial situations, in the report on the work to eliminate racial and cultural discrimination, and again in the brief description of community self-surveys.

Group dynamics, we have said, is interested in knowing how groups form and how they may be changed. When we focus our attention on techniques or programs for effecting orderly and desirable changes in groups and institutions, we are concerned with action research. This aspect of group dynamics may be defined, accordingly, as that phase of our inquiry which (1) studies the conditions under which group changes take place and (2) indicates how best to utilize our knowledge of how to control and direct these changes in the interests of the group. So conceived, action research is the integration of scientific facts about groups and the practical means of changing them in the desired direction. For this reason it is sometimes called by the not-too-happy term "human engineering." This term implies that scientific facts and methods are applied to changing real-life situations. It is founded on one of Lewin's well-known observations which we have stated before, namely, that when people discover the source of their own hatreds and prejudices toward others they are more likely to change them, because these are their own discoveries instead of external impositions. People believe truths of their own finding, according to Lewin, in a manner similar to their belief in themselves.

While we recognize Lewin's contribution to recent action research, he has only revitalized it and brought it up to date. We agree with Laura Thompson's estimation that action research is very old, even though we do not follow her in saying that it is as old as human society.[11] Her description of its leading characteristics, however, is sound. It originates from the need of people in a group to solve urgent practical problems, such as race discrimination, for example. For its solution it requires the cooperation and participation of both scientists and "user-volunteers." The scientists, or "human engineers," play a dual functional role in the effort, that is, they must be "scientist-technicians" and integrative leaders at the same time. They must, as Thompson states it, stimulate, draw out, and foster the leadership qualities of members and subordinate their own roles "except as catalysts of group potentialities."[12]

As scientist-technician, the practitioner of action research must be a *fact-finder.* As we said before, good will, while good, is not good enough. Recommended actions must be based on facts or reliable information. In the self-survey of Northtown which is described in Chapter 10, we stressed the importance of fact-finding. The fact-finding consisted of interviews with families, real estate men and other businessmen. The fact-gathering covered, the reader will recall, discrimination in housing, in employment, in the public schools, and in public services.

However, facts alone, like good will, do not take us far enough. Bare facts are meaningless until they are shared with others and their implications are understood. This involves *feedback* and *interpretation.* Both are important because they generate group awareness of the problem and elicit critical evaluation of the data.

[11] L. Thompson, Action research among American Indians, *Sci. Monthly, 70* (1950), 34–40. For Kurt Lewin's initial discussion of action research, see his Action research and minority problems, *J. soc. Issues, 2* (1946), 34–46.

[12] *Ibid.*, p. 34.

Feedback is a communications technique by means of which the information-giver may observe the effect of his information upon others. This may be done directly by the fact-finder or by means of a recording machine which plays back to the entire group the activities during a period of time. In this way everyone engaged in the project is familiarized with everyone else's contribution to it. We have indicated some of the errors and distortions that result when the communication channels are not functioning adequately, and we have described the negative and destructive effects of poor transmission of messages among the members of a group. The purpose of the feedback is to share all the facts and lay them open to analysis and evaluation. This sounds easy enough, but it requires experience to inform a group of all the ramifications of facts and ideas that come together in the course of an investigation.[13]

Interpretation, or *evaluation* of facts or data, is essential in all scientific research. Contrary to a popular notion, facts and figures do *not* speak for themselves. We are reminded of the trenchant observation by Alfred Marshall, the famous economist: "The most reckless and treacherous of all theorists is he who professes to let facts and figures speak for themselves."[14] Facts, in other words, have to be interpreted and evaluated before they can be purposefully used.

In action research interpretation is not confined to an examination of and acquaintance with the facts. Perhaps even more important, as far as eventual action is concerned, is the evaluation of the degree of member-participation, the kinds of tensions, conflicts, and rivalries which are generated in most active groups, the quality of the leadership, the extent to which each member appraises his own shortcomings, and the like. Interpretation, in the final analysis, is the act of *group self-evaluation.* The chief merit of this self-evaluation by the group is that it leads the members "to

[13] For a lucid description of feedback and examples illustrating its operation, see D. H. Jenkins, Feedback and group self-evaluation, *J. soc. Issues, 4* (1948), 50–60.

[14] A. C. Pigou (ed.), *Memorials of Alfred Marshall* (New York: The Macmillan Co., 1925), p. 108.

become more sensitive to the difficulties in interaction and discussion . . . their causes, and some techniques for avoiding them."[15]

This brief overview of group dynamics, reviewing the numerous but not well-integrated concepts, principles, and research problems of its development during the past half-century, shows that group behavior is always a function of two inseparable and extraordinarily complex factors, namely, *persons* and the *set of relations* among them which we call the *group*. Although the attitudes and other individual characteristics of persons are modified when they interact with other persons, these attitudes and characteristics are not dissolved or obliterated. To some extent the person remains autonomous even when he is deeply involved in subtle and intricate relations with others. Personality is modified but not eliminated.

The group that emerges out of—or better, that is comprised of—the dynamic relations of persons to one another, is defined by its psychological structure or organization, its leadership structure, its social climate, its attracting or repelling valences, its system of roles dynamically conceived, and so forth. While research has furnished us with a far better understanding of group behavior than men possessed fifty years ago, until we have empirical descriptions and experimental demonstrations of the complicated *relations between persons*, we shall be unable to predict successfully the behavior of either persons or groups.

Anyone who has embarked on the tangled road to a coherent systematization of group dynamics, as has the present writer, must be ready to face disappointment. In the present stage of its development a complete systematization cannot be successfully achieved. Any attempt to do so would be tantamount to superimposing upon the study of group dynamics a conceptualization which is not justified by the

[15] Jenkins, Feedback and group self-evaluation, p. 60. For an illustration of its concrete use in the Northtown survey, see the reference by C. Selltiz and M. H. Wormser (issue eds.), Community self-surveys: an approach to social change, *J. soc. Issues, 5,* No. 2 (1949).

piecemeal experimentation by which it has come into being. We hazard the opinion that if such a conceptualization were indeed imposed upon it, many—perhaps most—of the intelligent and devoted workers in the field would hardly recognize their own formulation. Meanwhile, no one need sit around waiting, for to declare an intellectual moratorium until our concepts and principles are more meticulously systematized and defined would be utterly fatal.

SOME CRITICAL CONSIDERATIONS

Group dynamics is a heady wine which easily beclouds evaluation by some of its investigators. Some of the latter have made pronouncements that at times sound like the shibboleths of a new doctrine. They have infused group dynamics with an obscurantism that it ill deserves. Group dynamics is neither a cult nor a doctrine, but a serious attempt by many capable researchers to attain an understanding of group behavior by means of careful and controlled research.

Some workers, carried away by their uncritical excitement, have understandably alienated serious psychologists and other social scientists. Many of the latter are repelled by the fad-like character of some aspect of group dynamics and many more are unreceptive to its unsupported claims.[16]

The Nonrelevance of Its Conceptual Basis. Many recent ideas and applications of group dynamics have their source in the theories and researches of Kurt Lewin. These we must examine critically. It is a scientific commonplace that the concepts with which one investigates a given phenomenon must touch or converge somewhere in the process. If there is no functional connection between them, then the concepts, while interesting in themselves perhaps, have no logical place in the system which purports to explain the events. This is flagrantly the case when fundamental con-

[16] While Gunderson's evaluation is somewhat of a caricature, its serious strictures deserve attention. As a teacher of speech he has been thoroughly exposed to its excesses. See R. G. Gunderson, Dangers in group dynamics, *Relig. Educ.*, *46* (1951), 342–44. See also his article This group-dynamics furor, *Sch. & Soc.*, *74* (1951), 97–100.

cepts in one branch of science are inappropriate or inapplicable in another. This situation is not uncommon in the social sciences when they borrow concepts from the physical sciences. As a consequence of this practice many descriptions and explanations of social and psychological phenomena in physical science terms are only analogical, not fundamental.

There is no objection in principle to the use of such concepts in the behavioral sciences. The only requirement is that in their use they not be distorted or falsified. But such distortions and falsifications are ever present dangers and frequent occurrences. Philosophers of science, whose business it is to investigate such problems, have frequently called attention to this error.[17] Lewin, it is now widely recognized committed this error in his theoretical analysis of behavior. He did not, contrary to the opinions of some of his followers, establish a functional relationship between the "mathematical" constructs which he used and the individual and social behavior which he described by means of them. Let us critically examine these constructs.

The concept of force. In a devastating criticism of the use of physical and mathematical concepts in psychology, which may well prove to be definitive, London takes Lewin severely to task for the latter's indiscriminate and inappropriate use of physical and mathematical constructs.[18]

The construct of *force* was used liberally by Lewin, despite the fact that modern relativity has outgrown the need for it. The concept of force was invented by Newton to account for the deviation of a free particle from its straight line of motion. Newton, having no other geometry to draw upon, was impelled to this type of explanation because he

[17] See, for example, M. Planck, *The philosophy of physics* (New York: W. W. Norton & Co., Inc., 1936); P. Frank, *Modern science and its philosophy* (Cambridge, Mass.: Harvard University Press, 1949); and H. Margenau, *The nature of physical reality* (New York: McGraw-Hill Book Co., Inc., 1950).

[18] I. D. London, Psychologists' misuse of the auxiliary concepts of physics and mathematics, *Psychol. Rev., 51* (1944), 266–91. Our own critique owes much to this article.

was bound by the Euclidean geometry of physical space. Modern relativity, not being similarly bound but able instead to draw freely on the constructs of non-Euclidean geometry, can account for motion without positing a hypothetical "force" to explain it. The deviation of a free particle from its line of motion is an artifact of Euclidean geometry, the geometry of straight lines. In a geometry of curved lines, or "geodesics," there is no such deviation; and since there is no deviation, the concept of force, which was invented to explain it, is superfluous.

If he looks back to Chapter 2 in which we briefly described Lewin's theoretical constructs for group dynamics, the reader will see that we omit the concept of force. This omission can be understood in the light of the foregoing remarks.

How did Lewin define this construct? It is not easy to state Lewin's definition of force because Lewin himself stated it in different ways. One of his definitions is "the direction and strength of the tendency to change."[19]

There are several types of forces, according to Lewin. *Driving* forces impel a person toward a positive or away from a negative valence, or attraction center. They are the sources of locomotion, or goal-directed behavior. When locomotion is hindered by physical or social obstacles, these barriers are called *restraining* forces. They do not lead to locomotion, but they influence the effect of driving forces. A driving force may be the desire to take a leadership position in the group, and the restraining force may be the resistance of others or the limitations of the individual, or both. An *induced* force is one that goes counter to a person's driving forces, but upon which he acts nonetheless because of social and other pressures. When this force operates, one acts in accordance with another's wishes, rather than according to one's own needs, or self-forces.[20] When forces corre-

[19] K. Lewin, *Field theory in social science* (New York: Harper & Bros., 1951), p. 256.

[20] This is not Lewin's but the writer's own term to describe the former's "forces corresponding to own needs."

spond neither to self-needs nor to the demands of others, they are called *impersonal* forces. The presence or absence of the latter determines the reaction of the individual and the atmosphere of the situation or group.[21]

It is clear that the phenomena described by the concept of force can be represented by other terms, such as *tension,* or excitation state, and *valence,* or attraction to and repulsion by an object, individual, or situation. These are psychological variables which are known to operate in human behavior, both individual and collective.

The concept of *field,* at once so useful and ill-defined, can be neither wholly accepted nor rejected. As originally defined by Lewin it presents, in the face of modern relativity field theory, a paradox. In field theory everything is in motion in relation to something else, and yet the concept of field in modern physics is essentially a *static* one.[22] The past, present, and future of any motion exist simultaneously in a static field. Motion is a curve, a "world line" or "world path," or a set of successive "now's" of an observer stationed in space-time.[23] London makes the telling point that an event in relativity is "a point in a static space-time continuum which is connected with prior and future events by means of world lines. It does *not* result from the dynamic interaction of physical factors, as Lewin would aver, but from the intersection of an observer's world cross-section with the world lines embedded in the static four-dimensional space-time continuum."[24]

Our own definition of the concept of field in Chapter 2 is not a mathematical one. It is descriptive, explanatory, and pragmatic. A social field, we said, is any acting or changing group to which the behavior of individuals, regions, and subgroups may be ordered. Thus conceived it is dynamic, rather than static.

[21] See Lewin, *Field theory in social science,* pp. 256–60.

[22] London, Psychologists' misuse of auxiliary concepts, p. 273.

[23] *Ibid.,* p. 273.

[24] *Ibid.,* p. 274. Lewin's position on this point is stated in his *Principles of topological psychology* (New York: McGraw-Hill Book Co., Inc., 1936), p. 33.

Closely related to the notion of a field is the concept of space, which has regions, subregions, and barriers. Inasmuch as we have no need for Lewin's concept of *hodological space,* we omitted it from our discussion in Chapter 2. London is quite right in asserting that Lewin invented the concept of hodological space in order to get around the inconsistency between vectors and other directed locomotions in a topological space which is *directionless.* Moreover, the concept is not admitted in pure topology. It had, accordingly, to be invented. Hodological space refers to the direction through the path of locomotion within a field. It is the individual's "life-space" in a particular situation at a particular moment of time. It is, accordingly, not infinitely divisible but is composed of certain units or regions.[25]

Not only has the concept of hodological space been thus far resistant to strict mathematical formulation, but it has been unproductive empirically. We can describe individual and group behavior by means of social and psychological vectors; no other "directional" concept is necessary. When people direct their actions toward a common goal, they are behaving vectorially; that is, they are moving in a certain direction with all the psychological energy that is available to them by the character of the field situation at the moment. This is a nonmathematical and purely descriptive use of the concept of vector. It does not commit us to anything more than the notion that all behavior has directional properties in that it is aimed toward a goal. From our point of view, the "energy" behind the impulsion toward a goal is not measurable in physical quantities but in terms of an interval scale; for there is no assumption in our interpretation that it has mass and velocity, as in the case of physical vectors.

Enough has been said, we think, to describe the ambitious attempt by Lewin to recast psychology, including group behavior, along rigorous mathematical lines. He not only failed, but his efforts show that its mathematization is not only spurious but probably impossible along Lewinian lines.

[25] Lewin, *Field theory and social science,* p. 26.

SCIENCE AND THE DEMOCRATIC BIAS. No one familiar with the early formulations of group dynamics, especially those of Lewin, doubts that they were motivated by powerful scientific and theoretical interests. Lewin's labors along these lines alone are sufficient to attest to this conclusion. Despite his failure—in our judgment, of course—to reconstruct psychology along mathematical lines, the prodigious efforts and the lively scientific imagination which he displayed in constructing a science of individual and social behavior are eloquent tributes to Lewin's stature as a scientist and theoretician. Aside from a few distinguished sociologists, there have been no psychologists who have as uncompromisingly stressed the inseparability of the group and its members; and that all problems of individual conduct, when comprehensively viewed, turn out to be problems of group behavior.

There is, however, another side to Lewin's many-sided interests which has created confusion and considerably aided in creating ambiguities regarding the foundation and the aims of group dynamics. In this he has been overwhelmingly helped by some of his students, followers, and enthusiastic devotees. That some of the latter have carried his own enthusiasm to unwarranted extremes is no fault of Lewin's, of course; but that his own bias has given them a strong moral justification, there can be little doubt.

A fundamental bias of Lewin's was his rather panacean conception of democracy. From his valid premise that by himself man cannot discover, let alone validate, truth he inferred that scientific propositions are social in character. No one today quarrels with this conclusion. But working together to discover and validate truth is an activity that can be, and has been, successfully carried out in other than "democratic" climates. Lewin mistakenly ascribes a maximum efficiency to democratic groups. This assertion is contraverted by the examples of autocratic and totalitarian regimes. Because of the cooperative and generally acceptant atmosphere of democratic groups, because of their essentially *humanizing* value, Lewin prefers them to all others.

So do we. But these groups do not automatically foster efficiency, productiveness, and good will. These results, as Lewin knew, have to be worked for. Consequently, the egalitarian groups in which he had boundless faith must be "controlled" or "manipulated"—words which are disagreeable to the "democratic" purist. Lewin was very well aware of this fact, and saw no way to escape from it. He recognized that management, for example, can fulfill its function only by means of "group manipulation."[26]

The preference for democratic groups is based on the fact that their manipulative acts are forms of inducement not coercions. The inducement is performed by "democratic" leaders. Democratic groups thus depend significantly on "good" or "right" leadership. This emphasis on the need for "good" leadership is not, however, based on the idealized conception of democracy which permeates the bulk of the theoretical and operational research in group dynamics; but rather, it reflects the stubborn realities of political experience. In this infidelity between ideal and fact—if fact it is—Lewin and his followers betray a surprising inconsistency. For while group dynamicists write enthusiastically about the dignity of man, they here embrace a view of him that by implication, if not expressly, denies it. Twenty years ago Lewin showed this wavering belief in the capability of men in groups to direct their own destiny by saying that men need to be guided in the way of social righteousness by leaders who understand the former's interests better than they do themselves. Man does not know where his "true" interests lie; therefore he has to be guided by leaders who will protect him from himself.[27]

A condition of indecision, not to say ambivalence, runs through a great deal of the writing on group dynamics concerning the foregoing problem. We are reminded on every

[26] K. Lewin, *Resolving social conflicts* (New York: Harper & Bros., 1948), p. 83. Since this chapter was written, the scientific achievements of the Russians support our criticism of Lewin.

[27] K. Lewin, Field theory and experiment in social psychology: concepts and methods, *Amer. J. Sociol., 44* (1939), 868–96.

side that people in groups will not automatically generate group movement and participate in collective deliberation. A central person or change agent, usually a leader, is necessary to initiate deliberation or action. Even in the most democratic group, especially in complex organizations, directives must be issued and control maintained from above. Hierarchization, we saw in Chapter 2, is probably a characteristic of all viable groups with a history, however short it may be. Control by "higher-ups," for example, is assuredly a characteristic of modern industry, even of that with the most democratic worker-management relationship, as we saw in Chapter 9. Even the most ardent exponent of democratic relationships in complex organizations cannot deny that people have to conform their behavior with the standards and expectations of those in authority.[28]

At the same time that they recognize the inescapability of control by others, many group dynamicists repeatedly stress the necessity of leadership-sharing, the importance of diffused leadership—on occasion even talking as if the leader had no place in a democratic group at all. "Leaderless" groups, to which we have already referred in Chapter 6, come perilously close to "liquidating" the leader altogether.[29] There is no logical, and certainly no moral, objection to encouraging the development of leaderless groups. The difficulty lies in demonstrating the fact that they are indeed "leaderless." In some of the groups studied some individuals, while in no sense designated as leaders or invested with leadership properties, nevertheless became central persons and initiated interaction. This situation is no doubt due to the fact that the central persons brought into the group with them, as we all do inescapably, some of their status qualities

[28] See R. R. P. French, Jr., in G. Murphy (ed.), *Human nature and enduring peace* (Boston: Houghton Mifflin Co., 1945), p. 325.

[29] The reader should consult the references on leaderless groups in Chapter 6. We suggest in addition, the following: L. F. Carter, Leadership and small group behavior, in M. Sherif and M. O. Wilson (eds.), *Group relations at the crossroads* (New York: Harper & Bros., 1953); and M. E. Roseborough, Experimental studies of small groups, *Psychol. Bull.*, *50* (1953), 275–303.

as individuals, their attitudes, their ascendant personalities, and the like.[30]

The indecision and ambiguity regarding freedom and control is reflected, finally, in the difficulty of fully harmonizing the advocacy of leaderless groups and the importance of leadership-training. It is hardly logical for group dynamics to stress diffuse leadership and leaderless groups and at the same time espouse and set up programs for training group leaders. If groups can perform their functions without leaders, or if leaders are bound to emerge in certain interactive situations anyway, then training persons to become leaders becomes a dubious enterprise.

At the Training Laboratory in Group Development, work with so-called leaderless groups has been experimented on with great interest. Its "leaders"—this is a paradox—believe that as the group develops the central person whom we usually designate as the leader will become unnecessary. But too often this does not happen. Still the believers in leaderless groups are sure that the confusion resulting from the absence of an established leadership would eventually lead to agreement. A virtue is even made of the confusion in one case by calling it "feeling-draining," the kind of imprecise and dubious but superficially reassuring term that is invented with great facility by a few practitioners of group dynamics. But as Whyte in describing a case which he observed points out, no agreement came, for "the group could not agree on a topic to agree upon."

Whyte continues: "The intellectual hypocrisy of the leaderless groups has brought forth a new breed; into the very vacuum that they bespeak have moved the professional expediters. The end they seek is compromise and harmony, but in their controlled way they can be just as militant as any desk-pounder of old, and a lot more self-righteous."[31]

[30] See B. M. Bass and C. R. Wurster, Effects of company rank on LGD performance of oil refinery supervisors, *J. appl. Psychol.*, *37* (1953), 100–104; W. Haythorn, The influence of individual members on the characteristics of small groups, *J. abnorm. soc. Psychol.*, *48* (1953), 267–84.

[31] W. H. Whyte, Jr., *The organization man* (New York: Simon & Schuster, Inc., 1956), p. 55.

There is a certain incompatibility between the scientific approach to the problems of group harmony and creativeness and the ethical dispositions of some group dynamicists, which is similar to that between their fundamental ideas and the pseudo-mathematical framework in which they cast them. The stress on the value of democratic procedures, on democratic leaders, on leaderless groups—in short, the whole emphasis on the pervasive democratic ethic in which Lewin and some others ardently believe—has no logical and functional connection with the methodology they have employed, nor does this methodology establish the validity of such concepts. The democratic atmospheres of which they speak, sometimes to the point of wearisomeness, is an ideal. In the light of our country's own historical development this ideal is, of course, both a challenge and a reproach to liberal democracy. But the fact is that nowhere in Western civilization does democracy resemble the semivisionary conceptions of some of the extremists. In theory the democratic harmony which some group dynamicists espouse is devoutly to be wished; but to believe that the experiments with democratic groups have established the validity of that harmony is to permit ethical and humanitarian considerations to overshadow scientific objectivity.

We believe that democracy will be greatly furthered by humanitarian ethics when it joins forces with scientific methods and values. It is thus ironic, in retrospect, to contemplate the fact that, while this is explicitly the goal toward which Lewin was so indefatigably aspiring, the net result of his efforts was that in his last years he showed himself to be a better humanitarian than a social scientist. Whether, had he outlived the barbarous decade which so deeply troubled his sensitive spirit, he might have turned his energies once more to the area of scientific theory wherein his genius lay, we cannot know. We know only that in his most productive years he also applied his gifts to fighting for the cause of democracy, and especially that of the minorities and the spiritually dispossessed, whose sufferings touched his deep humanity.

Perhaps nowhere else are the excesses of group dynamicists more evident than in the field of education. In Chapter 8 we made a largely impersonal exposition of education from a group-dynamics point of view. We wish to add now that the untiring stress which group-centered educators place on democratic procedures in administration, curriculum-building, and classroom-teaching deserves to be pushed to the limit. It is one thing, however, to recognize the value of democratic decision-making and the creation of an acceptant atmosphere in teaching, and another to stress the belief in democracy in education at any price. The extreme advocates of group dynamics in education have displayed a dogmatism that disparages the very democracy which they profess to espouse. Research evidence is too divergent, inconsistent, and contradictory to permit the confident conclusion that, for example, group discussion is superior to, say, the lecture method.

Some of the studies, especially that of Wispe, which we described in Chapter 8, challenge the alleged superiority of discussion to lecturing as classroom techniques. In a recent study by Bennett its superiority is even more sharply questioned. Stating one of her several findings regarding group decision, she writes: "Group discussion, as an influence technique, was *not* found to be more effective inducement to action than a lecture or no influence attempt at all."[32] It is, we think, a fair question to ask how it is that many people have become well educated, refined, and humanistic before the advent of group dynamics in education? Common sense and experience have shown that people may become well educated and assimilate the finest democratic values in lecture rooms, laboratories, recitation periods, and, yes, even by teachers with *ex cathedra* inclinations. In demonstrating that the teaching-learning process is best furthered in a democratically free and permissive atmosphere, where suppression and authoritarian discipline are eschewed, and where cognizance of the dignity of the learner is notable,

[32] E. B. Bennett, Discussion, decision, commitment, and consensus in "group decision," *Hum. Relat.*, 8 (1955), 251–73. Italics in original.

group dynamics has performed a very important function in education. However, there is no royal road to education, to borrow a well-known platitude; and this applies to its group dynamics variant with equal force.

A fatal weakness of much discussion in group dynamics, from both the ethical and scientific vantage points, is that it encourages as many zealous defenders of the faith as it does critical students of a system of generalizations. This is most evident in the tireless efforts of many group dynamicists to achieve consensus, harmony, and agreement, efforts which tend to blind men to the stubborn fact that, in reality, such goals are only rarely achieved, and are often achieved at the price of crippling conformity. The concept of universal harmony is a noble ideal, but it must be recognized for what it is: a myth.

Bennis and Shepard, in the article we have already cited, while concerned with the attainment of consensual validation, show how difficult it is to achieve it. For our part, we believe that the condition of consensual validation is never fully reached, for this condition could mean only sterility and death for the group. Describing the difficulty in reaching consensual validation, the authors call attention to the hostilities and unresolved tensions, and the aggressive attitudes which this effort induces. But, as they point out, the appearance of harmony must be maintained at all costs. In open group discussions, they show, this requirement is imperative: "either the member does not dare to endanger harmony with the group or to disturb the *status quo* by denying that all problems have been solved."[33] There are, of course, many devices by which the illusion of harmony is sometimes maintained, and while outwardly consensual groups appear harmonious, someone's wishes are frustrated, someone's disagreements are held in abeyance.

Scientific thinking is itself not immune to the myth of maintaining solidarity. Bronfenbrenner and Devereux describe an interesting example of this condition. In a pre-

[33] W. G. Bennis and H. A. Shepard, A theory of group development, *Hum. Relat.*, 9 (1956), 417.

liminary report on an interdisciplinary research team[34] they call attention to the difficulty it experienced in reaching agreement and the concomitant compulsion to appear to be in agreement. Two years did not prove long enough for the group of researchers to function together as a team. Let us look at some of the reasons.

First, cooperation became *an end in itself*. It is obvious to anyone that persons who have agreed to work together on a common problem should conscientiously try to understand and be receptive to one another's point of view. What is not obvious, as the authors point out, is that *this effort can be self-defeating*. "In our case," they write, "it resulted in a compulsion to hear out, approve, and somehow incorporate into the total plan every major idea proposed by a staff member." The staff was further burdened by the feeling that no meeting was successful if everyone had not participated.

A second difficulty, which sharply highlights the over-idealized and therefore distorted view of the democratic process, is the members' *deferential overdependence on others*. They did not want to propose a decision affecting the whole group because it was thought to be "presumptuous and 'undemocratic.'" Accordingly, rather than facing the potentially conflicting decision-making, the members of the team convinced themselves that they should invite outside experts to help them in their discussions. It is apparent that the "wrong" kind of democracy can paralyze constructive thinking and action.

An *overreliance on group activity*, an anxious concern with universal sharing of every idea, also impaired the team's effectiveness. Everything had to be "checked" with everybody. To make matters worse, any act performed by an individual alone "lacked status." *Interaction* was their watchword. Their quotation from a personal communication from

[34] U. Bronfenbrenner and E. C. Devereux, Interdisciplinary planning for team research on constructive community behavior, *Hum. Relat.*, 5 (1952), 187–203. The members of the team represented psychology, sociology, anthropology, psychiatry, and social work.

John Useem describes the investigators' situation with deadly finality: "'We spent too much energy interacting and not enough in thinking.'"[35]

Group self-analysis is much extolled in the literature of group dynamics. The members of the above-mentioned team used it to get a better knowledge of how the latter was functioning. The results were generally disastrous. The analysis "evoked self-consciousness and resistance both at explicit and covert levels which, for some team members at least, disrupted communication, enhanced insecurity, dampened spontaneous expression, and delayed stabilization of roles and responsibilities." This is in line with the experience of others that group self-observation not infrequently closes the channels of communication and arouses hostility and anxiety.[36]

Bronfenbrenner and Devereux describe additional examples of difficulties in reaching agreement and the need to appear as a coherent group, but these are specifically related to the methodology of research and are not germane to our specific theme. It is apropos, however, to add one of their important discoveries, a phenomenon which was duly noted in Chapter 1. The research team, they point out, "suffered from the lack of a concrete focus outside itself which would free the individual team member to express his convictions, propose courses of action, and engage in a job of work." Particularly significant, we believe, is their discovery that "the creative aspects of research activity were best carried out individually or in pairs rather than as a total group."[37]

GROUP PROBLEM-SOLVING: AMBIGUITY OF FINDINGS. One of the most important theoretical and practical issues in group dynamics concerns the relative superiority of individual and group problem-solving. Many findings, some of

35 *Ibid.*, p. 190.

36 In fairness to the authors and to the practice of group self-analysis it should be remarked that its damaging effect may be attributed to inadequate skill on the part of the group leaders. See *ibid.*, p. 191.

37 *Ibid.*, p. 193. Similar findings regarding creative work, it will be recalled, were made by F. H. Allport many years ago. See Chapter 1.

which are reported in Chapter 7, favor the superiority of the group; others, the superiority of the individual. An early study by Watson, as we have shown, adduces evidence that shows that groups "think" more efficiently than individuals.[38] A few years later Marjorie Shaw came to a similar conclusion, although her results were somewhat ambiguous.[39]

The studies of Thorndike and of McCurdy and Lambert, described in Chapter 7, add to the ambiguity, if not confusion. Thorndike, the reader will recall, found the group generally superior to the individual, especially if the task presents a wide range of alternatives.[40] Yet he also found in the same study that "a high level of complexity limits the effectiveness of group work."[41] Shall one conclude from this that, generally speaking, as the problem becomes increasingly more complex its solution must be given over to single individuals? There is no clear answer.

In the study by McCurdy and Lambert, which we also described in the chapter on collective problem-solving, the reported results are quite different. They found, the reader will remember, that individuals were markedly superior to three-person groups.[42]

A rigorous study by Lorge and his associates strongly undermines the claim for group superiority in problem-solving. Their experiment with Air Force personnel revealed that individuals make better solutions for *complex human relations problems* than do groups.[43]

[38] G. B. Watson, Do groups think more efficiently than individuals? *J. abnorm. soc. Psychol., 23* (1928), 328–36.

[39] M. E. Shaw, A comparison of individual and small groups in the rational solution of complex problems, *Amer. J. Psychol., 44* (1932), 491–504.

[40] R. L. Thorndike, On what type of task will a group do well? *J. abnorm. soc. Psychol., 33* (1938), 409–13.

[41] *Ibid.*, p. 413.

[42] H. G. McCurdy, and W. E. Lambert, The efficiency of small human groups in the solution of problems reqiuiring genuine cooperation, *J. Pers., 20* (1952), 478–94.

[43] I. Lorge, J. Davitz, D. Fox, and K. Herrold, *Evaluation of instruction in staff action and decision-making,* Report of the Air Research and Development Command, Human Resources Research Institute, Maxwell A.F.B. Alabama, Technical Res. Report, No. 16, 1953.

Food for further thought regarding the problem is supplied by the recent findings of Fox, who took the important factor of time into account. He found that, generally speaking, the best decision by Air Force officers was written by an individual. He states that, although the average group significantly exceeded the average individual in performance, there were individual officers who, working alone, did as well as or better than any group. Conversely, he found, the worst decisions were written by individuals. Thus, according to Fox, organized groups assure a level of decision quality better than those written by most individuals, but not superior to those written by the best individuals. When groups were given more time, however, their solutions were as good as those of individuals.[44]

It would be unrealistic to question the superiority of group problem-solving on the basis of inconsistent results alone. But reliance on group problem-solving alone is equally unrealistic. The danger in overemphasizing the group lies in the failure to realize that it gives us only a partial knowledge of the learning and thinking processes. The group-superiority view relies too much on *validation by consensus.* There are, however, other tests of the validity of thinking and judging, among them those that Bruner, Goodnow, and Austin refer to as (1) recourse to an ultimate criterion, (2) the test of consistency, and (3) affective congruence.[45]

The *ultimate criterion* for determining the edibility of a mushroom is whether it will either make a person ill or kill him. The *test of consistency* is too obvious to need explanation. The *test by affective congruence* is a special case of the test by consistency. It is a test based on "subjective certainty or even necessity." Conclusions based on it are difficult to disprove, and they gain their certainty consider-

[44] D. Fox, The effect of increasing the available time for problem solving on the relative quality of decisions written by individuals and by groups, Ph.D. Dissertation, Columbia University, 1955, p. 30. The last point was made by Lorge in a Seminar taught jointly by Lorge, the present writer, and others, at Columbia in 1955.

[45] J. S. Bruner, J. J. Goodnow, and G. A. Austin, *A study of thinking* (New York: John Wiley & Sons, Inc., 1956), pp. 17–21.

ably from this fact. Religious convictions are good examples. Thus a person may be convinced of the existence of God by the order of the cosmos, or by the great beauty of a mountain or of the sea.

We should like to sum up our view regarding much that has been said concerning the superiority of the group to the individual by saying that too many studies suffer from overgeneralization. It does not detract from the effectiveness of problem-solving by groups to agree with the well-balanced conclusion of Bennett that "group discussion and public commitment are not necessary components of successful 'group decision' operations."[46]

EXCESSIVE VENERATION OF GROUP DYNAMICS. Group dynamics, we have shown, is not new, but some of its believers and practitioners seem to forget the fact. While deplorable, this fact is understandable. What is not acceptable are the unsupported generalizations which some of them make and the unwarranted faith which they have in some of the applied aspects of the subject. The things which they perform are not necessarily scientific, for they do not pay sufficient attention to the need for scientific rigor. The words they use are descriptive rather than formally defined concepts. The concepts they use are practical rather than fundamental. In sampling their terminology Gunderson observes humorously that such terms as "gatekeeper," "blocker," and "play boy," "which are chosen indiscriminately from the sporting arena, the theater, and the fraternity lounge do not convey precise meaning even when intermingled with the vocabulary of topological and vector psychology."[47]

Role-playing, which is an important and insightful aspect of contemporary social psychology and group therapy, is sometimes carried to ludicrous lengths. Some of the practices in this connection are not merely useless; since they are communicated in the name of science, they are also fraudulent. We are indebted to Gunderson for calling our attention to a not atypical example published in the *Educator's*

[46] Bennett, Discussion, decision, commitment, p. 272.
[47] Gunderson, Dangers in group dynamics, p. 344.

Washington Dispatch.[48] In one session the teacher changed places with a problem child in a class. While acting out the role, the teacher pinched the little girl sitting next to her, and acted in other unpleasant ways. Allegedly, as a result of this interchange of roles, the problem child had improved at least enough to become more cooperative. We are given no supporting evidence, and no hint that other factors might have played a part. If a problem child can be helped that easily and quickly, then we have indeed entered a new era of human relations improvement!

The veneration of group dynamics reaches its height, it seems, with some of the workshop trainees of the National Training Laboratory on Group Development, which meets every summer on the campus of Gould Academy, in Bethel, Maine. Here research science, experimentation in group living, and democratic participation freely and intelligently mingle. Interaction and discussion, however, seem to be trusted too implicitly, so that whatever cannot be agreed upon in formal groups can be continued in "buzz sessions."

The buzz session as a leaderless group where "democratic participation" is alleged to reign supreme, is a good illustration of the great faith in the power of group dynamics, even if the results do not always warrant it. We shall permit Whyte to describe his experience with one of them at a management convention by quoting him at length.

> . . . It had started conventionally enough with a panel discussion in which I and two other men spoke. Halfway through the proceedings, the program chairman called an intermission and, with the assistance of several helpers, began rearranging the seating so that the audience would be divided into groups of four, with the chairs turned around so that they faced each other. . . . When I asked him what was going on, he seemed surprised. Hadn't I ever heard of a "buzz session"? . . . He explained that rather than have a "directed" discussion, we would stimulate ideas through interaction. By breaking the audience into a constellation of face-to-face groups, he said, we would create this interaction. The fact that the seating would be a random mixture of strangers would make no difference; the interaction itself would produce many provocative insights.

48 A portfolio of teaching techniques (1949), 1–31; edited by its staff.

At last he banged down the gavel, and some two hundred grown men turned and faced each other for the discussion period. Minutes went by. There was no buzz. . . . The chairman was not chastened. After the meeting he told me that the trouble was simply that the groups were too small. Four wasn't up to the ignition level. Next time they would do it with six to eight men.[49]

There is a great deal of practical value to be gained from participation in such workshops. But for some of its enthusiasts to claim that what they are doing is also a scientific investigation of human relations is to pervert the meaning of science. We have already shown the value of group-dynamics principles for the elimination or reduction of ethnic and racial tensions; but we challenge the claim that this is any more *scientific* than building skyscrapers and bridges. Role-playing may serve as an aid in certain types of human relationships, but it can hardly be described as scientific. Science and technology, while related are scarcely identical. The practitioners do not take the time to permit themselves to realize that the relation between science as a set of testable hypotheses and the work which they are performing is greatly oversimplified.

The excessive veneration of group participation, finally, has led to the view in some quarters that unless man is perpetually interacting with his fellows he cannot be happy and normal. The relentless stress on group harmony has taken on the character of a minor crusade. Thus group-belongingness, which is as old as mankind, is raised to the status of an all-embracing principle. A person should and must belong we are repeatedly told—as if normally he would not wish to do so. This comes perilously close to demanding that an individual *sacrifice himself* for the questionable privilege of always belonging. It comes close to saying that unless he always participates in a group he can do little constructive thinking. A scientific thinker, however, would investigate the value premises of participation and agreement. Overzealous advocates, by contrast, are "certain" of the "right-

[49] W. H. Whyte, Jr., *The organization man* (New York: Simon & Schuster, Inc., 1956), pp. 55–56.

ness" of the premises, for these premises are "democratic." A scientific thinker would also inquire into the need for participation or to ascertain its goal. Participation would be seen as a means toward something else; but to the devotee it seems to be its own excuse for being.

We must agree with Whyte and many others, that it is "the price of progress that there never can be complete consensus. All creative advances are essentially a departure from agreed-upon ways of looking at things, and to overemphasize the agreed-upon is to further legitimize the hostility to that creativity upon which we all ultimately depend."[50]

The extreme veneration of group-dynamics techniques and the dogmatism to which it tends to lead is not infrequently a subtle control of others parading behind the banner of the democratic process. The advocate of leaderless groups in practice often really decides and directs. By means of his group skills and facile use of the jargon of his profession, the practical worker unwittingly intimidates other group members. Because, furthermore, of the high value placed on consensus, and because of the demand to be hypersensitive to the group's purpose, many ascendant and imaginative persons throttle their initiative out of fear of being labeled "authoritarian" or "undemocratic."

THE TYRANNY OF THE GROUP AND THE TWILIGHT OF THE INDIVIDUAL. Neither group dynamics nor any other science develops in a social vacuum. We now have much documented evidence to prove that science is conditioned by the times in which it originates and flourishes. Perhaps no other discipline reflects the social ideology of our time in a more pronounced way than group dynamics; and no other, surely, more strongly supports it. The psychology of human behavior has been supporting the doctrine of social adjustment for almost half a century, but it has remained for group dynamics to raise it to its present glory. The latter's preoccupation with group belongingness and group harmony,

[50] *Ibid.*, p. 58.

its insistence on the "superiority" of the group over the individual, and its effort to turn human relations, through "social engineering," into one happy brotherhood are contemporary trends. They describe in essence what Whyte has called the "organization man," the man who completely belongs—the well-adjusted, gregarious, and group-centered man *imprisoned in brotherhood.*[51] There is also a strong tendency today, especially among some group dynamicists, to equate personal independence with individual recalcitrance and antagonism. It is obvious that some of them confuse group-centeredness with individual capitulation.

We have referred to the preoccupation with group-mindedness as a contemporary trend. The need to be liked, and the whole philosophy of group integration, is part of our contemporary heritage. It is found in the nervous concern with acceptance by the peer group, the reference group, and almost every other group to which we belong or aspire to belong. *Group integration,* which is a normal social process, has been inflated to the point where it has become an all-encompassing ethic. This is a sure way of undermining the worth of the individual, an almost certain means of intimidating him and causing him to lose confidence in himself. If his ideas are constantly at the mercy of group evaluation, he will gradually learn to become silent. Nothing is more dangerous to the fragility of creative ideas than to have them relegated into outer darkness by an intolerant group.

It is a commonplace that American society has been characterized by heterogeneity and has encouraged irreverence toward entrenched authority. The premium which some group dynamicists place on conformity to group standards can help to destroy the individual spontaneity which has described American democracy from its very inception. The conformity of which we speak is, of course, not deliberately imposed; it is effected by subtle pressures from peer groups and reference groups which identify deviation with wrongdoing. The anxiety and sense of guilt thus generated have

[51] The arresting phrase, italicized by the present writer, is Whyte's. See *ibid.,* p. 12.

not been investigated by group dynamicists, and their study is long overdue.

It is difficult to determine antecedence in the process which we are describing. Ignoring the cause-and-effect relationship we merely call attention to the fact that the transition from group consensus to mass culture, from group conformity to social standardization, is easier than one might think.

It is true that participation in constructive groups may lead to expansion of the self and to an increasing acceptance of individual differences. This fact has been documented in this book. Like all serious students of individual and group behavior we believe in the integration of the individual with the group; he cannot live outside it and survive psychologically. But there are kinds and degrees of integration. It is the business of group dynamics to determine what forms and degrees of integration are self-enhancing and which are self-constricting. This is something, however, concerning which we still need a great amount of experimental research, not the pseudo-humanitarianism of the extremists. Until we do, no practitioner of group dynamics is morally justified in branding as maladjusted or antagonistic any individual who prefers aloneness and solitude. Not even a fool can live in glorious isolation, and the solitary individual often knows this better than his "group-integrated" neighbor.

In all the writings of the extremists there is not one hint regarding the value of individualism and privacy. Indeed, often the stress is clearly on *anti-individualism.*[52] It is a fact, nonetheless, that recent studies of mental health cite the value of privacy. Apartness can be as much a psychological restorative as group belongingness is a source of pleasure and security. Maslow's study of the self-actualizing person, who is generally a mentally healthy individual, describes this type as not only able to identify himself with mankind but as uncommonly loving privacy and detachment.[53] Group re-

[52] See Chapter 8, and K. D. Benne, Democratic ethics in social engineering, *Progress., Educ., 26* (1949), 204–07.

[53] See A. H. Maslow, The authoritarian character structure, *J. soc. Psychol., 18* (1943), 401–11.

latedness and apartness need not be antithetical. Together they constitute a priceless art. But in an age when social participation is raised to the level of an ethical principle, individualism can be enjoyed only by persons of exceptional independence and moral courage. We commented at length on this quality in Chapter 10, calling particular attention to those creative people who added to the world's heritage in solitude.[54]

The group-integration ideology is also reflected in science, with respect to both its ideas and its success in recruiting prospective workers. Because of the cultural emphasis on group life, cooperation, and teamwork, social scientists tend to see group phenomena in expected ways. This is a case on a collective level of having one's perceptions determined by the expectancies of the group. We see the group as superior to the individual, for example, because our minds are "set" to so perceive it.

In a recent article on the effect of "groupism" on the exceptional individual, Michael makes a trenchant observation which we shall quote in full. Deploring the decrease in "inner-directed" students he writes that

> . . . it is becoming more and more difficult in these days of "group adjustment" for a youngster to be idiosyncratic in the eyes of his peers, his parents, and teachers, and still maintain the sense of inner security and inner drive that will permit him to go about his independent way as a "meat ball" in high school and an "egg-head" in adult society, devoting himself singlemindedly to science.[55]

Michael goes on to reflect along lines of argument similar to our own. It is entirely possible, he continues, that the contemporary other-directed view of life is incompatible with genuine scientific creativity. We do not know, of

[54] Some months ago, toward the end of a program, the writer happened to turn on his television which was featuring a woman speaking on the same topic. At the risk of being charged with using it to imply guilt by association, *which is utterly false,* we quote one of her significant statements: "Only the communists and ourselves are banishing the individual into outer darkness."

[55] D. N. Michael, Scientists through adolescent eyes: what we need to know, why we need to know it, *Sci. Monthly, 84* (1957), 137.

course. A few studies, however, show that the single-mindedness which is ascribed to the creative scientist *and* a social environment sympathetic to it have been essential to scientific productiveness. If this should prove to be generally so, then the means of maintaining inner-directedness in an outer-directed society will require all the knowledge and skill that we can bring to bear upon the task. Group dynamicists must ponder this deeply and unrelentingly.

The foregoing considerations naturally bring us back to the problem of group creativity. We must agree with Whyte, in describing many current efforts to see the group as a creative vehicle, as "the most misguided attempt at false collectivization." "People," he says, "rarely *think* in groups; they talk together, they exchange information, they adjudicate, they make compromises. But they do not think; they do not create."[56]

Advocates of group thinking know this is so, but they consider it a limitation to be overcome. It is a "bug of human relations to be cured." But why the insistence on it? Why impel people to think and create in groups? Why, if the grass is green should anyone wish to make it purple? Perhaps the group advocate, like the mountain climber, wants to do the job because "it is there!"

To repeat: The criticism of group-oriented life is not directed toward its groupness as such, but toward the tyranny which it can easily inflict upon genuine individualism. Moreover, the concern of some group-dynamics advocates is not with the human community, as we have described it in Chapter 10; it is not "neighbor-responsive." It is frequently spurious, for "it results in the abdication of personal freedom and a progressive dwindling of the self as an authentic center of decision and action. The individual person is in danger of so blending into the group that *his thought and action become but a reflection or echo of the group*—all this going on, perhaps, in the name of 'community.' "[57]

[56] Whyte, *The organization man*, p. 51.

[57] W. H. Kirkland, Fellowship and/or freedom, *The Christian Century*, *74* (1957), 490–92. Our italics.

The danger of an indiscriminate luring of persons toward consensus and conformity lies partly in its insidiousness. Having yielded to the group's initial pressure, there is a diminishing reason for not yielding still more until, at last, there remains neither the will nor the logic not to surrender completely. The need for belonging and approval, while normal and desirable in its place, can be so manipulated by group pressures as to obliterate individuality and effective personal freedom. This is the more true when resistance to conformity is regarded as maladjustive and evil. We submit that it is as difficult for the overzealous group dynamicist to become aware of the potential harm to the individual of perpetual group impact as it is for the nonparticipant to realize that his distortion of the motives of others is a product of his isolated existence. Personal and social inadequacy is the consequence of each.

CONCLUSION

We have now reviewed for the reader the subject matter, the methodology, the value preferences, and some of the limitations and defects of group dynamics. Considered as a whole, and despite the strictures placed against it in this chapter, it is a field of investigation worthy of the attention of the best psychologists and sociologists. Anyone who is not easily discouraged by or contemptuous of many of its fuzzy ideas will find group dynamics a challenging field of study and investigation. Perhaps here, as in other areas of life and thought, one test of the truly democratic individual is his "tolerance of ambiguity." Certainly, if during the formative stages through which it is still going he can tolerate its sometimes exasperating imprecisions, he will find it stimulating. We are speaking largely of group dynamics as a scientific discipline with hypotheses to pose and to test by means of systematic and controlled experiments. We are not referring to some of the weird applications to which we have referred in this chapter, nor even to group dynamics as an applied science. This book does not suggest a group-dynamics practicum. Anyone who is interested in the latter must first master the principles, generalizations, and experimental data which we have placed at the reader's disposal in the pages of this book.

If group dynamics is to become what it now only approximates, namely, a science of group behavior, it must construct a system of theory or principles by means of which its phenomena can be rationally ordered. It is our belief that the principles which it must formulate will have to be consistent with the principles that account for individual behavior. Social psychology has not yet reached this level of rigorous, abstract conceptualization. The task of integrating the two awaits future investigation.

A besetting evil in psychology, we believe, is the determination, *in the absence of adequate facts and data,* to force our discipline into a rigid mold for which it is as yet unfitted. Thus, for example, we hear on almost every side that concepts must be operationally defined. The term has become, indeed, a part of the *façons de parler* of pretentious technical discussions of individual and group behavior. Bronfenbrenner and Devereux say of operationism that for the American social scientists it is "both a source of security and a standard of scientific virtue."[58] It would make an interesting study to investigate how extensively the social scientist hides his occupational neuroses behind this concept's reassuring façade. No one doubts the imperative need for conceptual rigor in any of the social sciences, including the area of group dynamics; but it is unrealistic to believe that it can be attained at the present stage of their development. Bronfenbrenner states the matter perfectly when he writes that,

> . . . to exact this requirement at the very outset is to make the dubious assumption that scientific wisdom increases by steps at the 5% level. In the face of such exacting standards, . . . it is difficult for the would-be scientist to avoid being forced in one of two dissociated directions. If he covets his professional reputation, he is under pressure to confine himself to the analysis of relatively simple phenomena where the variables are few, discrete, and susceptible to rigorous experimental control. The most significant aspects of human

[58] Bronfenbrenner and Devereux, Interdisciplinary planning, p. 192.

behavior, however, are not likely to be found in this category, for they are characteristically elusive and multi-determinate. To wrestle with these at a realistic level and at the same time to face up to the expectations and criticisms of fellow scientists take more time, energy, patience, and self-integration than many able men command. It is far easier to remain free of such demands by doing one's theorizing in a non-scientific context. As a result, it is perhaps possible to say—with only moderate exaggeration—that the study of human behavior in America shows a bimodal distribution with undisciplined speculation at one mode and rigorous sterility at the other . . . Viewed in the perspective of this discussion, hypotheses should do more than serve as cannon fodder for the statistician . . . If we wish to grapple with the molar as well as the molecular problems of human behavior, we must be ready to start with vague gropings which only gradually begin to approach the clarity and specificity we have come to require of hypotheses.[59]

Should the cynic describe the foregoing explanation as the rationalization of a shortcoming, we respectfully ask him to try to do the job himself. If he succeeds, group dynamicists will owe him a signal debt.

[59] U. Bronfenbrenner, Toward an integrated theory of personality, in R. R. Blake and G. V. Ramsey, *Perception: an approach to personality* (New York: The Ronald Press Co., 1951), pp. 208–9, quoted in U. Bronfenbrenner and E. C. Devereux, Interdisciplinary planning for team research on constructive community behavior, *Hum. Relat.*, 5 (1952), p. 192.

Name Index

Subject Index